Globalization and Civilizations

Edited by Mehdi Mozaffari

Routledge
Taylor & Francis Group

LONDON AND NEW YORK

First published 2002
by Routledge
11 New Fetter Lane, London EC4P 4EE

Simultaneously published in the USA and Canada
by Routledge
29 West 35th Street, New York, NY 10001

Routledge is an imprint of the Taylor & Francis Group

Typeset in Baskerville by Taylor & Francis Books Ltd
Printed and bound in Malta by Gutenberg Press Ltd

British Library Cataloguing in Publication Data
A catalogue record for this book is available from the British Library

Library of Congress Cataloging in Publication Data
Globalization and civilizations/edited by Mehdi Mozaffari.
  Includes bibliographical references and index.
  1. Civilization, Modern–1950– 2. Globalization.
  3. Civilization–Philosophy. 4. East and West. I. Mozaffari, Mehdi.

  CB430 .G58   2002
  909.82–dc21   2002075155

ISBN 0–415–28614–X (hbk)
ISBN 0–415–28615–8 (pbk)

303.482 MO2

Globalization and Civilizations

Are we experiencing a "clash of civilizations"?

Can the Islamic and Western worlds be reconciled?

Has globalization eroded differences between civilizations?

The notion of a "clash of civilizations" has never been more topical or contentious. This edited collection challenges stereotypes about the nature of civilizations and the supposed inevitability of the conflict between them.

Globalization and Civilizations critically interrogates the concept of "civilization" by asking whether it is still valid in today's globalized world economy. The book provides an historical and theoretical context within which we can understand the idea of civilization in political science, and demonstrates how the various social, economic, political and cultural processes of globalization have radically altered perceptions of the concept. It includes case studies looking particularly at examples of the interaction between globalization and civilization and contains chapters focusing on Islam, China and India among others.

This book is a significant contribution to two of the most important debates in international relations today – globalization and the "clash of civilizations" – and provides a wide variety of Western and non-Western views.

Mehdi Mozaffari is currently head of the Department of International Relations at the University of Aarhus, Denmark. He has written books and articles on global civilization, ethics, political Islam and theory of international politics. His latest book is *FATWA: Violence and Discourtesy.*

Contents

Contributors

Djamshid Behnam obtained his PhD from the Sorbonne, University of Paris. He was Professor, Dean of the Faculty of Social Sciences, and Vice Chancellor of Teheran University. Subsequently, he was appointed Chancellor of Farabi University. Since 1981 he has been living in Paris where he was Visiting Professor at Paris V, Sorbonne (1980–84); Deputy-Secretary General: International Social Science Council; staff member of UNESCO's Population Division (1984–91) and Dean of Mediators at UNESCO (1992–95). He is the author of several books and articles on population, family and modernity and has participated in numerous international conferences.

Niels Brimnes is Assistant Professor in the Department of History, University of Aarhus. He works on Asian history in general, but his special research interests are Indian history in the early colonial period. He is the author of *Constructing the Colonial Encounter. Right and Left Hand Castes in Early Colonial South India* (Richmond, Curzon Press, 1999).

Robert W. Cox is Professor Emeritus of Political Science at New York University, Toronto. He is the author of *Production, Power, and World Order: Social Forces in the Making of History* (Columbia University Press, 1987) and a collection of essays prepared with Timothy J. Sinclair, *Approaches to World Order* (Cambridge University Press, 1996). His works also include the issues of civilizations and civil society.

Richard Falk is currently Visiting Professor at the University of California at Santa Barbara, after retiring as Milbank Professor of International Law at Princeton University in June 2001. His most recent books are *Law in an Emerging Global Village: A Post-Westphalian Perspective* (1998); *Predatory Globalization: A Critique* (1999); *Human Rights Horizons* (2000); and *Religion and Humane Global Governance* (2001).

Gerrit W. Gong is Assistant to the President at Brigham Young University in Provo, Utah, with responsibility for Planning and Assessment. He is also Senior Associate at the Center for Strategic and International Studies (CSIS) in Washington, DC. He holds PhD and Masters of Philosophy degrees in

International Relations from Oxford University, where he wrote and published his book on *The Standard of "Civilization" in International Society* (1984). At the US State Department, he served as a Special Assistant to the Under-Secretary of State and Consultant to the State Department Policy Planning Staff, Rumsfeld Commission on Ballistic Missile Threats, etc. In addition, Gerrit W. Gong has testified before Congress on a range of Asian issues, and consults, lectures, and writes on East Asian developments, especially in Europe, Asia, and North America.

Xiaoming Huang is Senior Lecturer at Victoria University of Wellington, New Zealand. He received his PhD from the University of Southern California, and has been Research and Teaching Fellow at: the East–West Center in Honolulu; the University of Tampere, Finland; the University of Trondheim, Norway. He teaches Asian politics and political economy at Victoria University. His recent research interests focus on the problem of culture, institutions, and social orders, and his latest publication is *The Political and Economic Transition in East Asia* (Georgetown University Press).

Jan Ifversen holds a PhD in History from the University of Aarhus, Denmark. He is Associate Professor and the Director of Studies at the Centre for European Cultural Studies, University of Aarhus. He is the author of articles on the idea of Europe, and on key concepts in European self-understanding. Among his publications is *Hjem til Europa* [Home to Europe] (Copenhagen, Gyldendal, 1992) (with Anne Knudsen). He is currently working on a book on twentieth-century perceptions of Europe.

Edgar Morin is a philosopher and a sociologist. He was a member of the resistance movement and Lieutenant of the Forces Françaises Combattantes (1942–44). In 1945 he was appointed General Staff Attaché of the French First Army in Germany (1945), then "propaganda" Bureau Chief at the Information Headquarters of the French government in Germany (1946). Since 1995, Edgar Morin has been Professor Emeritus and Head of Research. He has been President of the European Agency for culture (UNESCO), and President of the Association for Complex Thought. He is the author of many books among which are *L'Esprit du Temps*, *L'Homme et la Mort*, *Le Paradigme perdu*, *Penser l'Europe*, and *Terre Patrie*. His most recent book is *La Méthode* (vol. 5) (2001).

Michael Mousseau is Assistant Professor of International Relations at Koç University in Istanbul, Turkey. Michael Mousseau received his PhD in Political Science from the State University of New York at Binghamton (1998). His research focus is the impact of market-oriented development on social and political processes, including the emergence of liberal political culture, democratic institutional stability, and the peace among democratic nations. He has published articles in the *Journal of Peace Research*, *Journal of Conflict Resolution*, and *International Interactions*.

Mehdi Mozaffari is Docteur d'État en Science Politique (Sorbonne-Panthéon). He is a former Professor at Tehran University and a lecturer at the

Sorbonne, University of Paris. He is currently Head of the Department of International Relations at the University of Aarhus, Denmark. He is the author of several books and articles among which are *Authority in Islam: From Muhammad to Khomeni* (New York, M.E. Sharpe, 1987); *Security Policy of the Commonwealth of Independent States* (ed.) (London, Macmillan, 1997); *Fatwa: Violence and Discourtesy* (Oxford, Aarhus University Press, 1998); and *Pouvoir Shi'ite: Théorie et évolution* (Paris, l'Harmattan, 1998). He is continuing his work on globalization and civilizations as well as on the issue of global terrorism.

Preface and acknowledgments

This book is the fruit of reflections from a number of scholars discussing globalization, civilizations and world order. Contributors stem from different disciplines, have different nationalities, and various cultural, religious and philosophical backgrounds. In a world marked by an unprecedented speed of communication and dominated by uncertainty and unpredictability, there is a vital need for reflection and criticism. Reflection helps us better understand the meaning of events, to establish a comprehensive connection among them and to extract the real essence of our time. Consequently, it is no over-statement to underline that reflection is an absolute necessity of our epoch. Reflection, of course, must be qualified. The contributors' writings are based on their academic research. In this book, argument stands as the prevailing method, and criticism is the dominating trend. Generally, the reader is exposed to a plurality of approaches and points of views. Subsequently, through the means of argument, the author presents his own approach and standpoint. The reader may select among the options presented; or he/she may produce his/her own independent idea. In this way, the book offers an opportunity to stimulate reflection and to challenge long established concepts and ideas.

The first chapters discuss relations between civilizations and world order under the process of globalization. Chapter 1 by Robert W. Cox represents a model of interdisciplinary study. In this chapter, history, economy, political science, international politics, culture and religion are carefully woven together so as to spotlight the architecture of civilizations in the new era of human history. Chapter 2 by Mehdi Mozaffari is an attempt to explain the evolution of the world order parallel to the plight of civilizations and the rise of globalization. Inspired both by world system theory and social constructivism, he attempts to unveil how the rise of capitalism in Europe has contributed to the rise of the standard of European civilization and its spreading to other parts of the world. He argues that the current world order can best be described as a "democratic-hegemonic anarchy".

Globalization is a profound ongoing process embracing all aspects of international relations. This process considerably affects international norms, rules and institutions. Richard Falk, a prominent pioneer in the field who has been advocating for decades the appropriateness of global governance, consecrates

Chapter 3 to raising the question of the emergence of the first normative global revolution. In spite of the manifest despair and complacency of the age, he propounds whether or not we are embarked upon a relatively soft, normative revolution of values as well as of legal procedures and institutions, transforming above all our understanding of global justice. Subsequent to a critical analysis of the very concept of *revolution* and progress in the normative field, he brings forth several activating conditions necessary for a normative global revolution. Gerrit W. Gong's Chapter 4 is in fact a continuation of Falk's discussion. Gong, author of *Standard of "Civilization"* (1984), now a classic, explores in his chapter whether the "old" standard of civilization embraces meanings and merits as normative and organizing principles in today's globalized international system. Gong argues no less that the continuing, self-conscious definition of international standards of civilization is a natural and necessary consequence of international interaction. Studying dimensions of the "new" standard of civilization in domains as different as human rights, rules of war, sustainable development and environment, he pays particular attention to international trade standards (GATT and then WTO). In Chapter 5 Michael Mousseau explains from an anthropological point of view how globalization, markets, and democracy are interconnected. In this endeavor, the school of cultural materialism inspires him to emphasize (the well-known) three layers of all social systems: the infrastructure, the structure, and the superstructure. From this perspective, understanding global structural changes begins with grasping the infrastructure of the influential sectors of the global economy. Mousseau argues that the common infrastructure is the reason why all advanced industrial nations share a common political structure (democracy) and superstructure (liberal political culture). Accordingly, the real source of failure of democracy and liberal political culture in all other states lies in the absence of this common infrastructure.

After an overall survey, the book moves on to study specific civilizations. Chapter 6 by Edgar Morin opens this section on European civilization. A number of important concepts, questions and challenges are elegantly put forward. The subject of Morin's inquiry raises explicit yet crucial questions: when did Europe become Europe? Is European culture identical with European civilization? Is European civilization "universal" or "universalisable"? What is the difference between "dialectic" and "dialogy"? He unfolds a historical, sociological, philosophical and political analysis. Morin exposes strong arguments in favor of European civilization that do not in the least derive from a European ethnocentric point of view. On the contrary, Morin's thesis is that European civilization originates from a "coincidence" of history, without a preconceived itinerary. Therefore, this civilization possesses an increased potential to be open towards different cultures; old and new. Most importantly, this chapter contains justifications why Morin who had previously been "anti-European", ultimately became a convinced "pro-European". European civilization has also undergone a number of crises. The strong and deep impact of WWI on European civilization made a few European thinkers doubt the survival of this civilization. Jan Ifversen, in Chapter 7, retraces the paths of the crisis between WWI and WWII. His aim is essentially to analyze the discursive and conceptual frameworks within which European intellectuals and politicians could express their ideas on Europe. He argues that these frameworks were held together by the conceptual triangle around the concepts of "crisis," "civilization" and "Europe". To demonstrate his point, Ifversen goes through a systematic analysis of the writings of several prominent inter-war year European thinkers such as Paul Valéry, Oswald Spengler, Ernst Robert Curtius and H.G. Wells. At the end of the chapter, he tries to connect this debate to the current initiated by Samuel Huntington's *Clash of Civilizations*. The study of European civilization is followed by the study of several non-Western civilizations. Djamshid Behnam in Chapter 8 introduces this section by analyzing the Eastern perception of the West. This perception is limited, however, to the Iranian and the Ottoman world. He demonstrates that Eastern intellectuals and politicians have different perceptions of the West: ranging from "idealization" to "demonization". Attitudes to the West oscillate from fascination to criticism, rejection and even negation. These trends did not always occur in a regular fashion, one after the other. They overlapped from time to time causing further confusion and complication. Behnam's study sheds a light on the tensions prevailing on the one hand *within* some of the Eastern societies concerning their attitude *vis-à-vis* the West, and, on the other hand, *within* the overriding turmoil *between* East and West. Chapter 9 by Mehdi Mozaffari on Islamic civilization is a sequel to Behnam's chapter. When did the Islamic civilization rise? What were the causes of its decline? Should it be re-constructed? And how? What is the impact of globalization on the current Muslim intellectual mainstream? These are some of the questions shaping Mozaffari's map of investigation. In this chapter, Islam's formative and axial periods are examined, their main characteristics are analyzed and the different theories on causes of the decline of the Islamic civilization are systematically reviewed. Mozaffari states that Muslims moved for centuries between two antagonistic points that metaphorically may be seen as Medina and Athena. The violent tension within Muslim societies is partially explained by this still ongoing movement. In this respect, he identifies three main trends among Muslims: reproductionists, communalists, and universalists.

Chapter 10 begins with a challenging question: "What is 'Chinese' about Chinese civilization"? Right from the start, Xiaoming Huang points out that the central point of his study is neither about the glory of Chinese civilization nor about how the non-Chinese should understand and respect this civilization. The main purpose of his study deals, on the one hand, with the impact of globalization in relation to the moral approach (Confucianism) of Chinese civilization, and, on the other, the institutional approach. Hence, Huang's questions relate to classical theories on civilizations. Civilizationalists built their theory upon the notion that a general breakthrough had occurred within the Axial Age civilizations. The question is whether China experienced such breakthroughs in the Axial Age. Huang puts forward a subtle answer to this question. Subsequent to the clarification of his concept of "civilization" based on "human nature", "institutions" and "culture", Huang attempts to identify different components of Chinese civilization and the role played by the Chinaman, the Confucian Man and the Singaporean.

The final chapter deals with Indian civilization with a particular focus on Hindu nationalism. In Niels Brimnes' view, the reason for insisting on Hindu nationalism is to be found in a parallel process in India. In fact, India witnesses two simultaneous challenges: the increasing challenge from globalization and the rise of Hindu nationalism. The established and widespread notions of Indian civilization reputed to be peaceful, syncretic and tolerant is challenged by Hindu nationalism. Brimnes casts a light on this problematic by questioning the very notion of "civilization" and its usefulness in analyzing the current events in Indian society. After a general critique on different theories on the concept of civilization, or in Brimnes' words, "de-essentializing civilizations", he demonstrates how Indian civilization was constructed. Brimnes bases his analysis on studies and views of some of the most influential "architects" of this civilization. Hence, we are introduced to the views of authorities such as William Jones, the "father" of Indology and founder of the Asiatic Society (1784), and James Mill, author of the monumental *History of British India* (1818). In the late nineteenth century, the notion of Indian civilization acquired a new significance. Deriving from the romantic notions of the authentic cultural nation, Indian intellectuals began to formulate ideas about a particularly spiritual Indian–Hindu civilization. This angle became a source of inspiration for Gandhi who adopted Indian spirituality and tolerance. In the same vein, Brimnes studies Nehru and Louis Dumont's approaches. At the end of the chapter, the relationship between Hindu nationalism and Indian civilization is unraveled.

Acknowledgments

This book was made possible thanks to the Danish Social Research Council's financial support. Professor Georg Sørensen who heads the overall project on "Globalization" proved to be a valuable source of inspiration and permanent encouragement. Many of my colleagues at the Department of Political Science of the University of Aarhus were a major source of advice and support. I would like to express my gratitude to the contributors of this volume who patiently reviewed their chapters. I acknowledge a special debt to Robert W. Cox, Edgar Morin and Richard Falk for their invaluable advice and inspiring discussions and correspondences. I am thankful to Édition Gallimard, who kindly permitted inserting a section of *Penser l'Europe* into Morin's chapter, and to Oxford University Press for permission regarding Robert W. Cox's contribution. I thank Angélique Armand-Delille for her excellent work in translating Morin's chapter. I also owe a special debt of gratitude to Ann Davenport for her help and encouragement. Finally, I wish to record my special gratitude to my secretary Lone Winther for her outstanding contribution throughout the long course of writing and editing this book. Her meticulous proofreading of the manuscript and standardizing of each chapter in accordance with the guidelines from Routledge were an enormous help in completing this project.

Mehdi Mozaffari

1 Civilizations and the twenty-first century

Some theoretical considerations

Robert W. Cox

We look to the past in the light of the problems of the present. This is the sense in which Benedetto Croce wrote that all history is contemporary history.[1] Civilizations represent continuities in human thought and practices through which different human groups attempt to grapple with their consciousness of present problems. At some times, these continuities appear to be vigorous, reaffirmed, even redefined. At other times, they are obscured, subordinated to other dominant modes of thought and practices. At such times and for such groups talk of civilizations is absent, suppressed, or seemingly irrelevant. When and why do civilizations become a significant object of knowledge?

For three decades and more, knowledge about world affairs was constructed predominantly with reference to the Cold War. Its pre-eminent form in international relations theory, particularly in its American expression, was neorealism, a problem-solving form of knowledge applicable to superpower rivalry. Neorealism was a technology of power based upon the premiss of a common rationality shared by both sides in the US–Soviet conflict in which game theoretic exercises and rational choice hypotheses could be taken as guides for policy understandable in the same way by both sides.

Once the overarching control of the Cold War was lifted, the underlying but obscured diversity of the human situation became more fully apparent and neorealism lost its monopoly of explaining the world and proposing action. But the salience of the Cold War was succeeded by the salience of globalization: the vision of the inevitable homogenization of economic and cultural practices, driven by competitiveness in a global market and by new technologies of communication. As an ideology, globalization is the ultimate form of alienation: something created by people that has come to wield absolute power over them.

There is, however, an historical dialectical resistance to this vision of global homogenization – an affirmation of diversity through many forms of identity: gender, ethnic, religious, linguistic, attachment to the land, and a sense of historical grievance and humiliation. The two most prevalent forms of identity of the earlier twentieth century – nationality and class – are submerged, though not eliminated, in these other forms. The largest aggregate of identity is the civilization. Globalization is countered by the affirmation of civilizations in this dialectic of homogenization and diversification. This is the basic reason for a revival of concern about civilizations in international studies.[2]

How should we theorize civilizations and their role in this future world? What are the implications for international studies? In an attempt to begin answering these questions, I discuss four points in this chapter:

1   To consider reflexively the changing awareness of civilizations in Western thought, in other words, to historicize the concept of civilization. For someone born into the Western tradition, this is a necessary exercise in self-awareness as a precondition to awareness of others.
2   To propose a workable definition of the entity "civilization". What is a civilization?
3   To consider the dimensions of the entity "civilization" as an approach towards analyzing the dynamics of civilizational change.
4   To propose a research program as an heuristic guide to the study of present and future encounters and transformations of civilizations.

Historicizing the concept of civilization

The origin of the word "civilization" is traceable to eighteenth-century France (Braudel 1994: 3–8; Elias 1995). In German, the word *Kultur* assumed comparable significance about the same time. Both had the connotation of a process of increasing civility, the antithesis of barbarity. The context was the emergence of the bourgeoisie as a strong social force – in France more closely linked to state power, in Germany more separate and having its stronghold in the universities. The civilizing process was conceived as a universal phenomenon characterizing the Enlightenment of eighteenth-century Europe, at one with universal reason and natural laws applicable in the physical sciences, economics, law, and morality. The finality of the process was civilization in the singular.

The Enlightenment perspective of civility was soon challenged by the Romantic movement which rejected the notion of an objective world governed by universal laws and striving towards the attainment of universal norms of law and morals. Romantic thinkers gave more place to subjectivity and uniqueness. Each distinctive national culture had its own aim and destiny in world history. Herder in Germany, Michelet in France, Burke in England voiced this counter-perspective to the universalism of the Enlightenment. The theme was developed later during the nineteenth century by German historicism (e.g. by Wilhelm Dilthey). The European expansionism of the nineteenth century gave substance to these philosophical leanings. *Les bourgeois conquérants* (to borrow the phrase of Charles Morazé, 1957) encountered other civilizations. Civilization in the singular gave way to civilizations in the plural. But imperialism and its accompanying scholarship now defined the non-European civilizations as objects of knowledge. European civilization (and its American offshoot) were to be thought of as dynamic, an active agent inspired by the doctrine of progress. Non-European civilizations were thought of as passive and fixed.

Conditions during the later nineteenth century – the long depression of the last three decades, the social conflicts arising from urbanization and industrialization, the social transformations that Tönnies described as from *Gemeinschaft* to *Gesellschaft* and Durkheim as from mechanical to organic solidarity, and ultimately the imperialist rivalries that led to WWI – encouraged skepticism about the doctrine of Progress. Oswald Spengler's *The Decline of the West*, the first major European work of the twentieth century on the theme of civilizations, reflected this more pessimistic mood. The manuscript was substantially completed just before the outbreak of WWI and was worked over and published in 1918 in the context of German defeat. The English translation was published in 1926 and 1928. Its pessimism resonated to the era of the Great Depression and the rise of fascism.[3]

Spengler saw history as recording the birth, maturity and decline of a number of civilizations, each with a distinct spirit. This he called his "Copernican revolution". Europe and the West were not the center around which other societies revolved; they were one among other civilizations, each of which followed a predetermined sequence of stages and European civilization was entering into its final phase. His approach elaborated upon the visions of Giambattista Vico and the Romantics of the earlier nineteenth century. Spengler's thoughts for his own time focused on what remained possible for Western civilization to achieve during its inexorable decline.

The other great work on civilizations of the first half of the twentieth century, Arnold J. Toynbee's *A Study of History* (1946, 1957), was more optimistic in tone since it envisaged the possibility of rebirth of civilization through a religious revival. This monumental work was published in a series of volumes through the 1930s. Its major impact came after WWII and was quite important especially in the United States.[4] A major promoter of Toynbee's work in America was Henry Luce, the publisher of *Time*, *Life*, and *Fortune* magazines. Luce seized upon Toynbee's concept of the "universal state" as the ultimate stage of a civilization and put the United States in the role of creator of a new universal state for the world. He signed an editorial in *Life* entitled "The American Century" which reflected the internationalist and interventionist views of the Eastern Establishment against American isolationism. *Time* published an influential summary of Toynbee's work by Whittaker Chambers, the ex-communist soon to attain renown as the principal witness in the trial and conviction of Alger Hiss. Luce undoubtedly enhanced Toynbee's reputation but his use of the work deviated from Toynbee's own preoccupation with religion as the road to salvation for civilizations as well as individual souls (McNeill 1989).[5]

Luce's appropriation of Toynbee placed emphasis once again upon civilization in the singular – the creation of a single all-embracing American-inspired world order. As the Cold War came to dominate thinking about the future of the world, the choice seemed to be between two universalisms, capitalism and communism, both derived from the European Enlightenment. The sense of coexistence of a plurality of civilizations was obscured. Whatever was not pertinent to the Cold War did not matter in the top levels of world politics. Of course, at the lower levels, the Cold War was less a matter of concern than the daily struggle for survival in conditions of poverty and deprivation, the subordination of peoples to imperialism, and various forms of discrimination. But such sentiments were obscured in the top-down view of the Cold War. With the formal end of the Cold War these other sentiments began to be more clearly articulated as forms of identity. A plurality of civilizations re-emerged as the largest aggregates of identities. However, these new burgeoning identities were contradicted by the triumphant universalism of the Cold War victor: the ideology of economic globalization.

Western consciousness has been split between a dominant universalistic perspective that sees civilization as a *Western* civilization encompassing the whole world, and a pluralistic perspective that sees Western civilization (variously defined) as coexisting with and interacting with other civilizations. In the Western historical trajectory, the pluralistic conception is recurrent as counterpoint to major historical upheavals: the affirmation of national cultures in response to the conquest and containment of the French Revolution, the *fin de siècle* pessimism of the late nineteenth century, and the loss of certainty in the exhaustion of the certainties of WWII and the Cold War in the late twentieth century. The universalistic notion of civilization has, however, remained a characteristic of Western consciousness and an intellectual obstacle to recognition of the ontological equality of other civilizations.

What is a civilization?

Archeologists who have studied ancient civilizations have defined them in material terms (Childe 1942). The process of civilization is associated with urban life, state structures, and technological innovation, from neolithic through copper to bronze eras, including invention of the wheel, the ox-cart, and the sailing ship. Such material civilizations are recorded *c.* 2500 BCE in the Nile Valley, Fertile Crescent, and the environs of Mohenjo Daro, other such sites of autonomous civilizations being in China, Africa, and Central and South America.

These material, technological, economically organized and class-structured entities were unified by religion, myth, symbols, and language, which were all the same thing until the rationalization of language distinguished among them. Those sets of symbols which made possible meaningful communication among the participants in a material civilization can be called sets of inter-subjective meanings. *So a working definition of a civilization can be a fit or correspondence between material conditions of existence and inter-subjective meanings.*

The notion of a "fit" does not imply a base/superstructure relationship in a "vulgar Marxist" sense. Different sets of inter-subjective meanings may correspond to the same material conditions of existence. The requirement is that they make sense of these material conditions for the people concerned and make it possible for them to conceive their future and to concert their activities towards certain ends. The relationship is more like Max Weber's "elective affinity" between religions and social groups (Weber 1948: 267–301). Some implications flow from this definition: epistemology; theories of history; boundaries in time and space.

Epistemology

The emphasis on inter-subjectivity implies that there are different perspectives on the world, different understandings about the nature of the world, different perceptions of "reality". Accordingly, the "real world" is not a given, external to thought. "Reality" is socially and historically constructed as part of thought interacting with its material environment. Different civilizational perspectives perceive different "realities"; and these different realities are constantly changing and developing. One inference from this is the need for reflexivity, for self-awareness of the social and historical conditioning of our own thought. Another inference is the need to be able to enter into the mental frameworks or inter-subjective meanings of others (Vico 1970: para. 338).[6] It leads to the postmodern dilemma: if there are no absolute foundations for social knowledge, where is truth?

Theories of history

Various theories of the development of civilizations may yield heuristic hypotheses but must be rejected as laws of history. Giambattista Vico posited that each civilization had a distinct origin and a history independent of other civilizations.[7] These separate histories, however, followed a common pattern, the "ideal eternal history" which, from heroic creative origins out of the barbarism of the senses evolved a rationalized society under universal laws, which in time descended into the "barbarism of the intellect" in which pursuit of self-interest was unconstrained – a condition more depraved than the original barbarism of the senses. Vico minimized contacts and borrowing among civilizations, placing all the emphasis on the internal dynamics of development activated primarily by class struggle. He formulated the classical statement of the cyclical concept of the history of civilizations.

Oswald Spengler's view of the distinctness of civilizations was similar to Vico's. Each civilization had its distinct spirit, but each also went through the same phases of birth, creativity, rationalization, and decline. The characteristics of these phases were somewhat different from Vico's but the pattern was the same. Toynbee introduced more interaction and borrowing among civilizations. He was interested in the process of succession linking one declining civilization to another emerging civilization; but he retained the essentials of the cyclical hypothesis.

A triadic view of the history of civilization preceded and coexisted with the cyclical hypothesis. The fascination with the number three in Western conscious-ness as a key to history can be traced to the twelfth-century Calabrian monk Joachim of Floris and may well derive from the Christian doctrine of the Trinity. Joachim of Floris divided history (there was only one history, i.e. the history of

Christianity) into three periods: the reign of the Father, the rule of the unincarnate God, an authoritarian pre-Christian era; the reign of the Son or the Christian era in which political institutions were necessary to constrain people's behavior in conformity with the revelations of religion; and the reign of the Holy Spirit which he imagined as a communitarian future in which harmony would naturally prevail without the need for political constraints. This triadic form, entrenched in Western consciousness, lent itself to the dialectical theories of Hegel and Marx. In simplified form, it became a linear, progressive doctrine of history. Triadic and linear forms conceive of only *one* civilizational trajectory.

In non-Western perspectives, a dyadic picture of history has been more common. Its foremost expression is in the Chinese conception of a fundamental rhythm of the universe alternating between *yin*, a quiescent phase of unity and harmony, and *yang*, a phase of activity, conflict and fragmentation. The fourteenth-century Islamic diplomat and philosopher Ibn Khaldun posited a recurrent swing between two forms of social and political life, *'umran badawi* and *'umran hadari* (Khaldun 1967; Lacoste 1984).[8] The first derives from rural life and the second from urban life but the meanings go far beyond those terms. *'Umran badawi* is the origin of social organization and is conceived of as an ascetic form of life in which may arise a spirit of solidarity (*'asabiya*) through which people become capable of creating a state. The aim of the state will be enjoyment of sedentary, urban civilization or *'umran hadari*; but urban life and the affluence it generates are corrupting and ultimately erode the spirit of solidarity which created it. Thus history, in both Chinese and Ibn Khaldun's conceptions, is cyclical rather than progressive. Both conceptions refer to the dynamics of one civilization and say nothing about the coexistence of civilizations.

Boundaries in time and space

Spengler and Toynbee do not agree about the number or the boundaries of civilizations which suggests this is not a matter about which any categorical statements can be made. Fernand Braudel insists that each civilization develops from a specific geographical zone:

> To discuss civilization is to discuss space, land and its contours, climate, vegetation, animal species and natural or other advantages. It is also to discuss what humanity has made of these basic conditions: agriculture, stock-breeding, food, shelter, clothing, communications, industry and so on.
>
> (Braudel 1994: 9–10)

Certainly, historically civilizations have evolved upon specific geographical sites and have, as Braudel remarks, been colored by these origins. Today, however, with demographic expansion, migratory movements, the diffusion of ideas, and the proliferation of diasporas, geographical definitions become more problematic. Susan Strange has referred plausibly to a non-territorial "business civilization" (Strange 1990). Different civilizations coexist within the geographical space of one country, even within the personal space of one individual. Nowadays it makes more sense to think of a civilization as a community of thought, taking up the inter-subjectivity side of my proposed definition, while acknowledging that inter-subjective meanings evolve in relation to material conditions in which geography continues to play a role alongside transnational economic networks and world-spanning communications technologies.

Braudel also wrote: "The history of civilizations … is the history of mutual borrowings over many centuries, despite which each civilization has kept its own original character" (1994: 8). One can agree with this statement and at the same time acknowledge that it leaves unresolved problems. If civilizations are continually borrowing and changing, how do we recognize the core identity? How do we know the boundaries?

Thinking of a civilization as a community of thought allows for the physical intermingling of civilizations. It loosens the analogy of civilizations to nation–states and the notion that one can plot the "fault lines" between civilizations on a map.[9] I would therefore rather focus on inter-subjectivity and the dynamics shaping different forms of inter-subjectivity.

Dimensions of civilizations: what are the factors that shape inter-subjectivity?

What follows has no pretensions to completeness. I signal here some of the factors that influence the ways in which peoples understand the world in which they live. These are factors which seem to be at work within all civilizations. They may differentiate civilizations that coexist but they also account for changes within each civilization. There may well be other factors that the following itemization overlooks.

Social economy (or social relations of production)

The way people are organized to satisfy their material needs is a basic aspect of civilization. Both liberalism and Marxism see capitalism as an economic system functioning according to inherent laws, although they differ, of course, in their evaluation of that system. Karl Polanyi's view was different. As a social anthropologist, he studied "substantive economies", i.e. the various historically created forms through which people had become organized to satisfy their material needs. In these different substantive economies, economic processes were embedded in social relations. They served the social goals or conformed to the social norms of the community. In consequence, different substantive economies, different modes of social organization of production and distribution, have come into existence throughout history, each conforming to a particular form of society.

Polanyi's concern centered upon the attempt initiated in England in the early nineteenth century to sever that historically prevalent connection between economy and society: the attempt to create a self-regulating market over and above society. This "utopian" venture, according to Polanyi, tore at the fabric of society, reducing whole classes to the condition of isolated and helpless individuals. It provoked a reaction from society that later in that century began to re-establish social protection against the destructive effects of economic processes: factory acts, organized industrial relations, social security, ultimately the welfare state (Polanyi 1957). Another effort to introduce the self-regulating market on a world scale is now happening through economic globalization. There is an implicit conflict between the dominance over society of abstract economic laws and the construction of substantive economies that organize economic activity in compatibility with the norms of existing societies. That conflict is expressed in practical policy issues in different parts of the world today. In that conflict civilizational perspectives challenge the dominance of the global self-regulating market.

Globalization is in practice challenged by resistance from below, from the aroused consciousness of people hurt by globalization; and also by the affirmation of different forms of capitalism rooted in different cultural traditions or different and conflicting views of the future. Instances of resistance from below include strike waves (France in December 1995 and South Korea in January 1997) that were consciously directed against globalization; the rebellion of the *Zapatistas* in Chiapas that broke out significantly on the day the North American Free Trade Agreement (NAFTA) came into effect (New Year's Day 1994); what Fantu Cheru has called the "silent revolution" in Africa or the turning away from the state and international institutions by local self-help movements (Cheru 1989); and the mobilization of civil society movements that blocked the proposed Multilateral Agreement on Investment.

Capitalism is global to the extent that it seems to function according to certain general laws, specifically the behavior of markets in respect of supply and demand. This common nature of capitalism is reinforced as governments have lost both the power and the will to intervene in market behavior. Capitalism remains culturally specific insofar as its institutionalization in different parts of the world has been shaped by different historical experiences and different conceptions of social purpose. Herein lies the conflict between globalization and civilizations, for civilizational forces work towards the social embedding of different forms of capitalism.

This conflict is most salient today in Europe as the European Union (EU) on a variety of issues is confronted by the choice between hyperliberal and social market (or social democratic) conceptions of capitalism.[10] The debate in the institutions of the EU over "social Europe" and the "democratic deficit" is propelled by social and political forces in the different countries. Lionel Jospin seized the point when he qualified the unexpected Socialist Party victory in the June 1997 elections as "un choix de civilisation" (*Le Monde*, 7 June 1997).

The Asian financial crisis of 1998 may well give rise to conflict between global capitalism, which has created conditions for Western firms to gain financial control over Asian productive resources, and Asian governments and people determined to regain control over their economic and political future

(Richardson 1998). The distinctiveness of Asian, and particularly Japanese, capitalism in terms of the social relations of production has been well established (Johnson 1982; Tsuru 1993; Fallows 1994). The relationship of individual to group, the roles of state and society, and of consensus and competition, are understood differently from the way these things are understood in hyperliberal capitalism. Resentment against global finance, perceived as western controlled, could stimulate determination to construct more indigenous forms of social and political economy.

In Russia, a predatory capitalism infiltrated by mafia-type enforcement methods has grown up in the space left by the collapse of "real socialism". In China, a more managed transition from socialism seems to be taking place. Other projects of substantive economy exist outside the realm of capitalism in the perhaps utopian goal of an Islamic social economy, in the movements towards self-sufficiency and internally determined development by indigenous peoples, and in the support to be found among "Green" dissenters in more affluent areas of the world for a social economy subordinated to maintenance of the biosphere.

A conventional Marxist would say it is all capitalism, and in one sense that is probably a fair statement but it obscures the fact that the differences in social organization and in widely accepted values and norms of behavior and expectations may be very significant for people living and working under these different forms of society. Civilizations confront the economic imperatives of capitalism and move social economies in different directions.

Dominance and subordination

Edward Said (1979) described the Western approach to Eastern civilizations as "Orientalism" by which he meant a form of knowledge through which Eastern civilizations were seen as subordinate to the West.[11] Western scholarship, assuming a position of universalist objectivity, defined the characteristics of dominated civilizations and had the power to transmit to the dominated this knowledge of themselves. The elites of the dominated could thus become absorbed into an alien universalism. Kinhide Mushakoji has used the term "occultation" to describe the manner in which the thought processes of one civilization have been displaced by those of another dominant one. Yet the thought processes of the dominated civilization are not totally suppressed but remain latent, ready to be aroused by some crisis (Mushakoji 1996).

Antonio Gramsci's concept of "passive revolution" has some relevance here, although Gramsci was not discussing civilizations (Gramsci 1971: 105–20). Gramsci took the term from Vincenzo Cuocuo, the historian of Naples under Napoleonic rule for whom passive revolution was the introduction of ideas from an alien society which were embraced by a local elite though they did not resonate with the common people. The result was a situation Gramsci called revolution/restoration in which the newly adopted ideas and modes of behavior were never securely entrenched since they never penetrated thoroughly to the mass of the people. One might draw a parallel with British intellectual and institutional influence in India, seemingly secure in the Nehru era but subsequently contested by the Hindu nationalists when they gained power.

Oswald Spengler, despite his thesis that civilizations were separate and did not impinge upon one another, put forward an interesting concept that suggests how an impetus from one civilization penetrating into another can partially transform that other but be constrained by the persisting structures of the other. Borrowing a term from mineralogy, he called the process "pseudomorphosis" and applied it to the formation of the European Middle Ages from the time of Augustus to the tenth century.[12] A nascent Arabian spiritual energy became configured by a fixed and persistent Greco-Roman political form. Spengler discerned a similar phenomenon in the way Westernization imported into Russia by Peter the Great framed and shackled the Russian spirit.[13] All of these concepts – Orientalism, occultation, passive revolution, and pseudomorphosis – evoke the phenomenon of dominance of one civilization over another but also of the continuing latency of the dominated culture and the potential for reaffirmation of its authenticity. A most important object of enquiry is thus to trace the evidence of linguistic and conceptual superposition, to try to assess the different meanings given to these superimposed concepts in the discourse of subordinate groups, and to identify the kinds of crisis likely to precipitate a rejection of the superimposed discourse by subordinate groups.

Spiritual consciousness

The sociologist Pitrim Sorokin contrasted two types of culture: the sensate and the ideational (Sorokin 1957).[14] The sensate culture admits only observation of external phenomena. The observer achieves "objectivity" by classifying and plotting the relationships among the data observed. The ideational culture posits the existence of a spiritual world behind the observable phenomenal world – the thing-in-itself or noumenal world of Kant. For Sorokin, these were ideal types, neither of which has ever existed in a pure form, but always in combinations stressing the one tendency or the other.

The notion "spiritual" here need not mean mystical; it can just as well mean a world animated by thought both at an individual and a collective level. Nor need "ideational" imply "idealism" in the sense that the world is the concrete expression of ideas alone. Recognition of a spiritual element behind observable phenomena is consistent with a recognition that the specific form the spiritual may take in different times and places responds to the material conditions of existence that people have experienced and the social practices they have devised to cope with these material conditions. Max Weber recognized this in his sociology of religions (Gerth and Wright Mills 1948; Bendix 1960: 49–281). It is the common feature of historicist thought in the West from Giambattista Vico, through the German historicism of Wilhelm Dilthey and the English of R.G. Collingwood, to the Italian of Croce and Gramsci. The common theme is that thought is the point of access to an understanding of the continuing interaction of mind and material conditions in the making of history. As method, the ideational hypothesis is the obvious key to an understanding of civilizations, since civilizations represent the ways large aggregates of people interpret the world, respond to it, and shape projects for acting in it.

Pitrim Sorokin had in mind something more than a method for understanding, however. He saw an alternation between a predominance of the ideational culture and that of the sensate as marking changes of era. All the main components of a culture: science and philosophy, law and ethics, forms of social and political organization – all these he saw as changing synchronously and in the same direction (1957: 223). The ideational was characteristic of a creative, poetic initial phase of a culture (Sorokin always speaks of culture rather than civilization). The sensate emerged in a mature phase and fully characterizes a post-mature culture. This reading of the process of civilization is similar to that of Vico and Spengler. Spengler used the term "culture" (which has that special connotation of creativity in German) for the initial phase of the historical entity which, in its mature and declining phases, he called a civilization. Sorokin, writing in the 1930s, like Spengler, writing somewhat earlier, predicted a crisis of the prevailing sensate culture of the West.[15] In his thinking, as in the *yin* and *yang* of Chinese culture or in the alternations of rural and urban in Ibn Khaldun's thought, the demise of the sensate culture should make way for a revival of the ideational.

As suggested above, such notions of historical laws may be taken as heuristic hypotheses though not accepted at face value. Whatever value may be placed upon a notion of historical sequence or alternation of cultural perspectives, it is useful in the study of the dynamics of inter-subjectivity to reflect upon the implications for human understanding and action of different types of spiritual consciousness. Theology, over the centuries, has given us three types that have contemporary applicability: monotheism, polytheism, and pantheism.

The monotheistic idea may have been derived from the centralized power of ancient hydraulic empires where everything appeared to flow from a single source. The idea took root in the Eastern Mediterranean and spread worldwide through the three monotheistic religions: Judaism, Christianity, and Islam (Armstrong 1993).[16] The monotheistic mentality, however, is not limited to adherence to one of these three religions. Its most important aspect is belief in absolute truth which may be retained by people who have severed any formal religious affiliation.[17] The absolutist cast of mind not only affirms with certainty; it also excludes and anathematizes heresy. This cast of mind impresses an indelible character upon the civilization it shapes.

Polytheism admits of multiple truths and accepts the coexistence of non-exclusive religions. Polytheism is relative where monotheism is absolutist and it has been more characteristic of Eastern civilizations. The point is not to stereotype civilizations with the monotheistic or polytheistic mode of thought, but rather to examine the way such tendencies may be indicators of change in the evolution of civilizations. Postmodernism in Western civilization may be seen as a polytheistic development to the extent that postmodernists accept that different individuals and different groups have their own "truths", that "truth" is socially and historically constructed.[18]

Pantheism sees a spiritual unity to the cosmos which is manifested through the manifold variety of existences. Everything is linked to and dependent upon the whole. This has been a common feature in the religious consciousness of indigenous peoples. It is also present in the Hindu *upanishads* which posit a single Reality or Unity that manifests itself in multiple ways.[19] Pantheism has arisen within contemporary Western civilization in deep ecology or the sense of unity and interdependence of all forms of life and life sustaining substances within the biosphere (Lovelock 1979).

Modern societies have also known an extreme form of spiritual consciousness that takes the form of doomsday cults. These cults mix science or science fiction with doctrines of salvation under the supreme authority of their leaders. They have attracted technically sophisticated people, which suggests that some formally educated people do not find sufficient meaning in their lives within the contemporary world. Some, like the Solar Temple and Heaven's Gate, have led to mass suicide of their members. Others, like the Aum Shinrikyo have actively sought to make their doomsday prophesy self-fulfilling (Iida 1997).

No civilization is ever reducible to a single form of spiritual consciousness. Civilizations are shaped through a mingling of different forms and a shifting predominance of one or other of these forms; and this mingling and shifting consciousness is related to the development of the material world. Monotheism is not powerful through a resurgence of church-going but through the absolute certainty of the ideological exponents of global capitalism.[20] The strengthening of alternative forms of social economy could encourage an acceptance of diversity reminiscent of polytheism. The advancement of Green economics gives substance to pantheism; and the alienation from society of the cultist is not unrelated to anomie produced by modern economies.

Time and space

Harold Innis, from his study of civilizations, inferred that the relative emphasis on time and space gave a bias affecting broad aspects of a culture. A stable society, he concluded, had a proper balance between a time orientation and a space orientation (Innis 1951, 1986). Innis saw space orientation as being derived from an emphasis on administration, law, and military power. A time orientation derived from the sense of continuity in religion and an oral tradition. Innis was troubled by what he saw as the "present-mindedness" of his contemporary world, the dominance of the ephemeral. He urged recovery of a time orientation to restore a proper balance.[21]

Time is a most complex idea. The more one reflects upon it, the less certainty there is about it. According to Henri Bergson, whose philosophical work is of the late nineteenth century, there were two contrasting conception of time (Bergson 1945). One was the common-sense notion of time, what we can call "clock time", the notion of a universal homogeneous medium measuring from outside whatever is happening. This was, as Bergson thought about it, time reduced to space, the space traveled by the hands of the clock. The other kind of time, which interested Bergson more, he called *durée*. The term is not very adequately rendered into English as "duration", since duration may also have the spatial meaning of an externally observed trajectory between two points, a beginning and an end. *Durée*, for Bergson, signified rather lived time, experienced time, the subjective feeling of acting and choosing and of pressures limiting action and choice.

Modern physics since Einstein has destroyed the common-sense absoluteness of clock time. Time and space, since Einstein, are seen as interrelated and relative to each other. Time, with the universe, has a beginning, and so will have an end. There are different times depending on the relative motion of bodies in space. Time is not an absolute in the mind of God but a construct of the minds of human beings. The post-Einsteinian physicist John Wheeler has said: "The word Time came not from heaven but from the mouth of man" and he reduced the concept to the rather modest definition that "Time is nature's way to keep everything from happening at once" (Davies 1996: 236–67). There is for modern physics no absolute standard against which happenings in the physical world, let alone the human and social worlds, can be plotted.

In the history of time, the European Middle Ages held time to be an organic, subjective thing, a part of nature. The Enlightenment, with Newton, initiated the idea of time as an abstract independent standard of measurement, divorced from nature. Einstein put time back into nature and at the same time deprived it of the common-sense certainty inherited from the eighteenth century.

The subjective notion of *durée* has also undergone development. Bergson's work was related to the individual's consciousness of time. Fernand Braudel expanded it to cover historical time (Braudel 1979).[22] For Braudel, different aspects of human and social life have different tempos. Economic change moves at a different pace from art and architecture or from change in law and mores. In this he differs from the vision of Vico or Spengler in which all aspects of society change simultaneously from a single impetus. For Braudel, changes in these different departments of life are not unrelated, but they are not synchronous. So there is a history of mentalities moving at a different pace from a history of material life but nevertheless interacting with it.

In all these different histories – these different "times" – there are three levels of time according to Braudel. The level of immediacy is the time of events (*l'histoire évenmentielle*). Events can be recorded but they do not explain themselves. To be explained, they must be understood within their context in time and space. The first level of explanation is what Braudel called *conjonctures*, an intermediate time-frame such as that of a long economic cycle, a persisting configuration of social forces, e.g. Fordism or social democracy, or the duration of a scientific paradigm. The *conjoncture* in turn is explainable within the framework of the *longue durée*, an historical structure created by collective human activity over long periods of time which comes to be regarded in common sense as the natural order of things. Language, the moral code, property relations, the state and the interstate system are all constructions of human collective activity in the *longue durée*, though they come to be regarded as enduring foundations of human life. They are all, however, subject to slow change through collective human activity and that change can, often in retrospect, reach points of radical transformation into new historical structures.

An historical structure of the *longue durée* is to be understood in both synchronic and diachronic dimensions – both in terms of the interactions and interdependencies of its different component elements, and in terms of its development over time. Braudel's magnum opus on the world-economy of capitalism seemed to privilege the synchronic, the understanding of this economy as a world system but one can read into it that the purpose of understanding the synchronic dimension is to be able to see the contradictions out of which structural transformation could come. Braudel's theorizing of history bridges the gulf between the homeostasis of structural–functional sociology and the change through conflict of Vichian and Marxian dialectic. It brings us back to Harold Innis' problematic of balance between a space orientation and a time orientation.

In our own world, the time–space balance is having a profound effect on economic behavior and through the economy on all other aspects of life. Money is a symbol of economic power. The real economy is the actual production of goods and services. Money is fungible and mobile at the speed of electronic communication. Production is fixed in specific enterprises and it takes a long time to develop – technological innovation and building of producer goods, training of workers. The symbolic economy of finance operates in a synchronic dimension; it is space-oriented. The development of production takes place in a diachronic dimension; it is time-oriented. As the world economy has become global in extent, global finance has come to dominate production. Globalization means the triumph of space over time, the victory of the transitory and the ephemeral. The economic basis for the subordination of the time orientation is reinforced by the globalization of the media which propagate a consciousness of an eternal present. This is the psychological meaning of "the end of history".

Revival of civilizations would shift emphasis from space to time. Civilizations are entities of the *longue durée*. In part, this involves a sense of continuity and development from past origins but primarily it implies the construction of alternative visions of a future – an escape from the inevitability of the eternal homogenized present of globalization into an active collective construction of future economies re-embedded in self-conscious societies.

A research program

To study civilizations and their role and potential in the world today implies both an approach to knowledge and a focus on topics that enable us to assess how the aforementioned dimensions of civilization are interacting in the process of civilizational development.

Epistemology

Two propositions stand out as implicit in the very notion of civilizations:

1   *There are alternatives for the human future.* Mankind is not bound into an inex-
    orable expansion of globalization determined by competitiveness in a global
    market which will lead inevitably to a homogenized global society on the
    model of contemporary America. Civilizations embodying different values
    and different patterns of social organization are conceivable, for good or ill.
    There is still a problem of moral and social choice.
2   *If different civilizations do coexist, the problem of mutual comprehension becomes
    paramount for the maintenance of world order.* This arises in an epistemological
    context far different from the game theoretic and rational choice notions
    popular during the Cold War which assumed a single shared rationality. An
    ability to enter into the mental framework of the Other becomes an essen-
    tial ingredient in peaceful coexistence.

R.G. Collingwood, in his book *The New Leviathan* (1942), put forward a relevant
thought. The book bears the marks of its conception during WWII in its insistence on the struggle between civilization (in the singular) and barbarism.[23] But
it contains a thought about the process of civilization – the process of generating
civility – that is relevant to a coexistence of civilizations (in the plural).
Collingwood refers to the distinction made by Plato between two kinds of discussions: eristical and dialectical. In an eristic discussion each party tries to prove he
was right and the other wrong. In a dialectic discussion each party hopes to find
that initial disagreement will, through the process of discussion, lead to a perception by both parties that they are both right (1942: 181–3). Each sees one aspect
of a truth that both, through the process of dialectic, may ultimately share. To
Collingwood, dialectic discussion was especially appropriate in a Heraclitean
world, i.e. a world of change in which reality, the object of discussion, was in
constant transformation. Dialectic was, he argued, the means of absorbing non-
social elements into a larger society; but it might also, extrapolating now from
Collingwood, become a means of understanding among coexisting civilizations
each of which had different perspectives on a world common to both.

   Mikhail Bakhtin, using a different vocabulary, takes a not dissimilar but
perhaps more fully applicable approach to the problem of coexistence (Bakhtin
1984). Bakhtin rejects the term dialectic insofar as it has been appropriated by
Hegelian and Marxist theories of history in which the dialectic is determined by
a single central impulse, whether ideal or material. He uses the term "dialogue"
which derives from the Socratic dialogues of Plato (Collingwood's source for the
term "dialectic"). For Bakhtin, the Hegelian and Marxian dialectics are mono-
logues, the expression of a single thought interpreting and explaining the world.
Bakhtin's world is peopled by self-conscious beings, each with its own perspective on the whole. In his reflections on Dostoevsky, these beings were the
characters of the novels, each of which brings a distinctive perspective to the
action; and there is no overarching "author's" interpretation. But we may also

think of civilizations as beings each with its own inter-subjectivity, together engaged in an interaction in which there is no authoritative overarching theory of historical change. These civilizational perspectives evolve in time; and the world of coexisting perspectives is open-ended. There is no closure, no end of history. No one being (individual or civilization) may legitimately reify the Other, i.e. treat it as an object (as in Orientalism). The condition of dialogue is mutual recognition of self-conscious beings. Referring to Dostoevsky's novels, Bakhtin writes: "there stands in place of a single cognizant and judging 'I' to the world, the problems of the interrelationship of all these cognizant and judging 'I's' to one another" (ibid.: 100).

Civil society

The formation of inter-subjectivity may be examined both from the top down and from the bottom up. Established institutions – state, church, media and family – tend to stabilize and reproduce inter-subjectivity, the common-sense view of reality, morality, and the sense of what is normal. Change in inter-subjectivity – in a sense of injustice and of new social norms – comes from the bottom, from civil society. Movements for emancipation of women, for human rights, and for action to relieve poverty come from civil society. Changes in the social relations of production come about through a reaction by civil society to initiatives from dominant economic forces. Study of these movements can trace changes in the balance of power in production, in dominance and subordination of civilizations, in forms of spirituality, and in orientations to space and time. Civil society is the site in which change in inter-subjectivity is generated and in which the basis of political authority at all levels from local to global is grounded. Study of civil society is thus fundamental to knowledge about the dynamics of civilizations.

Civic solidarity

The effectiveness of civil society in promoting change depends upon the degree of civic solidarity. This is a classic problem of political theory. The historian and political theorist Charles Cochrane, in his book *Christianity and Classical Culture*, traced a shift in mood from the creative politics of the Augustan empire, accompanied by notions of commonwealth, reason and justice, to the fatalism of the late empire when life seemed dominated by circumstances, and the state, far from being the creation of human beings in their collectivity was thought of as imposed by a heroic individual of the past.[24] The sense of self-conscious human efficacy, once dominant, was emptied and replaced by determination of the external force of fate. People, once the creators and supporters of political authority, become its passive objects.

The reasons for this transformation have been discussed in a sequence of historical interpretations, each one of which may tell us at least as much about the historian's own time and its preoccupations as about the imperial transformation of Rome.[25] Classical humanism, e.g. in Cicero and Virgil, sought a balance between "virtue" and "fortune", but in the late empire "fortune" had overwhelmed "virtue". Machiavelli hoped for a revival of *virtù* in his time – the creative energy needed to overcome internal fragmentation and conflict and to resist external invasion. He thought his contemporaries too corrupt to provide it from what we could now call civil society; and so he looked to a Prince as a surrogate for civic *virtù* (Chabod 1958; Pocock 1975; Machiavelli 1977). The fourteenth-century Islamic diplomat and historian, Ibn Khaldun, discussing the history of North Africa, saw the collective solidarity of the austere rural community, which he called *'asabiya*, as the force necessary for the creation of a new state. *'Asabiya* was, however, a fragile force, subject to decay in the security and affluence of urban life (Khaldun 1967; Cox 1992). In twentieth-century America, the sociologist Robert Putnam has pointed with concern to a decline of the spirit of association that de Tocqueville credited with the strength of American nineteenth-century society (Putnam 1995).

The strength of civic solidarity is a measure of a society's capacity for civilizational development and therefore of its capacity to resist becoming overwhelmed and "occulted" (Kinhide Mushakoji's term) by another civilization. To understand more about the factors that underpin civic solidarity is thus a key element in the understanding of civilizational dynamics.

The biosphere

Maintenance of the material conditions propitious for human life is the fundamental prerequisite for any form of civilization. At the close of the millennium, awareness of the fragility of the biosphere – the ultimate material constraint – is more vivid than at any earlier period of history. This poses a challenge to develop practices and inter-subjective meanings conducive to maintenance of the biosphere.

Where globalization fosters the synchronic space orientation of global finance, maintenance of the biosphere involves a sense of time, a way of thinking and acting that foresees the consequences of economic practices in terms of their ecological effects. Where globalization is accompanied by absolutist precepts of economics, maintenance of the biosphere involves a mode of spirituality that contemplates the interdependence of all forms of life. And this sense of global biological interdependence would exclude any form of environmentalism that merely shifts the problem from one place to another, from dominant to subordinate economy, cleaning up affluent areas and polluting among the less powerful.

Concern for the biosphere also becomes a central issue in the social relations of production. When corporate interests make competitiveness the supreme criterion, they subordinate both ecological consequences of production and employment and human welfare to it. Taking the biosphere seriously will involve transforming conventional economics into a science that gives priority over competitiveness to nature and society – in Polanyian terms, re-embedding the economy in society and nature. Different civilizational developments may be capable of achieving this in different ways.

Global governance

To think of world order in terms of a coexistence of civilizations poses the problem of global governance in a new way. One aspect of what is happening now is a transformation of the inter-state system (Bull 1977; Sakamoto 1994). A multi-level structure of governance is emerging: institutions of the global market limit the rights of states to intervene; political authority is fragmented among regional, national, and sub-national entities; the principle of "subsidiarity" (as consecrated in the EU) applies more and more widely, whereby authority in specific fields descends to the level most able to effect it; weak states descend into chaos; and one reluctant superpower acts or refrains from action insofar as it is motivated or obstructed by the intensity of purpose of elements of its domestic opinion.

Given these conditions, the most feasible form of global governance may be that of a weak center in a fragmented system. Such a pattern is not without precedent. It existed in phases of the Chinese empire, and also of the Japanese, and in the European Middle Ages with the dual centers of Empire and Papacy. In the present world, the United States appears to be acting as that kind of center, albeit uncertainly and without clear and general acquiescence on the part of others. This form of governance underwrites economic globalization and the concept of a single civilization into which other civilizations would ultimately be absorbed.

The alternative would be an even weaker center like a reconstructed United Nations freed from US unilateralism that conceived its purpose as to search for common ground among coexisting civilizations and to define and promote the material conditions requisite for the development of any and all forms of civilization. The minimal objectives of such a center of global governance could be: (1) maintenance of the biosphere; (2) avoidance of major violence; and (3) mutual recognition of difference among civilizations. From that minimum, objectives could extend to facilitating alternative forms of social and economic organization consistent with a minimal understanding of human rights and welfare. Such a "United Nations" would operate with an epistemology on the lines sketched out above, one which recognizes a multiplicity of "realities" and "truths" and which works not to bring about their convergence but their reconciliation.

Notes

1

> The practical requirements which underlie every historical judgment give to all history the character of "contemporary history" because, however remote in time the events there recounted may seem to be, the history in reality refers to present needs and present situations wherein those events vibrate.
>
> (Croce 1955: 17)

2 In *The Clash of Civilizations and the Remaking of World Order*, Samuel Huntington gives a different reason that future conflicts will be "clashes" of civilizations. This leads to a refurbishment of Cold War mental structures, with a new enemy (a putative Islamic/Confucian alliance) to replace the Soviet threat and with the basic Cold War strategies reaffirmed.

3 A one-volume edition of *The Decline of the West* was published by Knopf, New York, in 1939. For the context of this work, see Hughes (1952).

4 The publication in 1946 of Somervell's abridgement of the first six volumes of Toynbee's *A Study of History* made his ideas more accessible to the general reader.

5 McNeill's *magnum opus The Rise of the West* (1963), obviously entitled as a rejoinder to Spengler's *Decline of the West* (1939), was expressive of the American *hubris* of the post-war decades. His theme was that the principal factor promoting historical change is contact with foreigners possessing new and unfamiliar skills. Civilizations result from a diffusion of skills and knowledge from a central point such as the United States appeared to be following WWII. Twenty-five years later, in a more reflective mood, McNeill came to regard this thesis as "a form of intellectual imperialism". (The retrospective essay which first appeared in the *Journal of World History*, I, 1990: 1–21 is reproduced in the 1991 re-edition of *The Rise of the West*.)

6 R.G. Collingwood called this process "rethinking the thought of the past" (1946). Collingwood applied this notion to different temporal epochs in a continuous history but it is equally applicable to different cultures or civilizations. Indeed, it is the method used and advocated by Giambattista Vico (1970) who wrote that his effort to discover the way in which the first human thinking arose "cost us the research of a good twenty years" in which it was necessary "to descend from these human and refined natures of ours to those quite wild and savage natures, which we cannot at all imagine and can comprehend only with great effort".

7 Vico did not use the word "civilizations" more than a century before it became current in European discourse. Rather, he spoke of "nations", although with a meaning very different from that of nineteenth- and twentieth-century nationalisms. "Nation" for him meant an entity with a common origin and a common set of institutions, in the sense of common social practices, not formal institutions, and a common language, not in the sense of English or French but as a common means of communicating meaning, or what we have here called "inter-subjectivity."

8 The meanings of Ibn Khaldun's concepts are discussed in Yves Lacoste, *Ibn Khaldun: The Birth of History and the Past of the Third World* (1984: 92–117).

9 This is one of the difficulties I have with Samuel Huntington's metaphor of civilizations as tectonic plates colliding along specific geographical fault lines and his picturing of civilizations as states writ large.

10 See e.g. Michel Albert (1991).

11 See also his more recent *Culture and Imperialism* (1993).

12 Spengler (1939: vol. II, 189):

> In a rock stratum are embedded crystals of a mineral. Clefts and cracks occur, water filters in, and the crystals are gradually washed out so that in due course only their hollow mould remains. Then come volcanic outbursts which explode the mountain; molten masses pour in, stiffen, and crystallize out in their turn. But these are not free to do so in their own special forms. They must fill up the spaces that they find available. Thus there arise distorted forms, crystals whose inner structure distorts their external shape, stones of one kind presenting the appearance of stones of another kind. The mineralogists call this phenomenon *Pseudomorphosis*.
>
> By the term "historical pseudomorphosis" I propose to designate those cases in which an older alien Culture lies so massively over the land that a young

> Culture born in this land, cannot get its breath and fails not only to achieve pure and specific expression-forms, but even to develop fully its own self-consciousness. All that wells up from the depths of the young soul is cast in the old moulds, young feelings stiffen in senile works, and instead of rearing up in its own creative power, it can only hate the distant power with a hate that grows to be enormous.

13 The tragedy of the Russian pseudomorphosis, in Spengler's analysis, has been the continuing dominance of Western imported thought over a suppressed and barely articulate Russian spirit. By analogy, the current "market reformers" are but an extension of the Western-inspired communist managers, themselves natural successors to Peter the Great's modernization. In the post-communist débâcle, opposition to the advocates of "shock therapy" have revived awareness of non-Western *narodnik* sentiment. One literary instance is in a revived interest in the work of Nicholas Berdyaev (1947). Those with a longer historical perspective could trace the phenomenon back to the Varangians!

14 Pitrim Sorokin, *Social and Cultural Dynamics*, revised and abridged in one volume by the author (1957). Original four-volume edition published in 1937.

15 According to Sorokin:

> The crisis is far deeper than the ordinary; its depth is unfathomable, its end not yet in sight, and the whole of the Western society is involved in it. It is the crisis of a Sensate culture, now in its overripe stage, the culture that has dominated the Western World during the last five centuries. It is also the crisis of a contractual (capitalist) society associated with it.
>
> (1957: 622)

Against this prediction, it can be argued that the three decades following WWII saw a flourishing of the sensate culture, especially in American social science, and the collapse of "real socialism" appears to negate a crisis of capitalism. In favor of it, it can be argued that the crisis was only postponed and that movements like postmodernism and deep ecology redefine the crisis in more meaningful contemporary terms.

16 For a concise statement, see Karen Armstrong (1993).

17 As an instance of absolutist thinking Louis Althusser has written: "It has been possible to apply Marx's theory with success because it is 'true'; it is not true because it has been applied with success" (Althusser and Balibar 1979: 59). The French Catholic philosopher Jean Guitton, who had been Althusser's professor in his preparation for the *Ecole normale* and was his companion in *l'Action catholique*, remained his friend after Althusser's conversion to atheism and Marxism. The two maintained a close relationship and correspondence thereafter. In 1980, just before the psychiatric crisis in which he strangled his wife, Althusser came to Guitton with a premonition of human catastrophe which, he thought could only be avoided by a union of Rome with Moscow. Reflecting on this strange and enduring friendship, Guitton (1988) wondered whether from his days with *l'Action catholique* to his role as foremost exponent of Marxism in post-1968 France Althusser had fundamentally changed *"dans son intimité secrète et profonde"*.

18 David L. Miller writes:

> Polytheism is not only a social reality; it is also a philosophical condition. It is that reality experienced by men and women when Truth with a capital "T" cannot be articulated reflectively according to a single grammar, a single logic, or a single symbol-system. It is a situation that exists when metaphors, stories, anecdotes, puns, dramas, movies, with all their mysterious ambiguity, seem more compelling than the rhetoric of political, religious, and philosophical systems.

They seem more compelling than tightly argued and logically coherent explanations of self and society because they allow for multiple meanings to exist simultaneously, as if Truth, Goodness, and Beauty can never be contained in a logic that allows for only one of the following: good versus evil, light versus dark, truth versus fiction, reality versus illusion, being versus becoming. In a philosophically polytheistic situation the "new science" of the time will break forth with principles of relativism, indeterminacy, plural logic systems, irrational numbers; substances that do not have substance, such as quarks; double explanations for light; and black holes in the middle of actual realities.

(1974: 5)

19 For a discussion of how this concept of unity in diversity has influenced Indian political history, see Satish Chandra (1997).
20 For a critique of this certainty, see George Soros (1997).
21 David Harvey (1989: 204) sees a compression of time and space as the present condition. Time, he sees as privileged over space in social theories; and space over time in aesthetics. Space is compressed in the awareness of global interdependencies. The compression of time comes about through the shrinking of decision-making horizons into a non-historical present. (One might say, inspired by Innis, that time is being compressed into space.) Harvey's strongest point is that our consciousness of both time and space is dependent upon material processes:

> From this materialist perspective we can then argue that objective conceptions of time and space are necessarily created through material practices and processes which serve to reproduce social life ... The objectivity of time and space is given in each case by the material practices of social reproduction, and to the degree that these latter vary geographically and historically, so we find that social time and social space are differentially constructed. Each distinctive mode of production or social formation will, in short, embody a distinctive bundle of time and space practices and concepts.

Harvey relates present-day concepts of time and space to the reorganization of production from Fordism to Postfordism; the fragmentation of production processes in what he calls "flexible accumulation" enhances the sense of the ephemeral.
22 Braudel's theoretical reflections on time and history are to be found in Braudel (1980); and in Braudel (1979) vol. III especially Chapter 1 and Conclusions.
23 The subtitle to the book is *Man, Society, Civilization and Barbarism*.
24 Cochrane was a student of R.G. Collingwood. Harold Innis' work on civilizations was informed by his conversations with Cochrane, his colleague at the University of Toronto.
25 E.g. Edward Gibbon (1776–88); and the work of Jacob Burckhardt (1852), the Swiss cultural historian.

References

Albert, Michel (1991) *Capitalisme contre capitalisme*, Paris, Seuil.
Althusser, Louis and Balibar, Etienne (1979) *Reading Marx*, London, Verso.
Armstrong, Karen (1993) *A History of God*, New York, Ballentine Books.
Bakhtin, Mikhail (1984) *Problems of Dostoevsky's Poetics*, Minneapolis, University of Minnesota Press.
Bendix, Reinhard (1960) *Max Weber: An Intellectual Biography*, New York, Doubleday.
Berdayaev, Nicholas (1947) *The Russian Idea*, London, Geoffrey Bles.
Bergson, Henri (1945) *Essai sur les données immédiates de la conscience*, Geneva, Skira.

Braudel, Fernand (1979) *Civilisation matérielle, économie et capitalisme XVe–XVIIIe siècle: Le temps du monde*, Paris, Armand Colin.

—— (1980) *On History*, Chicago, University of Chicago Press.

—— (1994) *A History of Civilizations*, London, Allen Lane.

Bull, Hedley, (1977) *The Anarchical Society: A Study of Order in World Politics*, New York, Columbia University Press.

Burckhardt, Jacob (1852) *The Age of Constantine the Great*, London, Routledge & Kegan Paul.

Chabod, Federigo (1958) *Machiavelli and the Renaissance*, London, Bowes & Bowes.

Chandra, Satish (1997) "The Indian Perspective", in Robert W. Cox (ed.), *The New Realism: Perspectives on Multilateralism and World Order*, London, Macmillan for the United Nations University.

Cheru, Fantu (1989) *The Silent Revolution in Africa: Debt, Development and Democracy*, Harrare and London, Zed/Anvil Press.

Childe, Gordon (1942) *What Happened in History?*, Harmondsworth, Penguin.

Cochrane, Charles (1944) *Christianity and Classical Culture: A Study of Thought and Action from Augustus to Augustine*, Toronto, Oxford University Press.

Collingwood, R.G. (1942) *The New Leviathan*, Oxford, Oxford University Press.

—— (1946) *The Idea of History*, Oxford, Clarendon Press.

Cox, Robert W. (1992) "Towards a Posthegemonic Conceptualization of World Order: Reflections on the Relevancy of Ibn Khaldun", in James N. Rosenau and E.-O. Czempiel (eds) *Governance Without Government: Order and Change in World Politics*, Cambridge, Cambridge University Press.

Croce, Benedetto (1955) *History as the Story of Liberty*, New York, Meridian Books.

Davies, Paul (1996) *About Time: Einstein's Unfinished Revolution*, New York, Simon and Schuster.

Elias, Norbert (1995) *The Civilizing Process: The History of Manners and State Formation and Civilization*, Oxford, Blackwell.

Fallows, James (1994) *Looking at the Sun: The Rise of the New East Asian Economic and Political System*, New York, Pantheon.

Gerth, H.H. and Wright Mills, C. (eds) (1948) *From Max Weber: Essays in Sociology*, London, Routledge & Kegan Paul.

Gibbon, Edward (1776–88) *The History of the Decline and Fall of the Roman Empire*, 8 vols. London, The Folio Society.

Gramsci, Antonio (1971) *Selections from the Prison Notebooks*, New York, International Publishers.

Guitton, Jean (1988) *Lire. Le magazine des livres*, no. 148, January 1988.

Harvey, David (1989) *The Condition of Postmodernity: An Enquiry into the Origins of Cultural Change*, Oxford, Basil Blackwell.

Hugues, H. Stuart (1952) *Oswald Spengler: A Critical Estimate*, New York, Scribners.

Huntington, Samuel (1996) *The Clash of Civilizations and the Remaking of World Order*, New York, Simon and Schuster.

Iida, Yumiko (1997) "Virtual Kingdom and Dreams of Apocalypse: Contemporary Japan Mirrored in *Aum Shinrikyo*", paper presented at the 10th Annual Conference, Japan Studies Association of Canada, Toronto, Ontario, 3–5 October.

Innis, Harold A. (1951) *The Bias of Communication*, Toronto, University of Toronto Press.

—— (1986) *Empire and Communications*, Toronto, Press Porcépic.

Johnson, Chalmers (1982) *MITI and the Japanese Miracle*, Stanford, CA, Stanford University Press.

Khaldun, Ibn (1967) *The Muqaddimah*, Princeton, NJ, Princeton University Press.

Lacoste, Yves (1984) *Ibn Khaldun: The Birth of History and the Past of the Third World*, London, Verso.

Lovelock, J.E. (1979) *GAIA: A New Look at Life on Earth*, Oxford, Oxford University Press.

Machiavelli, Niccolò (1977) *The Prince*, New York, W.W. Norton.

McNeill, William H. (1963) *The Rise of the West*, Chicago, University of Chicago Press.

—— (1989) *Arnold J. Toynbee: A Life*, New York, Oxford University Press.

Miller, David L. (1974) *The New Polytheism*, New York, Harper & Row.

Morazé, Charles (1957) *Les bourgeois conquérants*, Paris, Armand Colin.

Mushakoji, Kinhide (1996) "Multilateralism in a Multicultural World: Notes for a Theory of Occultation", in Robert W. Cox (ed.), *The New Realism: Perspectives on Multilateralism and World Order*, London, Macmillan for the United Nations University.

Pocock, J.G.A. (1975) *The Machiavellian Moment*, Princeton, NJ, Princeton University Press.

Polanyi, Karl (1957) *The Great Transformation*, Boston, Beacon Press.

Putnam, Robert D. (1995) "Bowling Alone: America's Declining Social Capital", *Journal of Democracy*, vol. 6, no. 1, January, pp. 65–78.

Richardson, Michel (1998) "West Snaps Up Asian Businesses: As Crisis Deepens, U.S. and European Firms Move In", *The International Herald Tribune*, June, 20–1.

Sakamoto, Yoshikazu (1994) *Global Transformation. Challenges to the State System*, Tokyo, United Nations University Press.

Said, Edward (1979) *Orientalism*, New York, Vintage Books.

—— (1993) *Culture and Imperalism*, New York, Knopf.

Sorokin, Pitrim (1957) *Social and Cultural Dynamics*, Boston, Porter Sargent.

Soros, George (1997) "The Capitalist Threat", *Atlantic Monthly*, February.

Spengler, Oswald (1939) *Decline of the West*, New York, Knopf.

Strange, Susan (1990) "The Name of the Game", in Nicholas X. Rizopoulos (ed.), *Sea Changes: American Foreign Policy in a World Transformed*, New York, Council on Foreign Relations.

Toynbee, Arnold J. (1946, 1957) *A Study of History*, London, Oxford University Press.

Tsuru, Shigeto (1993) *Japan's Capitalism*, Cambridge, Cambridge University Press.

Vico, Giambattista (1970) *The New Science of Giambattista Vico*, Ithaca, NY, Cornell University Press.

Weber, Max (1948) "The Social Psychology of the World Religions", in H.H. Gerth and C. Wright Mills (eds), *From Max Weber*, London, Routledge & Kegan Paul.

2 Globalization, civilizations and world order

A world-constructivist approach

Mehdi Mozaffari

Why are the three concepts of globalization, civilization and world order relevant? How are they related to each other? This chapter seeks to answer these questions. Answering the first one is simple. Obviously, the current world order cannot be fully understood without taking "globalization" into consideration. The effects of globalization reach every corner of the world in different scope and degree. Why is "civilization" important? It is important because civilization incorporates the essence of world order. Civilization, as we will see later on, contains and reflects economic, social, cultural and political aspects and dimensions of the world order. We define a great civilization as the junction between a world vision and a historical formation. The answer to the second question constitutes the main subject of this chapter. We will (1) analyze the relations between civilization and world identity; (2) explain how globalization is related to world economy; and finally (3) we will bind the three concepts (globalization, civilization and world order) together by proposing three models on world order.

Before going through our study, our theoretical approach will be outlined in brief. There is a general consensus among scholars that globalization is first and foremost of economic character. The advanced technological progress contributes largely to the acceleration of economic globalization as well as globalization of certain sets of values; e.g. human rights. In this respect, the world system theory may be applied to explain the evolution of parochial economic systems to the rise of capitalism and the world economy. The world system theory – especially in its Braudel–Wallerstein ramification – goes even further and deals with questions related to civilization, culture, democracy, etc. (Braudel 1979, 1993; Wallerstein 1992, 1995). However, the primary focus remains on economy without paying much attention to the international system, to phenomena such as anarchy, polarity, international law, international ethics, and in general to questions about the identity of the world. A main part of these aspects of the problematic enters within the field of social constructivism which focuses sufficiently on the interaction between international actors as well as on the quality of anarchy and the identity of states. However, the sphere of economy does not represent a priority for the school of social constructivism. Therefore, a synthesis of these two approaches is assumed to be a useful theoretical explanatory tool to clarify relations between globalization and civilizations, the rise of a new standard of civilization, and also the question about the new identity of the world. These two different sets of theories will be operationalized without entering into a theoretical discussion on the selected theories. In other words, theories are not applied here for the sake of theories; they are used with regard to explaining relations between globalization, civilization and world order.

Civilizations and the new identity of the world

The crucial question concerns the compatibility/non-compatibility of the current unprecedented global system with a world made up by a plurality of civilizations. In other words, can the world become economically global without having any substantial impact on civilizations? Such crucial and complex questions require profound and detailed investigation which is beyond the scope of this chapter. However, two elements of this problematic must be mentioned. First, as a general rule, trade will automatically increase the intensity of cultural exchanges. Trade carries along the culture of the traders. The history of humanity stands as proof of the importance of cultural exchange through trade. Second, what is valid for traditional and primitive trade, is *a fortiori* valid for a highly sophisticated system such as capitalism. Capitalism does introduce profound structural transformations in a society. Capitalism requires the division of labor, networks of distribution, banking systems, etc. Such transformations entail social and hence mental and cultural changes. A deep and constant implementation of capitalism in a society will shape the world vision of the people. When a global economic system (capitalism) functions through a system experiencing technological revolution, the mentality and attitude of the people on existential questions (life and death, conflict and cooperation, time and space, etc.) will consequently be influenced. To continue this discussion, the problematics of civilization as a phenomenon must be addressed.

There are small civilizations and great civilizations depending upon their scope, length and depth. There are abortive civilizations (e.g. the Nestorian Christian civilization in the past, and the Soviet civilization in modern times). Cumulative civilizations are of *longue durée* stretching over many centuries (e.g. the Roman and Islamic civilizations). Great civilizations belong to the last category. It is this kind of civilization which will continue to shine, even a long time after their decline. New civilizations are often reconstructed versions of great and cumulative civilizations. In our days, the Western political philosophy is still inspired by ancient Greek philosophers, and its existing legal system is deeply inspired and influenced by the legacy of the Roman Empire. The Muslims, on the other hand, continue to refer to their heritage with the purpose of making and remaking their social, economic and political life.

There was a time when different great civilizations could coexist. Their coexistence was not always peaceful but often dominated by war. At that time, each civilization was unique in the sense that it had its specific set of values, applicable social and political concepts, and a specific idea of its own identity as well

as of that of other civilizations. The characteristics of each civilization constituted its standard of civilization. Globalization broke the cyclical theory
defended by Toynbee (1995) and Quigley (1961). Globalization is now progressively blurring characteristics between different civilizations. It is globalization
which selects various characteristics of civilizations, making of them a sort of
symbiosis.

Civilization is often defined in vague and ambiguous terms: "The inevitable
destiny of a culture" (Spengler, in Huntington, 1996: 42); "The kind of culture
found in cities" (Bagby 1958: 162–3); "Civilizations are invisible, just as constitutions" (Toynbee 1995: 46), etc. In reality, such definitions say nothing tangible
and workable about civilizations. Fernand Braudel provides us with a better definition when defining civilization as "both moral and material values" (1995: 5).
Immanuel Wallerstein, who is also skeptical about the various definitions of civilization, makes a distinction between "historical system" and "civilization".
Civilization, in his view, refers "to a contemporary claim about the past in terms
of its use in the present to justify to heritage, separateness, rights" (Wallerstein
1992: 235). Despite the differences of opinion among scholars, there is at least
unanimity over civilizations being broader than a single culture and larger than a
group of cultures. In other words, civilization is "macro-formation" composed of
"patterns", systems, and movements

> that are again broken down into various schools and movements. The
> patterns are the arrangements that give the parts a relationship to one
> another and to the civilization as a whole, whereas systems have their own
> unity, regardless of whether they happen to form a part of a still larger
> system.
>
> (Melko 1995: 30)

Therefore, the inclusion of "historical formation" or "material" dimension into
the cultural body and memory seems indispensable, at least when the objective is
a workable concept.

In our view, great and cumulative civilizations are composed of two inseparable parts. The first part is made up by an explicit world vision which may be a
set of cultural systems, an ideology, or a religion, which is generally the case. The
second is represented by a coherent political, military, and economic system
often concretized as an empire or a historical formation. I define civilization as a
junction between a world vision and a historical formation. In other words, when
a specific world vision is realized through a historical formation, this fusion is
called civilization. When a historical formation is brought into being without a
comprehensive world vision, such a formation shapes tribes, empires, states, and
other forms of political entities, but not a civilization. Similarly, when a world
vision stands without a body – a "physical" shape – it is merely ideology, culture
or religion. A real civilization is necessarily a generative entity; in its discourse
(world vision) as well as in its historical formation/system. By way of example,
the Roman civilization with its elaborated cosmopolitan vision was seconded by

an imperial institution: the Islamic civilization, with the Koran as a world vision and Umma/Caliphate as a historical formation.

Each civilization possesses its own standard. The standard of Chinese civilization is different from the standard of Islamic civilization, just as the standard of European civilization is different from the standard of Indian civilization. Put simply, the standard of each civilization represents the identity card and the DNA of the same civilization. Furthermore, the standard of civilization is the criterion determining who is "uncivilized" and who is "civilized". "Uncivilized" in one civilization could be considered "civilized" in another, and vice versa.

There is a direct correspondence between the real power of a civilization and the extension of its standard. When one civilization becomes stronger than another, its standard will prevail as the dominant standard. The dominant standard is often imposed on others (e.g. "capitulation", "unequal treaties"), but it can also be "interiorized" and voluntarily accepted (conversion to a religion, adherence to democracy, etc.). Rejecting the dominant standard or opposing it is a sanctionable offense. The sanction can take different forms: Jihad against non-Muslims, economic sanctions against Iraq, universal condemnation of human rights conditions in China, etc. Weak civilizations produce only weak standards in terms of degree and scope of applicability and acceptance. The standard of a declined civilization cannot be revived after its fall.

Continuing our discussion on civilization, there is no historical evidence that the primary aim of civilizations is establishment of internal peace. Historically, all civilizations have been subjected to severe internal conflicts resulting in war. In fact, internal conflicts have been the main source of the decline of civilizations. In other words, a clash within a civilization has been more frequent and more damaging than a clash between civilizations. This is a general remark, valid for all civilizations including the Western civilization. In fact, the Western civilization has been one of the most war-haunted civilizations. Here, we are not referring to the innumerable, bloody and horrifying external wars related to Western colonialism and imperialism. We refer to internal wars such as the Hundred Years' War, the Thirty Years' War (1618–48), the Napoleonic Wars, WWI, and WWII. Similarly, the Greek civilization experienced multiple wars; e.g. the Peloponnesian War between Athens and Sparta, and war between the Athenians themselves. Also the powerful Roman Empire could not escape their fate of division and the rise of the Byzantine Empire as a new rival. The Islamic Empire followed the same path and was divided into many parts (Abbasids, Fatimids, Seljuqs, etc.) causing her final decline as an empire and a civilization. Now, the question is why did the horrifying war history of the Western civilization not cause the decline of Western civilization? Why did the West become paradoxically stronger, and why is its civilization still shining, not like a dying star but as a dominant and unchallenged civilization? Which characteristics of this specific civilization make it so unique? These are crucial and highly sophisticated questions requiring an extensive and multi-disciplinary investigation. Some Western scholars argue that Western civilization is actually in decline. Spengler and Huntington represent this tendency. However, if we consider the West as a whole (USA, Europe, Canada, Australia, Japan, etc.), no serious symptoms indicate a coming decline. On the contrary, the arrow is moving in the opposite direction. As any other civilization, the current Western civilization could of course also be subject to decline. However, this has not happened yet and probably never will. Essentially because what characterizes this civilization and differentiates it from all other previous civilizations resides in the fact that the Western civilization represents a unique and unprecedented example in the history of humankind by the fact that it is a democratic civilization. Since democracy is based on freedom of speech and mind and rule by the people, it possesses crucial qualities of self-discipline. Consequently, as long as the West remains fully democratic, Western civilization will be capable of avoiding decline. Thus, due to the specific nature (democracy) of the Western civilization, a fall, should it ever occur, will be completely different from the fall of all other previous civilizations. In this connection, one may distinguish between the strength of Western powers and the destiny of Western civilization. At present, Western civilization and Western powers are almost identical. A possible decline of Western powers will of course negatively influence Western civilization. However, Western civilization as a civilization would probably survive in other parts of the world; as it happened for Christianity which survived as a hegemonic religion outside its original place of birth.

Globalization combined with the expansion of Western civilization has created a specific world order. This world order is not merely limited to a mechanical stability. The new world order goes beyond stability. It requires legitimacy which is quite different from the legitimacy related to absolute and perpetual sovereignty; a legacy of the Westphalian order. The novelty is that the current changes are more substantial and more general than any time before in history. The new changes in state identities are both horizontal and vertical. Both *Gemeinschaft* and *Gesellschaft*. The identity of states such as e.g. the Czech Republic, Poland, Romania, Bulgaria, and the Baltic republics are quite different from before the end of the Cold War. The most important identity transformation is unquestionably the changes in the identity of the Russian nation. This change has had a considerable number of consequences for peace and stability in the world. As a result, we may claim that Russian missiles today are culturally different from the earlier Soviet missiles. However, there is some resistance to the general change. China, North Korea, Iran, Iraq and some other states are in different degree resisting transformation of the identity in their respective states. However, the change in state identities has not so far affected the structure of the international system. A system changes only if its ordering principle is changed. The ordering principle of the system is still anarchy and the system therefore remains the same. Has the bipolarity changed? Not in military terms. More than a decade after the fall of the Berlin Wall, we still have a nuclear balance of power between the USA and Russia as the successor of the USSR. If the ordering principle of the system has not changed, and the nuclear balance of power remains unchanged as well, wherein lies the actual change? In this respect, the structural–realism gives contradictory messages. On the one hand,

Kenneth Waltz, the foremost figure in structural realism, admits that "[c]learly something has changed" (2000: 30). On the other hand, he says that "[the] world, however, has not been transformed; the structure of international politics has simply been remade by the disappearance of the Soviet Union and for a time we will live with unipolarity" (ibid. 39). From this argumentation we may deduce that the change at the unit level (in this case the Soviet Union) can cause a change in the structure of the international system. Surprisingly, when admitting to this proposition (above quotation), Waltz contradicts himself by saying that "[c]hanges in the structure of the system are distinct from changes at the unit level" (ibid.: 5). The latter proposition is correct, thus is in clear contradiction with Waltz's other proposition that "the structure of international system has been remade". The only way to solve this contradiction is to admit the fact that the structure of the international system has not changed. Despite the hegemony (and not "unipolarity") of the USA, the system still remains anarchical. Clearly, change does not lie in the structure of the international system. The change lies precisely in the world and the identity of the world, and consequently the identity of the global system. It means that the identity of the system can be subject to change whereas the structure remains unchanged. Consequently, we still have anarchy, although not the same kind; we still have a balance of powers, but not the same kind; and we still have states, but they no longer have the same authority and sovereignty. Yet, it is obvious that the world before and after the fall of the Berlin Wall is a quite different place. The balance of power between a democratic bloc, on the one hand, and a non-democratic bloc on the other differs from a balance of power between two democratic blocs. More specifically, the US–USSR balance of power is completely different from a possible US–EU balance of power. It is equally true that a democratic anarchy is quite different (in terms of functioning, communications, and consequences) from a mixed anarchy (democratic and non-democratic). In an anarchical system there are two ways of categorizing states. One is power-based and the other is quality-based. Most theories, realism (old and new) in particular, classify states according to their respective material (power) capabilities: superpowers, great powers, medium powers, and small powers. From this point of view, nuclear weapons are nuclear weapons independent of the immaterial attributes of their possessor. Some nuclear weapons are less destructive than others. There is neither "good" nor "bad" in a Machiavellian universe, only "friends" and "enemies", amity and enmity. Waltz is convinced that states' interests have nothing to do with their identity. The interest of a democratic state is identical with the interest of a non-democratic state. However, he admits that "all governments have their faults, democracies no doubt fewer than others, but that is not good enough to sustain the democratic peace thesis" (Waltz 2000: 12). If it is so, why does President George W. Bush consider Russia a friend of the USA? What happened which turned the arch-enemy of the USA to its friend? To state the reason to be Russia's weakness would be a realistic argument. In this case, why does the President of the USA not consider countries such as China, North Korea or Iran as friends of the USA? These states are even weaker in military terms than

Russia. The main reason why these countries are not perceived as "friends" is to be found rather in their specific identity than in their military capabilities. Therefore, the most logical and reasonable explanation resides in fact that the change in Russia's identity has been the real cause for the change of the US perception of Russia. This remark brings us directly to the quality-based approach. This approach operates with the identity of states as well as the identity of missiles. There are "uncivilized" ones, just as there are "democratic" and non-democratic missiles. While all civilized and democratic missiles are friends because they share the same democratic values, the uncivilized and undemocratic missiles are hostile not only to each other, but certainly also to civilized and democratic missiles. One could argue that the "uncivilized" missiles share the same value – the uncivilized element – which will restrain them from going to war against other barbarians. Against this argument we may say that uncivilized "values" do not create durable "common interests" and lack a cooperative culture. For decades, the USSR and the People's Republic of China shared the same ideology (Marxism–Leninism) and pursued the same objective: the realization of communism. Obviously, this was not sufficient to establish durable common interests between them. Furthermore, a schism actually produced "fratricide", antagonism and hostility between Beijing and Moscow. Since they were non-democratic, their "common cultures" were negative. And negative common cultures are insufficiently capable of establishing "uncivilized peace".

The main reason for the lack of long-term common interests and peaceful cooperation between non-democratic states is that their "culture" is alien to the concept of voluntarily entering into contracts. While the entire underpinning of democracy is based on a liberal contract system, non-democratic constructions are arbitrary products of force, and are thus incapable of generating common interests. One could also argue that the Warsaw Pact and Comecon, created in 1955 and 1949 respectively, are evidence that runs counter to the argument presented here. In response to this, we emphasize the substantial difference between a military alliance, on the one hand, and a collective security arrangement or security community, on the other. In Alexander Wendt's words, "alliances are temporary coalitions of self-interested states who come together for instrumental reasons in response to a specific threat. Once the threat is gone, the coalition loses its rationale and should disband" (1994: 386). It is true that both the Warsaw Pact and NATO initially possessed the same characteristics. A significant difference between the two is that while the former was dissolved before the end of the "threat" from NATO, the latter transformed from an alliance to a community thus changing its *raison d'être* from working against a specific threat to working against non-specific threats. When comparing the Comecon with the EU, we arrive at the same conclusion that the auto-dissolution of Comecon was a result of its mechanical and abortive character, while the progress of the EU is due to its integrative and cumulative character.

Based on the quality criterion, John Rawls divides states (people in his terminology) according to the degree to which they have internalized "liberal culture". He divides states into (1) reasonably liberal people; (2) decent [non-liberal] people; (3) outlaw states, and (4) societies burdened by unfavorable conditions (1999: 4). He thinks that peace should be possible between the first and the second category of states, and obviously with the third one. Rawls does not assign much importance to nuclear weapons, but what in his model makes peace possible between categories (1) and (2) are again the "basic cultural affinities" between them (respect for basic human rights, moral duties, obeying the law, etc.). The most important requirement to obtain classification as a decent state is to be non-aggressive (ibid.: 64–70). In civilizational terms, Rawls' classification of states is based on "cultural identity" rather than material power. From this point of view, the world consists of the "civilized" or "semi-civilized" and the "uncivilized" or "savages" (Rougier 1910; Oppenheim 1912; Gong 1984). In both approaches, actor identity determines the quality of anarchy and not the reverse. Our argument is that the change in the international arena that we are witnessing in the post-Cold War period is primarily due to the transformation of the Russian identity rather than the disintegration of the USSR. The former gave rise to the latter and not vice versa. The USSR could disintegrate and yet remain the same (with a Marxist–Leninist identity). According to this hypothesis, the USSR would surely have been a weaker challenger without this tangible effect on the identity of the system. NATO could hardly have intervened in Yugoslavia and Poland, and the Czech Republic and Hungary could not as easily have become full members of NATO. The reason is that the USSR challenged not only the military power of the USA (and hence the entire West), but also and especially the very identity of the West. It was only when the USSR changed her identity by giving up the adversarial position towards Western identity, slowly moving in the direction of Western "civilization" and sharing the same inter-subjectivity that the sense and meaning of Russia's military challenge changed in consequence. In short, "Russian missiles" are culturally different from the earlier "Soviet missiles" independent of their technical performance. It is only from this angle that President George W. Bush's statements on Russia can be correctly understood. He has repeatedly announced that "Russia is our [USA/Western] friend." What happened that Russia became USA's friend? Is it not precisely because of the fundamental change in Russia's identity?

How can structural realists explain this change?

At present, there are no tangible signs indicating China's possible return to Maoism, Vietnam's to the Ho Chi Minh era, or Iran's to the Khomeini era. On the contrary, numerous indicators show that these countries intend to pursue policies of reform. We have an ongoing process towards global convergence which also affects inter-state relations. This convergence is not tactical, nor is it a contextual convergence of merely materialist interests between states. Convergence is too broad a concept and cannot be reduced to temporary "alliances" (e.g. the alliance between Nazi Germany and Stalinist USSR in 1939). Convergence is a product of change in the orientation of states. We are not saying that it is complete, nor that it is perfect, but the trend towards convergence is unprecedentedly great. Contemporary state orientation moves roughly in the direction of capitalism and liberalism. This tendency is more immediately noticeable in the "center" of the world system (the West) as well as in countries such as Russia, China, Vietnam, and Iran. These countries have yet to "internalize" the norms associated with the Global Standard of Civilization, but they are at the stage of pre-internalization or "norm cascade" (Finnemore and Sikkink 1998: 902–4). This factual observation does not necessarily imply that all these countries share the same ideas and values and have similar approaches to human rights, democracy, and liberalism. On the other hand, it is undeniable that, in a historical sense, the gap between different world visions is now as narrow as it has ever been. Two pillars of the current mega-civilization remain unchallenged, and also adherence to liberalism and capitalism (in various ramifications) is on the increase. In other words, globalization has considerably reduced the differences between various world visions. Not yet complete convergence or complete divergence.

Globalization and world economy

Contemporary globalization is a result of a long cumulative complex and multi-dimensional process which can be traced back to the fifteenth and sixteenth centuries. In fact:

> Capitalist development is a process that was put together gradually over a period of some five centuries, beginning in Western Europe from the four-teenth century, before it became, in nineteenth, a coherent expansive force on a world scale. The expansive force at the mid-nineteenth century point was in its competitive phase. From the late nineteenth century, capitalist development entered a new, monopolistic phase. Each of these phases was associated with new modes of social relations of production.
>
> (Cox 1987: 51)

During the past six centuries, the world has completely changed in every think-able and unthinkable way. It is a profound and immense change. Within the social and political fields, the crucial question is to establish which elements among the most general ones have been constant during the entire period from the fifteenth to the twenty-first century. If we ignore a number of elements, two will be identified as being the most constant. By "constant", we do not mean that elements have not been subject to evolution. On the contrary, they have been submitted to challenge (by communism and fascism/Nazism/fundamentalism). However, these elements maintain their strong position – which is almost hegemonic – causing substantial changes in all aspects of human social life. These constant elements which emerged in Europe (the epicenter of a new civilization which became Western before becoming global) are: (1) a specific and unique economic system referred to as capitalism; and (2) a specific set of ideas about social and political engineering which – in contemporary discourse – is referred to as liberalism. We argue that the world today and globalization in particular are best understood by taking these two elements into consideration.

It is a fact that capitalism is the absolute dominant economic system, as it is a fact that despite great lack of perfection, the world has never been as democratic as today. Furthermore, the respect for human rights has never been as weighty even though horrifying violations of human rights still take place. Following the Freedom House Survey (2000–2001), at the end of year 2000, there were 86 free countries (2,465.2 billion people; 40.69 percent of the world population) in which a broad range of political rights was respected. There were 59 partly free countries (1,442.2 billion people; 23.80 percent of the world population) in which there was a mixed record of more limited political rights and civil liberties. There were 47 countries rated not free (2,151.1 billion people representing 35.51 percent of the world population) where basic political rights and civil liberties were non-existent. In sum, the survey shows that in the year 2000, there was significant progress towards freedom in 25 countries and significant setbacks for freedom in 18 countries. Moreover, 40.69 percent of the world population living in freedom is the highest score in the history of the Freedom House Survey which was founded in 1941. This brings us to ask ourselves whether this state of affairs is purely a matter of coincidence, or whether there is any logical and historic connection between globalization on the one side and capitalism–liberalism on the other.

Fernand Braudel, the architect of the world system theory, makes a distinction between two concepts: world economy (*économie mondiale*) and world-economy (*économie-monde*). The former is simply what we call international economy or "universal market". The latter – more important in his view as a historian – is equivalent to the German *Weltwirtschaft* and is applied to an economy of a portion of the world standing by itself as a *tout économique*.

> A world-economy is defined by a triple reality: 1) it is limited to a given geographic area; 2) it is related to a political pole or center (e.g. New York) or even to multiple centers (London, New York, Tokyo, Paris, etc.); and 3) it is also composed by a center and different peripheral zones.
>
> (Braudel 1985: 85–6)

Immanuel Wallerstein, the most prominent of Braudel's disciples, argues that a world system is a multicultural network of exchange of necessities which include food, raw material, bullion, and protection. In his view, there are two types of world systems: world empires and world economies which shape and control production and distribution (Wallerstein 1974: 63).

The reason why Braudel attaches more importance to world-economy is the particular evolution of European world-economy which as a single regional system is the only one that expanded and incorporated all parts of the world. None of the other world systems became global despite the fact that they shared some structural similarities with the European system. "Many of them had core–periphery hierarchies in which core regions, usually those areas with the biggest cities and the strongest states, dominated and exploited adjacent peripheral regions" (Boswell and Chase-Dunn 2000: 19–20). Along this line, we may ask why Europe stands as a unique system which became global. World system theorists explain it by the fact that, only in Europe, capitalism became the dominant mode of accumulation, and this fundamentally altered the nature of the international system.

Consequently, as the vehicle of structural transformation in Europe, capitalism in this context is a *longue durée* phenomenon *par excellence*, and the vehicle is defined as "historical capitalism" quite different from all previous historical social systems. What distinguishes historical capitalism is that "in this historical system, capital came to be used (invested) in a very special way. It came to be used with the primary objective or intent of self-expansion" (Wallerstein 1995: 13–14). Another difference resides in the non-availability of one or more elements of the process: the accumulated stock in money, the labor to be utilized by the producer, the network of distributors, the consumers. More specifically, in the pre-capitalist formation:

> One or more elements were missing because, in previous historical social systems, one or more of these elements was not "commodified" or was insufficiently "commodified". What this means is that the process was not considered one that could or should be transacted through a "market". Historical capitalism involved therefore the widespread commodification of processes – not merely exchange processes, but production processes – that had previously been conducted other than via a "market".
>
> (Wallerstein 1995: 15)

To Marx, capitalism is a system of commodity production. "In the capitalist system producers do not simply produce for their own needs, or for needs of individuals with whom they are in personal contact; capitalism involves a nation-wide, and often an international, exchange market" (Giddens 1971/1990: 46). In Marx's own words, "capitalism withdraws from the spheres with low rates of profit and invades others which yield a higher profit" (quoted by Giddens 1971/1990: 51).

Following the path of expansion of capitalism, the treaties of Westphalia (in 1648) and subsequently the rise of nation–states are interpreted by world system theorists as a necessary, even inevitable consequence of historical capitalism in expansion. It is explained by the fact that the capitalist world system from being among many worlds is becoming the historical social system of the entire world needed to construct "territorial organizations capable of regulating social and economic life and of monopolizing means of coercion and violence" (Arrighi 1997: 5–6). On the other hand, the concentration of capital in the core zone created a fiscal base as well as a political motivation for establishing relatively strong state machineries, the many capacities of which ensured that the state machineries of peripheral zones became or remained comparatively weaker

(Wallerstein 1995: 32). In short, national states are a differentiated form of capitalist power. It must be stressed that the capitalist system based on the Westphalian national state, which led to the world economy is distinct from the global economy. While the former was predominantly about movements in trade, investments, and payments crossing national frontiers regulated by states and by international organizations created by states, the latter, in contrast, "was the sphere in which production and finance were being organized in cross-border networks that could very largely escape national and international regulatory powers" (Cox 1996: 22). In other words, the Westphalian world economy was based on territoriality, while the "global economy" is at work in a de-territorialized universe (Hassner 1993: 53). The distinction between the two stages of evolution of capitalism is crucial to grasp the real sense of globalization. Globalization is not about intensification of the classic international economy since the global market is not the sum of national markets. The whole is more than the sum of its parts. Globalization is about the expansion of the world economy which became a reality during the nineteenth century. In its elementary form, globalization is what Lenin called imperialism which emerged as the development and direct continuation of the fundamental characteristics of capitalism in general (Lenin 1946: 366–85). Lenin was far from being the only thinker who was preoccupied by the idea of the expansion of capitalism. Before and after him, a range of specialists, thinkers and theorists focused their study (some of them their entire life) on this topic. To give an idea of the importance Marxist authors attached to capitalism, nothing is perhaps more revealing than the title of Marx's own seminal work: *Das Kapital* and not *Das Beruf*! In a sense, one could argue that Marxism (and with it communism) was not an alternative to capitalism; actually it was a reaction to it. As a matter of fact, this reaction is apparent already in their Manifesto calling and preaching for the "unification of proletarians" against the "unified front of capitalists". Marx himself and Marxist theorists of the nineteenth century and the beginning of the twentieth century did in general correctly predict the development and expansionist tendencies of capitalism. What they failed to predict was the extraordinary capacity of capitalism to overcome its contradictions ... so far. Rudolf Hilferding is among the authors (i.e. Bukharin, Luxemburg) who in his major work *Finance Capital* (1910), explained the new mechanism of expansion of capitalist economy and its evolution from international economy to world economy. To Hilferding:

> Finance capital marks the unification of capital. The previously distinct spheres of industrial capital, commercial capital and bank capital are henceforth under the control of high finance, in which the magnates of industry and the banks are closely associated. This association, which is founded on the suppression of competition between capitalists by great monopolistic combines, has, of course, the effect of changing the relations between the capitalist class and the state.
>
> (*Finance Capital*: 40 in Brewer 1980: 85–6)

The further expansion of capitalism during the twentieth century confirmed Hilferding's prediction. Capitalism continued its way towards more expansion, it became a world economy by ignoring national borders and by making the states the agents of globalization from which they (at least states in the high developed capitalist economy) drew substantial benefice. The empirical work is also beginning to "confirm the expectation that highly mobile capital may place limits on the ability of governments to choose not only an autonomous monetary policy but an expansionary fiscal policy as well" (Simmons 1999: 64).

It is in the same spirit that Robert W. Cox retraces the evolution of capitalism. He writes:

> The monopoly phase of capitalist development begins with the long depression of 1873–96. Its salient characteristics have been (1) the concentration of capital into large corporate units; (2) the growth of a dual structure of economy in the industrialized countries ... (3) increased importance of the role of banking consortia ... (4) increased concern of states ... for ensuring the conditions in which production and capital accumulation can continue without distributions ... (5) an international division of labor brought about by capital in the most industrialized countries.
>
> (1987: 69)

The above discussion shows that capitalism evolved from European world-economy into global economy. A global economy is "an economy with the capacity to work as a unit in real time on planetary scale" (Castells 1996: 92). In this definition, all three elements of globalization are present in a unified form. "Unit" means a comprehensive system with its internal logic and its own dynamics. "Time" is real and synchronic. "Space" is planetary and no longer limited to national, regional or even cultural borders. In such a system, capital is managed around the clock in globally integrated financial markets working in real time. The labor markets are not yet global; thus the arrow goes in direction of globality. In a world becoming more and more mobile, the labor follows production and services which in turn follow cheaper wages and favorable taxation. Of course, it does not imply that protectionism is history or that every company sells worldwide. It merely implies that trades, productions and transactions in the core (the USA, the European Union and Japan) of the system are becoming predominantly global, giving birth to what Susan Strange called a non-territorial "business civilization" (Strange 1990). In her view, the key aspect of globalization involves neither trade nor investment: it is the adoption of common practices and standards (Strange 1996). In many respects, the rise of a global economy drastically transformed the face of the global world. It stimulated the homogenization and standardization of products which in turn produced a "global life style". It also established a framework and guidelines for good conduct in international trade (6.6 trillion US dollars in 1997). The general and multilateral rules on trade are now considerably reinforced by the World Trade Organization (WTO). Among these rules are: reciprocity, non-discrimination, decreasing tariffs (not increasing), consulting and dispute resolution, etc. The third and perhaps most significant consequence of global economy is the time-conditioned gap between finance and production. Money is fungible and extremely mobile. New technologies allow billion dollars worth of transactions to take place in seconds in the electronic circuit around the globe. Capital flows become global and are operating in synchronic dimensions. The development of production takes place in a diachronic dimension. As a result of this gap, global finance has come to dominate production (Cox, see Chapter 1: p.14; Castells 1996: 93). Consequently, changes in the mobility of capital will inevitably influence the development of the nation–state, by the fact that while capital flows globally, the nation–state is fixed. In this situation, "the different states compete to attract and immobilize the flow of capital. The relation of particular national states to global capital is mediated through the competitive process of attraction-and-immobilization" (Holloway 1996: 130). The problem with global finance is that it is not bound to any global regulatory institution. Disconnected from economic realities, global finance is left to the uncontrolled financial market mechanism, which only takes care of individual interests; causes turbulence (e.g. the financial crisis in Asia and Latin America in 1998) and misery for millions of people. The *laissez-faire* orientation of the market has taken refuge in the lame conviction that, in due course, the invisible hand associated with economic growth would overcome economic hardship, a view completely lacking in empirical support (Falk 1999: 423). George Soros (who is an "insider" of the global finance and a beneficiary of the lack of regulations in this domain) thinks that the present international economic system is highly unstable, and that it has within it the makings of another catastrophe like 1929. Furthermore, in his new book, he criticizes the current situation in the financial market, because "instead of acting like a pendulum, financial markets have recently acted more like wrecking balls knocking over one economy after another" (Soros 1998: xvi). Other commentators such as Paul Hirst, who are skeptical about the ungovernability of financial markets, admits, however, to the urgency and necessity of its regulation by "extending public governance at both national and international levels, with the aim of combining growth with fairness within and between nations" (1997: 425). The lack of rules and principles for a sector on which the future of humanity may depend justifies the necessity of common civilization. A common civilization, universally accepted, is not yet established. However, strong indicators attest the emergence of at least a common standard of civilization.

Globalization, civilization and world order

"World order" is a human phenomenon. Like other human phenomena, it is a social construction. Social constructed phenomena are best understood when they are studied in broader scope than what they are in reality. Describing a phenomenon provides little information about its identity, its spirit, its essence, its history and its possible transformation in the future. To reach such a stage, we need to go beyond description. We need to put the target phenomenon into a broader perspective and take sufficient distance from the phenomenon itself. We need also to look to some deep structures in what the phenomenon (in this case the "world order") is rooted. It requires reaching general principles and durable regular movements that determine the shape of the world order. Such a *démarche* is necessary, because simply the world order cannot be explained by the world order itself.

To begin this process, there needs to be a workable definition of world order. Hedley Bull defines "world order" as "those patterns or dispositions of human activity that sustain the elementary or primary goals of social life among mankind as a whole" (1977: 20). Furthermore, Bull makes a correct distinction between "world order", on the one hand, and the 'international system", on the other. In his view, the former is broader than the latter. He argues that "international order [system] is order among states; but states are simply groupings of men [and women] and men may be grouped in such a way that they do not form states at all" (ibid.). Elaborating further his argument, Bull states:

> World order is wider than international order because to give an account of it we have to deal not only with order among states but also with order on a domestic or municipal scale, provided within particular states, and with order within the wider world political system of which the states system is only part.
>
> (ibid.: 22)

We have to say that Hedley Bull's great contribution to understanding the "world order" remains at an analytical level. Explaining the causes of different world orders through history did not constitute Bull's first priority. Simplifying Bull's statements, the "world order" and order in international society exist because it is necessary (ibid.: pp. 4–5 and Chapter 3). What Bull has not done, we find in Robert W. Cox's works, in his seminal *Production, Power, and World Order* in particular. Cox tried to demonstrate that the variations in "world order" are caused by reciprocal relations between production and forms of states. Relations that are both related to the rise and development of capitalism. He states: "In focusing on the transformation in forms of state that bring about changes in production relations, we are led to discover the relationship between changes in forms of state and changes in the structures of world order" (Cox 1987: 108). And, on the other hand, "In examining changes in world order, the alternation between hegemonic and non hegemonic structures is of particular significance. The hegemonies of the Pax Britannica and the Pax Americana both constituted interstate systems that gave free rein to the expansion of the world economy" (ibid.). Opposite to this, "in the intervening non hegemonic and more turbulent structure, the interstate system reasserted itself so as to subordinate and control world-economy influences" (ibid.). Following this schema, Cox retraced three successive structure of world order: (1) the coming of the liberal international economy; (2) the era of rival imperialism; and finally (3) the neoliberal world order. From an international political economy angle, other scholars come to the conclusion that capitalism went through four periods: (1) the mercantile phase; (2) the colonial period; (3) the neo-colonial period; and finally (4) post-imperialism (Hoogvelt 1997: 17).

The above definitions contribute to a better understanding of the concept of "world order". We find that while Bull's approach to "world order" is strong in the description and analysis of this concept, it is equally weak because of the lacking explanation of the dynamism of world order. How has the world order changed? What are the relations between world order and world economy? Cox does not give any definition of "world order". Thus, he proceeds to a deep analysis of the dynamism underlying the transformation of the world order. In this connection, what we are proposing is: (1) considering economic factors (i.e. capitalism) as the primary cause for the shape and evolution of the world order; (2) considering "civilization" as the commonplace for both economic formation and cultural–political identity. It is with these two remarks in mind that we mean that "globalization" and "civilization" together are determining the shape and transformation of the contemporary world order. What could then be a new definition of "world order"? Do we have a better definition than the one by Hedley Bull? We tried and tried again to find a better and more comprehensive definition. One outcome of our search is this: the "world order" is an arrangement of the most general structures that shape general paths of actors' identity and behavior. Comparing this definition to Bull's, we must admit the great superiority of Bull's definition. Especially, because Bull's definition "is not definitionally limited to political and economic considerations; it allows normative ways in which individual and collective actors can incorporate into themselves the cognitive and behavioral dispositions associated with particular world orders" (Alker *et al.* 2001: 8).

Therefore, we consider Bull's definition as valid and workable *faute de mieux*. In this connection, our contribution will be to go beyond Bull's definition to find out what underlies the "world order". How is the "world order" shaped? How can it be that under some world orders, international norms and ethics become more relevant and more visible, while under others, international law and ethics become considerably marginalized?

When looking at the evolutionary process of world economy from the birth of capitalism until our days, we may trace the progressive trends between the evolution of world economy, on the one hand, and a set of common norms and rules, on the other. In general, this evolution has gone through three phases or models which will be presented in the following.

Model 1: European world-economy and Westphalian order

Model 1 exemplifies the rise of the European world-economy and the phasing out of multiple world-economies where different regional and autonomous economies could coexist: a Chinese, a Japanese, an Arab-Islamic, and a European world-economy as examples. Under this type of world configuration, multiple civilizations could also live side by side. What happened during the long sixteenth century was that only one of these world-economies emerged as a system with extraordinary capacity of expansion: the European world-economy. Because of its highly dynamic nature, the European system extended to multiple spheres internally (in Europe) as well as externally (colonialism and imperialism). Here, only two elements of European origin directly related to our current study are mentioned. The first is called the Westphalian model based on state sovereignty, and the second is the absolute autonomy of politics. On the first, there is a vast literature (Krasner 2000; Sørensen 1999, among others). Thus, our focus is on the second element – the autonomy of politics – since sovereignty, despite its importance, does not represent a crucial element in the present study. Autonomy of politics is rooted in Aristotelian and more precisely in Machiavellian traditions. It is astonishing, however, that the reformulation of autonomy of politics by Machiavelli happened during the Renaissance; coinciding with the birth of capitalism in Europe. According to the world system theory, capitalism needed a well-defined political sphere which did not exist at the time. Emergence of the Westphalian system and consequently the sovereignty of state was in this perspective an economic exigency. It means that politics were not separated from the economic system but rather from religion and later on from the feudal system. In other words, multiple chains of loyalty gave place to a single political one. In this way, all the essential aspects of capitalism (banking, communications networks, investment, distribution, etc.) could be assured by administration of a responsible and sovereign nation–state. It is a fact that until the Treaty of Westphalia, questions related to ethical and/or legal principles were incorporated into religion: (the Church/the Canon). The right and wrong, the just and unjust (war) as well as principles of legitimacy, contracts, conquests, relations with non-Christians, etc., were decided upon and justified by the ecclesiastic institutions. During this period, the international society as Hedley Bull noticed "was identified as European rather than Christian in its values or culture. Reference to Christiandom or to divine law as cementing the society of states declined and disappeared, as did religious oaths in treaties" (1977: 33). The secularizing movement was accelerated by the French Revolution of 1789. Even the salvation that, up to that time, was an exclusive religious (Christian) property, became public property (*salut public*).

When the European system went through a secular process, Europeans were faced with a new task of devising a new set of ethical and law principles: predominantly non-religious. The result was the formulation of a standard of civilization. The standard of civilization was European, and it was first and foremost directed to regulating inter-European relations. Thus, the standard was exclusive and discriminatory. With the intensification of international trade, military and political expansion of Europe, the European standard of civilization (ESC) became progressively the international criterion for "civilized" international behavior. As a result, the absolute exclusive character of ESC was scaled down. Japanese, Persians, Chinese adhered to the ESC, at least partially. However, the ESC conserved its discriminatory character segregating human beings in terms of slave and master, man and woman, and race. It was not until the proclamation of the Universal Declaration of Human Rights in 1948 that the rights of human beings as human beings were officially recognized. Under model 1, the identity of the world was in general terms asymmetric: Europe on the one side (subsequently together with North America) and the rest of the world on the other. This configuration changed with the outbreak of WWI and WWII. The following model is consecrated to a brief review of the transitory period.

Model 2: Competing global world-economies and world empires

Model 1 continued to dominate the international system submitted to modifications and improvement (Hague Conventions 1899 and 1909, League of Nations, etc.). The European world-economy changed to capitalism and was increasingly challenged by the rise of Soviet socialism. Thus, the challenge was limited. Geographically, the Soviet regime was limited merely to Russia. Politically, it was also of a limited scope. It was only after WWII that the Soviet world-economy expanded to comprise the political and military spheres, hence becoming an alternative to the world order dominated by Western powers. The Western world order embraced three related components: economic, cultural and political. The Western economic system included the developed market economies of North America, Western Europe, and Japan. "These states were [and still are] wealthy, highly developed and capitalistic. They had [and still have] their major international economic interactions with each other and were involved with each other in a dense system of mutual economic interaction" (Spero 1981: 12).

To improve the management tools to control the increasing economic interaction, financial arrangements were set up through the Bretton Woods system. This system was in reality an up-to-date version of the former European world-economy. It was rooted in economic liberalism and supplanted by Keynesianism. The IMF and the World Bank (apart from IBRD and the late GATT) constituted the institutional pillars of the whole system. Culturally, liberalism and consequently the primacy of individual rights constituted the cultural identity of the Western system. Politically, the Western system was basically a world empire governing the Western hemisphere and large parts of Asia, Africa and South America. The system was protected by nuclear weapons and a network of regional alliances (such as CENTO and SEATO). The Western world empire and the Western world-economy reflected each other in an interactive movement.

This system was challenged by the competing socialist system led by the USSR, and was seconded by China. For the sake of convenience, we may call it the Eastern system. Equivalent to the Western system, the Eastern had economic, cultural, as well as political elements. The Eastern economic system was a planned economy; a derivative version of the European world economy. Socialist states established their own economic international institutions in which the Comecon played a central role. Culturally, the Eastern system elaborated a highly developed doctrine based on the primacy of community and the absolute submission of the individual to the rule of community. Politically, just as its Western rival, the Eastern system succeeded in creating a world empire armed with nuclear weapons.

Under model 2, the identity of the world is best described as a schizophrenic symmetry. Two independent holistic systems stand face to face. In a world like this, each part has its own set of norms and ethics used as instruments for the destabilization of the other. There were two concurrent standards of civilization: Western ("imperialist" according to the socialist vocabulary), and Eastern ("evil empire" according to the Western vocabulary). During the transitory period, relations between international ethics and international politics were paradoxically drawn together as compared to the previous period; however, not in general or in global terms. The criterion of Western standards was primarily security-bonded. States which were against communism were considered members of the "free world". Non-communist states which were not necessarily anti-communist (India, Egypt, Indonesia, etc.) were considered more or less civilized. Consequently, the repetitive instrumental use of ethical principles prevented the establishment of a procedure in this field which is a necessary condition for socialization between actors. Without socialization, the ethical dimensions of international relations are almost isolated from the international political arena. During this period, the world witnessed improvements in the international legal system, and in particular in technical and commercial domains such as the Law of the Sea and regulation of trade.

In short, when describing the main trends of this period in only one word, primacy of security seems to be a qualified choice since all other elements in the economic, cultural and political spheres were dependent variables of security. The end of the Cold War put an end to this period inaugurating a new era (model 3).

Model 3: The rise of a global world order and world civilization

The fall of the Soviet Empire was not simply the fall of an empire as history has witnessed with other mighty empires. It was also the end of a civilization which possessed all the necessary elements of a great civilization: a powerful and sophisticated ideology (Marxism) constituting a complete world vision; a well-defined project for a historical formation (communism); an immense and rich geographic territory; and an empire to which a number of countries in Eastern Europe and elsewhere were subjugated. Nuclear deterrents protected the entire system. What is the point of interest for us is why this civilization declined. Among many explanations (sociological, economic, military, historical, etc.), a revised world system theory could offer a qualified explanation. The Soviet civilization failed because it emerged and lived at the wrong time. While the European world economy seconded by its standard of civilization was able to transform and expand to the outside world; the Soviet world economy was quite unable to do so. The system's "no go" nature and dogmatic character prevented renovation and innovation. At the same time, the capitalist system once again demonstrated an extraordinary capacity to create new favorable environments for further expansion. David Harvey, a Marxist geographer, gives a good example of the flexibility of capitalism. He argues that the radical fall in transportation and communications costs was related to reorganization of the nature of capitalist accumulation since around 1968–69. These changes have had important consequences for the culture of capitalism. Harvey focuses on the contrast between Fordist mass production and "flexible specialization" for the global market. He claims that "flexible accumulation" is much more revolutionary than was Fordism (quoted in Boswell and Chase-Dunn 2000: 159, Hoogvelt 1997: Chapter 5). A similar argumentation is found in Brooks and Wohlforth's well-documented article. They see the Soviet Union's decline as a consequence of the changing structure of global production resulting in a change in the perception of the Soviet elite and ultimately in the transformation of Soviet identity. The shifts in the globalization of production in the late 1970s and 1980s became particularly evident in three ways: "1) the upswing in the number and importance of inter-firm alliances; 2) the increased geographic dispersion of production; and 3) the growing opportunity cost of being isolated from foreign direct investment" (Brooks and Wohlforth 2000/01: 34). The fact is that the Soviet Union and its allies were completely isolated from this trend. This gap between the Western accelerating globalization of production, on the one hand, and the Soviet Union's critical backwardness, on the other, could only be filled by ideas. The problem was that the Soviet ideas at that time were not appropriate to find new remedies for the economic crisis. Hence, "Gorbachev became increasingly disposed to undertake a radical shift toward retrenchment" (ibid.: 50). A process that resulted in the fall of the Soviet Union.

The fall of the Soviet empire and civilization resulted in an increasing globalization of the world order. The current world order is interpreted differently. Samuel Huntingon argues that, "[i]n the post-Cold War world, for the first time in history, global politics has become multipolar and multicivilizational" (1996: 21). As a consequence of the rise of the new world "the most pervasive, important and dangerous conflicts will not be between social classes, rich and poor, or other economically defined groups, but between peoples belonging to different cultural entities" (ibid.: 28). Kenneth Waltz is still insisting that the traditional balance of power will be re-established (after the Cold War) and that business will continue as usual. "Realist theory," he emphasizes, "predicts that balances disrupted will one day be restored … One does, however, observe balancing tendencies already taking place" (Waltz 2000: 27). Richard Falk believes that the world is going through a "Grotian moment" and the "dynamics of globalization has rested its normative case for acceptance on the promises of liberal economics and the benefits claimed for sustained economic growth on a quasi-global scale" (1998: 24). Our approach is closer to Falk than to Huntington and Waltz. We argue that the "Grotian moment" is a reality. Reality in the sense that it happened as a rupture in human history as a consequence of the end of the Cold War; a phenomenon due to the change in Russian identity rather than to the disintegration of the USSR. This critical change also marked the beginning of change in the world dominant culture. Alexander Wendt identifies three cultures of anarchy: the Hobbesian, the Lockean, and the Kantian. While it is impossible for a Hobbesian anarchy based on enmity, to have any kind of shared culture, the Lockean culture is different because it is based on a different role structure, rivalry rather than enmity. The Kantian culture is based on a role structure of friendship (Wendt 1999/2000: 246–312). So, theoretically, a global civilization based upon respect for human rights and individual freedom is more likely to arise in a Kantian culture than a Lockean culture. Hence, the Hobbesian culture is private and not shared, and as a culture is unqualified to produce or generate a global civilization. Here we face a crucial question. How does the culture of the international system change from one epoch to another? Do Hobbesian, Lockean and Kantian cultures represent different phases of cultural progress? Is this progress irreversible? There are no easy answers to these central questions. What we do have is a variety of approaches to these questions. Realists reject any progress. From their point of view, the contemporary international system is fundamentally similar to the world of Thucydides. Opposite to this approach, the Kantians argue for progress that implies irreversibility. Social Constructivists situate themselves between the first and the second approach. They recognize that the contemporary international system represents considerable progress over that of 500 or even 1500 AD. But "there is no historical necessity, no guarantee, that the incentives for progressive change will overcome human weakness and the countervailing incentives to maintain the status quo" (ibid.: 310–11).

The existing world order as the product of the end of the Cold War can be described as a democratic hegemonic anarchy. It remains anarchical, yet dominated by the hegemony of the USA. It is true as Kenneth Waltz puts it that "[a] state that is stronger than any other [USA] can decide for itself whether to conform its policies to structural pressures and whether to avail itself of the opportunities that structural change offers, which little fear of adverse affects in the short run" (2000: 24). Certainly, the USA can decide for itself, thus not without any cost. The cost could be loss of prestige and diminished influence in certain domains. Certainly, the USA can decide for itself, but cannot always successfully impose its will on others. Furthermore, the highly critical point is that the current hegemony is quite different from the previous hegemony in history. As mentioned before, the hegemony of the USA represents the first and unique historical example of a democratic hegemony. A democratic hegemony in an anarchical society operates differently from a non-democratic, dictatorial and totalitarian hegemony. Certainly, the USA is bound to lead the world, but it is also bound to observe democratic rules and free elections in its own quarters. Furthermore, despite the obvious fact that the USA dominates the world in military, political, economic, technological and cultural domains, there is, however, a paradox that the USA is not always (even often not) able to impose its will, especially in normative and ethical spheres. Some scholars argue the American defiance to international law and its problematic commitment to international organizations may be explained by "US exceptionalism". It is argued that the USA has a unique destiny to lead the world. "Translated into actions in respect of international law this means that the United States is an exception to what we might expect of a state as being accountable in terms of international law for its actions" (Scott 2001: 4). Exceptionalism describes the perception of Massachusetts Bay colonists that, as Puritans, they were charged with a special spiritual and political destiny: to create in the New World, a church and a society that would provide the model for all the nations of Europe as they struggled to reform themselves (Deborah L. Madsen quoted in Scott 2001: 7). Furthermore, the reluctance of the USA towards international institutions is not a recent attitude. It has in fact been an integral component of US policy since Versailles in 1919. At that time, the USA did not yet occupy the dominant position that it gained after the Cold War. Furthermore, the Nixon years (1968–74), especially with the Vietnam War, and the Reagan years (1981–89) were periods of particular concern at what was widely perceived to be a pattern of unprecedented lawlessness and unilateralism in the conduct of American foreign policy. Before these years, the Bay of Pigs invasion of 1961, and the Dominican Republic intervention of 1965 must be remembered as actions disrespectful to international law. These examples show that the current US position is not new and, the new position of the USA cannot stand as the sole explanation for the American reluctance.

At present, when looking at the general situation, we see that the USA itself is challenged by norms proposed and established by other actors. For example, in the case of the International Criminal Court, the USA did a triple flip: participating in the negotiations, not signing, and finally signing just before the deadline (31 December 2000, together with Israel and Iran). Another example is US opposition to the Kyoto Protocol on the environment, which has not prevented other states carrying on with their efforts by adopting a document, similar to Kyoto with some modifications (Bonn, Germany, July 2001). Furthermore, pressure on the USA is growing (especially from its European allies) concerning the abolition of death penalty. One of the consequences of this pressure was reflected by the unprecedent decision resulting in the non re-election of the USA as a member of the UN Human Rights Committee (April 2001). The US Congress is still reluctant to pass a resolution on payment of US debt to the UN. Such an attitude is embarrassing for the US administration and causes damage to the prestige and reputation of the country. The terrorist attacks of September 11 have finally changed the American policy. The US Congress accepted to pay a large part of the American debt to the UN. Another example is the non-participation of US Secretary of State (Colin Powell) at the UN's anti-racism gathering in Durban, South Africa (August 2001). These examples demonstrate that in reality USA is challenged instead of being the challenger. Therefore, the current world order is not fully identical with Pax Americana. In this respect, Robert W. Cox who admits that, "[t]he second Gulf War – the US and coalition campaign against Iraq – made transparent a change in the structure of global politics" (Cox 1996b: 33). However, he seems skeptical about the depth and magnitude of the change. In his view:

> The change was not the transition to a post-Cold War order proclaimed by US political leaders. Rather it was the shift from a hegemonic to a tributary system. This change had been going on since the early 1970s. Retrospectively, it had begun with the US defeat in Vietnam, and the "Nixon shocks" that undid the Bretton Wood system. Since that time, the more or less spontaneous consensual hegemonic leadership the United States had commended in the non-Soviet world turned into a sequence of bargained deals, mostly taking the form of financial quid pro quo for US military cover.
>
> (ibid.)

In reality, what Cox calls a "tributary system" is almost the same that Joseph S. Nye talks about as an ability to get what one wants through attraction rather than coercion. Discussing the position of the USA, he states that "one source of soft power is our values. To the extent that we are seen as a beacon of liberty, human rights and democracy, others are attracted to follow our lead" (*New York Times*, 3 January 2000). This is obviously an optimistic assessment of reality. A less optimistic evaluation of the current situation as well as for the future is based on lessons from history. From a historical angle, the dominant empire, in general, has a strong tendency to excessive expansion which in itself creates/accelerates dramatic dissension within the empire. This rule is valid for empires: the Roman Empire, the Islamic Empire as well as the late Soviet Empire. For Montesquieu, what initially caused the fall of the Roman Empire was the grandeur of Rome and the internal divisions within the metropolis Roma (Montesquieu [1951]: vols II, 111 and 119). One could easily say the same for the Islamic and for the Soviet Empires, in particular. In this respect, Waltz is completely right in claiming that "dominant powers take too many tasks beyond their own borders, thus weakening themselves in the long run" (2000: 28). Which was precisely the case for the Soviet Union's engagement in Afghanistan from 1979 until 1989. An adventure which essentially caused internal dissension among the Soviet leadership and ultimately the fall of the USSR. Precisely, the fall of the USSR was also related to the Soviet Union's non-democratic identity. The lack of free press, free elections and other forms of media for the Soviet public opinion gave the USSR's leadership a free hand to conduct the catastrophic war in Afghanistan. Compared to this, the USA survived the absurd and horrific war in Vietnam. Why? Because US intervention was defeated not on Vietnamese but on US territory. An increasing majority of Americans against the Vietnam War, together with the opposition of world public opinion, forced the US administration to end the war. Such things did not exist in the USSR. Consequently, we have to conclude that the survival of the USA (after the Vietnam War) and the collapse of the USSR (after the invasion of Afghanistan) are partly due to the non-democratic character of the USSR and the democratic character of the USA. Based on historical evidence, we may conclude that a dominant Empire (a hegemonic power *a fortiori*) usually plays a double role. It is the main guardian of the stability of the world, and at the same time it is the main threat to it. Everything being equal, and in absence of a better alternative, it seems apparent that a democratic hegemony is preferable to a non-democratic one.

Under model 3, the world order became global as well as the world-economy and the standard of civilization. The international system remained anarchical, yet under a democratic hegemony. The ethical and normative issues also became more powerful than ever before. The magnitude of hegemonic power (USA) is, however, limited and fixed to a set of rules. Violation of these rules will be costly for the decision-makers of the USA, both internally and on an international arena.

Conclusion

This chapter suggests that globalization has reached a stage where the international normative set is on the way to becoming global. As a result of the emergence of a new global standard of civilization, world identity as well as the culture of anarchy have been transformed accordingly. These changes, however, left the ordering principles of the international system unchanged. It has also been argued that the international system constitutes a construction which is the product of a causal chain: the rise of capitalism and liberalism caused globalization, which in turn shaped the new standard of civilization. The chapter also focused on the interaction between international ethics, law, and politics. This "interaction" is not itself new. It actually dates from the seventeenth century. What is new is the increasing importance of ethics as well as new rules and norms. The role played by new technology and more efficient communications facilities considerably enhanced the dynamics of this interaction. Globalization together with the change of the Russian identity has pushed the world into a transitory phase best described as a "Grotian moment". What is hiding behind the Grotian veil of course remains to be seen at this stage. However, based on the knowledge that we possess today, the overthrow of globalization seems highly improbable. Globalization can be adjusted and corrected; its disastrous consequences can also be contained and repaired. Nevertheless, it can hardly be halted. The logical deduction of this assumption indicates a progressive replacement of coercion by attraction, and gradual reformulation of interests in terms of value rather than physical force. This is not to claim that every problem will be solved and that a peaceful world will suddenly emerge. It is only to suggest that the elements of convergence are becoming stronger than the elements of divergence. The following remarks presume the world constellation under three different phases of the evolution of the parochial world-economy to the global economy as well as the impact of the latter on the identity of the world:

In a world with multiple and different world-economies, in Braudelian terminology, the standard of civilization as well as the world order became consequently regional. This was the case, for example, in the fifteenth century. In Europe, this situation led to the Westphalian order. Under this model, the standard of civilization is both exclusive and discriminatory and the logic of consequences based on conquest and expansion prevails.

In a world with two concurrent and dominating world-economies, security issues determine the quality of relations between international politics, ethics, and law. This was the case during the Cold War. In this type of situation, the logic of consequences based on security will prevail. It should be noted that economy alone is not enough to fully explain the rivalry between the West and the East. This was equally a struggle or a clash between two competing civilizations.

In a world with a global economy, the logic of consequences and the logic of appropriateness are used alternatively. The standard of civilization will follow the pace of globalization. International ethics and international law will take more room and attract more attention than before because of a more or less pronounced degree of homogenization of the world identity and consequently the progressive transformation of state identity.

References

Alker, Hayward R. *et al.* (2001) "Twelve World Order Debates which Have Made Our Days", paper presented at the International Studies Association, Hong Kong, 25–8 July.

Arrighi, Giovanni (1997) *Globalization, State Sovereignty, and "Endless" Accumulation of Capital*, New York, Fernand Braudel Center.

Bagby, Philip (1958) *Culture and History*, London, Longmans.

Boswell, Terry and Chase-Dunn, Christopher (2000) *The Spiral of Capitalism and Socialism: Toward a Global Democracy*, Boulder, CO, Lynne Reinner.

Braudel, Fernand (1979) *Civilization matérielle, économie et capitalisme Xème–XVIIIème siècles: Le Temps du Monde*, Paris, Armand Colin.

—— (1985) *La dynamique du capitalisme*, Paris, Flammarion.

—— (1993) *A History of Civilizations*, New York, Penguin Books.

—— (1995) *A History of Civilizations*, USA, Penguin Books.

Brewer, Anthony (1980) *Marxist Theories of Imperialism*, London, Routledge & Kegan Paul.

Brooks, Stephen G. and Wohlforth, William C. (2000/01) "Power, Globalization, and the End of the Cold War: Reevaluation a Landmark Case for Ideas", *International Security*, vol. 25, no 3, pp. 5–53.

Bull, Hedley (1977) *The Anarchical Society*, London, Macmillan.

Castells, Manuel (1996) *The Rise of the Network Society*, Oxford, Blackwell.

Cox, Robert W. (1987) *Production, Power, and World Order*, New York, Columbia University Press.

—— (1996a) "A Perspective on Globalization", in James H. Mittelman (ed.), *Globalization: Critical Reflections*, Boulder, CO, Lynne Reinner.

Cox, Robert W. with Timothy J. Sinclair (1996b) *Approaches to World Order*, Cambridge, Cambridge University Press.

Falk, Richard (1998) *Law in an Emerging Global Village: A Post-Westphalian Perspective*, New York, Ashley.

—— (1999) "The Pursuit of International Justice: Present Dilemma and an Imagined Future", *Journal of International Affairs*, vol. 52, no. 2, Spring, pp. 409–41.

Finnemore, Martha and Sikkink, Kathryn (1998) "International Norm Dynamics and Political Change", *International Organization*, vol. 52, no. 4, Autumn, pp. 887–917.

Giddens, Anthony (1971/1990) *Capitalism and Modern Social Theory*, Cambridge, Cambridge University Press.

Gong, Gerrit W. (1984) *The Standard of "Civilization" in International Society*, Oxford, Clarendon Press.

Hassner, Pierre (1993) "Beyond Nationalism and Internationalism", *Survival*, vol. 35, no. 2, pp. 49 65.

Hirst, Paul (1997) "The Global Economy: Myths and Realities", *International Affairs*, vol. 73, no. 3, pp. 409–25.

Holloway, John (1996) "Global Capital and the National State", in Werner Bonefeld and John Holloway (eds), *Global Capital, National State and the Politics of Money*, London, Macmillan.

Hoogvelt, Ankie (1997) *Globalization and the Postcolonial World*, London, Macmillan.

Huntington, Samuel P. (1996) *The Clash of Civilizations and the Remaking of World Order*, New York, Simon & Schuster.

Krasner, Stephen (2000) *Sovereignty: Organised Hypocrisy*, Princeton, NJ, Princeton University Press.

Lenin, Vladimir I. (1946) *Marx and Engels' Marxism*, Moscow, Foreign Languages Publishing House.

Melko, Matthew (1995) "The Nature of Civilization", in Stephen K. Sanderson (ed.), *Civilizations and World Systems: Studying World-Historical Change*, Walnut Greek, Altamira Press.

Montesquieu, Charles-Louis de (1951), *Considérations sur les Causes de la Grandeur des Romains et de leur Décadence*, œuvres Complètes, Paris, Gallimard.

Oppenheim, Lass Francis Lawrence (1912) *International Law*, London, Longmans & Co.

Quigley, Carrol (1961) *The Evolution of Civilizations: An Introduction to Historical Analysis*, New York, Macmillan.

Rawls, John (1999) *The Law of Peoples*, Cambridge, MA, Harvard University Press.

Rougier, Antoine (1910) "La Théorie de l'Intervention d'Humanité", *Revue de Droit International*, pp. 408–526.

Sanderson, Stephen K. (ed.) (1995) *Civilizations and World Systems: Studying World-Historical Change*, Walnut Greek, Altamira Press.

Scott, Shirley (2001) "The United States and the Ongoing Quest for Legal Security". paper presented at CISS/ISA conference, Heidelberg, 25– 6 June.

Simmons, Beth A. (1999) "The Internationalization of Capital", in Herbert Kitschelt *et al.* (eds), *Continuity and Change in Contemporary Capitalism*, Cambridge, Cambridge University Press.

Sørensen, Georg (1999) "Sovereignty: Change and Continuity in a Fundamental Institution". *Political Studies*, vol. 47, no. 3, pp. 590–604, Special issue, Blackwell Publishers.

Soros, George (1998) *The Crisis of Global Capitalism*, New York, Public Affairs.

Spero, Joan Edelman (1981) *The Political International Economic Relations*, New York, St. Martin's Press.

Strange, Susan (1990) "The Name of the Game", in Nicholas Rizopoulos (ed.), *Sea Changes: American Foreign Policy in a World Transformed*, New York, Council of Foreign Relations.

—— (1996) *The Retreat of the State: The Diffusion of Power in the World Economy*, Cambridge, Cambridge University Press.

Toynbee, Arnold (1995) *A Study of History*, London, Oxford University Press

Wallerstein, Immanuel (1974) *The Capitalist World-Economy*, Cambridge, Cambridge University Press.

—— (1992) *Geopolitics and Geoculture*, Cambridge, Cambridge University Press.

—— (1995) *Historical Capitalism with Capitalist Civilization*, London, Verso.

Waltz, Kenneth N. (2000) "Structural Realism after the Cold War", *International Security*, vol. 25, no. 1, Summer, pp. 5–41.

Wendt, Alexander (1994) "Collective Identity Formation and the International State", *American Political Science Review*, vol. 88, no. 2, pp. 384–96.

—— (1999/2000) *Social Theory of International Politics*, Cambridge, Cambridge University Press.

3 The first normative global revolution?

The uncertain political future of globalization

Richard Falk

The sudden advent of global war

The events of September 11 alter fundamental calculations about the future of global governance, the role of the state, and the policy agenda that is likely to dominate the debate in various national, regional, and global arena. Whether the impact of mega-terror attacks on the World Trade Center and the Pentagon initiate a civilizational war between the West and Islam is highly uncertain at this time, but what seems beyond doubt is that the substantive and symbolic harm inflicted on the United States by Osama Bin Laden's al-Qaida network, a non-state enemy with visionary goals, forever changes our sense of historical context and of the nature of war and power.

Before September 11, the preoccupations of the era seemed captured by the terminology of globalization, and the tensions produced by economistic emphasis on global economic growth as the foundation of a new geopolitics, possibly also providing a vehicle for a unified world culture built on the pillars of secularism, market economics, and constitutionalism at the level of national governance. Security concerns were seen as matters of law enforcement and peacekeeping rather than matters of war and peace, with the major challenges increasingly being associated with the rise of transnational crime. International terrorism was viewed as part of this challenge, a matter of finding the perpetra-tors, although the most virulent forms of terrorism seemed to be associated with ethnic, religious, and national struggles that were being waged to determine the destiny of a particular state. During the late 1990s, there were think tanks in the United States and public officials warning the public about bioterrorism and the danger of terrorists acquiring nuclear weaponry, but such scenarios were widely discounted as exaggerations or as efforts by the government to identify new threats to justify high defense budgets in the absence of any serious strategic rivalry, and the widely shared general sense that war among leading states was not likely to recur. The American effort to build a defense shield was justified against such a background as a check against the danger of attack by "a rogue state", but not as a capability that could be effective against a major adversary.

Since September 11, this understanding has been radically revised, at least for now. The pursuit of security is again in the domain of "war" rather than "law enforcement". Global economic concerns no longer dominate the policy scene, and even the emphasis on globalization is temporarily in eclipse. What is more striking is the degree to which the new global war has seemed to sideline the normative preoccupations that appeared so important during the 1990s: human rights, the accountability of leaders, redress of historic grievances, and the prospects for global democracy. My argument in this chapter is that these initiatives of the 1990s taken together were mounting the first normative (humane values as expressions of ethics and law) revolution in world history that was of global scope, and that these developments were an outgrowth of modernity that could not be reversed. The events of September 11 seem to contest such an interpretation, but I believe that their impact, while overwhelming in the short run, will be temporary, delaying rather than terminating the overall effort to establish the norms and institutions of humane global governance as the foundation of world order in the twenty-first century.

Such a reading of the future may seem overly optimistic, especially considering the possibility that mishandling the response to September 11, either by under- or over-reaction, could induce an inter-civilizational war of long duration and savage intensity. I think the danger of under-reaction is virtually non-existent, and that the scale of reaction, while risking over-reaction, will be moderated by prudence in the months and years ahead. If such a line of anticipation is correct, then it remains useful to comprehend the underlying trends that gave rise to the speculative hypothesis that we were witnessing the first ever normative revolution of global proportions (Lewis 2001: 50–63).[1]

A revolutionary prospect

Jacques Barzun (2000: 3) warns us at the outset of *From Dawn to Decadence* that "[w]e have gotten into the habit of calling too many things revolutions", and so we have. To claim, then, a revolutionary prospect on the horizon of international political and cultural life is to accept a heavy burden of persuasion. It is not only a matter of not contributing further to the dilution of the idea of revolution as entailing a fundamental transformation, but also of countering a historical mood of post-utopian skepticism about large jumps for the better in the human condition. The disillusionment that accompanied the failures of state socialism as reinforced by the defeat of the cultural revolution that was at the core of the turmoil of 1968, makes doubters of us all. This anti-revolutionary mood extends even to the point of admitting that seeking a promised land tends to make modest ethical gains of an incremental character unlikely, and certainly more difficult. This is due to a conservative backlash that generally achieves strict control of thought and action in the aftermath of failed revolutionary projects. This pattern of hostility to progressive social change, whether domestic or international, in the main, captures the spirit of the times during the 1990s and the early twenty-first century.

If revolutionary rhetoric survives at all during this period as a positive prospect, it is with reference to a set of materialist claims that market forces, integrating via computer, satellite, and optic fiber, will generate an era of abundance and health on a global scale. Cumulatively, these radical technological innovations are now, according to this view, in the process of establishing an organic form of "globalization" that will indeed diminish the role of the territorial state to the point that it is no longer satisfactory to consider world order as constituted by sovereign territorial states. Even these most extreme globalizers do not foresee the disappearance of the state, but rather its increasing virtuality, a redesigned role to facilitate world trade and investment, providing security to the extent that disruptive actors mount threats to the established order (Rosecrance 1999; Held *et al.* 1999).[2] In the background of such dramatic conceptions of the global integrative process underway is the related idea that globalization carries with it a cultural and normative code that homogenizes world society in a coherent and beneficial manner.[3] The global media socializes people everywhere to a common consumptive lifestyle, and more ambitiously promises, that in time, due to economic growth and technological innovation, poverty will disappear and material well-being will become attainable for everybody.[4] Such developments may over time even lead to a system of global law and morality taking hold of the political imagination. There is an irony that such a materialist vision of the future has generated such mainstream enthusiasm at this stage of world capitalism, despite its resemblance to Marxist conceptions of human and societal fulfillment.

There is the dark flipside scenario that sees the same forces of globalization moving toward self-destructive catastrophe as energy use, pollution, warming, and demographic pressure overwhelm the carrying capacity of the global ecosystem. In this understanding, the impotence of the state to stem such a globalizing juggernaut is part of our collective inability as a species to slow the human stagger toward the abyss. The plaintive and shrill calls for help associated with anti-globalization militancy, initiated in a vivid manner in late 1999 during World Trade Organization meetings at Seattle, and continued ever since, raise many questions about the viability and legitimacy of globalization. This movement from below has gained such strength that its presence at any notable gathering of globalizers from above dominates the occasion, making the encounter overshadow the substantive issues and policy changes under discussion in the official sessions. So far, these demonstrations against corporate globalization have succeeded as media events but have yet to prove themselves capable of qualifying as political events that bring about change or even offer a confused public an alternative. For the first time, in the wake of the violent riots accompanying the July 2001 G-8 meetings, heads of state began to evaluate their approach to the management of the world economy. The leaders assembled at Genoa and their retinue of advisors seemed determined that in view of the political turmoil generated, such meetings should no longer be held, at least within the setting of major urban centers.[5]

There is another series of emergent innovations that have been identified as possessed of revolutionary potential, and these are associated with the frontiers of science and technology. The advent of super-intelligent machines, of really smart and versatile robots, and of human cloning and breakthroughs in biogenetics challenges our sense of the human condition and of species survivability in profound ways. These prospects can give rise to either the excitement of a cyber-world of abundance and longevity or a bladerunner world of sheer destructivity.[6] I think we need as a matter of civilizational urgency to assess with great care the political, ethical, and spiritual impacts associated with this radical technology, but I do not propose to do so in this chapter.[7]

My attempt here is to consider whether, despite the manifest despair and complacency of the age, as well as the disruptive and diversionary effects of September 11, we are not embarked upon a relatively bloodless, normative revolution of values, as well as legal procedures and institutions, which is transforming above all else our understanding of global justice. This process is also profoundly affecting our sense of political authority, accountability, and structure of relations in fundamental respects. Such a hypothesis is easy to fault, even to scorn as totally discredited by the evidence of failed and flawed efforts to pull off humanitarian interventions during the past decade or to hold leaders of states consistently accountable for crimes of state.

In a recent highly articulate repudiation of such normative projects, James Mayall (2000: 155) writes, "[t]he revolutionary view of the future is the least plausible". Mayall wants to argue that the continuities of international society based on the coexistence and cooperation of sovereign states, although stretched in places, remain the best hope, and only realistic prospect, for sustaining even the current moderate world order that has the capacity to make modest ethical advances. This view carries forward Hedley Bull's rejection of those normative innovations that attempt, prematurely and regressively in his view, to curtail the sovereignty of states (Alderson and Hurrell 2000: 95–124). Mayall's skepticism is explicitly grounded in the thought of David Hume about the international society of his time, with its primary insistence that we do not allow our moral expectations to exceed our experience of what is attainable in the world as we know it (Mayall 2000: 28–31). Of course, such Humean rhetoric is largely question-begging as the issue as to what our experience allows is a speculative matter that is constantly proving our most august pundits unable to see the handwriting on the wall. Consider, in this regard, how "experience" failed to show that East Europe would be liberated peacefully from Soviet control and domestic oppressive rule in the 1980s, that South Africa would find a way to overcome apartheid without enduring bloody civil strife, and that the standards of international human rights would emerge from their declaratory incubator to become genuine levers of influence. To the extent that experience in global affairs is demonstrative at all, it is to confirm our inability to identify the boundaries of the possible, or to give comfort to either optimistic or pessimistic turns of mind.[8] The non-anticipation of the mega-terrorism of the sort manifested on September 11 suggests that our negative imagination is as deficient as is our sense of what is possible in a more positive sense. It also discloses the inadequacies of intelligence gathering by the state, despite billions of dollars devoted to identifying and preventing threats of a terrorist character. We should, in these respects, encourage receptivity to a wide range of hopeful and dangerous future scenarios, acknowledging the inadequacy of knowledge as a foundation for prediction. In effect, we need to learn to trust the imagination and the political will if we wish to be better prepared to address the future, both its promise and its menace.

It is true that revolutionary processes rarely reveal themselves in advance, and seem to unfold with such rapidity that participants are taken by surprise. Only in retrospect does a revolution disclose its efficient causes and antecedent conditions. Barzun notes "[h]ow a revolution erupts from a commonplace event – tidal wave from a ripple – is cause for endless astonishment" (2000: 7).

Revolutionary precursors or liberal delusions?

If we look back on a century of efforts to achieve global reforms, it is possible to reach quite opposite conclusions. The Bull–Mayall view is that efforts at reform are dysfunctional to the extent that they do not respect the essential hierarchical character of an international society dominated by sovereign states of unequal size and influence. The view associated with international liberalism has been more optimistic, a confidence that small steps of an ethical and institutional character can over time produce a more peaceful and equitable world order. The view being mainly explored here is whether such reformist steps, whether implemented or not, reflect an intensifying revolutionary impulse to reconstruct world order along more normative and globalist lines that express its integrative character. The conclusion reached is that at this point such initiatives are inherently ambiguous, susceptible of interpretation along any of the three lines. The ambiguity is not likely to be removed for at least a few decades as the fuller impact of globalization is disclosed.

The path of such an interpretative effort leads backwards to Woodrow Wilson and the League of Nations, founded without US participation after WWI, as a tribute to Wilson's stature and popular following in the aftermath of a senseless, cruel, and devastating experience of prolonged warfare in Europe. Was not this enactment of Wilson's vision a normative revolution of global proportions? Perhaps, if only words count. Grandiose claims were made at the time for its transformative effects, especially its project to supersede the balance of power diplomacy and war as the arbiter of change through the institutionalization of collective security. But was Wilson's vision ever enacted in a form, with capabilities and constitutional processes that might have had a reasonable chance of upholding its claims? Is there any evidence that Wilson himself understood or accepted the transfer of capabilities to the international level implied by his proclaimed commitment to end the war system? Did the political elites of the leading states of the world, aside from Wilson, believe that the old realist interplay of dominant sovereign states, could be or should be put aside? Not much energy has to be wasted responding to such questions (Knock 1992; Kissinger 1994). A resounding "No" is all that is necessary. At the same time, there is no doubt that the League experience, as sustained by its more elaborate and successful sequel, the United Nations, provides part of the background that helps make the present argument for a normative global revolution more plausible than it would otherwise be. There has been over the course of the last century a growing institutionalization of governance at the international level, a process expressing the increasing complexity of international life, especially in economic domains, along with the search for the security and stability of transactions across the borders of sovereign states.

The same can be said about the Nuremberg and Tokyo war crimes trials held after WWII. On one level, these events did put into question the idea that states were the ultimate arbiters of legality and responsibility, as well as the protective notion granting immunity from prosecution to those individuals who acted on behalf of the state. But the one-sidedness of these inquiries into criminality gave these proceedings an inevitably shaky normative status. They were vulnerable to attacks as "victors' justice" and pure hypocrisy, which could be deflected by contending that a principled framework of generalized accountability would soon follow, with codes and tribunals applicable to all members of international society (Jaspers 1978). When there was no implementation of this Nuremberg Promise, cynicism seemed justified, and the experience of imposing accountability was limited to the circumstances surrounding the outcome of WWII.

As with Wilsonianism, so with the Nuremberg, a normative idea with strong potential claims was validated to a certain degree under special conditions, but not in a manner that would induce durable and consistent change in the behavioral practices of world order as conceived along Westphalian lines of territorial sovereignty. As such, these normative impulses, although capable of arousing extremes of enthusiasm and opposition, were not "revolutionary" in either intention or effect. The means to reach the lofty goals proclaimed were not willed into being. No suitable political project that might challenge statist world order or hegemonic patterns took shape in a credible form.

To suggest the possibility of a global normative revolution is to be aware of this background of disingenuous gestures that are made on an *ad hoc* basis without an accompanying will and social forces to make structural changes. Without relevant agency and the structural changes, the rhetoric of revolution is hollow sentimentality, or a politically irrelevant utopianism. The structural changes responsive to a normative agenda challenge several aspects of political realism embedded on a global scale in such ideas as sovereignty, statism, hegemony, marginality of law and morality, and the absence of a clear and agreed conception of *global* justice.

My position is that this normative agenda of challenge has emerged in the last decade or so, building on these earlier impulses, but now reinforced by the global setting in an unprecedented manner, making the idea of a normative revolution more politically grounded than ever before. Such grounding does not ensure its success, hence the question mark in the title, and there are evident significant contradictory tendencies. Yet, for the first time in human history, a combination of social forces and practical pressures is giving the current manifestation of a project for normative revolution serious credibility, if not yet robustness. This credibility mainly arises because multi-dimensional forms of resistance to market-driven globalization need to be neutralized by making the emergent order legitimate in the eyes of the peoples of the world.

It remains to ask what is meant by "normative global revolution". The idea of normative is associated with justice, moral values, and legal order, while that of global is connected with the scope of what is being proposed, but in the manner of stacked Russian dolls. Contextualizing such an outlook requires that we consider the Westphalian framework of territorial sovereignty as the established order against which the revolution is being undertaken. As such, it is not a modification of a reformist sort that will enable that inherited and resilient framework to adapt yet again to altered conditions, but something that is so fundamental as to revise our perception of the core features of "the real". We will partly come to appreciate the transformative character of this process by expressing the need for and seeking out a new language of explication and appraisal that conveys the new realities in more satisfactory ways.

Barzun, quoted earlier, portrays the history of the West as a sequence of revolutions, but carried on within the boundaries of states taken as the stable elements of an established order. As expressed, "[a] revolutionary idea can succeed only if it can rally strong 'irrelevant' interests, and only the military can make it" (Barzun 2000: 10). My view explored here is that a revolutionary idea under contemporary conditions needs to rally strong support throughout global civil society, which can be conceived from a statist perspective as a domain of the internationally "irrelevant", but no longer depends on violence for its success.

This possibility is a result of three mutually reinforcing developments. The first of these, and the most encompassing, is the evolution of international human rights from a pious promise made in an unconvincing and nominal form back in 1950, and even earlier, to a serious claim directed against inconsistent behavior in the early twenty-first century (Falk 2000). In this regard, I take seriously as the second development the empirical spread and universal endorsement accorded a democratizing ethos, although I dissent from the view that "democracy" is properly delimited in minimalist and statist terms of electoral consent in this era of globalization (Marks 2000).[9] The third development is the anti-globalization movement with its implicit indictment of the illegitimate character of the manner in which global policy is being formed and implemented, as well as with the inequities alleged to result from such processes, especially with regard to the peoples of the South. This combination of international human rights (including distinct movements of women, indigenous peoples, and sexual identity), the democratic ethos, and the anti-globalization movement is what gives the normative global revolution its political shape and relevance. It is predicated upon an underlying engagement with the attainment of global justice, or alternatively phrased, "humane global governance".[10]

Imagining a normative global revolution: some activating conditions

The first set of normative impulses can be best understood as a continuation of WWII by the victorious coalition of states led by the United States. This meant the war crimes trials at Nuremberg and Tokyo, establishment of the United

Nations, the Genocide Convention, and the Universal Declaration of Human Rights. Partly, these initiatives represented efforts to learn from the mistakes of the past, particularly they reflected the failures of the punitive approach to Germany embedded in the Versailles Treaty and the non-participation of the United States in the League of Nations. Partly, these initiatives resulted from a belated sense of shame about the failure of the liberal democracies to oppose the genocidal politics of the Nazi regime in Germany, or even to proffer aid to the victims in their quest for places of refuge, that is, criminalizing genocide and internationalizing human rights were symbolic steps in the direction of imposing limits on sovereignty as exercised *within* territorial limits. But in the main, these initiatives taken between 1945 and 1950 were problematic, being tainted by the victors' insistence on exempting their own behavior from legal scrutiny, failing to transfer any peacemaking capabilities to the United Nations, and through the intense adherence to notions of sovereign rights as modified by geopolitical prerogatives (most notably the vet power of the five permanent members of the UN Security Council). The year of 1945 was still very much of a Westphalian world, its statist logic accentuated by Soviet concerns associated with their plausible anxiety about being outmaneuvered and outvoted in any consensual procedure established at the global level.[11] It is also the case that the main learning experience arising from the WWII experience was that idealistic approaches to international order do not succeed in providing either security or peace. The paradoxical conclusion is that the best prospects for peace result from the maintenance of deterrent strength rather than by way of demilitarizing disarmament, which tempts aggression. The so-called "lesson of Munich" was formative for Western leaders in this period, creating anxiety about placing any serious reliance on the UN as possibly diverting resources and energies from the need to rest world peace in the future on a balance of power logic. Neither legal nor moral norms of constraint, but only countervailing power could induce moderation based on assumptions that leaders of states are generally guided by rational assessments of gains and losses associated with recourse to force and by a prudent approach to risk-taking.

The two most radical innovations in world order that were launched in this period were not widely perceived as such at the time, and perhaps for this reason were able to develop beyond most expectations of what seemed realistic. The first of these innovations was to overcome some of the weaknesses in world economic coordination that were thought to have contributed to the Great Depression of the 1930s, especially currency volatility. A complementary institutional innovation was designed to ensure that there would be ways to assist poorer countries of Asia and Africa in meeting their needs for foreign capital so as to overcome their backwardness while respecting their political independence, and without appearing to be constructing new variants of economic imperialism. The IMF and the World Bank, the so-called Bretton Woods institutions, as much later complemented by the World Trade Organization, designed to institutionalize periodic moves toward freer international trade and exchange rate stability, evolved into a powerful institutional triumvirate. Unlike the UN, global economic governance was seen as a capitalist enterprise, and was controlled by the Western liberal democracies from its inception. These institutional actors, along with the leading capitalist governments, provide a measure of global economic governance that has evolved over the decades in response to changing conditions, and recently functioned quite explicitly to disseminate neoliberal ideas and practices about state/society policy. This includes facilitating the adoption of market-oriented priorities of corporate globalization by countries in the South such as privatization, fiscal austerity, and the free transnational flow of capital.

The second radical innovation with enduring implications for global governance was the establishment of a regional approach to Western European recovery and reconstruction that began modestly with cooperation in relation to iron and steel production and trade among a small number of Western European countries.[12] By the year 2001, European regionalism has matured into a quasi-confederal European Union that will launch a common currency in 2002, impressively upholds human rights of Europeans even against abuses by their own national government, contemplates a European constitution, and may in the years ahead incorporate much of Eastern Europe into an enlarged "Europe". Whether to view international financial and trade institutions and European regionalism as normative initiatives are themselves complicated and controversial matters that required extended and nuanced analysis. Certainly both initiatives have important normative implications, especially in relation to two crucial concerns: the character of global governance, the role of the state, and a concept of justice that is not limited to state/society relations. Their relevance will be assessed in the concluding section.

Undoubtedly, the great normative achievement of the Cold War era involved the delegitimation of colonial rule, and the emergence of almost universal support for the right of self-determination. Of course, this achievement was rendered more difficult and remarkable because it cut against the grain of geopolitical alignments, placing the colonial powers, particularly Britain and France, as pariahs of the old order, and putting the United States in an ambivalent position. The extent of this ambivalence became evident in the setting of the Indochina Wars in which the United States supplanted France in a sustained and futile effort to prevent indigenous nationalism from strengthening the Communist bloc.[13]

The bipolar split of the Cold War era (1945–89), combined with a realist turn in the diplomacy of major states, kept other normative developments of an inter-governmental character at a minimum: a consensus in support of the modernizing quest of the developing world and an ethos of coexistence flourished from time to time that encouraged formulating an over-arching framework of shared normative ideas. The adherence of the United States to a realist understanding of global security was particularly influential, especially as the United States had traditionally challenged the European geopolitical orientation as war-prone premised on shifting alliances and the balance of power. This turn encouraged the substitution of "arms control" for "disarmament", in effect, seeking to reduce risks associated with unintended behavior without challenging the essential role of power in sustaining peace and stability within "the anarchical society" of states. This managerial diplomacy of prudence mainly focused on the distinctive problems of managing rival arsenals of nuclear weaponry, especially the dual role of this weaponry in relation to deterrence and to a resolve to forego actual use. Hence, the fascination with the acronym MAD, mutual assured destruction, but as well the crazed condition of threatening a course of action that would also lead to catastrophic self-destruction. MAD was complemented by an anti-proliferation approach to nuclear weaponry, in effect, trying to prevent additional states joining the nuclear club rather than seeking to abolish the club altogether. The prevalence of nuclearism tended to marginalize normative efforts in the security domain, especially given the implicit adoption of omnicidal prerogatives in the name of the security of state or ideological identity ("better dead than red") and the reluctance of the existing nuclear state to seek ways of reliably denuclearizing world politics.[14]

Yet in this period, despite the ideological cleavage that affected all dimensions of global policy as coupled with the realist *Zeitgeist*, there were important developments that set the stage for later developments. First of all, initiatives in civil society challenged statist approaches to both international human rights and environmental protection. Civil society actors (earlier known as NGOs), with transnational links began to promote adherence to weak, yet existent, international norms, exerting pressure especially in democratic societies for their implementation. Starting with the Iranian Revolution at the end of the 1970s, non-violent populist pressures for democratizing change were mounted under the extreme conditions of authoritarianism prevailing in Eastern Europe, as well as in relation to the racism associated with apartheid in South Africa. Second, militant opponents of Cold War policies believed to violate fundamental norms of international law and morality began to invoke the Nuremberg idea as the basis of their refusal to support official policies. This process took place in America especially during the latter stages of the Vietnam War and later on with respect to symbolic acts of resistance by individuals seeking to prevent the deployment of nuclear weapons with first strike characteristics. In both instances, feeble or flawed inter-governmental undertakings relating to accountability that were supposed to be confined in their application to their original facts, were kept alive in a mutated form, while being generalized by civil society activists. These activists, often associated with deeply religious backgrounds, gradually came to view "democracy" through neo-natural law eyes as the spontaneous exercise of "popular sovereignty" in deference to the authority of a normative order higher than that of the secular state.[15] Such attitudes, particularly as vindicated by varying degrees of success, helped set the stage for subsequently mounting a normative revolution of global proportions.

A final stage-setting development was the totally unexpected visionary global outlook provided by Mikhail Gorbachev during the last years of the Cold War. In seeking to undertake drastic reforms internally and diplomatically, including a negotiated end to the Cold War, Gorbachev revived a normative global agenda with a sweep and passion that recalled Woodrow Wilson. Unfortunately, this visionary call by Gorbachev for a more cooperative and demilitarized world order, sustained by a stronger United Nations and an increased acceptance of the rule of law, was dismissed at the time either as "propaganda" or as a feeble effort by the Kremlin to conceal the mounting evidence of Soviet decline. Unlike the efforts to deepen the commitment to human rights norms and to keep alive the Nuremberg tradition, this Gorbachev crusade led nowhere, despite its humane and sensible content, and has been barely acknowledged.[16] Most regretfully, the United States, the most satisfied of superpowers, saw no need to respond to this Gorbachev approach either by way of endorsement or at least with a reform agenda of its own. Even after the collapse of the Soviet Union, Washington failed to seize the occasion to promote a system of humane global governance. Unlike the endings of major hot wars over the centuries, the end of the Cold War did not induce the victorious powers to offer the peoples of the world a program of global reform that would contribute to future human well-being. The two most tangible opportunities for global reform as of the 1990s were a serious effort to achieve phased nuclear disarmament and a commitment to strengthening the capabilities and independence of the United Nations system. Despite this disappointment at the inter-governmental level, other positive developments ensued to make the hypothesis of a normative global revolution seem well worth entertaining.

The previously mentioned trends toward global economic governance and European regionalism were accelerated due to favorable geopolitical conditions for their evolution. Without Cold War preoccupations, greater attention could be turned toward the coherent management of the world economy and the effective participation of Europe in a global trading and financial system that was dominated by the United States and Japan. Overall, the end of the Cold War brought to the fore an economistic outlook toward the goals of global policy, particularly given the absence of serious strategic or ideological conflict. China's moves to enter the world economy and submit to the discipline of world capitalism has operated as a major factor in reorienting world order around global economic policy.

These developments taken together with a series of technological developments, especially in the broad area of information technology (IT) – the computer and Internet, as well as the rise of networking organizational schema in business operations – led to the realization that there was a sufficient disjunction between past and present to require a new descriptive vocabulary. Hence, globalization. In some respects, the advent of globalization, especially as historically enacted according to quite contingent neoliberal precepts, represented a serious normative regression: a declining willingness to divert resources to overcome poverty and social deprivation combined with a reliance on the market and private sector to address human suffering. The point here is that the technological infrastructure that has made world integration feasible and beneficial could occur in relation to a more socially compassionate set of presiding ideas. Other "globalizations" more normatively acceptable than neoliberal globalization were possible, and yet may be negotiated to bring "peace".[17]

This regression associated with the rise of neoliberal ideas was offset to some controversial extent by an effort to make democratic patterns of governance, by which was meant periodic multi-party elections and free markets, the foundation of legitimate state/society relations. Leaders of Western states, whether knowingly or not, became unwitting (although partial) adherents of Immanuel Kant's ideas about "democratic peace", and conditioned their enthusiasm for globalization by this call for democratization.[18]

Also important was the changed role of violence in world society. There seemed to be a growing sense of obsolescence associated with major warfare as territorial gains were rarely worth the effort, and the backlash could be severe. In this sense, the Gulf War of 1991 was an anomaly, and it also demonstrated the point that aggressive undertakings could generate massive responses to achieve a reversal. Of course, unsettled borders and unresolved territorial disputes still threaten future wars, but for limited ends that do not threaten international stability, with the possible and highly unlikely exceptions of wars fought by China to gain control of Taiwan or of North Korea to take over the entire Korean Peninsula or the renewed outbreak of Indo-Pakistan warfare relating to the future of Kashmir. Despite these lingering concerns, the prospect of strategic warfare is receding from the political imagination, although not smoothly as ongoing debates about missile defense systems and regimes for the prohibition of biological weaponry suggest.

As a result of this tendency, and in view of the large number of persisting forms of violent encounter, there has grown a focus on intranational violence, and on the limits of sovereign power and authority. There has emerged the awareness that international law and the UN as now constituted fit awkwardly into the new paradigm of political conflict.[19] Both international law and the UN Charter accept the idea of territorial supremacy and sovereign rights of the state, thereby rejecting any external accountability of a government or responsibility on the part of the world community to protect an abused society or ethnic minority. This tension between moral imperatives and the constitutional order generates efforts to find new normative ideas that will bridge the gap.

A further actuating circumstance is the emergence of global problems that can only be solved by the logic of collective action. The US refusal as of 2001 to back the Kyoto Protocol relating to global warming without offering a substitute measure is indicative of the vulnerability of the peoples of the world to a normative framework that is conditioned on the right of a single state to defy the collective will of the world community. The issue raised is whether collective action can be arranged either by way of a revised US assessment of its own interests or by way of procedures that take precedence over its refusal to accept a global regime of restraint. The short-term outlook is not promising, but as the evidence of harm from continued emissions of greenhouse gases at current levels mounts, there is likely to take shape a strong political effort to insist that the United States in its behavior act as "a responsible sovereign", which might include cutting back aspects of its way of life that are globally damaging.

A further background consideration is the dual realization that armed struggles have difficulty gaining their goals, and that governments are not able to prevail over their citizenry by reliance on coercion alone. The 1980s and 1990s bore witness to a post-Gandhian rise in non-violent revolutionary challenges to established political orders and an abandonment of armed struggle strategies. The trend toward negotiated compromises was a promising, although not consistent, development. Non-violent challenges were turned back in several Asian countries, most prominently in China during 1989, and armed struggle tactics succeeded in some instances, as in inducing the NATO intervention in Kosovo that resulted in the expulsion of the Serb oppressive police and military forces.

My argument is simple: that a series of developments have set the stage for the unexpected surge of normativity that has taken place *globally* (and *regionally* to an uneven extent) during the last decade or so. The next section will identify the main dimensions of this normative phenomenon, to be followed by a short section assessing its sustainability.

The normative surge since 1989: a quest for global justice

Although the hypothesis being explored is that the cumulative impact of the normative initiatives underway *may* amount to a global revolution if sustained for the next decade or so, it may also fizzle out, and there are also present some lively possibilities of normative global regression. The main elements of what is being presented here as the elements of the normative revolution are, by and large, not novelties, but extensions of earlier initiatives that had appeared to be stillborn with only a historical significance. That is, the *latent* normative potential of the Westphalian evolution of statism during its latest phases are the main building blocks of a possibly emergent normative global revolution. The political project associated with achieving global justice and humane global governance amounts, then, to activating these latent elements.

Accountability: justice for the perpetrators

Undoubtedly, one of the most striking developments with moral/legal/political implications involves a multitude of efforts to hold those who act on behalf of sovereign states *internationally* accountable for their behavior, at least to the extent of severely abusive behavior.[20] The substantive scope of "abusive" is unclear, and will undoubtedly evolve to incorporate shifting sentiments, but seems now definitely to extend to genocide, crimes against humanity, torture, rape as a military tactic, and possibly crimes against peace and severe violations of human rights. Such efforts to impose international accountability is a direct and fundamental challenge to the central Westphalian idea of territorial supremacy of the sovereign state, and the related doctrines of act of state, sovereign immunity, and superior orders. This impulse to hold leaders, and their subalterns, accountable for adherence to norms is not new, tracing its origins to medieval efforts to uphold codes of chivalry in times of war. In the last century, the half-hearted insistence by the Allies that Kaiser Wilhelm of Germany be prosecuted as a war criminal for his role in starting WWI suggested a rudimentary type of international accountability, which came to nothing.

The true precursor to the recent initiatives was, of course, the Nuremberg/Tokyo trials held after WWII. At the time, these trials seemed to promise a radical innovation in international relations, but turned out to be limited to their historical circumstances associated with the outcome of a war deemed just by its victors (Minear 1971; Taylor 1992). Or were they? The benevolent virus of international criminal accountability had been released into the body politic, and it spread unpredictably, establishing its authority as a standard of criticism and self-judgment. This was especially the case for the United States, which was the main architect of the Nuremberg approach, and also the state most vulnerable to claims from within its own society, as well as from the broader community of liberal democracies. In fact, Cold War priorities inhibited allies from complaining about US departures from the rule of law with respect to the use of international force, but it did not similarly constrain outraged citizens, especially in response to growing domestic and international opposition to the Vietnam War in the late 1960s. Notable in this regard was the convening in Europe of a tribunal composed of well-known moral authority figures to assess the criminality of American conduct in Vietnam by the British philosopher, Bertrand Russell.[21] Also significant was Daniel Ellsberg's much publicized release of the Pentagon Papers, which he explained in public and under oath at the time as responsive to the text and teachings of the Nuremberg Judgment.

But the 1990s witnessed the inter-governmental revival of international accountability procedures, at the formal initiative of the United Nations Security Council, initially with respect to the break-up of the former Yugoslavia and then shortly thereafter in relation to genocide in Rwanda. The establishment of the International Criminal Tribunal for the former Yugoslavia at The Hague in 1992 led to a renewed interest in international accountability. This interest was intensified some years later when Slobodan Milosevic was indicted in the midst of the Kosovo War, along with other high-ranking officials in Belgrade, while he was officially head of state, and again in 2001 when Milosevic was handed over for prosecution as a result of a change of government in Yugoslavia.[22] These developments stimulated civil society and moderate governments to seek the institutionalization of international accountability through the establishment of an international criminal court. Surprisingly, this collaboration resulted in the Rome Treaty of 1998 that comes into force once it secures 60 ratifications, which seems likely within the next year or so, but without the participation of such vital states as the United States, China, Russia, and Israel. There is still prevalent the idea that accountability is a selective instrument that cannot be used to judge the behavior of individuals acting on behalf of the powerful states. The silence of the West in relation to Russian behavior in Chechnya is revealing of the extent to which normative principles are subordinated in favor of economistic and geopolitical goals.

Of comparable interest, and even greater salience, have been the efforts by national courts in Western Europe to claim the legal competence to punish foreign governmental officials for criminality even if committed within their own country. The landmark experience involved the criminal indictment of Augusto Pinochet for crimes committed in Chile during his period as dictatorial ruler, and his later detention in Britain for the purpose of assessing whether he could be extradited to face prosecution. This effort yielded some notable legal decisions in Britain, including a final determination by a Law Panel of the House of Lords, that Pinochet was subject to extradition, but for a very portion of the criminality charged (Brody and Ratner 2000; Falk forthcoming). In the end, Pinochet was returned to Chile, being declared by the British Home Secretary as unfit to stand trial, a conclusion also reached later on slightly different grounds by Chilean courts.

Subsequently, in 2001, Ariel Sharon, Prime Minister of Israel, is under investigation with regard to his allegedly criminal role in connection with the massacre of Palestinian refugees at Sabra and Shatila in 1982 while he was Defense Minister. The massacre occurred in the last stage of the Lebanon War, perpetrated in West Beirut with alleged Israeli complicity by the Phalange Militia, while it was under the control of the Israel Defense Forces. The Israeli Foreign Ministry in August 2001 has reportedly prepared a map for its officials and diplomats that points out which countries have empowered their courts to prosecute for crimes against humanity and other crimes of state, and have warned of possible embarrassment to Israel (Goldenberg 2001: 6; Hitchens 2000).

A group of scholars and legal practitioners has formulated a set of guidelines as to the extension of universal jurisdiction to allegations of this type.[23] There is a definite movement underway to challenge the traditional idea of sovereign immunity when it comes to crimes of state, which if it becomes established in the years ahead, will represent a major step in the struggle to bring law to bear on the behavior of governments. It will also give pause to leaders who could no longer count on immunity or asylum. It is notable that national courts function as agents of both global civil society and of an international society of states to the extent that such accountability is implemented.

It is important to ask why such a momentous set of developments has taken place in the last decade, especially given the failure during the prior half century to follow up on the Nuremberg precedent. The obvious answer relates to the absence of geopolitical inhibitions of the sort that existed during the Cold War. With the fall of the Berlin Wall, it seemed to become more tenable to assert universal standards of accountability whose application would not be seen as a propaganda victory or defeat, and would not be an occasion for a heightening of superpower tensions. Also relevant was the increasing importance of international human rights, with the exemption of crimes of states thus seeming like an anomaly.

Redress of grievances: justice for the victims

Parallel, yet seemingly disconnected from these extraordinary moves toward international accountability, has been an unprecedented effort in an array of settings to achieve on behalf of victims some measure of redress for past grievances. It is possible to view the imposition of criminal liability on the perpetrator of abuses as also simultaneously responding to the pleas of victims and their families. Indeed, capital punishment in the United States is often defended as a form of justice for the victims, particularly since other arguments based on deterrence and prevention seem so unpersuasive. Yet it seems helpful to separate the efforts to hold perpetrators individually accountable from the efforts to obtain redress from a variety of actors associated with perpetrators (and entities such as banks and industrial firms, and even governments) in various ways.

The most salient instance of redress was associated with the efforts of Holocaust survivors and descendants to recover their share of gold that had been confiscated from them by the Nazi regime in Germany and deposited in various European banks, especially those in Switzerland. These claims along with related claims to unclaimed bank deposits seemed suddenly to receive moral backing from important governments, including that of the United States. The Swiss Government and a consortium of its leading banks negotiated a large settlement, and "redress" became an idea whose time had definitely come. A variety of claims followed seeking recovery of earnings from slave labor, insurance proceeds, and art objects.[24]

The experience of pursuing Holocaust claims seemed inspirational for other communities of victims. Most obviously, those in Asia/Pacific who had suffered at the hands of Japanese imperial power sought redress with a special intensity. Japan, far less than Germany, took the first step toward redress, which is an acknowledgment of wrongdoing. At present, in Japan more than fifty-five years after the end of WWII, school textbooks continue to whitewash the past, which itself has kept from healing the wounds of victims and those who identify most closely. Some of the Asian efforts are merely to coerce remembrance and accurate historical reconstruction through such devices as books, films, museum exhibits, and conferences detailing the Nanking Massacre of 1937.[25] And from remembrance, the impulse to obtain redress seeks informal acknowledgments of wrongdoing, which eventually will produce a formal apology by the responsible government, and possibly some sort of offer of compensation.

The more monetary approach to redress associated with the Holocaust survivors was also emulated by Asian/Pacific survivors who have been seeking to recover damages for slave labor and other abuses endured at the hands of Japan. So-called "comfort women" abducted in various Asian-occupied countries to satisfy the sexual appetites of Japanese military forces have also sought to obtain some sort of belated compensation for the abuses sustained, so far failing to find satisfaction from the Japanese judicial system.[26] From an international law perspective, the redress process directed at Japan has encountered special difficulties arising from the waiver provision in the Japanese Peace Treaty that purported to extinguish all claims of individuals on both sides of the conflict. There are important ways around this apparent barrier, but they are yet to be accepted by courts.

A form of redress that has achieved great prominence, and can be viewed also as a diluted approach to accountability, is the establishment of truth and reconciliation commissions to record and document past wrongs, as well as to elicit testimony and expressions of remorse by confessed wrongdoers. These commissions were established in Latin American countries in the process of making peaceful transitions from dictatorial regimes to constitutional democracies, and seemed to offer a more stable way to walk the tightrope between impunity and accountability in societies where the old order was still entrenched in the military and security forces. Ever since Nuremberg, the argument has been made that one of the main functions of criminal prosecution is to build a documentary record of past wrongdoing, both to avenge the feelings of the victims and to educate the society and the world in the hope of avoiding repetition. South Africa's remarkable transition to a multi-racial democracy relied on a truth and reconciliation commission as an alternative to seeking "justice" by prosecuting those who carried out the criminal policies of the apartheid regime. Such an attempt to make transitions to democracy successful is not without controversy, with the most severely victimized elements of the society exhibiting bitterness about letting the perpetrators of unforgivable crime get off so easily. On balance, the truth and reconciliation approach has proved to be a creative compromise, repudiating past criminality without treating those associated with the former regime so harshly as to provoke their resistance. Of course, there is no incompatibility between engaging in a truth and reconciliation process and relying on accountability procedures to deal with certain unrepentant or severe offenders.

Redress as a moral and political tactic is definitely in the mind of victim communities. Without surveying the vast array of claims, it is worth observing the issuance of apologies by leaders of dominant countries for such past abuses as colonial rule and the institution of slavery. Refusal of acknowledgment, as with respect to Armenian allegations of "genocide" by Turkey in 1915–16, has been treated by segments of international public opinion as tantamount to an endorsement of the historic abuse.

Among the most militant and persistent pursuers of redress have been indigenous peoples acting in various ways through their representatives. These initiatives have been notable for their assertiveness without any strong base of military or economic power, but through a moral and legal crusade to enjoy the protection of property and other rights, including respect for sovereignty and traditional way of life. Indigenous peoples have been able to establish a forum for networking, expressing their grievances, and positing a protective regime based on a legitimated normative order.[27]

The logic behind the redress movement is that the victims of severe wrongdoing are entitled, even with the passage of decades or even centuries, to obtain some sort of symbolic or material form of compensation for past injustice. The relevant actors are both individual and collective, with various entities engaged as claimants and responsible party. This validation of a redress ethos reverses an earlier dominant cultural and political view that the past is a closed book as to rectification of wrongs. The new context has lent credibility to claims and contentions that were formerly dismissed as frivolous, as was the case with efforts by African-Americans to demand reparations (in billions of dollars) for the suffering endured due to the practice and institution of slavery.

The significance of this redress ethos is difficult to assess at this stage. It does clearly form part of an increased sensitivity to issues of justice wherever and whenever, and the relevance of their resolution to a peaceful and equitable world order. Why during the 1990s? It seems evident that the end of the Cold War, coupled with concerns about accountability, human rights, and democracy, led those who identified as victims improperly acknowledged toward adopting activist positions. In addition to this normative atmosphere, two other factors seem worth noting: the relativizing of sovereignty made states and their representatives more vulnerable to legal and moral claims than previously; and the preoccupation with the future imparted a new salience to time and history, giving to the past a present relevance.

None of these considerations is conclusive. It remains to be observed whether the redress movement is sustainable, and achieves enough tangible results to influence our understanding of the nature of global justice. What can be agreed upon is that diverse redress claims are being asserted to an unprecedented degree during this period, and that this process contributes to the impression that a normative global revolution is underway.

Humane global governance: justice for the peoples of the world

In the background of this quest for global justice is the effort to achieve humane global governance within a political setting that can no longer be conceived or dealt with as an assemblage of nation–state communities. In this regard, the normative global revolution is accompanying a transition from a pluralist world of sovereign states to a solidarist world of peoples.[28] The sites of struggle and controversy are complex, inter-linked, and diverse, and can only be indicated here in the most cursory manner. Several sites can be mentioned: the legality and legitimacy of humanitarian intervention; the movement to globalize democracy; the resurgence of religion; and the struggle for people-oriented development.

Humanitarian intervention

The NATO involvement in Kosovo in 1999 heightened an awareness of humanitarian intervention, occasioning intense debate that persists. To the extent that humanitarian intervention is justified on ethical grounds, it expresses the right and duty of collective action on an international level to protect victims of crimes of state, including victims of gross violations of human rights. Humanitarian intervention overrides territorial sovereignty, implying a use of international force in circumstances other than self-defense. If underwritten by a

United Nations mandate that is processed by the Security Council, then there is a general acceptance of legality associated with humanitarian intervention despite the UN Charter's promise in Article 2(7) that the Organization will not intervene in matters that fall within the domestic jurisdiction of member states. Implicitly, the severe abuse of people by a territorial government no longer insulates the behavior from international coercive protective action.

The more difficult challenge arises when a Security Council mandate is not forthcoming despite overwhelming evidence of catastrophic human abuse. Such was the case, as understood by those who supported the Kosovo intervention. As the Independent International Commission on Kosovo argues in its report, the Kosovo intervention disclosed a troublesome gap between legality and legitimacy in relation to claims for humanitarian intervention. The Commission approach was to propose a set of guidelines to shape such an intervention and its assessment, but the possibility persists that a humanitarian intervention can appear to be legitimate from the perspective of morality and politics and yet illegal from the perspective of international law.[29]

On a purely conceptual level, the idea of humanitarian intervention suggests the emergence of a protective global regime that responds to the vulnerability of peoples being victimized by a government that does not respect international law in dealing with its own territorial population, usually a dissident minority. It reflects the pressure for normative revolution by subordinating claims of territorial sovereignty to those associated with humane governance. But humanitarian intervention of the Kosovo variety is highly contested in theory and practice. It is attacked for its defiance of international law and the UN Charter on a matter of cardinal importance – the unconditional prohibition on uses of non-defensive force in international relations. It is viewed as a new modality of imperial control by the strong in relation to the weak: if Kosovo, why not Chechnya, or Tibet? It is attacked as a cover for old geopolitics repackaged for public relations (Chomsky 1999). And it is opposed on pluralist grounds of support for sovereign rights as the most consistent means to protect the well-being of peoples at the present stage of international history.

Global democracy

If the normative revolution is to succeed, it will need to extend the principles and practices of democracy to the main arenas of decision and policy-making operative in the world. "Globalization" is a shorthand for suggesting that many of these arenas fall outside the statist framework. The anti-globalization movement, although unfocused, does emphasize its refusal to accept the authority of institutional actors who do not act in accordance with the precepts of global democracy: transparency, participation, and accountability.

One idea for advancing the agenda of global democracy involves the establishment of a Global Peoples Assembly (GPA) either within the UN System or as a free-standing institution (Falk and Strauss 2000; 2001). There are many formats that could be used to get such an institution into being, with various methods available to select representatives. A GPA could start modestly as "a coalition of the willing", and gradually improve the quality of its representative-ness. The experience of the European Parliament is instructive, both in terms of its evolution and the degree to which it has gained in respect and authority through time despite being dismissed as irrelevant at various points by cynical and realist-minded critics.

Global democracy to be realized implies a solidarist world order, which in turn presupposes the completion of a normative global revolution. It is connected with earlier discussions of accountability and redress, and connects democratic process with global justice. As with other aspects of the revolutionary possibility, it is premature to draw firm conclusions. It seems evident that resistance to globalization is likely to lead its managers to offer some coopting gestures of democratization, but whether these amount over time to "governance" is the critical and now unanswerable question.

Religious resurgence

Perhaps even more controversial than other aspects of the argument relating to a prospective normative revolution is the inclusion of a religious dimension. It is controversial, to begin with, because many commentators on the international scene regard religion as a divisive element, and closely connected to the Huntington postulate of "a clash of civilizations". The view favored here is that religion has a dual aspect, partly destructive of the prospects for humane global governance, but partly *indispensable* to its attainment (Falk 2001). The contribution of religion is to mobilize mass sentiment around several themes: the spiritual and moral context of the human condition; the unity of the human family; the shared perspectives – what Aldous Huxley called "the perennial philosophy" – being promoted by Hans Küng and others (Küng 1998).

What is not in doubt is the reality of the religious resurgence as a worldwide phenomenon that suffuses all of the great world religions, although unevenly and with differing impacts. The preoccupation with religious extremism, especially in the Islamic world, diverts our attention from the degree to which the rise of religion is a normative reaction to the material and secular fundamentalisms embedded in economic globalization.

Calls for inter-civilizational and inter-religious dialogue are part of the effort to construct a shared human identity that could combine an understanding and acceptance of differences with an affirmation of common values and goals. It builds normative networks outside the domains of conventional transnational activism, and emphasizes cultural and civilizational boundaries more than those of sovereign states. As such, the religious resurgence could contribute to humane governance within a variety of regional frameworks. The positive sides of religious consciousness also affirm responsibility for the poor and afflicted, providing a normative antidote to those who believe that economic growth and private sector charity can handle human suffering. Finally, the religious approach to the global challenges posed by such divergent realities as global warming and human cloning suggest the insufficiency of reliance on either economistic or secular modes of problem-solving.

People-oriented development

More utopian than other aspects of the current revolutionary turmoil is the demand that *people* and not *profitability* shape the allocation of resources for development, particularly in countries of mass impoverishment. There is some shift in the rhetoric of such international institutions as the World Bank and the IMF that seems responsive to such a demand. To the extent that such an approach to development is accepted by influential actors, it adds to the impression of an emergent normative climate in world politics.

At present, such a re-orientation of the developmental ethos away from profitability and growth seems utopian in the sense that almost everywhere the prevailing mood and allocational patterns governing the use of resources continue to be capital-driven. Banking principles and financial markets exert direct influence on the behavior of governments, even to the extent of overwhelming traditional postulates of economic sovereignty. Even a country as strong and nationalist as Turkey has ceded substantial control to external decision-makers implementing a neoliberal view of development. Commenting on a visit to Turkey by Stanley Fischer, a former high-ranking IMF official, in July 2001, a journalist named Mehmet Ali Birand writes: "Fischer's trip revealed something of great importance: The Turkish economy it transpires is being run from Washington. As if nobody knew already. What was not clear was the degree of detail involved" (Birand 2001: 5).

No normative global revolution can succeed unless it address directly and as a matter of priority issues of economic deprivation, but also the degrees of disparity between countries, regions, and classes. It may be both the most obvious and elusive issue as its resolution would require the substantial revision, if not the abandonment, of the current ideological orthodoxy embedded in globalization.

Conclusion

The presentation above tried to make credible the case for believing that a normative global revolution is underway, but that its sustainability and outcome are highly uncertain and beset by contradictory evidence and trends, especially given the onset of the war on global terror. The goal of such a revolution is the establishment by stages of humane global governance that is responsive to the functional needs of an era of globalization. Whether the sovereign state can adapt to this revolution, or mounts a counter-revolution on behalf of a pluralist world order, is a major area of uncertainty. It would seem that rates of adaptation are uneven, with interesting collaborative opportunities evolving for states favoring normative reforms joining with civil society actors to achieve such ends as an international criminal court or a ban on anti-personnel landmines.

Another crucial uncertainty involves the direction taken by the United States, and the manner in which it chooses to discharge its global leadership, especially now that it has shifted its focus to a decidedly militarist pursuit of security. Its present anti-solidarist unilateralism and reliance on a militarist view of global security are discouraging, but they may generate counter-tendencies within the United States and elsewhere that are supportive of the normative global revolution.

In the end, the secular prospects for the normative global revolution will depend on the degree to which the anti-globalization movement converges with the struggle to promote and achieve global democracy. But even if this movement evolves in a constructive manner, its ultimate success will depend on its capacity to relate positively to the creative and visionary aspects of the religious resurgence, and not get trapped into an embrace of secular fundamentalism as a reaction to religious extremism and its mega-terrorist enactments.

Notes

1 But some influential voices, most notably the celebrated Islamic scholar Bernard Lewis, warn of under-reaction as the main danger even in the wake of the war against the Taliban regime in Afghanistan.

2 A sophisticated presentation of the spectrum of opinion relating to the character and impact of globalization from the perspective of global change is found in Held *et al.* (1999).

3 For an assessment along these lines, see Mozaffari (2000).

4 Perhaps, the most prototypic account of globalization in this vein is that of Friedman (1999).

5 Note that in the 1990s, challenges of a comparable sort were raised at global conferences held under UN auspices. These challenges were addressed at particular policy concerns: environment, women, human rights, population pressure, and were directed mainly at prevailing statist policies. The anti-globalization movement, although in evidence at these conferences, especially at the Social Summit of 1995 in Copenhagen, was subordinated to substantive concerns with particular social issues. This earlier set of calls for democratization and grassroots participation in global policymaking processes did not include violent anarchistic elements that have been given such attention in the anti-globalization movement, diverting attention from the substantive objections to globalization as currently constituted.

6 Most vividly depicted in its ominous potentialities by Bill Joy, "Does the Future Need Us?", *WIRED*. The same realities are viewed positively by Ray Kurzweil, *The Age of the Spiritual Machine: When Computers Exceed Human Intelligence*.

7 I am indeed attempting such an understanding in a book-in-progress entitled *Killer Technologies*, to be published by Polity Press in 2002. See also the report of efforts by Ismail Serageldin, the Director of the Bibliotheca Alexandria, to convert this ancient center of learning into a place of research and debate on the ethical implications of scientific discoveries and technological innovations. Also Schneider (2001).

8 Such humility in the face of international reality is not meant as a leap in the opposite direction – affirming that whatever seems desirable to the imagination is attainable. Such misplaced rationalism has made the advocacy of world government seem so banal over the years. "Experience" does show that there must be a political conception connecting the present state of affairs to the future, a politics of transition that distinguishes a serious *project* from a figment of the *moral* and *literary* imagination.

9 For a more satisfactory understanding of the nature of the democratic ethos see Archibugi and Held (1995).

10 I have tried to interpret these developments from the perspective of humane governance in a series of books: Falk (1998, 1999, 2000, 2001).

11 But note that there has been little disposition by P-5 to dispense or even curtail the exercise of their veto in the aftermath of the Cold War, and despite Russian membership in the G-8. Even the efforts to make the Security Council more representative of the world as it exists today have foundered mainly on the unwillingness of the existing permanent members to dilute their status, and secondarily on an inability to agree upon a formula for an expansion of permanent membership.

12 On the origins and evolution of European regionalism, see Sidjanski (2000); of course, there were regional visionaries such as Jean Monnet and Schuman, but the consensus was that nationalist rivalries would place strong limits on the expansion of the European idea.

13 This ambivalence was also evident in the Suez Campaign of 1956 in which the United States sided with the Third World and neutralist Nasser government of Egypt in the face of an attack by its closest allies, the United Kingdom and France (along with Israel).

14 Most significantly analyzed by Thompson (1982); see also Lifton and Falk (1991); Schell (1982).

15 In essence, the notion of sovereignty associated with the French Revolution animated the initiatives in transnational civil society, thereby challenging the statist view of sovereignty that derives from the Westphalian legacy.

16 Gorbachev's views were clearly set forth in his address to the UN General Assembly, 7 December 1988.

17 It is notable that Seattle demonstrations were described in the media as "the battle of Seattle" and that a war terminology was widely relied upon to portray the confrontations between protesters and police at the Genoa meeting of the G-8. What is increasingly evident is that if social peace is to be restored, neoliberal globalization will have to make significant normative concessions to the demands of the protesters. Of course, as has been pointed out, there is currently a lack of coherence in the anti-globalization movement both as to tactics and with respect to grievances. The violent component of the movement is a small fragment of the whole, yet its unsettling and disproportionate impact, yet may provide the nonviolent majority with the political leverage they need to achieve results.

18 On the application of Kantian ideas to contemporary international relations see Doyle (1983). See also Knock (1992) and Kissinger (1994) for criticism of this way of conceptualizing the democratic imperative in the era of globalization.

19 This awkwardness has been highlighted in the debate occasioned by the 1999 NATO intervention in Kosovo, especially the contention that the intervention was "legitimate" even if "illegal". See Report of the Independent International Commission on Kosovo (2000).

20 Domestic or internal accountability had also been a struggle against claims of sovereign immunity and absolute monarchy. Historically, the theory of sovereignty was designed as a principle of order designed to centralize authority in the personage of the monarch, thereby enlarging the sphere of governmental control and curtailing local authority and the power of the nobility. These ideas are most associated with the work of Jean Bodin. The American constitutional procedure of impeachment was connected with a non-technical conception "high crimes and misdemeanors". It was significant in the Bill of Impeachment drawn up to charge Richard Nixon after Watergate that the allegation associated with illegal bombing of Cambodia was dropped in the final version, suggesting that despite the seriousness of the infraction, accountability for international actions was not regarded as a basis for impeachment.

21 The story of the Russell Tribunal and its main findings are contained in Duffett (1970).
22 For an insightful discussion of the complexity, legally and morally, of a forthcoming prosecution and trial of Milosevic, see Wechsler (2001).
23 See "The Princeton Principles on Universal Jurisdiction" (2001).
24 For an excellent overview of the dynamic and significance of the redress phenomenon, see Barkun (2000); Barkun sees these developments as having a potentially transformative effect on international relations of a beneficial kind. For some commentary on Barkun's view see unpublished paper delivered at a UCLA conference by R. Falk, "The Holocaust and International Human Rights". Other commentators are more skeptical such as Finkelstein (2000) who sees redress as a corrupting mercenary undertaking that exhibits the worst features of the existing political order.
25 See, for instance, Chang (1997). Although the book has been criticized on grounds of accuracy, its spirit and message, even its title, express the essence of that form of redress that is concerned with acknowledgment, and at most, apology.
26 A people's tribunal on the ordeal of comfort women was held in Japan during the year 2000.
27 This process is admirably described and analyzed in Lam (2000). The normative efforts of indigenous peoples have culminated in the formulation of a Declaration of the Rights of Indigenous Peoples, which has been under formal consideration within the United Nations for several years, apparently stuck in the bureaucracy because of the reluctance of some states to confirm a right of self-determination as inhering in those indigenous communities that qualify as a "people", as that term is understood.
28 It is precisely this transition that realists are denying: see Mayall 2000, also, Jackson (2000); such conceptualizations also underlie Wheeler's (2000) important contribution to the literature on humanitarian intervention.
29 See Report discussed in note 19.

References

Alderson, Kai and Hurrell, Andrew (eds) (2000) *Hedley Bull on International Society*, New York, St. Martin's Press.

Archibugi, Daniele and Held, David (eds) (1995) *Cosmopolitan Democracy*, Cambridge, Polity Press.

Barkun, Elazar (2000) *The Guilt of Nations*, New York, Norton.

Barzun, Jacques (2000) *From Dawn to Decadence*, New York, HarperCollins.

Birand, Mehmet Ali (2001) "Time for Government Revision", *Turkish Daily News*, 31 July.

Brody, Reed and Michael Ratner (eds) (2000) *The Pinochet Papers: the case of Augusto Pinochet in Spain and Britain*, The Hague, Netherlands, Kluwer.

Chang, Iris (1997) *The Rape of Nanking: The Forgotten Holocaust of World War II*, New York, Basic Books.

Chomsky, Noam (1999) *The New Military Humanism: Lessons from Kosovo*, Monroe, ME, Common Courage.

Doyle, Michael (1983) "Kant, Liberal Legacies and Foreign Affairs", *Philosophy and Public Affairs*, no. 12, pp. 203–34, 323–53.

Duffett, John (ed.) (1970) *Against the Crimes of Silence: International War Crimes Tribunal*, New York, Simon & Schuster.

Falk, Richard (1998) *Law in an Emerging Global Village: A Post-Westphalian Perspective*, Ardsley, NY, Transnational.

—— (1999) *Predatory Globalization: A Critique*, Cambridge, Polity Press.

—— (2000) *Human Rights Horizons: The Prospects of World Order*, New York, Routledge.

—— (2001) *Religion and Humane Global Governance*, New York, Palgrave.

—— (forthcoming) "The Pinochet Litigation", in Stephen Macedo, (ed.), *Principles of Universal Jurisdiction*.

—— (2000) " The Holocaust and International Human Rights", unpublished paper presented at a UCLA conference.

Falk, Richard and Strauss, Andrew (2000) "On the Creation of a Global Peoples Assembly: Legitimacy and the Power of Popular Sovereignty", *Stanford Journal of International Law*, vol. 36, no. 2, pp. 191 219.

—— (2001) "Toward Global Parliament", *Foreign Affairs*, vol. 80, no. 1, pp. 212–20.

Finkelstein, Norman G. (2000) *The Holocaust Industry: reflection on the exploitation of Jewish suffering*, London, Verso.

Friedman, Thomas (1999) *The Lexus and the Olive Tree: Understanding Globalization*, New York, Farrar, Straus, Giroux.

Goldenberg, Suzanne (2001) "Israel Reveals its Fear of War Crimes Trials", *The Guardian*, 27 July, p. 6.

Held, David and McGrew, Andrew *et al.* (1999) *Global Transformations*, Cambridge, Polity Press.

Hitchens, Christopher (2000) *The Trial of Henry Kissinger*, London, Verso.

Jackson, Robert H. (2000) *The Global Covenant: Human Conduct in a World of States*, Oxford, Oxford University Press.

Jaspers, Karl (1978) *The Question of German Guilt*, Westport, CT, Greenwood.

Joy, Bill (2000) "Why the Future Doesn't Need Us?", *WIRED*, Archive, 8.04.

Kissinger, Henry (1994) *Diplomacy*, New York, Simon & Schuster.

Knock, Thomas J. (1992) *To End All Wars*, New York, Oxford University Press.

Küng, Hans (1998) *A Global Ethic for Global Politics and Economics*, New York, Oxford University Press.

Kurzweil, Ray (1999) *The Age of the Spiritual Machines: When Computers Exceed Human Intelligence*, New York, Viking.

Lam, Maivan Clech (2000) *At the Edge of the State*, Ardsley, NY, Transnational Publishers.

Lewis, Bernard (2001) "The Revolt of Islam", *The New Yorker*, 19 November, pp. 50–63, esp. 60–3.

Lifton, Robert Jay and Falk, Richard (1991) *Indefensible Weapons: The Political and Psychological Case Against Nuclearism*, New York, Basic Books.

Marks, Susan (2000) *The Riddle of All Constitutions*, Oxford, Oxford University Press.

Mayall, James (2000) *World Politics: Progress and its Limits*, Cambridge, Polity Press.

Minear, Richard (1971) *Victors' Justice: The Tokyo War Crimes Trial*, Princeton, NJ, Princeton University Press.

Mozaffari, Mehdi (2000) "A Triangle of International Ethics, Law and Politics: Global Standard of Civilization", pamphlet, September, Aarhus, Department of Political Science, University of Aarhus.

"The Princeton Principles on Universal Jurisdiction" (2001) Program in Law and Public Affairs, Princeton University.

Report of the Independent International Commission on Kosovo (2000) Oxford, Oxford University Press.

Rosecrance, Richard (1999) *The Rise of the Virtual State: Wealth and Power in the Coming Century*, New York, Basic Books.

Schell, Jonathan (1982) *The Fate of the Earth*, New York, Knopf.

Schneider, Howard (2001) "Chief of Alexandria's New Library Builds Up a 'Lighthouse for Thought ' ", *International Herald Tribune*, 25 July, 2.

Sidjanski, Susan (2000) *The Federal Future of Europe: From European Community to the European Union*, Ann Arbor, MI, University of Michigan Press.

Taylor, Telford (1992) *The Anatomy of the Nuremberg Trials*, New York, Knopf.

Thompson, Edward P. (1982) *Beyond the Cold War: A New Approach to the Arms Race and Nuclear Annihilation*, New York, Pantheon Books.

Wechsler, Lawrence (2001) "The Defendant", *The New Yorker*, 16 July, pp. 27–8.

Wheeler, Nicholas (2000) *Saving Strangers*, Oxford, Oxford University Press.

4 Standards of civilization today

Gerrit W. Gong

This chapter explores whether and how standards of civilization, which first emerged with practical validity during the nineteenth-century internationalization of the states system with its origins in Europe, have meaning and merit as normative or organizing principles in today's globalized international system.

This inquiry is not so much a search for continuity in the evolution of international standards, though such may become apparent. Rather, it is an assertion that the continuing, self-conscious definition of international standards of civilization is a natural and necessary consequence of interaction among politically and culturally diverse states in search of common interests, rules, values, and institutions.

Hobbesian realists may see such definitional efforts as seeking the lowest common denominators of system functionality that *Realpolitik* calculations require. Kantian idealists may see such definitional efforts as seeking the greatest common denominators that expanding common international purposes can conceive. And Grotian pragmatists may see such efforts to define international standards of civilization as both descriptive and prescriptive, as seeking both to set lower limits of common understanding necessary for the system to function effectively and to push those limits in the search for widened, positive-sum international cooperation.

Regardless of one's underlying political or philosophic approach, the globalization of the international system from one centered in Europe (nineteenth century), in Europe and North America (twentieth century), to one increasingly centered in Europe, North America, and Asia clearly represents the juxtaposition (sometimes jarringly so) of an emerging global cosmopolitan culture with politically and culturally divergent state and non-state actors. Paradoxically, as has been generally recognized, the emerging global cosmopolitan culture transcends many traditional aspects of sovereignty, just as the diversity of state and non-state actors themselves represent pragmatic but often divergent hybrids of traditional and modern social-cultural interests, rules, values, institutions, and modes of perceiving and making decisions. In the everyday collectivity of international interactions and their underlying values lies the international system's essential intermediation role, including, by the way it defines, consciously and not, standards of civilization for the system and its constituent members.

Today's global international system renews the questions of how, where, and to what extent global standards of civilization establish identity boundaries for those included within and those left on the outside of a self-determined international society, whether it is called "civilized society" or goes by some other name. Enduring questions also include the extent to which global standards of civilization imply, perhaps largely unspoken, normative values rooted in specific, rather than universalist, societal, or cultural patterns. Alternatively, international society may have reached a point where meaningful assertions of generally accepted standards of civilization now hold.

Paradoxically, in such interactions, those espousing particular standards of civilization frequently underestimate the normative aspects of those standards, due to the perceptual dilemmas of ethnocentrism, synchrocentrism, and geocentrism. The concept of ethnocentrism is well established and does not require further elaboration. Synchrocentrism is the tendency to view events, including their causes and consequences, from the perspective of one's own historical time-frame. Likewise, geocentrism tends to view developments from the fixed point of one's own regional geography.[1]

This chapter proceeds in three sections, as follows:

1   to define and outline the international standards of civilization that emerged during the nineteenth- and early twentieth-century development of the international system;
2   to review international standards of civilization today;
3   to explore the role of contemporary international financial standards.

We begin by defining and outlining the concept of an international standard of "civilization" as it emerged during the nineteenth century, when the international system, with its origins in Europe, expanded to become geographically global for the first time.

The standard of civilization and the expanding international system

The confrontation that occurred as Europe expanded into the non-European world during the nineteenth and early twentieth centuries was not merely political or economic, and certainly not only military. It was fundamentally a confrontation of civilizations and their respective culture systems (Gong 1984).

At the heart of this nineteenth-century clash were the standards of civilization by which these different civilizations identified themselves and regulated their international relations. In the nineteenth century, practices generally accepted by "civilized" European countries, and therefore by the international system centered in Europe, took an increasingly global and explicitly juridical character as that international system developed. The standard of "civilization" that defined nineteenth-century international society provided a purportedly legal way both to demarcate the boundaries of "civilized" society and to differentiate among "civilized", "barbarous", and "savage" countries internationally.

Indeed, this chapter subsequently considers the parallel practice some see in the global expansion of the twentieth-century economic and financial system, now defined by a standard of economic and financial "civilization". Though perhaps not by judgmental intent, today's economic and financial standards may nevertheless *de facto* demarcate a global hierarchy of "non-market", "emerging market", and "developed market" entities. And, just as the nineteenth-century standard of civilization raised questions about how to define traditional and modern, European and non-European, so today's standard of economic and financial "civilization" renews enduring issues of whether and how distinctions among Anglo-Saxon, European, Western, and modern roots can and should influence standards of civilization in today's global international society.

Generally speaking, a system of states (or international system) is formed "when two or more states have sufficient contact between them, and have sufficient impact on one another's decisions, to cause them to behave – at least in some measure – as parts of a whole" (Bull 1979: 9–10). A society of states (or international society) is measured in terms of certain fundamental commonalties: common interests and values, commonly binding rules, and common institutions (ibid.: 13). A standard of civilization is thus an expression of the assumptions, tacit and explicit, used to distinguish those that belong to a particular society from those that do not.

Three distinctions pertain. First, by definition, those who fulfill the requirements of a particular society's standard of civilization are brought inside its circle of "civilized" members, while those who do not so conform are left outside as "not civilized" or possibly "uncivilized". Second, standards of civilization apply to individual states or individual societies, as well as to systems of states or international societies of states. Third, standards of civilization derive from the recognition that interactions among states or among systems of states occur at both the transactional and normative levels. While a continuum exists between practical, common transactional practices (e.g. the regulation of international posts and telecommunications), a distinction also applies between specific practice and general principles, because the latter often extend the former in embodying normative value regarding international behavior. It is the aggregation of these normative values regarding international behavior which reflect and shape, by whatever name, international standards of civilization today.

The emerging codification of an international standard of civilization is thus itself symbolic of a larger global transformation – the result of an effort to define in explicit terms common interests, values, and ways of interacting, which characterize different international systems, particularly as they confront countries, states, or other actors with differing interests, values, or organizational patterns.

In pre-1914 customary international law, a standard of "civilization" emerged as Europe's response to two problems – one practical, one philosophical – which had arisen with Europe's expansion into the non-European world. First, in response to the practical problem of protecting European life, liberty, and property in sometimes hostile non-European countries, the nineteenth-century standard of "civilization" sought to guarantee certain basic rights, the "observance of which, at least in relation to foreign nations, could be expected from civilized states" (Schwarzenberger 1976: 114). Second, in response to the philosophical problem of determining which countries deserved legal recognition and legal personality under international law, the standard of "civilization" provided a doctrinal rationale for limiting recognition in international law to those candidate countries that "recognizing states, rightly or wrongly, regarded as being civilized" (ibid.).

Again, as this chapter explores in its third section, a parallel may exist in the contemporary international financial system's efforts to protect foreign investments abroad, including, by guaranteeing ownership against expropriation, by protecting local operations from arbitrary interference, and by providing transparency and the free flow of information crucial to commercial operations.

By 1905 at the latest, a standard of "civilization" had emerged as an explicit legal principle and integral part of the generally accepted doctrines of prevailing international law. This standard of "civilization" included the following five requirements:

1   a "civilized" state guarantees basic rights (i.e. life, dignity, and property; freedom of travel, commerce, and religion), especially those of foreign nationals;

2   a "civilized" state exists as an organized political bureaucracy with some efficiency in running the state machinery, and with some capacity to organize for self-defense;

3   a "civilized" state adheres to generally accepted international law, including the laws of war; it also maintains a domestic system of courts, codes, and published laws that guarantee legal justice for all within its jurisdiction, foreigners and native citizens alike;

4   a "civilized state" fulfills the obligations of the international system by maintaining adequate and permanent avenues for diplomatic interchange and communication;

5   a more subjective element was also included: a "civilized" state, by and large, conforms to the accepted norms and practices of the "civilized" international society; for example, suttee, polygamy, and slavery were considered "uncivilized" and therefore unacceptable.

Especially from a non-European point of view, one cannot speak of "modernization", or the "process of becoming modern", in a historical perspective without referring to what an earlier age called "civilization" and the process of becoming "civilized". This historical perspective emphasizes that there are no value-free models of development.

The processes by which an international system establishes standards to define and codify its operating interests, rules, values, and institutions are continuing ones. Yet, not surprisingly, changes within an international system – such as those represented by the globalization of the international system and society, particularly in the latter half of the twentieth century – frequently produce new working standards. Thus, continuity of process can produce a change of standard, although elements of the nineteenth- and early twentieth-century standard of civilization remain deeply embedded in international standards of civilization today.

International standards of civilization today

In many regards, both the international transactional rules and the normative values of the nineteenth-century standard of "civilization" have been broadly accepted as universal. They are now generally seen as a part of state practice and international law. Every state seeks to avoid the opprobrium of being labeled "uncivilized" by the international community, even while recognizing that the normative elements of that international society continue to develop.[2]

Thus, while foresighted publicists frequently expressed themselves in broad, universalist terms, the realities of sustained international interaction have changed the discourse on international standards. These realities make the theoretical more practical, the general more specific, and the straightforward more complex and subtle. To the observations of Kant, Grotius, Vitoria, and others, regarding the sources, roles, and stipulations of international standards are added contemporary perspectives. Realists discount the notion that norms affect self-interested behavior; neoliberals see state behavior constrained by the norms that self-interested states have previously accepted.

Constructivism posits an ontological relationship between the actors and the norms of the system or structure of which they form an integral part.[3] To take the case of state actions: statesmen carry out foreign policy according to the dictates of "national interest". But it is always in the national interest for a state to be, and to be seen as, law-abiding and civilized. And international norms dictate part of what it means to be civilized. Only when a regime faces exceptional circumstances will it risk clearly illegal acts, even then usually rationalizing them within some international legal ambit.

International law constrains state behavior by explicitly prohibiting certain actions. Standards of civilization are more subtle. States, wishing to render credible their self-descriptions of being civilized, must adhere to internationally recognized standards of civilization – as well as to their own principles of civilization. The society of states sets standards of civilization, although individual states interpret such standards within their own national and cultural identity. According to constructivism, in such mutually constitutive relationships, states, systems of states, and international societies each create and shape the norms by which they understand their own behavior and identity.

Other developments in sociology, psychology, identity theory, epistemology, and international organization contribute to a better sense of where and how norms develop, and the roles they play internationally, including when civilizations interact.

The debate continues as to whether this is simply law-abiding behavior, or whether, as traditionally, the standard of civilization specifies norms for state interaction premised on sovereign equality.[4] And there are new and multiplying subjects of international law, including individuals and international organizations, as well as new areas of concern, which both result from and contribute to the breakdown of strict sovereignty. In some regards, a return of naturalism is perceived in peremptory legal norms, independent of state consent, in areas such as non-discrimination, human rights, genocide and other crimes against humanity, apartheid, piracy, slavery, or forcible aggression.

International standards of non-discrimination and human rights

A recognized sensibility on the moral and practical imperative of non-discrimination and, although with weaker agreement, on the protection and promotion of human rights represents a significant continuity of the nineteenth-century standard of "civilization" into today's international standards.

This standard of respect for human rights and non-discrimination is ensconced in the UN Charter, Articles 1, 55, 56, and especially the preamble (paragraph 2); practices of states and UN organs; and the Universal Declaration of Human Rights and International Covenants on Human Rights, as well as other international conventions, court rulings, and resolutions. Through these documents, one can trace a progression from vague aspirations (UN Charter Articles and the Universal Declaration) toward a more comprehensive and binding regime.

For example, two international covenants (Economic, Social, and Cultural Rights; and Civil and Political Rights) aim to constitute a binding international bill of rights. Especially since the removal of Cold War ideological barriers, both covenants have gained signatories. Today, the UN, in various forms, continues to promulgate declarations and covenants regarding human rights, such as the Vienna and Bangkok conventions on human rights, the World Conference on Human Rights (June 1993, Vienna); international worker rights (International Labor Organization, GATT); and children's rights (International Labor Organization).

Some argue that, unlike the classic standard of "civilization", the new standard of civilization, based upon the UN human rights regime, is inclusive (Donnelly 1998). This regime emphasizes the universality of human rights – applicable to all human beings – rather than any colonial interpretation amounting to extraterritorial discrimination favoring "civilized" non-citizens.

In the field of human rights, the most progressive regimes are regional ones, notably the Inter-American System (institutions under the Organization of American States, Inter-American Commission of Human Rights, and Inter-American Court of Human Rights) and the European System (institutions under the Council of Europe, European Commission of Human Rights, and European Court of Human Rights).

In the European system, individuals can raise cases without state sponsorship. Provisions of the European Convention on Human Rights were later incorporated in the International Covenant on Civil and Political Rights. Between 1960 and 1995 the European Court of Human Rights handed down 439 decisions, of which 320 found at least one violation (Council of Europe, 1995). This self-consciously European standard was also used as rationale for exclusion, for example, refusing to admit Turkey on the grounds that Ankara's treatment of its citizens did not meet European and "universal" standards.

During the Bosnia war, powerfully, though not without controversy, flanked by a supportive US Secretary of State, even Germany's foreign minister at the time gave "No more Auschwitzes" as a reason justifying Berlin's involvement with the allied efforts. On the one hand, this statement reiterated that modern Germany's foreign policy is constrained by the memory of Nazi Germany's egregious racial and ethnic discrimination, including, at its extreme, genocide. On the other hand, this statement argues that modern Germany's adherence to a contemporary international standard of non-discrimination compels Berlin's participation in contemporary efforts, even involving war, to limit genocide or ethnic cleansing in Europe. Thus, an international standard of non-discrimination has also become closely connected in practical ways with international standards regarding crimes against humanity.

International standards regarding crimes against humanity and the rules of war

"The rules of war," Michael Walzer asserts, "consist of two clusters of prohibitions attached to the central principle that soldiers have an equal right to kill. The first cluster specifies when and how they can kill; the second whom they can kill" (Walzer 1978: 41). While the first cluster is "susceptible to the transformations brought about by social change, technological innovation, and foreign conquest," the second is "more closely connected to universal notions of right and wrong" (ibid.: 42). Indeed, international lawyers have long recognized the "continuous tug-of-war between the requirements of the standard of civilization and military necessities" (Schwarzenberger 1976: 82).

The rules of when nations can go to war are foundational to the UN system. The UN Security Council claims the authority to preserve international peace and security, including, if necessary, by the use of force.[5] Its jurisdiction covers even non-UN members.[6] The ability for states legally to use force outside Security Council authorization is limited to the inherent right of individual or collective self-defense given under customary law, and preserved in Article 51 of the UN Charter.[7]

In short, the norm that prohibits state aggression, non-existent as an international standard before the twentieth century, sketched out in the flawed League of Nations, and affirmed in the Kellogg–Briand Pact, has, in the latter part of the twentieth century, been strongly asserted as an international standard by which modern "civilized" states abide.

A corollary is the enduring norm that, even in war, humanity requires that combatants and non-combatants be distinguished, particularly women and children, and that transgressing these "bounds of civilized behavior", whether against combatants or especially against non-combatants, can constitute crimes against humanity.[8]

The natural conclusion of the process of judging war criminals, whether at Nuremberg, Tokyo, or most recently in Bosnia (where military forces under NATO authority pursued those charged with crimes against humanity), is the creation of the International Criminal Court as a permanent entity charged with the trial of war criminals worldwide (Pace 1998). This court seeks to strengthen norms concerning war and the use of force by creating a deterrent for would-be war criminals to consider their actions in the light of potential post-conflict trials. Though neither the USA nor China intend to become court members, it symbolizes the effort to promulgate and institutionalize a shared standard. Effectiveness will be crucial to its credibility and hence deterrent power, but this can only be demonstrated over time.

It is worth noting that a shared standard of European civilization recently gave rise to the extended concern that no one connected with Nazi crimes against humanity be given political standing. More specifically, it provided compelling motivation for fourteen European Union countries to withhold recognition of the otherwise democratic election of an extreme right-wing individual in Austria's elections. The willingness to overlook traditional sovereign boundaries in the name of political ethical imperative underscores how deep-rooted international standards of non-discrimination and international standards opposing crimes against humanity have become, in Europe and elsewhere.

Emerging international standards on sustainable development and environmentalism

Not only individual, but also societal and/or group rights have become a twentieth-century focus of efforts to establish generally recognized international standards. One possible emerging international norm centers on the need to recognize and promote sustainable development and environmentalism, now increasingly incorporated in international agreements such as NAFTA.

Such concerns create cross-pressures between developed and developing countries, such as those evident in the 1972 Stockholm Conference for the Human Environment, in the 1992 Rio de Janeiro UN Conference on Environment and Development (UNCED), and most recently in the 1997 Kyoto Conference of the Parties of the UN Framework Convention on Climate Change (UNFCCC). Though clearly global in their implications, environmental concerns such as global warming and ozone erosion have yet to build a consensus on their nature, urgency, or potential division of cost for any agreed upon remedy. Beyond narrow cost concerns are genuine differences in social values regarding development and ecological priorities.[9]

International trade standards[10]

Following WWII, blamed in part on global economic and financial depression, the international community sought to build a liberal trade regime supported by stable currencies and to institutionalize them in the 1948 General Agreement on Tariffs and Trade (GATT) and International Monetary Fund (IMF) processes. Thus was born a succession of GATT negotiations (including the Kennedy, Tokyo, and Uruguay rounds), culminating in agreements to bolster free and open trade. As the rounds continued, GATT international trade standards emerged to include the following:

- Reciprocity: states offer to free up trade in a certain area if other states free trade in return (not always in the same area).
- Non-discrimination: under the *most-favored-nation* principle, a state must offer all GATT members the lowest tariff rate it sets with any one of them (customs unions have a special exemption). Under *national treatment*, a state must treat foreigners on the same terms as its own nationals, for example, taxation, and handling and distribution of products after customs.
- Tariffs decrease not increase: if tariffs change, they must decrease, with limited exceptions, for example, for national security purposes or infant industries.
- Tariffs over quotas: if a state must take protective measures, tariffs are preferable to non-tariff barriers (e.g. quotas, or worse, non-transparent measures, such as national procurement). Tariffs are thought to be more predictable and more subject to negotiated reduction.
- Consultation and dispute resolution: members agree to use GATT procedures, although ineffective enforcement became a key reason for creating the World Trade Organization (WTO) with more credible dispute resolution procedures.
- Multilateral over unilateral measures: if a state breaks the rules, other states may be authorized to take necessary and proportionate countermeasures, such as restricting trade, but only as a concerted, rather than unilateral, enforcement mechanism.

Over the course of the protracted Uruguay Round (1986–94), states decided to create a World Trade Organization – born on 1 January 1995 – to oversee the international trade regime and national trade policies. WTO dispute resolution includes structured, defined, and staged procedures. Countries losing disputes cannot block the adoption of the ruling unless a consensus to reject the ruling occurs.[11] The WTO's Dispute Settlement Body (DSB) has the sole authority to establish an expert panel to consider cases and to accept or reject panel findings or appeal results. The DSB can also authorize retaliations when countries fail to comply with rulings.[12]

Unlike the IMF or the World Bank, the WTO does not have a board of directors or bureaucracy; instead, it is administered by member governments themselves, with major decisions made on a consensus basis by the membership as a whole through authorized ministers or officials. For instance, if sanctions are necessary, the member countries, not the organization, impose the sanctions.[13] The fact that states bind themselves through bilateral and multilateral WTO-negotiated obligations marks a significant difference with other international standards, which often evolve as a matter of customary state practice. Although GATT and subsequent WTO rules and their implementation remain imperfect, they now incorporate better the interests of developed and developing countries, through broader consensus decision-making on new rules.

In sum, over the fifty years of the GATT's existence and now the WTO, though disagreements and hard bargaining inevitably continue, the importance and value of an international trade in goods and services are now virtually universally accepted.[14] However, as is the nature of the international society, even as these international trade practices seek universal acceptance, new arenas of international activity are contributing to emergent global practice that may in time set new international standards.

International norms of capital risk and return as a new standard of civilization?

Today, capital flows move as much according to market logic as to political decisions. The global financial regime comes with its own evolving institutions and rules, and its own organizing principles. Although challenged by Asia's financial crisis and its aftermath, these organizing principles reflect (a) open, liberalizing domestic markets; (b) coordinating intergovernmental organizations; (c) dynamic, private-market actors; and (d) efforts to maintain local practices and values.

The transactional features of this global financial system may constitute simply a standard of current success, although the interface of financial capital with diverse political, economic, social, and cultural structures clearly impinges on elements of civilization and may thereby contribute to a contemporary standard of financial civilization. At a minimum, it is clear that countries wishing to be considered credit-worthy, attractive investment and trade partners must adapt and adhere to new financial standards increasingly ensconced in the international system. Indeed, today's international system contains criteria for "financially modern" states, including:

- a "financially modern" state has a defined territory, population, and governmental authority, including popular political and economic participation and stability;
- a "financially modern" state has a reasonably sized, relatively clean government that responsibly accepts sovereign obligations, engages in budget processes, and ensconces its economic system in predictable tax and regulatory regimes;
- a "financially modern" state participates in international financial institutions and maintains at least semi-independent financial institutions as part of

transparent, legally defined and operated, government and private decision-making processes;

- a "financially modern" state enforces title to physical and intellectual property in all their various forms, with fair and effective adjudication processes to reconcile disputes and to remedy infringements;
- a "financially modern" state respects economic and financial information openness and adheres to generally accepted accounting principles.

As in the nineteenth century and early twentieth century, it is the spoken and unspoken general international practices and principles embodied in today's international financial institutions, agents, and normative values which shape contemporary standards of financial civilization. Accordingly, this section outlines the contributions to today's financial standards and the international roles played by rating agencies, the International Monetary Fund (IMF), the World Bank, and the Bank for International Settlements (BIS).

Rating agencies[15]

By design or otherwise, rating agencies play a significant role in providing and promulgating a new, financially based standard of civilization, with their rating measures representing new *de facto* criteria for countries seeking to conform to modern standards of "civilized" credit worthiness. The top five include Moody's, Standard and Poor's, Fitch IBCA, Thomson BankWatch, and Duff and Phelps. Taking Standard and Poor's as a representative example, rankings range from AAA (best) to CC (worst), with both qualitative and quantitative assessments that include "worst-case" scenarios over a three-to-five year horizon. Ratings of BB and below signify obligators who have "significant speculative characteristics". These are "junk bonds" because they do not meet the "investment grade". A BB rank is the lowest investment grade; though many companies specify higher thresholds for their investments. Each agency may have refinements or slightly different notation, but the basic system remains the same.

At first glance, rating agencies would appear to function in a value-neutral way. They provide investors with information, namely the risk of default for a specific security. From the borrower's perspective, the credit rating is vitally important because it will determine the cost of borrowing, namely the interest rate on the debt. If the rating falls below "investment grade", then many credit lines may actually be cut off. The rating agencies wield influence based on the credibility of their reputations. Ratings entail financial judgments of companies and countries, organized and operating in diverse political, economic, social, and cultural settings. What each must demonstrate and disclose to an exceptional extent is their likely future ability to repay obligations. Thus the incentive of good ratings pushes businesses toward stringent standards of disclosure and, in so doing, encourages them to use international accounting practices, if not one of the major accounting firms.[16]

Like the major accounting firms, the major rating agencies – those accredited by the US Securities and Exchange Commission (SEC) – are Anglo-Saxon in origin. Four, including the two most prominent – Moody's and Standard and Poor's – are New York-based. Thomson BankWatch and Duff and Phelps are also American, while Fitch IBCA is London-based. While numerous local rating agencies exist, few have significant operations outside their country of origin. One exception is the Japan Credit Rating Agency, which has international operations, due to Japan's many investments abroad. Credit rating agencies have only recently begun rating sovereigns, other than a limited number of rich, developed countries. The credibility of these sovereign ratings seems to be based on the rating agencies' broader, well-established reputations. Because no international sanction mechanism exists in the case of sovereign loan defaults, there are few alternative grounds to judge the accuracy of sovereign ratings. A main incentive for countries not to default is the wish to preserve their reputation and thereby their future credit ratings and access to capital. In the United States, the Securities and Exchange Commission has sought to monitor, if not regulate, new rating agencies according to SEC criteria, including:

- operational capacity and reliability;
- organizational structure and staffing;
- financial resources;
- independence from the companies it rates and extent of contact with the management of issuers;
- use of systematic rating procedures;
- policies and procedures to prevent the misuse of public information.

Sovereign ratings purport to assess a government's capacity and willingness to repay debt, with economic risk measuring the ability to repay, and political risk the willingness (Standard & Poor's 1997). Key risks include:[17]

- stability of political institutions and degree of popular participation in the political process;
- income and economic structure (equity, markets);
- fiscal policy and budgetary flexibility;
- monetary policy and inflation pressure;
- public debt burden and debt-service track record.

One econometric study found six factors played important roles in determining country credit ratings (Cantor and Packer 1996):

- per capita income;
- GDP growth;
- inflation;
- external debt;
- level of economic development;
- default history.

Clearly, financial markets and credit ratings are interactive. Many leading US and European investors do not invest in countries with less than agency investment-grade ratings. For example, when the Republic of Korea's ratings were downgraded below the investment-grade threshold during the Asian financial crisis, many investors and institutional funds automatically left. As gatekeepers to international capital markets, rating agencies set standards that affect the financial viability of countries around the world. Without an investment-grade rating, a company often cannot obtain international credit. Less than an investment-grade sovereign rating limits the access of a country's companies and banks to international finance markets, because a country's rating becomes the ceiling for its nationals. Especially in emerging markets, companies, and particularly banks and firms, are beholden to credit agency standards. The debate has and will continue regarding the extent to which credit raters change judgments according to opaque criteria and subjective judgments. Likewise, discussion continues regarding the extent credit raters, in fact, facilitate financial markets by providing essential comparable information.

The World Bank[18]

The World Bank's objective is to strengthen economies and expand markets to improve quality of life, especially in poorer nations. The Bank does not grant aid, but lends money to developing countries at two rates: first, at near-market rates for developing countries able to afford borrowing money loaned from investors worldwide; second, at more favorable rates for the poorest countries that have a limited ability to borrow in international financial markets. The World Bank is comparable to a global cooperative, owned by member countries, whose shares are determined by the size of their country's respective economy relative to the world economy. The G-7 own about 45 percent of World Bank shares, with the USA holding an often decisive 17 percent. The World Bank group includes the International Bank for Reconstruction and Development (IBRD) and the International Development Association (IDA).

The IBRD, established in 1945, is owned by 181 governments, each having joined the IMF and its capital stock and regional shares quota. The IDA was established in 1960 to lend to the governments of poorer developing countries (about 70 are eligible) unable to meet the IBRD's near-commercial terms. The repayment period for no-interest IDA credits is 35–40 years, though commitment charges range from 0–0.5 percent of undisbursed balances. The World Bank also provides advice and technical assistance to borrower countries and governments through the International Finance Corporation (IFC) and the Multilateral Investment Guarantee Agency (MIGA).

Established in 1956, the IFC helps mobilize domestic and foreign capital so private investors and commercial enterprises can promote development. It has 172 members and is legally separate from the World Bank, but it does draw upon the World Bank for administrative and other services. The IFC does not accept government guarantees for its financing, instead sharing project risk with private-sector partners. Now with 141 members, MIGA was established in 1988 to promote the flow of foreign direct investment (FDI) in member countries by providing guarantees to private investors against major political risks and by offering host governments investment-marketing services to attract FDI.

Regarding international financial standards and regulations, some 10 percent of World Bank group structural adjustment loans have a financial sector component aimed at either bank restructuring or capital-market strengthening. During the Asian financial crisis, the Asian Development Bank (ADB) and World Bank together loaned some $26 billion US dollars.

The International Monetary Fund (IMF)[19]

The International Monetary Fund was established at the Bretton Woods (New Hampshire) conference, 1–22 July 1944. It officially came into existence on 27 December 1945 and it commenced financial operations on 1 March 1947. The IMF was created to promote international monetary cooperation; to facilitate the expansion and balanced growth of international trade; to promote exchange stability; to assist in the establishment of a multilateral system of payments; to make its general resources temporarily available to members experiencing balance of payments difficulties (under adequate safeguards); and to shorten the duration and lessen the degree of disequilibrium in the international balances of payments of members.

Its functions include the following:

- Surveillance – a process by which the IMF assesses its members' economic situations and policy strategies.
- Financial assistance – includes credits and loans extended by the IMF to member countries with balance of payments problems to support policies of adjustment and reform.
- Technical assistance – consists of expertise and aid provided by the IMF to its members in several broad areas:
    - design and implementation of fiscal and monetary policy;
    - institution-building;
    - handling and accounting of transactions with the IMF;
    - collection and refinement of statistical data;
    - training officials at the IMF Institute and Joint Vienna Institute.

Each IMF country's voting rights are determined by its monetary contribution, in turn based on its weight in the global economy. Each country's relative financial weight also determines borrowing capacity or drawing right.

The IMF provides advice and temporary financing to countries facing a wide range of problems and circumstances. Typical prescriptions involve:

- the deregulation of domestic economies and establishment of more-level playing fields for private sector activity;

- stronger financial systems and the development of effective regulation and supervision;
- reductions in unproductive government spending, such as costly military build-ups;
- increased spending on basic human needs, such as primary health and education; on adequate social protection for the poor, unemployed, and other vulnerable groups; and on key environmental problems;
- greater transparency and accountability in government and corporate affairs, and more effective dialogue on economic policy with labor and civil society.

In light of its perceived performance during the Asian financial crisis, the Fund also began internal reform and restructuring. As it did others, the Asian financial crisis caught the Fund off-guard, forcing intense self-examination and revised procedures, including:

- more effective surveillance over individual countries' economic policies and fuller disclosure of all relevant economic and financial data;
- regional surveillance because experience shows regional economic performance improves when countries help one another on a regional basis;
- financial sector reform, including better prudential regulation and supervision, by applying proven standards and regulations;
- more effective structures for orderly debt workouts, including better international ways to integrate private-sector assistance with official efforts in resolving sovereign debt problems;
- orderly capital-account liberalization so that more countries benefit from access to the international capital markets;
- a worldwide effort to promote good governance and fight corruption.

The Bank for International Settlements[20]

Founded by the central banks of Germany, France, Belgium, Britain, Italy, and Japan, and private banks from the United States, the Bank for International Settlements (BIS) was established in 1930 to channel German war reparations to other European countries, making it the oldest international financial institution. The BIS is headquartered in Basle, Switzerland, and current membership includes 45 countries, with total funds of some 6.25 billion gold francs. The bank's capital and reserves stand at 2.6 billion gold francs. As of 31 March 1998, it manages some 104.9 billion gold francs, 1 gold franc = US $1.94149. The BIS was created "to promote the cooperation of central banks and to provide additional facilities for international financial operations, and to act as trustee or agent in regard to international financial settlements entrusted to it under agreements with the parties concerned".[21] To this end, BIS standards are widely respected, by non-BIS members as well, even though it has no legal authority, only moral suasion, to induce compliance.

As a "central banks' bank", the BIS assists central banks (including non-members) in managing and investing monetary reserves; lends deposit funds to central banks (including non-members); provides traditional short-term investments for funds not required for lending; coordinates its policy with the monetary policies of member central banks; provides means for central banks to make settlements with each other; and conducts research, especially into monetary and financial questions, by collecting and publishing data on international banking and financial market developments through an automated intra-central bank economic database.

Historically, the BIS is known for having established minimum-capital requirements for banks, drafting international principles for bank supervisors, and writing a voluntary code of disclosure for the banks' derivatives trade. It also convinced international banks to set up a global clearing house to decrease the risk of a loss if large foreign-exchange trades were not completed as agreed. In the 1960s and 1970s, the BIS monthly meetings of central bank governors helped relieve currency crises through large loans to the UK and France when balance of payments problems affected their currencies. It also monitored Eurodollars and stabilized gold prices through active involvement in the "gold pool". In the period 1981–4, the BIS encouraged creditor commercial banks to act cautiously and assisted troubled debtor countries with short-term loans during the debt crisis by making loans to the IMF.

Conclusion

As in the past, today's international standards of civilization reflect dynamic change. Interestingly, as in the past, conditions and requirements in the arenas from which international standards emerge continue to evolve, often giving the impression to countries trying to approximate these standards that the standards themselves continue to change, sometimes unpredictably.

A current case is the increasing discussion, not only of the financial importance of capital, but also of a new taxonomy of capital to include financial capital, as defined in the Anglo-Saxon tradition, for example, through disclosure principles; intellectual capital, now recognized as extending beyond traditional measures of simply exogenous "technology"; human capital, including skills, "learning by doing", and other elements of judgment; and social/managerial capital, which recognizes the potential advantages and disadvantages conferred by various synergies among groups and society at large (Fukuyama 1995; Healey 1998).

Particularly as human organizational and value elements are defined and equated within capital equations (however imperfectly), traditional forms of financial capital become juxtaposed with the more subtle socio-culturally based means of production. In this juxtaposition lies a major modern interface of interacting civilizations – the history, self-identity, socio-organizational patterns of different people in different regional and cultural contexts with the standards that accompany global capital. Nor is this interface the unique province of "developing countries", because various forms of competing capitalism exist in Europe, North America, Japan and other parts of Asia (Peterson 1994).

In this view, the potential for a "clash of 'standards of civilizations'" is more fundamental than the juxtaposition of cultural values and approaches. Along some fault lines – for example, in contemporary Indonesia racked by financial crisis and multiple international institutions each with its own bitter medicine – there is resentment, and sometimes violence. As has always characterized standards of civilization as they have emerged in the rubbing together of divergent civilizations, this clash of civilizations contains an interacting, dual element.

First, there is the hierarchical and judgmental element of "more civilized" and "more modern" versus "less civilized" and "less modern". The notion of "civilization" has always contained, at least tacitly, an assertion that those who adhere most closely to the standard are somehow more modern, more progressive, more "civilized". There is another element as well. It is that methods of evaluation – in this case, using capital return, risk-hedging, and associated values such as the free flow of information and transparency – come implicitly and explicitly with the new criteria established for international financial values and institutions, some of which are purveyed in private-sector manifestations by the largest, most dynamic multinational companies.

Indeed, some far-sighted accounting firms posit that conventional profit and loss models of tangible company assets miss far more important assets, including collective training and judgmental abilities of company employees; organizational culture, values, traditions, and broader professional networks; and whatever advantages may accrue by socio-cultural operating context to the company's functions and functioning. By this logic, familiar accounting principles applied in conventional ways may miss the important asset values in a company or country. In turn, the interaction of multiple companies within the institutional and social framework of a particular country may convey advantages and disadvantages which entail costs and benefits. Questions also remain regarding the way in which financial capital may manifest itself differently as it interfaces with different human, organizational, and social patterns in new ways.

To use the financial metaphor, the interaction of financial capital with different political–cultural systems (dare we say, different forms of culture and civilization) in their distinctive human, organizational, and social characters gives rise to new issues regarding whether or not the standards established by those responsible for the returns on globalized financial capital are necessarily congruent with the values, objectives, or institutions in various alternative regions or civilizations. And yet, paradoxically, the very use of financial terms such as human capital (as though human value were reducible to financial asset valuations) marks the recognition that even complex business interactions represent more than the sum of disparate parts, including less physical criteria, such as human training and skill, organizational patterns, and social context.

It seems quite reasonable to broaden the areas of recognized input for success in economies that are increasingly knowledge, technology, and capital intensive. Still, the debate deepens about the social benefits of Japan's approach to capital use versus the seeming financial inefficiencies of its return on capital or return on equity approach (when judged by Anglo-Saxon Return on Equity (ROE) models). All this has enormous consequences if international ratings, exchange rates, and other transactions dance to a new standard of financial civilization that is truly universal or more culture-bound in its expression.

Other related issues still to be resolved are:

- the extent to which institutions, such as rating agencies, purvey Western or traditional, return-maximizing, Anglo-Saxon "capital-owner" values;
- the extent to which the IMF or the World Bank apply uniform and sometimes incorrect approaches to diverse country situations; and
- the extent to which shifts from multi-local to genuinely global operations imply international transactional commonalities that portend, but do not yet embody, shared global principles and values; all perhaps still reflecting and creating nascent standards of civilization.

This chapter began with the observation that, because the concept of a standard of "civilization" *per se* carries a unique nineteenth-century derivative implication of a smugly asserted "superior" European or Western civilization, the term standard of "civilization" has faded from general use. However, particularly when it is not restricted to a narrow legal definition, the concept of a standard of civilization (by whatever name) is not new, nor will it (this chapter has argued) ever become old. Some standard of civilization will remain a feature of any international society wherein cultural diversity and pluralism coexist with hierarchy and anarchy, regardless of how strong the ties of international society become.

Notes

1 It is, of course, not as though time and geography are insignificant factors in efforts to explain economic developments. Note, for example, Krugman (1998).
2 This section draws on research conducted by Duncan Wrigley when he worked at the CSIS Asia Program, the author expresses appreciation, while remaining responsible for the chapter's content.
3 See Finnemore (1996) – Chapter 1 for introduction and further constructivist literature references. Alexander Wendt's, "Anarchy Is What States Make of It: The Social Construction of Power Politics" (1992) is a seminal article.
4 For a related, but different, approach, see Reus-Smit (1997).
5 UN Charter, Chapter VII, especially Articles 41, 42.
6 UN Article 2(7).
7 See Burnett (1995), and Duncan Wrigley's "The Evolution of International Norms", CSIS Asia Program Working Papers.
8 The most recent weapon to be banned is landmines. See Price (1998).
9 See Rautiala (1997) on the international politics of the environment.
10 This section draws on Yang (1998c). Data taken from World Trade Organization webpage, at www.wto.org, unless otherwise specified.
11 See http://www.wto.org/wto/about/dispute.htm.
12 Ibid.
13 Whose WTO Is It Anyway? //www.wto.org/wto/about/organs1.htm.
14 Source: IMF webpage.

15 This section draws on Wrigley (1998a; 1998c; 1998d).
16 On the role of the big accounting firms, see Strange (1996: Chapter 10).
17 Ibid. This includes a more comprehensive ratings list.
18 See Lee (1998). Facts and figures taken from World Bank Group webpage, at www.worldbank.org, unless otherwise specified.
19 See Yang (1998a; 1998b). Facts and figures taken from the IMF webpage, at www.imf.org, unless otherwise specified.
20 See Woo(1998). Facts and figures taken from BIS webpage at www.bis.org, unless otherwise specified.
21 Article 3, Statutes of the Bank for International Settlements.

References

Bull, Hedley (1979) "The Anarchical Society", London, Macmillan.
Burnett, Michael (1995) "The United Nations and Global Security: The Norm is Mightier than the Sword", *Ethics and International Affairs*, vol. 9.
Cantor, Richard and Packer, Frank (1996) "Determinants and the Impact of Sovereign Credit Ratings", *Economic Policy Review*, vol. 2, no. 2, pp. 37–53.
Council of Europe (1995) *Yearbook of the European Convention on Human Rights*, vol. 38.
Donnelly, Jack (1998) "Human Rights: A New Standard of Civilization?", *International Affairs*, vol. 74, no. 1.
Finnemore, Martha (1996) *National Interests in International Society*, Ithaca, NY, Cornell University Press.
Fukuyama, Francis (1995) "Social Capital and the Global Economy", *Foreign Affairs*, September/October.
Gong, Gerrit W. (1984) *The Standard of Civilization in International Society*, Oxford, Oxford University Press.
Healey, Tom (1998) "Counting Human Capital", *The OECD Observer*, no. 212, June/July.
Krugman, Paul (1998) "America the Boastful", *Foreign Affairs*, May/June.
Lee, J.T. (1998) "World Bank Working Paper", *CSIS Asia Program Working Papers*, 21 June.
Pace, William (1998) "Globalizing Justice", *Harvard International Review*, Spring.
Peterson, Eric R. (1994) "Looming Collision of Capitalisms?", *Washington Quarterly*, vol. 17, no. 2.
Price, Richard (1998) "Reversing the Gun Sights: Transnational Civil Society Targets Land Mines", *International Organization*, vol. 52, no. 3, Summer.
Rautiala, Kal (1997) "States, NGOs, and International Environmental Institutions", *International Studies Quarterly*, vol. 41.
Reus-Smit, Christian (1997) "The Constitutional Structure of International Society and the Nature of Fundamental Institutions", *International Organization*, vol. 51, no. 4, Autumn.
Schwarzenberger, Georg (1976) *The Dynamics of Law*, Abingdon, Professional Books.
Standard & Poor's (1997) "Sovereign Credit Ratings: A Primer", *Credit Week*, 16 April.
Strange, Susan (1996) *The Retreat of the State*, Cambridge, Cambridge University Press.
United Nations (1995) "The United Nations and Human Rights 1945–1995", United Nations Department of Public Information.
Walzer, Michael (1978) *Just and Unjust Wars*, Harmondsworth, Penguin Books.
Wendt, Alexander (1992) "Anarchy is What States Make of It: The Social Construction of Power Politics", *International Organization*, vol. 46, no. 2.
Woo, Christopher (1998) "Bank for International Settlements Working Paper", *CSIS Asia Program Working Papers*, 15 July.

Wrigley, Duncan (1998a) "Working Paper on Rating Agencies", *CSIS Asia Program Working Papers*, 22 June.
—— (1998b) "The Evolution of International Norms", *CSIS Asia Program Working Papers*, 22 June.
—— (1998c) "Chronology on Rating Agencies in the Asian Financial Crisis", *CSIS Asia Program Working Papers*, 15 July.
—— (1998d) "Rating Agencies: A Think-piece", *CSIS Asia Program Working Papers*, 15 July.
Yang, Victoria (1998a) "Evolution of IMF", *CSIS Asia Program Working Papers*, 22 June.
—— (1998b) "Pros and Cons of the IMF in Dealing with the Asian Financial Crisis" , *CSIS Asia Program Working Papers*, 22 June.
—— (1998c) "The World Trade Organization", *CSIS Asia Program Working Papers*, 24 July.

Internet references

www.bis.org – Bank for International Settlements.
www.imf.org – IMF.
www.un.org – UN webpage has information on environment, international law and human rights.
www.wto.org – WTO.
U.S. Department of Agriculture brief on the WTO: ffas.usda.gov/info/factsheets/wto.html
www.worldbank.org – World Bank Group.
www.worldbank.org – The World Bank homepage:
–Facts and Figures of East Asia, Questions and Answers (2 pages)
–Facts and Figures of Mexico (1 page)
–Facts and Figures of the World Bank, WTO, and GATT (1 page)
–Fact and Figures of the UN and World Bank (1 page)
–Fact and Figures of the IMF and World Bank
–Financial Statement of the bank is included in folder (Balance sheet, statement of income, statement of cash flows, and summary of statement of loans).
–Speech to the Annual Dinner of the Japan Society – The World Needs a Strong and Internationally Active Japan – June 10, 1998 President of the World Bank, James D. Wolfensohn.
–Statement to the Bretton Woods Committee – The East Asia Crisis and the Role of the World Bank – February 13, 1998 Managing Director of the World Bank, Sven Sandsrom.
–Commemorative Lecture for the Golden Jubilee Year Celebration of Industrial Finance.
–PREMnotes: Economic Policy – What effect will East Asia crisis have on developing countries? (March 1998, Number 1) The World Bank
–Overview: World Bank Activities in Fiscal 1997.

5 Globalization, markets and democracy

An anthropological linkage

Michael Mousseau

In world politics "globalization" means the growing demise of the traditional power of the sovereign state. These challenges can be seen in the multiplying international pressures towards democratic and law-based governmental structures; the growing adoption among nation–states of liberal economic policies; burgeoning restraints on the unilateral use of coercion in foreign affairs; and a seemingly rising power of individuals as global actors. In short, in the field of international relations "globalization" means a changing inter-state system – changing from high state sovereignty to some other structural form.

What is the new structural form of "globalization"? In this chapter, I present a cultural materialist model of economic development and cultural change, and demonstrate its robust explanatory and descriptive power for grasping twenty-first century globalization. In brief, cultural materialist ontology posits a probabilistic interrelationship among economic conditions, institutions, and culture, but that in the long term economic conditions have predictable effects on institutions and culture (Harris 1979). In this way, cultural materialism identifies economic conditions as exogenous, and predicts that two indigenous cultures that have never been in contact yet share common economic infrastructures – such as pastorialists in Tuva and East Africa – will share some common core values and institutions. In the same way, the ontology also offers an extraordinary perspective on the growing adoption by nations of liberal economic policies and forms of government, the seeming replacement of global politics with law, and the rising power of individuals as global political actors. The model presented herein thus offers a unique insight on the processes of early twenty-first century globalization.

This chapter is structured as follows. After reviewing the emergence of the Westphalian inter-state system and the processes of late twentieth-century globalization, I introduce the ontology of cultural materialism. I then present the cultural materialist model, which identifies the origins of liberal political culture and democratic institutions with the rise of a market economy. Subsequently, a history of market civilizations is reviewed, including the rise of the market economy in sixteenth-century Europe and the origins of the modern inter-state system. I then trace the patterns of globalization – the changing inter-state structure – and explain these changes according to the increasingly complex divisions of labor in the advanced market economies. I conclude by showing how the model appears to be a true theory of world politics, in that it yields a large number of unambiguous, novel and empirically verifiable predictions.

Globalization and civilizations

Until the sixteenth century, most civilizations were hierarchical and doctrinal in nature. The Roman, Byzantine, Ottoman, Chinese, Indian, and a host of other civilizations, while encompassing vast differences among them, shared at least two traits in common. First, these past civilizations were structured hierarchically, with the power of central authorities near-absolute at the center, but diminishing the further a locality was from the center. Typically, this meant strong central control in the core, a distant relationship based on tribute in the periphery, and some mixture of the two in between. Second, the power of the central authorities was universally legitimated with an ethnocentric and hegemonic paradigm that left little room for opposing views and values. The Chinese emperor was the Son of Heaven; the Byzantine *basileus* was the viceroy of God on Earth; the leader of Persia was the "king of kings". While relations among the empires varied dramatically across time and space, one constant remained: few hegemonic leaders considered themselves socially or legally equal to anyone else (Watson 1992).

Fifteenth-century European civilization was not much different. The legitimacy of authority rested with the paradigm of Catholicism and the supposed infallibility of the Pope. With the collapse of Rome, however, political authority became relatively dispersed within the common paradigm, though often concentrated on a political hegemony legitimated by alliance with the Pope, such as the House of Habsburg. Whether the relative dispersal of political authority in Europe set the stage for the emergence of a market economy as some suggest (Wallerstein 1979) is a question beyond the scope of the present study. The focus here is not on explaining the rise of the market economy, but on discerning the impact of this rise on the subsequent emergence of Europe as the core of a new global civilization. For starting around 1450 began a rise of a market economy in northwestern Europe (Braudel 1979: 24), and soon after occurred an event that, with the benefit of hindsight, distinguished European civilization from all others: the Protestant rebellion against Catholic hegemony.

The importance of the Reformation and the Protestant-imposed settlement at Westphalia for the emergence of the modern inter-state system can hardly be overstated. During the course of the Thirty Years' War Protestant (and some Catholic) political entities allied against the hegemonial power of the Habsburgs in Vienna. In the course of this alliance, representatives of small states often met and negotiated with powerful ones as equals. Like the Byzantine Emperor and the Persian king of kings, however, the Habsburgs could hardly ally as equals with anyone, since their war aim was to restore their dominance in a hierarchy (Holy Roman Empire) legitimated with intolerant dogma (Catholicism). The Protestants, in contrast, were fighting in defense of their states, and thus had few qualms with allying with any political entity, including Catholic France, against the Habsburgs. The consequence was the emergence of a new political system with three revolutionary features: (1) equal, rather than hierarchical, legal status among member-states; (2) ideological pluralism based on religious tolerance among member-states; and (3) regularized meetings of representatives of the states to manage inter-state affairs. In this way, the Thirty Years' War launched the modern inter-state system of state sovereignty (legal equality) and diplomacy – with the latter managed with regulated or "legal" war – institutional structures codified with the Treaties of Westphalia (1648), Utrecht (1714) and Vienna (1815) (Watson 1992: 169–97).

It is noteworthy that during the course of the Thirty Years' War the nearby and powerful Ottoman Empire played a key role in the Protestant victory by allying with France, but the Ottomans never took part as equals in the alliance negotiations during the war, or in the settlement thereafter. Instead the Ottoman Empire remained aloof in its own hegemonic civilization, bordering on Europe but not a part of the European commonwealth of sovereign states. Over the following three centuries, however, the growing power of Europe caused the relatively decaying empires to join the now global European system, with entry ultimately associated with republican revolutions in China (1912), the Ottoman Empire (1923), and Ethiopia (1975), and genocide and de-colonialization elsewhere.

Whereas the Protestant Reformation launched the modern inter-state system of high state sovereignty and diplomacy, with globalization politics and diplomacy appear to be giving way to world law and institutions. The origins of this process can be traced to the middle of the nineteenth century with the emergence of new international governmental organizations (IGOs), such as the International Committee of the Red Cross (1863), the International Telegraph Union (1865), and the Universal Postal Union (1874). While these IGOs hardly constrain state sovereignty, subsequent IGOs do: the establishment of the League of Nations (1919) outlawed aggressive war and territorial aggrandizement; and the United Nations (1945) established new international regimes for economic cooperation, human rights, and the ending of colonization. Whereas the establishment of a law or regime does not mean that every state always abides by it, it is a true historical fact that most states at most times abide by the growing list of international laws and regimes. Moreover, some IGOs have the power to force their will on member-states: all United Nations members must abide by resolutions of the UN Security Council; the International Monetary Fund (IMF) has the power to sanction states that do not follow its recommendations; and an increasing number of international treaties impose direct legal responsibility on individuals who violate crimes against humanity.

It is in the seeming convergence of state institutional and economic structures, however, that the effects of globalization seem most apparent. With the demise of the Cold War democracy has emerged as a global regime. The influential Western democracies impose a system of rewards and punishments that encourage democratization; and many regional and global IGOs impose democracy as a condition for membership (Schmitter 1996). Some regional groupings even allow states to intervene in each other's internal affairs to protect democratic institutions, such as the European Union, the North Atlantic Treaty Organization, the Organization of American States, and the British Commonwealth of Nations. Globally, in 1994 the UN Security Council authorized military intervention in Haiti to restore the rule of democratic law.

Other visible aspects of globalization are the growing adoption of liberal economic policies worldwide; the dearth of unilateral uses of coercion in foreign affairs; and the seeming emergence of a global civil society. In recent years more and more states have opened their economies, liberalized their currencies, and reduced the size of their public sectors (Strange 1996). At the same time, the collective and overwhelming response to military aggression by Iraq in 1991 established a clear post-Cold War regime against the unilateral use of force for territorial aggrandizement. Finally, individuals are more and more global actors not only because they are increasingly protected by international institutions, but also as a result of an explosion of non-profit International Non-Governmental Organizations (INGOs) aimed at lobbying IGOs (Clark *et al.* 1998).

In this way, the structure of the international system has changed dramatically since the treaties of Westphalia, Utrecht, and Vienna. While the Protestant Reformation was fought for inter-state religious tolerance; with globalization there is little inter-state tolerance for non-democratic forms of government. Whereas in the seventeenth century *raison d'état* was a progressive notion based on inter-state pluralism, with globalization *raison d'état* is a reactionary doctrine superseded by severe constraints on the unilateral use of force. While the Westphalian settlement established the principle of non-interference in internal affairs, with globalization sovereigns may be held accountable for violations of human rights.

A leading trend in the globalization literature identifies a growing interdependence on trade and capital as the primary cause of change from high state sovereignty to globalization (Strange 1996; Williamson 1996); others emphasize the diffusion or evolution of Western cultural norms and values (Fukuyama 1995; Spybey 1996). While traditional Realism assumes the system established at Westphalia as unchangeable, hegemonic stability theory (Gilpin 1981) may explain globalization as a function of US hegemony. In contrast to these views but not necessarily contrary to them, I now turn to another possibility: an emerging global culture associated with the global rise of a market economy, a view with cogent roots in Anthropology and the ontological tradition of cultural materialism.

The ontology of cultural materialism

Cultural materialism, according to its leading advocate in Anthropology, Marvin Harris, is "based on the simple premise that human social life is a response to the practical problems of earthly existence" (1979: ix, cited in Murphy and Margolis 1995: 2). In this way, cultural materialism is far removed from the idiographic and interpretative direction that has gripped some of the current generation of anthropologists (Johnson 1995: 7). Rather, cultural materialism and science have a long history together, as "cultural materialism is a focused theoretical commitment to the causal primacy of infrastructural variables in explaining sociocultural systems" (ibid.: 9).

Cultural materialism highlights three layers in all social systems: the infrastructure, the structure, and the superstructure. The *infrastructure* is the base layer: the material conditions of human existence. How do people relate to their environment? How do humans produce and consume? The *structure* refers to a society's social and political institutions. What sort of familiar and non-familiar associations, organizations, and institutions are found in the society? The final layer, the *superstructure*, is a society's ideologies, paradigms, and values (Murphy and Margolis 1995: 2).

Cultural materialists assert that there are predictable and causal relationships among these three layers, the infrastructure, the structure, and the superstructure. At the same time, cultural materialists assume that "changes in a society's material base will lead to functionally compatible changes in its social and political institutions (structure) and in its secular and religious ideology (superstructure)" (ibid.). For example, while many would assert that the rise in the use of contraception in the United States is a result of declining moral values, cultural materialists would argue that a change in material conditions – the rise of the industrial and service economy – brought about a desire for fewer children. The change in material conditions caused large families to be an economic burden rather than an asset, and thus encouraged alternative social behavior (smaller families). Since human beings are social and thus tend to justify their behavior as socially proper, the material-induced change in social behavior yielded, over a period of time, a change in social institutions (structure/family size) as well as values (superstructure/moral acceptance of contraception) (ibid.: 2–3).

In this way, cultural materialists assert that it is the material conditions (infrastructure) that primarily cause change in social institutions (structure) and ideologies (superstructure). Cultural materialism is not, however, deterministic: it does not assert that *all* social and institutional change arises from material change. Nor does cultural materialism deny that changes in structure and superstructure can affect the infrastructure. Rather, cultural materialists view the relationship among all three layers as probabilistic, but the *primary* flow of causation is from the infrastructure to the structure and superstructure (Murphy and Margolis 1995: 3). This is because at a deep level human beings are assumed to be economically rational, and thus innovations that occur in the infrastructure are likely to be preserved and enhanced if they improve economic efficiency. If such innovations are incompatible with structures and superstructures, it is the latter that will adjust to the infrastructure. However, because the structure and superstructure do influence the infrastructure, change induced by the latter often happens slowly. As will be shown below, it is divergence among the three layers that offers a great deal of explanatory potential in world politics, with government (structure) and cultural norms and values (superstructure) seen as conservative forces acting against change induced from the material infrastructure.

Based on science, cultural materialist explanations have the potential to yield predictions that can be subject to empirical testing. Since it is the infrastructure that is considered the primary source of causation, it is infrastructural variables that are identified as exogenous, with social and political institutions (structure) and ideological values (superstructure) explained. In this way, cultural materialist ontology has been successfully applied across disciplines, including studies of Asiatic civilizations (Harris 1968: 672), archaeological discoveries in the American Southwest (ibid.: 674–5), explaining the sacred cattle in India, the *potlatch* of the Kwakiutl, warfare among the Yanomami (Fergusson 1995), and numerous other applications. Indeed, indicative of the power of cultural materialist ontology is the fact that it arose independently in two separate and disconnected disciplines, Anthropology and literary studies (Jackson 1996: 15–17).

Globalization is a pattern of structural change from the high state sovereignty instituted at Westphalia to some other emerging structure. From the cultural materialist perspective, therefore, to understand globalization (the structure) we must first grasp the underlying material (infrastructural) and cultural (superstructural) changes that accompany it. The next section explores these changes.

Infrastructure (markets) and superstructure (liberalism)

From the premise of cultural materialism, understanding global structural change begins with grasping the infrastructure – the material base – of the influential sectors of the global economy. From the perspective of cultural materialism, therefore, it is not a coincidence that all the advanced industrial nations share a common political structure (democracy) and superstructure (liberal political culture) – and that democracy and liberal political culture remain unstable or seemingly absent in all states without this common infrastructure. What is the infrastructure common among the advanced industrial economies?

The infrastructure (markets)

As mentioned, an application of cultural materialism to world politics begins by identifying the material conditions that are common to, and unique among, the advanced industrial states. Wealth is not unique to the industrial world: the tiny oil-rich kingdoms of the Persian Gulf, for example, have unusually high levels of per capita wealth, but relatively simple divisions of labor. While the advanced industrial states all have complex divisions of labor, several communist nations have also had complex divisions of labor. This fact indicates that a complex division of labor, like wealth, does not yield the predicted democratic structure and liberal superstructure. However, the advanced industrial states that have also had democratic structures and liberal superstructures appear to have had one material base that is both common and unique among them: the presence of *both* a complex division of labor and a market linking these divisions.[1]

How does a complex division of labor whose divisions are linked with the market yield democratic structures and the liberal superstructure? Transactions that occur on the market are sanctified by contracts, or agreements among individuals to cooperate and modify their behavior for mutual gains. In advanced market economies individuals regularly engage in contract when they sell their labor and skills, exchange their goods, and purchase what they consume. In an economy with relatively simple divisions of labor material production and consumption are less intense, as individuals are more likely to consume products that they themselves produced. For products not directly produced, successful acquisition often rests less with the fortunes of individualistic exchange than it does on non-market "discounts" arranged with familiar, clan, feudal, or other forms of collective linkages. In a non-market economy with a complex division of labor production and consumption may be relatively intense, but economic transactions are arranged not through contract but by monopolies, bureaucrats, and familiar and political linkages. It is almost axiomatic that in all economies without complex divisions of labor integrated with exchange, individual survival rests less on the successful and regularized engagement in contract than it does on the building and nurturing of various kinds of patron–client relationships.

In this way, what predominantly differentiates the day-to-day life of ordinary people in advanced market economies from virtually all other economies is the intensity in which they regularly engage in contract forms of economic cooperation. Thus, the infrastructure of interest – the material – is the proliferation of exchange unique to developed market economies. What norms and values arise from a socio-economy integrated with exchange?

The superstructure (liberalism)

In this section, I demonstrate how a society with an increasingly complex division of labor integrated with exchange will give rise to liberal norms and values. Specifically, the regularized engagement in contract affects the superstructure in at least five ways. It encourages the values of: (1) cooperation managed with exchange; (2) individualism and freedom; (3) negotiation and compromise; (4) equity, or legal equality, among individuals; and (5) a universal form of trust and respect for the rule of common law. I now address each of these separately.

Cooperation managed with exchange

In contract forms of cooperation each party to a contract explicitly and unashamedly pursues its own interests. In other forms of economic cooperation – as occurs within families, and in less prosperous societies within extended families, tribes, and other collectivities – economic arrangements are more likely to be consciously and explicitly rationalized by a common group utility.[2] As a consequence, as a society's division of labor linked with exchange becomes increasingly complex, individuals learn to value cooperation managed with exchange.

Individualism and freedom

Contracts are entered into by individual volition. If a person has little or no choice in a matter, or if the economic cooperation is based on notions of common utility, then the arrangement is not based on contract. Unfortunately, in developing societies too many people lack the economic leverage to engage in bargaining, and thus enter into economic arrangements without choice and hence without volition. If a person has little or no choice in a matter, the economic arrangement is not a contract but exploitation or slavery. However, in a socio-economy where most individuals have the economic leverage to regularly engage in contract, most individuals habitually enter into economic arrange-ments with choice and volition. Not only does your average individual have a choice in where to purchase potatoes, the individual – not the society, govern-ment, or collective – decides whether or not to consume potatoes. In this way, a market infrastructure gives rise to a superstructure that values individual choice and freedom.

Negotiation and compromise

Whether through a process of direct bargaining or with prices set by the market, individuals arrange contracts with negotiation and compromise. Among individ-uals sharing an explicit common utility, negotiation and compromise are not the normal methods that facilitate economic cooperation. This is because the processes of negotiation and compromise require each party to explicitly and unashamedly pursue its self-interest, and explicitly disregard the interests of economic partners. This neglect and unabashed self-interest are incompatible with a common utility explicit in economic collectives – as occurs within families – rendering the processes of negotiation and compromise not normal aspects of non-contract forms of economic cooperation.

Equity

Since a contract has no meaning in the absence of provisions that are equally binding for all members, a contract imposes equity among contractees. An equi-table agreement does not mean that all parties must be equal in wealth, nor does it mean that all parties derive an equal utility from the agreement. It simply means that contractees have an arrangement, such as the purchase of ice cream, in which the parties, the seller and the buyer, face explicit mutual obliga-tions – the buyer pays cash, and the seller furnishes the ice cream. Since each party is consciously equally obligated to fulfill its side of the deal, and each party has choice and free will whether to enter the contract, the arrangement is explicitly equitable. In this way, if a prince and a serf regularly engage in contract, each is aware that each is equally obligated to fulfill the terms of the contract, and their relationship becomes based not on a patron–client hierarchy but equity.

Universalism, trust and respect for common law

To enter into contract a person must have some element of trust that all contractees will fulfill their obligations. This is a form of trust present among individuals even though each explicitly pursues its own interests. This form of trust thus differs from the trust sanctified by common identities found within families, clans, and other collective economic units, and is therefore non-partic-ular. Moreover, all contractees expect all parties to the contract to fulfill their obligations *not* because they happen to be within a common in-group – your sibling, cousin, and so on – but because the contract commits everyone to the terms of the contract. In this way, contract forms of economic cooperation may occur across divergent within-group identities, and the form of trust derived from the regularized engagement in contract – the trust in the sanctity of contract (i.e. respect for the "law" of the contract) – is non-parochial, or universal.

In sum, if the material affects the superstructure as cultural materialists assert, then individuals in advanced market economies tend to share the liberal ideolog-ical values of exchange-based cooperation, individual choice and free will, negotiation and compromise, equity, universalism, and trust in the sanctity of contract or common law. Anthropological studies support this view: "[I]n indi-vidualistic societies individuals interact with others on the basis of such principles as competition, equity, and exchanges based on contracts" (Bierbrauar 1994: 246). Studies have shown that societies experiencing rapid economic devel-opment undergo a cultural change towards cooperation, compromise, and tolerance of different interests (Diamandouros 1997), that "people with more income, in complex and widely interdependent work situations … are more likely to ask for political freedom" (Lipset *et al.* 1993: 166), and that gross national product per capita is associated with higher levels of interpersonal trust (Inkeles and Diamond 1980).

Still, the relationship between the three layers in society is a probabilistic one, and hence changes in the infrastructure will not have immediate and determin-istic effects on the structure and superstructure. Instead, the structure (institutions) and the superstructure (culture) probably inhibit the impact of changes in the infrastructure as well as influence the infrastructure directly. This probabilistic interrelationship may, in fact, explain the "take-off" stage of devel-opment made famous by Rostow (1960). Once a rise of exchange, however small, fosters some change toward market culture in a society, then the increasing norm of trust in the sanctity of contract would likely lower transaction costs, fostering in turn an increase in exchange. In this way, a positive feedback loop renders the interrelationship among the three layers unstable, and after a certain point socio-economies "take off" – not unlike, in recent years, perhaps South Korea and Taiwan. If the environmental conditions do not favor economic growth, however – for reasons entirely exogenous to the model – then the rise in exchange is unlikely to diffuse through a socio-economy, and market culture is also unlikely to emerge. The important point is that the model does not explain a rise in exchange directly, as it identifies the primary flow of causation as moving *from* the infrastructure to the superstructure. The next section shows the power of the model in historical perspective.

Markets and civilizations

As discussed above, until the sixteenth century most civilizations were hierarchical and doctrinal in nature. The Roman, Byzantine, Ottoman, Chinese, Indian, and a host of other civilizations shared in common both hierarchical structures and one-dimensional hegemonic paradigms. There were several exceptions, however, and all of these appear to be associated with a market economy. The most notable case is classical Greece. Ancient Athens had an "extensive division of labor", and "banking, insurance, joint-stock ventures, and a number of other economic institutions that are associated with later epochs already existed in embryonic form in classical Greece" (Cameron 1997: 32–5). As did democratic government and liberal political culture: "The condition of the free man," wrote Aristotle, "is that he not live under the constraint of another" (quoted in Finley 1985: 40–1). Of course, Greek democracy was not perfect (nor is today's): the Greeks had slaves. But the market principles of exchange-based cooperation, individual freedom, universalism, and equity were evidently present among classical free Greeks.

While a scholarly consensus seems to agree that besides the present age, "the only other market-dominated society in history appears to have been the Hellenistic world" (Tandy and Neale 1994: 20), there are several cases in history where a market did emerge to some level of social and political influence. Twelve centuries after the Peloponnesian War precipitated the collapse of the Athenian market economy, Mecca appeared as the trading center linking the West with the East. Muhammad himself was a merchant, and the Koran places great stress on the values of equity, tolerance, and exchange-based cooperation (Mazrui 1990). In the thirteenth century the Black Death curtailed the global trading system and the economy of the Arab world declined. Soon afterwards the Italian city–states of Genoa and Venice emerged as the centers of Mediterranean trade, and hence it was the Muslim Arabs that introduced various trading concepts to them, such as the bill of exchange (requiring a high level of trust) (Abu-Lughod 1989: 93–4). As "urban economy and population reached their maximum growth [in Italy] in the course of the thirteenth century … social mores changed in subtle and in obvious ways" (Martines 1979: 63). Max Weber's "spirit" of modern capitalism emerged (Abu-Lughod 1989: 115), as did a rise in social equity, equitable law, and middle-class demands for direct representation in the new republican communes (Martines 1979).

As discussed above, fifteenth-century European civilization was not market-oriented but hierarchical and doctrinal – like the Indian, Ottoman, and Chinese civilizations. But starting around 1450 a rise in trade and commerce in north-western Europe began (Braudel 1979: 24). As predicted according to the market model, this change in infrastructure occurred just antecedent to the rise in the values of individualism, equity, and cooperative exchange that compelled the

Protestant Reformation against the collective hegemony of Catholicism. Whilst the Habsburgs insisted on imposing their Catholic hegemony throughout Europe, Cardinal Richelieu, despite his Catholicism, favored the interests of the French state and decided to ally with the Protestants against the Habsburgs. The result was the victory of the Protestants and their notion of equity, and the institutionalization of equal rather than hierarchical legal standing among Europe's political units with the Treaty of Westphalia. In this way, the model explains the origins of the modern inter-state system not as a semi-mythical or natural outcome of a struggle for power as Realists assert, but as an unambiguous consequence of the emerging liberal superstructure of equity (legal equality, in this case between nations) and tolerance (in this case religious). Indeed, at the time of the Treaty of Westphalia (1648), the notions of sovereignty and diplomacy were considered "Protestant" notions, and international law a "Protestant science" (Watson 1992: 188).

With the new universalism of the emerging liberal culture, European's began to think and act globally. Yet, like the Habsburgs, the notion of sovereign equality could hardly be understood in other regions of the world. Thus, diplomats sent from Europe to the hegemonial Ottoman, Chinese and other superstructures were perceived as sycophants of the court not unlike representatives from within these empires, and hence gifts were considered tribute and neither diplomatic relations nor gifts were treated with equitable exchange (Watson 1992). This may explain why the Ottomans, while allied with France to "balance" Austria, remained aloof from European affairs, did not follow European principles of law (e.g. they enslaved prisoners), did not send envoys in exchange for ambassadors (until much later), and had to set up a system of "capitulations" to deal with the European foreigners who, as outsiders, could not be expected to follow Ottoman structures and superstructures (ibid.). In this way, the model explains and connects the "capitulations" (arrangements to treat foreigners collectively outside local customs) made by the Ottomans, Chinese, and other hegemonial empires – and why capitulations were never instituted among the Europeans.

Markets and globalization

Just as the initial rise in the market economy in northwestern Europe can be seen to explain the Protestant Reformation and the origins of the modern inter-state structure of high state sovereignty and coercive diplomacy, the growing intensity of market economy and thus liberal culture in more recent times can be seen to offer a concise explanation for the processes of late twentieth-century globalization. To recall from above, these globalization processes are: (1) a growing adoption of liberal economic policies worldwide; (2) an increasing de-legitimacy of all but democratic forms of government; (3) burgeoning restraints on the unilateral use of coercion in foreign affairs; (4) the increasing emergence of global and regional governance as seen in the proliferation and power of global and regional inter-governmental organizations; and (5) an apparently rising power of individuals as global actors competing with, or possibly supplanting, the traditional charge of the sovereign state. I now address each of these separately.

The emerging global market economy

A constructivist far ahead of his time, in *The Great Transformation* Karl Polanyi documented how three forms of economic integration have been present in history: reciprocity, redistribution, and exchange. Each of these, in turn, is associated with a particular set of deeply embedded myths ([1944] 1957: 43–55). With reciprocity, common in hunting and gathering communities, societies are organized symmetrically and, since long-term relationships are more important than any particular transaction, individuals are motivated to express their worth to the community through fecundity and sharing. Redistribution is common in more complex socio-economies, as a central authority is needed to store goods for later consumption. These societies are thus organized hierarchically, and transactions are rationalized not with reciprocity but through social obligations confirmed with "gift giving" to the chief or lord. With market exchange transactions are rationalized not with gifts and sharing but by an "alleged propensity of man to barter, truck, and exchange" (ibid.: 44).

Polanyi's insights, now over five decades old, accord remarkably well with cultural materialist ontology in general, and with the market norms model in particular. Polanyi's *Great Transformation*, for example, was the emergence of market culture and institutions that occurred in seventeenth–nineteenth-century Europe. While the vast majority of Europeans through this time remained outside the market economy – as serfs, lords, or landless peasants integrated not with free exchange but with reciprocity and gift-giving – the tiny merchant class of Europe did have political influence. Perhaps this was a consequence of the intense political competition of Europe's sovereign states, which rendered a level of dependence on the trade and enterprise of the commercial classes (Tilly 1992).

If the market norms model is correct, then these merchants – like those around Muhammad in the seventh century – would have adjusted to some level of market norms. To use Polanyi's terminology, these merchants would assume as natural the "alleged propensity of man to barter, truck, and exchange" through processes of free choice, negotiation and compromise. It follows that with political influence, the merchant classes in northwestern Europe would have pressured political leaders for structural adjustments that accord with their growing market world views. Indeed, both Marx ([1867] 1952) and Weber (1978) observed how *common* law emerged because merchants needed an equitable procedure for enforcing contracts. In this way, political authorities in seventeenth–nineteenth-century Europe went about constructing a market economy, a structural change well documented as Polanyi's *Great Transformation*.

Like the monarchs of late feudal Europe, political leaders of developing countries at the turn of the twenty-first century face enormous pressures to reconstruct their economies along market assumptions. Some of these pressures may arise internally, emerging from domestic merchant classes.[3] Some of these pressures also arise, no doubt, externally. Until the end of the Cold War, systems of global tribute and reciprocity reinforced established reciprocal and redistributive infrastructures and superstructures across most of the developing world. For instance, economic aid flowed from Washington and Moscow or from various metropoles to national and colonial regimes, and then downward again with tribute and reciprocity to local officials, and so on. In more recent years, however, tribute from Moscow has disappeared, and Washington now makes its gifts conditional on efforts to re-construct recipient economies along market assumptions – a process known as "structural adjustment".

In this way, just as eighteenth-century merchants pressured political leaders to destroy Britain's traditional welfare system (Polanyi [1944] 1957: 77–86), the International Monetary Fund, foreign investors, and domestic merchants in the twenty-first century put pressure on political leaders of developing countries to demolish their welfare systems. The structural adjustment process, however, should not be viewed as only detrimental to the most vulnerable economic classes, and nor should economic elites be assumed to share market norms. The classic example is the banking sector. Before structural adjustment, a developing country's economy is integrated with complex systems of reciprocity typically observed as patron–client relationships. With weak market culture and norms, bankers – like everybody else – make some business decisions not according to the logic of a market (profits), but according to the logic of established norms of reciprocity (patron–client obligations) (Eichengreen 1996).

While such "non-market" activity is often referred to in the West as "corruption", it does not have the same connotation in cultures with deeply embedded norms of reciprocity, where corruption is a tool that makes "borrowed" market institutions fit established local customs. In this way we can see that when the banking sectors do collapse and IMF "shock therapy" is applied, (as occurred in Mexico, Indonesia, and South Korea), an important determinant on whether IMF policy is successful is the extent to which market culture prevails in the society. If the market culture is weak, in the long run reciprocating patron–client systems will re-emerge in the banking sector unless foreign interveners specifically monitor and control it.

Just as the structural adjustment in Britain destroyed the traditional social fabric across English classes, structural change – including rapid industrialization – fosters radical cultural change in today's developing countries. This is why the processes of late twentieth-century structural adjustment are associated with intense corruption, political upheavals, and anti-Western reactions. Consider what happens when an agricultural peasant or urban laborer, long accustomed to material survival through deeply embedded gift-giving and reciprocal relationships with family, village, neighborhood, and other forms of linkages, suddenly finds these support networks broken or otherwise unable to yield adequate material support. Unaccustomed and unaware of the notion of market competition and the principles of supply and demand, one's social constructions fall apart, as does society's superstructure.

A society without a superstructure is one not unlike that described by Hobbes as England was undergoing rapid infrastructural and thus superstructural change. Without established norms of social interaction order can be maintained only with brute force, as the absence of norms (liberal, religious, or what have you) leaves only power and fear to constrain social behavior. In most cases this environment of superstructural anarchy coincides with a material condition where the village peasant or urban laborer has little or no bargaining power, and thus little opportunity to engage in contract even if he or she understood its principle. Nor are the capitalists exploiting them engaging in contract, for when one side has little alternative neither side is engaging in an arrangement of mutual volition.

To survive in such poverty and social anarchy individuals seek refuge in various new forms of collectivities – if not the village, then political parties; if not a neighborhood association, then a union or mafia tie; or perhaps some form of religious, ethnic, or national identity. Unlike such groupings in civil society (see below), collective-oriented groups are not individualistic, and thus seek the total loyalty of their members to the exclusion of out-groups. The mafia, for instance, is an organization that no one can quit without becoming an enemy; as are communist parties. To get support, such collective groupings offer material rewards (jobs; food) and a hegemonic superstructure (religion; culture). With the dire inequities of the market before them, the more popular collectivist superstructures are those with anti-market appeals – such as anarchism, communism, fascism, Islamic and other religious fundamentalisms, and various forms of ethnic particularism.

In this way, the model explains the growing adjustment towards liberal economic structures in the developing world of the early twenty-first century as a process that actually began in sixteenth-century Europe. As Polanyi demonstrated, a market economy is not a natural but a human construction. Just as Europe's construction of a market economy was associated with class struggles and the rise of socialism and nationalism, today's structural and cultural adjustments in the developing world are associated with the rise of religious fundamentalism, ethnic parochialism, and nationalism. Whatever the form, the principle is the same: a volatile situation with great potential for extreme political violence and anti-market – often misunderstood as anti-Western – political upheaval. In this way, the market model also explains the Russian revolution and the Iranian, and predicts such anti-market revolutions to be more likely to occur during periods of rapid industrialization and structural adjustment.[4]

Democracy as a new global regime

Just as the market superstructure favors economic structuring, the market superstructure also favors political restructuring, for several reasons. First, if the formation of equitable or common law is rooted in market culture – that is, if democratic rule is perceived as a social contract of cooperation – then whatever is not signed away as an obligation in the social contract will remain a perceived individual *right* (i.e. no authority can legitimately take it away). Second, market culture yields the basis for tolerance in a society. Individuals that value individual free will and rights are less likely to impose their viewpoints on others, and more likely to tolerate opposing viewpoints and opposition electoral victories. Third, since rational individuals hope to place as few obligations as possible in their contracts, individuals in market cultures will tend to resist obligations to the social contract, or state, i.e. they will resist socialist or any other collective impositions by the state. Notably, this relationship becomes self-protective with an internal positive feedback effect: if a market culture constrains democratic leaders from significantly inhibiting the market, it follows that such elected governments will reinforce market culture and thus, in turn, democratic institutions.[5]

Fourth, democracy and equity go together, as democracy cannot be stable in societies that are socially structured in hierarchical forms – where individuals loyally vote according to the wishes of their patrons, be they ethnic leaders, feudal lords, mafia dons, warlords or priests. Fifth, as seen in the numerous attempts at liberal democracy in less developed countries, in the absence of respect for the rule of common law attempts at liberal democracy will fail. Too many individuals will flout the law, leaving the government with little choice but to establish a police state (e.g. Singapore), or tolerate chaos with most laws widely ignored and unenforced (e.g. Turkey). Either way, the state is no longer a liberal democracy. Sixth, in the absence of both equity and respect for the rule of law, corruption will be endemic, as it is the primary means to make "reciprocating" economic and cultural realities fit imported "market" state structures. For instance, without the value of equity the enforcement of law will not be in "common" but will vary according to social and economic class. Finally, in the absence of universalism, trust, and respect for the rule of law, there is little basis for voters to expect leaders to respect the rules and procedures of the democratic social contract. The median voter in less market-oriented democracies is less likely to vote for leaders that venerate the market norms of individual choice, free will, and the sanctity of the social contract than they are to choose leaders that revere particular religious dogmas or other parochial and hegemonic in-group identities and values.

In these ways, the stability of democratic rule in a nation depends on the strength of its market culture. This can be seen in the European historical experience. While the initial rise in trade and exchange in sixteenth-century northwestern Europe opened the social space towards equity (at least *among* the commercial classes), exchange, and universalism – and began the rise of common law and parliamentary government against the hegemony of the Pope – only a tiny minority of Europeans actually engaged in exchange, voted, and held market values. It took centuries for the division of labor to become complex enough that a clear majority of Europeans can be thought of as sharing the market superstructure. This is why few of the liberal states in Europe extended the franchise until industrialization created a society-wide complex division of labor. Simply put, until a clear majority of the people in a state has the opportunity to materially benefit from exchange, the majority will share not market but other more reciprocating and redistributive cultural mores, and democratic institutions will not work.

In this way, the model explains the well-known association of economic development and stable democracy (Burkhart and Lewis-Beck 1994; Przeworski and Limongi 1997): unless the society has an inclusive complex division of labor integrated with exchange (market development), voters will simply select non-liberal leaders that do not respect the democratic process. Unlike modern liberals, Europe's classical liberals understood this point very well. Kant, for instance, did not advocate democracy but feared it: "democracy is, properly speaking, necessarily a despotism", because democracy does not "conform to the concept of law" (Kant [1795] 1982: 14–15). The classical liberals never did grasp *why* some people shared liberal values and others did not and, like modern liberals, wrongly assumed the latter were simply "irrational" and not yet "evolved", "enlightened", or "civilized". With the market model, however, we can see that the issue is not "irrationality" or "evolution", but simply changing political preferences as a consequence of changing political mores associated with economic realities.

Nevertheless, with globalization democracy has emerged as a global regime because, with the end of the Cold War, the influential market democracies impose a system of rewards and punishments that encourage democratization (Schmitter 1996). The market democracies engage in this crusade because the market superstructure is so deeply embedded in these countries that their academics, voters, and policy-makers think everyone in the world thinks like them. They think the "propensity of man to barter, truck, and exchange" (Polanyi [1944] 1957: 44) is ingrained in human nature, as is the desire for individual-level freedom and democratic government. This is why when small demonstrations against an autocratic government in a developing country occur, Western media and academics tend to interpret these demonstrations as signs of mass democratic "enlightenment" and an emerging civil society. In fact, it is much more likely that the demonstration is a coalition of new rent-seeking patron–client networks seeking to replace the coalition of old rent-seeking patron–client networks (and this explains the passion in the politics of developing countries).

In this way, with the ontology of cultural materialism and the market model we can see that in the absence of market-oriented development the surge of global democracy will be both short-lived and false. In the absence of market culture voters will elect non-liberal leaders that are not capable of respecting the democratic process. The result, if not a return to autocracy, is "pretend" democracy: a democratic constitution that is widely ignored with extra-constitutional changes in government, non-liberal political parties banned, individual rights curtailed, laws not enforced, and real power ultimately resting in non-elected bodies, such as the military, foreign nations, or international organizations. In this way, with globalization is the emergence of a global regime of democracy – an illegitimacy of autocracy – but where democracy in the developing countries is also unstable and false.

The demise of inter-state war

Numerous studies have confirmed that nations with democratic governing struc
tures are less likely than others to engage each other in militarized conflict (Maoz
and Russett 1992; Gleditsch and Hegre 1997), and such states rarely, if ever,
engage each other in war (Babst 1964; Bremer 1992). Most explanations for this
pattern focus on democratic institutions, which are thought to either constrain
the leaders of democracies from fighting each other (Bueno de Mesquita *et al.*
1999), or encourage, over time, the democratic norms of negotiation and
compromise, which in turn constrain the leaders of democracies from fighting
each other (Maoz and Russett 1992; 1993; Dixon 1993; 1994).

As discussed above, the market model predicts democratic structures and the
liberal superstructure to be present in all states with complex divisions of labor
integrated with exchange. Democratic structures ensure some degree of popular
impact on public policy, including foreign policy, and numerous studies have
shown that the public does indeed affect the foreign policy behavior of democratic nations (Hinckley 1992; Page and Shapiro 1992; Knopf 1998). Nations
with both democratic structures and market infrastructures are thus predicted to
have foreign policy decision-makers constrained to behave in manners consistent
with the market-liberal norms of exchange-based cooperation, negotiation and
compromise, equity, trust, and respect for the rule of law. Nations sharing
common paradigms have less to fight about than those in divergent paradigms
(and conflict *between* paradigms can often only be managed with coercion), and
for those conflicts that do arise nations sharing a common superstructure are
jointly constrained to manage the conflict in accordance with the paradigm's
norms and values (whether the paradigm is liberalism, Confucianism, or what-
have-you).

The liberal superstructure is one of equity, trust, and law. It follows that relations between advanced market democracies are managed not with power and
coercion but with equity, trust, and law. Indeed, studies have shown that democracies are more likely than other kinds of states to settle their joint differences
with negotiation (Dixon 1994), compromise (Mousseau 1998), equity (Dixon
1993), and law (Raymond 1994). While none of these studies separated the
market-oriented from the other democracies, the model predicts that these
studies – including my own – are under-specified: that explanatory power would
be enhanced if the developed market democracies were not grouped with the
other democracies. In this way, the market model significantly departs from all
previous explanations for the democratic peace in that it yields several unambiguous novel predictions, the primary one being that the democratic peace is
driven predominantly by the democracies with contractual infrastructures: the
advanced market democracies. Subsequent research has since confirmed this
prediction (Mousseau 2000).

In short, just as democracy without market development is inherently
unstable, democratic nations without developed economies are not in the zone of
democratic peace. However, war is in retreat globally because, with the Cold
War over, the developed democracies use their overwhelming political,

economic, and military dominance over the rest of the world to bring a semblance of order and peace to world politics. Sharing the liberal superstructure, the market democracies perceive a common interest in global peace and prosperity, and thus seek to resolve conflicts arising elsewhere with their principles of negotiation, compromise, equity, trust, and law. It was the market-oriented democracies, for instance, that first attempted to outlaw war with the establishment of the League of Nations, and whose influence has established a global regime against the unilateral use of force for territorial aggrandizement. In this way, with the end of the Cold War the structure of the inter-state system is changing from one regulated with war and diplomacy to one managed by international organization and law.

The emergence of global governance

If the leaders of the market democracies are more likely than other leaders to pursue the values of exchange-based cooperation, individual choice and free will, negotiation and compromise, equity, universalism, and trust in the sanctity of contract as predicted, then the leaders of market democracies are constrained to think alike in global politics. They will share common perceptions of the value of equitable collective security networks, the enforcement of international laws, and the merit of international organizations (perceived as international social contracts). In short, if the advanced market democracies share the common liberal superstructure as predicted, then it follows that such nations are not in a state of anarchy but rather a *de facto* confederation and, because the structure must adjust to the infrastructure and superstructure, are in the process of forming a *de jure* confederation.

In the course of moving from formal anarchy to formal confederation we should expect to observe the appearance of equitable and multilateral alliance structures forming among the market democracies, including the formation of, and submission to, international organizations. Indeed, studies have shown that democracies are more likely than other states to ally (Siverson and Emmons 1991; Gaubatz 1996; Simon and Gartzke 1996; Bennett 1997; Thompson and Tucker 1997) and join international organizations (Russett *et al.* 1998). As above, the model predicts that these studies are under-specified: that explanatory power would be enhanced if the developed market democracies were not grouped with the other democracies. It also appears that "Northern" states are more likely than "Southern" states to delegate increasing power to international governmental organizations (Clark *et al.* 1998). Already a *de jure* confederation is forming among the European market democracies, and this pattern is identified here as having the same root cause as the one leading to the American federation of 1789.[6] In short, with the overwhelming economic, political, and military dominance of the market democracies, the structure of the international system is moving from high state sovereignty to state subservience to international law and organization, a process originated and driven by the liberal political culture omnipresent across the market-oriented democracies.

The rise of individuals as global actors

With roots in de Tocqueville, many theorists of democratic consolidation argue that civil society – citizen participation in government through formal organizations – is crucial for the success of democracy (Coleman 1988; Putnam 1993). From the perspective of the market norms model, however, civil society is not a cause of democracy but, like democracy, a consequence of the market infrastructure. Just as the market infrastructure gives rise to the proliferation of non-governmental domestic organizations (domestic civil society), the market infrastructure also gives rise to numerous non-governmental *international* organizations (international civil society). In this way, individuals are emerging as global actors.

In a society with a complex division of labor linked with the market, individuals regularly engage in a myriad of contracts: with one's employers; local vendors; bankers; utility companies; credit card companies, and so on. In all other societies, in contrast, individual survival rests less on the successful and regularized engagement in contracts than it does on the building and nurturing of one or a small number of intense patron–client relationships. Consider those few pockets of non-contract forms of cooperation that regularly occur in today's market cultures: that which occurs within families or, better yet, within mafia families. Individuals within such collectivities do not deal with their group in the same manner that they deal with local vendors and bankers. A collectivity is hegemonic: you are in a family – mafia or nuclear – for life, and survival rests on total loyalty to the family, including conformity to its beliefs and values (superstructure). The important point is that in socio-economies integrated with exchange individuals regularly engage in a wide range and level of overlapping contracting relationships, and each of these relationships is relatively weak compared to the small number of monolithic relationships individuals have with their collectivities and patron/clients in other kinds of socio-economies. As a consequence, individuals in market societies have a norm of entering contracts with little obligation (and the obligation is clear in the contract), and can thus freely join and quit organizations as they please.

Accordingly, the model predicts that in market economies and cultures individuals will frequently join (and quit) multiple associations of interest. In other socio-economies, in contrast, individuals will likely be members of far fewer groups, and each of these groups will tend to demand a much higher level of individual subservience to the group. In this way, non-market societies are structured two-dimensionally (society broken into groups much like geographic space is broken into nations), while market societies are structured multi-dimensionally, with a complex array of multiple layers of organizations with each making relatively light demands from, and for, its members. This explains, I suggest, why market development appears to cross-cut and abate traditional tribal, ethnic, religious and other kinds of identities, as individual interests rise over the collective. Indeed, consistent with model predictions, it does appear that those with strong social identities are also those who hold collectivist orientations (e.g.

Hinkle and Brown 1990), and strong social identities are associated with xeno-phobia and political intolerance (Gibson and Gouws 2000).

More importantly for the present purposes, we can see a clear distinction between civil society organizations and non-market collective groupings, and how civil society emerges in societies integrated with exchange. Since the model predicts civil society and democratic norms to co-vary, the evidence in the litera-ture is consistent with expectations. One study reports that "the causal sequence [of democratic norms and civil society], while not definitely established, appears interactional" (Booth and Richard 1998: 797). The same study also reports the "counter-intuitive" result that among urban Central Americans "formal group activism" (membership in unions, civic associations, cooperatives, and profes-sional groups) associates with higher levels of democratic norms and institutions, whereas "communalism *unexpectedly* associate[s] with lower rather than higher levels of democratic norms" (Booth and Richard 1998: 790, emphasis added).[7] The model predicts this "counter-intuitive" result, however, as the market super-structure should associate positively with formal group activism but negatively with communal, or collective, group activism.

Just as individuals from market cultures can and do organize into groups to influence local and state government, these same individuals have the political culture and world view that allows them to organize to influence international organizations. In this way, the market democracies – but not other democracies and not other states – are predicted to give rise to numerous non-governmental *international* organizations. Recent studies support this view: it appears that most international non-governmental organizations aimed at lobbying IGOs originate in the "Northern" states (Clark *et al.* 1998). Hence, the rise of international civil society and individuals as global actors.

In sum, just as the initial rise in the market economy in northwestern Europe can be seen to explain the Protestant Reformation and the origins of the modern inter-state system, the growing intensity of market economy and political culture in more recent times can be seen to offer a cogent explanation for the processes of late twentieth-century globalization. Just as merchants sharing market values and world views pressured seventeenth–nineteenth-century European states to construct a market economy, merchants and IGOs at the turn of the twenty-first century pressure developing countries to re-construct their economies along market assumptions. Whereas the division of labor with industrialization led to the democratization of the industrial states integrated with exchange, the prose-lytizing nature of market culture causes these countries to promote democratic rule as a global regime. Sharing norms of equity, universal trust, and respect for law, the market-oriented democracies have built a separate peace and, with the end of the Cold War, now use their overwhelming economic and political influ-ence to replace high state sovereignty and coercive diplomacy with international organization and law. Finally, market culture fosters civil society, and civil society may lobby national as well as international governmental organizations, and hence the rise of individuals and INGOs as global actors – and their origins in the market democracies. In these ways, globalization – the change in global structure – can be explained through changes in infrastructure (increasingly complex divisions of labor) and superstructure (increasing embeddedness of liberal culture).

Conclusion

I began this chapter with several historical observations. Until the sixteenth century most civilizations had been structured hierarchically, with authority legitimated with ethnocentric and dogmatic doctrine. The Chinese emperor was the Son of Heaven; the Byzantine *basileus* was the viceroy of God on Earth; the leader of Persia was the "king of kings". It was the Protestant Reformation against Catholic hegemony that broke this pattern in the modern context, with the settlement at Westphalia instituting a new civilizational structure based on legal equality among political units (sovereign states) interacting with diplomacy and limited war. Over the following three centuries the European states re-shaped the world in their own image, and the European commonwealth of sovereign states became the modern inter-state system.

At the turn of the twenty-first century, most observers of world politics report a transformation of the inter-state system, a change in structure known as "globalization". States around the world appear to be adopting liberal economic policies; there appears an emerging global regime of democratic government; we are witnessing an apparent demise of inter-state war and coercive diplomacy among nations; we see a proliferation and increasing power of global and regional inter-governmental organizations; and, finally, individuals and international civic organizations seem to be emerging as global political actors.

In this chapter, I sought to explain these global structural changes. Drawing on cultural materialist ontology in the field of Anthropology, I showed how communities with complex divisions of labor integrated with exchange may yield the embedded values of the liberal superstructure: exchanged-based cooperation, individual freedom, negotiation and compromise, equity, a universal form of trust, and respect for the rule of law. In this way market culture *is* liberal political culture. I then showed how the modern inter-state system may have emerged as a consequence of the rise in exchange that began in fifteenth-century Europe. While only a small minority of sixteenth-century Europeans actually engaged in exchange, Europe's small merchant class was politically influential and promoted the "Protestant" values of exchanged-based cooperation, individual equity, tolerance and universalism. It is well established that the initial advocates of individualistic reforms with the Protestant Reformation were drawn from the "merchants and townspeople" (Watson 1992: 172). In this way, the modern inter-state system is viewed as a consequence of the emerging liberal political culture of equity (legal equality, in this case between nations) and tolerance (in this case religious) that began with the rise of a market economy in northwestern Europe starting around 1450.

Just as the merchants are predicted to have pushed the Protestant Reformation, the tiny commercial classes of seventeenth to nineteenth-century

Europe would have lobbied hard for state re-structuring of national economies from reciprocating and redistributive forms of integration (feudalism) to exchange forms of integration (markets). Subsequent industrialization made the divisions of labor increasingly complex, bringing about society-wide transformations in political culture from feudal and other collective mores to market/liberalism. In this way, industrialization encourages democracy. Market democracies, in turn, do not engage each other in coercive diplomacy because not only do they think alike, but when in dispute they can easily resolve their differences with negotiation and compromise facilitated with the shared market norms of equity, trust and law (Mousseau 2000: 480–2).

With the end of the Cold War, the overwhelming economic and political dominance of the market democracies is again re-shaping the world in their image, with emerging global regimes of liberal economic restructuring, democratic governance, non-coercive international interactions, and an emerging replacement of global politics with international law and institutions. Civil society is a product of market political culture in the market-oriented democracies, and with the emergence of global and regional governance it follows that global and regional civil society is also emerging, but only in the market democracies that have vibrant market/liberal cultures – and effective only against the governments of market democracies because it is these states where law prevails over politics. In short, whereas the initial rise in exchange in Europe led to the institutionalization of equity *between* nations (the modern inter-state system), and industrialization fostered the institutionalization of equity *within* nations (democracy), the increasingly complex division of labor at the turn of the twenty-first century is fostering the institutionalization of equity *between people across nations* – globalization.

A number of alternative explanations may explain some of the phenomena herein, but I am aware of none that are both falsifiable and encompass such a wide menu of explanation. Balance-of-Power Realism does not explain the emergence of the Westphalian system nor globalization; it simply assumes the Westphalian system as constant. While Classical Liberalism accepts change, it does not explain the emergence of liberal political culture. Like Realism, Liberalism assumes the propensity to gain and the desire for freedom as ingrained in human nature. This is probably because most academics are from market cultures, and they simply assume everybody thinks like them. As Polanyi notes (1957: 44), this imposes "a strange attitude toward man's early history", as academics from market cultures re-write history to fit their myths. For instance, "primitive" man is assumed to be motivated for private gain (*à la* Hobbes, Locke, Rousseau), and the millions in the present age who do not seem to behave this way are deemed "uncivilized". While these cultural differences across economic worlds are well documented in Anthropology (Harris 1979), Sociology (Durkheim [1893] 1984) and economic history (e.g. Braudel 1979), economists and political scientists are trained to ignore this research, as their liberal–rationalist models are crucially dependent on the veracity of the Realist–Classical Liberal belief that the motive of gain and desire for freedom is in human nature

(Polanyi [1944] 1957: 44–5). The irony is, the market model explains the emergence of both the Classical Liberal and Realist paradigms – as logical inferences drawn by intellectuals from market superstructures living in the Westphalian inter-state state system.

In contrast to mainstream views, the market model predicts changing political preferences and, in the process, is easily falsifiable. For instance, as a society becomes increasingly integrated with exchange – as a market economy becomes more advanced – we should see an increase in social respect for exchange-based cooperation, individual choice and free will, negotiation and compromise, equity among individuals, universalism, trust in the sanctity of contract, and respect for the rule of common law. Process tracing of individual cases, survey analyses, and content analyses of political speeches, party platforms, and newspapers can verify the prediction that market political culture is associated with market development. In addition, a number of crucial, novel, and readily testable hypotheses emerge from the model: developed democracies – but not other states – are predicted to initiate, join, and submit to international organizations, form equitable alliance ties, engage in the highest levels of inter-state cooperation, vote alike at the United Nations, and rarely, if ever, engage each other in international violence.

Many suggest that political development and globalization are a function of the diffusion of Western culture (Fukuyama 1995) and education (Lipset 1959). From the cultural materialist perspective, this is to say that the primary flow of causation is not from the infrastructure but from the superstructure. This is the approach attributed to the modernization school: change the culture, and development (infrastructure) and democracy (structure) will follow. This was the path taken by many modernizing political leaders, such as Peter the Great in the late seventeenth century and Atatürk in the early twentieth century. Both leaders emphasized education and the adoption of European manners: just as Peter the Great levied a tax on Russian beards to make Russians more European, Atatürk banned Turks from wearing the fez.

However, these attempts at starting with the superstructure – at Westernizing the culture – did not result in the goals desired, for reasons that the market model now makes clear. First, the "modernization" approach confuses indigenous culture with political culture. Indigenous culture includes such matters as language, costumes, diets, and so on. Political culture is not about eating and drinking, but about political norms, values, and preferences. It just seems unlikely that political norms, values, and preferences can be taught in the classroom. More importantly, if we start with the superstructure, then it is difficult to determine what aspects of the "model" culture a developing country should import. The shaving of the beard, the wearing of the Western hat, and, as missionaries have thought, "the singing of Western hymns" will not change political culture.

Second, unlike virtually all models of democratic culture, the market model specifically identifies not only the content of liberal political culture without tautology (Kowert and Legro 1996), but also its origins in a market economy. If the model is correct, then liberal culture as not "Western" at all, but simply arises with a market economy. The market civilization of the present age originated in Western Europe by chance; it might just as easily have originated in twelfth-century Mali. But because it began in Europe, most everyone today confuses liberal political culture with "Western" indigenous culture. Third, this confusion is unfortunate, for once alleviated we can see that the emergence of liberal political culture is not a threat to indigenous culture and identity. The rise of markets and liberal culture in Ghana will not make Ghanians any more "Western" than the rise of a market economy in England made the British any more Dutch. Wearing Western suits may make Ghanians more Western, but engaging in contract and voting will not. While it is easy for any expatriate from a market socio-economy (such as myself) to observe cultural mores in a developing society inhibiting efficient production, consumption, and democracy, it is much harder to observe that it remains the material infrastructure, in the long run, that ultimately affects the structure and superstructure.

Notes

1   Even in Sweden, often acknowledged as the foremost "social democracy", the government share of gross domestic product (GDP) never exceeded 25 percent from 1950 to 1992 (Summers and Heston 1991). Note that government share of GDP can include capital that is exchanged on the market, and thus the market appears to constitute 75 percent *or more* of all economic activity in the industrial democracies during this period.

2   Some may object on the grounds that all forms of economic cooperation are in the form of contract. But what matters is that in advanced market economies actors tend to *perceive* their cooperation in the form of contract, while in other economies actors tend to *perceive* their cooperation as motivated, or rationalized, by some sort of common utility. Since most readers are from market cultures, I draw on one of the few non-contract forms of economic cooperation that regularly occurs in the modern market socio-economies: the cooperation that occurs within nuclear families. One provides food for their children or parents because one perceives a common utility with them. Relative to advanced market economies, in economies with more simple divisions of labor or which are not based on a market a higher portion of individual-level economic activity occurs within such common utility frameworks.

3   It might be useful at this point to make a distinction between merchants engaged in buying and selling on a market, and oligopolists, monopolists, and other types of rent-seeking organizations that survive not with market rules but with non-market influences, such as through market dominance, government connections, familiar linkages, mafia ties, and so on. Obviously, only the former are expected to share market norms. For a recent study documenting business pressures for constructing a market economy in Turkey, see Oniş and Turëm (2001).

4   The model may also explain a successful anti-market revolution in fifteenth-century China and, in this way, perhaps answer "the question that has perplexed ... serious scholars for the past one hundred years" (Abu-Lughod 1989: 321). Namely, why did China suddenly withdraw from the world? From the twelfth through early fourteenth centuries China experienced "a virtual explosion of 'private' trade" (quote found in ibid.: 320), but the Mings who succeeded in power in 1368 identified industry and trade with the previous rulers (ibid.: 341). Were the Mings fourteenth-century counterparts of the Russian Bolsheviks and Iranian mullahs?

5   It would be a mistake, however, to assume that the relationship is evolutionary or monotonic: an exogenous collapse of the market infrastructure associated with environmental conditions or war (as occurred in classical Greece) will precipitate a collapse of market culture and thus democratic institutions. Indeed, this may have come close to occurring in the Western democracies after the collapse of markets in the 1930s, and probably did occur in Germany between the world wars.

6   Note that the United States (northern states) enjoyed a thriving market economy in the pre-industrial era. Indeed, Gordon S. Wood argues that change in political institutions and ideas resulted from an "explosion of entrepreneurial power" in New England in the 1780s (*New York Review of Books*, 6 June 1994, cited in Dahl 1997). Note that the market model also explains the American Civil War as a clash of paradigms: the South had not a market but a hierarchical slave material infrastructure and superstructure.

7   While this pattern became insignificant with control added for GDP per capita, the market model predicts that low GDP per capita will cause communalism (collectivism), and thus both GDP per capita and communalism should not be in the same equation as independent variables.

References

Abu-Lughod, Janet L. (1989) *Before European Hegemony: The World System A.D. 1250–1350*, New York, Oxford University Press.

Babst, Dean V. (1964) "Elected Governments: A Force for Peace", *The Wisconsin Sociologist*, vol. 3, pp. 9–14.

Bennett, Scott D. (1997) "Testing Alternative Models of Alliance Duration, 1816–1984", *American Journal of Political Science*, vol. 41, pp. 846–79.

Bierbrauar, Gunter (1994) "Toward an Understanding of Legal Culture: Variations in Individualism and Collectivism between Kurds, Lebanese, and Germans", *Law & Society Review*, vol. 28, pp. 243–64.

Booth, John A., and Richard, Patricia Bayer (1998) "Civil Society, Political Capital, and Democratization in Central America", *Journal of Politics*, vol. 60, pp. 780–800.

Braudel, Fernand (1979) *Afterthoughts on Material Civilization and Capitalism*, Baltimore, Johns Hopkins University Press.

Bremer, Stuart A. (1992) "Dangerous Dyads: Conditions Affecting the Likelihood of Inter-state War, 1816–1965", *Journal of Conflict Resolution*, vol. 36, pp. 309–41.

Bueno de Mesquita, Bruce, Morrow, James D.,. Siverson, Randolph M. and Smith, Alastair (1999) "An Institutional Explanation of the Democratic Peace", *American Political Science Review*, vol. 93, pp. 791–807.

Burkhart, Ross E. and Lewis-Beck, Michael S. (1994) "Comparative Democracy: The Economic Development Thesis", *American Political Science Review*, vol. 88, pp. 111–31.

Cameron, Rondo (1997) *A Concise Economic History of the World: From Paleolithic Times to the Present*, 3rd edition, New York, Oxford University Press.

Clark, Ann Marie, Friedman, Elisabeth J. and Hochstetler, Kathryn (1998) "The Sovereign Limits of Global Civil Society", *World Politics*, vol. 51, pp. 1–35.

Coleman, James S. (1988) "Social Capital in the Creation of Human Capital", *American Journal of Sociology*, vol. 94 (supplement), pp. S95–S120.

Dahl, Robert A. (1997) "Development and Democratic Culture", in Larry Diamond, Marc F. Plattner, Yun-han chu, and Hung-mao Tien (eds), *Consolidating the Third Wave of Democracies, Themes and Perspectives*, Baltimore, Johns Hopkins University Press.

Diamandouros, P. Nikiforos (1997) "Southern Europe: A Third Wave Success Story", in Larry Diamond, Marc F. Plattner, Yun-han chu, and Hung-mao Tien (eds), *Consolidating the Third Wave of Democracies, Themes and Perspectives*, Baltimore, MD, Johns Hopkins University Press.

Dixon, William J. (1993) "Democracy and the Management of International Conflict", *Journal of Conflict Resolution*, vol. 37, pp. 42–68.

—— (1994) "Democracy and the Peaceful Settlement of International Conflict", *American Political Science Review*, vol. 88, pp. 1–17.

Durkheim, Emile ([1893] 1984) *The Division of Labour in Society*, Basingstoke, Macmillan.

Eichengreen, Barry (1996) "The Tyranny of the Financial Markets", *Current History*, vol. 96, pp. 377–82.

Fergusson, Brian (1995) *Yanomami Warfare: A Political History*, Santa Fe, NM, School of American Research Press.

Finley, Moses I. (1985) *The Ancient Economy*, 2nd edition, London, Penguin Books.

Fukuyama, Francis (1995) "The Primacy of Culture", *Journal of Democracy*, vol. 6, pp. 7–14.

Gaubatz, Kurt Taylor (1996) "Democratic States and Commitment in International Relations", *International Organization*, vol. 50, pp. 109–39.

Gibson, James L. and Gouws, Amanda (2000) "Social Identities and Political Intolerance: Linkages Within the South African Mass Public", *American Journal of Political Science*, vol. 44, pp. 272–86.

Gilpin, Robert (1981) *War and Change in World Politics*, Cambridge, Cambridge University Press.

Gleditsch, Nils Petter, and Hegre, Havard (1997) "Peace and Democracy: Three Levels of Analysis", *Journal of Conflict Resolution*, vol. 41, pp. 283–310.

Harris, Marvin (1968) *The Rise of Anthropological Theory*, New York, Thomas Y. Crowel.

—— (1979) *Cultural Materialism: The Struggle for a Science of Culture*, New York, Random House.

Hinckley, Ronald H. (1992) *Peoples, Polls, and Policymakers: American Public Opinion and National Security*, New York, Lexington.

Hinkle, Steve and Brown, Rupert (1990) "Intergroup Comparisons and Social Identity: Some Links and Lacunae", in Dominic Abrams and Michael A. Hogg (eds), *Social Identity Theory: Constructive and Critical Advances*, New York, Springer-Verlag.

Inkeles, Alex and Diamond, Larry (1980) "Personal Qualities as a Reflection of Level of National Development", in Frank M. Andrews and Alexander Szalai (eds), *The Quality of Life: Comparative Studies*, London, Sage.

Jackson, William A. (1996) "Cultural Materialism and Institutional Economics," *Review of Social Economy*, vol. 54, pp. 221–4.

Johnson, Allan (1995) "Explanation and Ground Truth: The Place of 'Cultural Materialsm' in Scientific Anthropology", in Martin F. Murphy and Maxine L. Margolis (eds), *Science, Materialism, and the Study of Culture*, Gainsville, FL, University Press of Florida.

Kant, Immanuel (1982 [1795]) *Perpetual Peace*, trans. and ed. Lewis White Beck, New York, Bobbs-Merrill.

Knopf, Jeffrey W (1998) "How Rational is the 'Rational Public'? Evidence From U.S. Public Opinion on Military Spending", *Journal of Conflict Resolution*, vol. 42, pp. 544–71.

Kowert, Paul and Legro, Jeffrey (1996) "Norms, Identity, and Their Limits: A Theoretical Reprise", in Peter Katzenstein (ed.), *The Culture of National Security*, New York, Columbia University Press.

Lipset, Seymour Martin, Seong, Kyoung-Ryung and Torres, John Charles (1993) "A Comparative Analysis of the Social Requisites of Democracy", *International Social Science Journal*, vol. 45, pp. 155–75.

Lipset, Seymour Martin (1959) "Some Social Requisites of Democracy: Economic Development and Political Legitimacy", *American Political Science Review*, vol. 53, pp. 69–105.

Maoz, Zeev and Russett, Bruce (1992) "Alliance, Contiguity, Wealth, and Political Stability: Is the Lack of Conflict Among Democracies a Statistical Artifact?", *International Interactions*, vol. 17, pp. 245–67.

—— (1993) "Normative and Structural Causes of Democratic Peace, 1946–1986", *American Political Science Review*, vol. 87, pp. 624–38.

Martines, Lauro (1979) *Power and Imagination: City–States in Renaissance Italy*, New York, Vintage Books.

Marx, Karl (1952[1867]) *Capital*, Founders' edition, Chicago, Encyclopaedia Britannica.

Mazrui, Ali A. (1990) *Cultural Forces in World Politics*, Portsmouth, NH, Heinemann Educational Books Inc.

Mousseau, Michael (1998) "Democracy and Compromise in Militarized Inter-state Conflicts, 1816–1992", *Journal of Conflict Resolution*, vol. 42, pp. 210–30.

Mousseau, Michael (2000) "Market Prosperity, Democratic Consolidation, and Democratic Peace", *Journal of Conflict Resolution*, vol. 44, pp. 472–507.

Murphy, Martin F. and Margolis, Maxine L. (1995) "An Introduction to Cultural Materialism", *Science, Materialism, and the Study of Culture*, Gainesville, FL, University Press of Florida.

Oniş, Ziya and Turëm, Umut (2001) "Entrepreneurs, Democracy and Citizenship in Turkey", paper presented at the 2nd Annual Social and Political Research Meeting, Florence, 21–5 March.

Page, Benjamin I. and Shapiro. Robert Y. (1992) *The Rational Public: Fifty Years of Trends in Americans' Policy Preferences*, Chicago, University of Chicago Press.

Polanyi, Karl ([1944] 1957) *The Great Transformation: The Political and Economic Origins of Our Time*, Boston, Beacon Press.

Przeworski, Adam and Limongi, Fernando (1997) "Modernization: Theories and Facts", *World Politics*, vol. 49, pp. 155–83.

Putnam, Robert D. (1993) *Making Democracy Work: Civic Traditions in Modern Italy*, Princeton, NJ, Princeton University Press.

Raymond, Gregory A. (1994) "Democracies, Disputes, and Third-Party Intermediaries", *Journal of Conflict Resolution*, vol. 38, pp. 24–42.

Rostow, Walt W. (1960) *The Stages of Economic Growth*, London, Cambridge University Press.

Russett, Bruce, Oneal, John R. and Davis, David R. (1998) "The Third Leg of the Kantian Tripod: International Organizations and Militarized Disputes, 1950–85", *International Organization*, vol. 52, pp. 441–8.

Schmitter, Philippe C. (1996) "The Influence of the International Context upon the Choice of National Institutions and Policies in Neo-Democracies", in Laurence Whitehead (ed.) *The International Dimensions of Democratization: Europe and the Americas*, Oxford, Oxford University Press.

Simon, Michael W. and Gartzke, Eric (1996) "Political System Similarity and the Choice of Allies: Do Democracies Flock Together or Do Opposites Attract?", *Journal of Conflict Resolution*, vol. 40, pp. 617–35.

Siverson, Randolph M. and Emmons, Juliann (1991) "Birds of a Feather", *Journal of Conflict Resolution*, vol. 35, pp. 285–306.

Spybey, Tony (1996) *Globalization and World Society*, Cambridge, Polity Press.

Strange, Susan (1996) "The Erosion of the State", *Current History*, vol. 96, pp. 365–9.

Summers, Robert and Heston, Alan (1991) "The Penn World Table (Mark 5): An Expanded Set of International Comparisons, 1950–1988", *Quarterly Journal Of Economics*, vol. 106, pp. 327–68.

Tandy, David W and. Neale, Walter C (1994) "Karl Polanyi's Distinctive Approach to Social Analysis and the Case of Ancient Greece: Ideas, Criticisms, Consequences", in Colin A.M. Duncan and David W. Tandy (eds), *From Political Economy to Anthropology: Situating Economic Life in Past Societies*, London, Black Rose Books Ltd.

Tilly, Charles (1992) *Coercion, Capital, and European States, AD 990–1990*, Oxford, Blackwell.

Thompson, William R. and Tucker, Richard M. (1997) "A Tale of Two Democratic Peace Critiques", *Journal of Conflict Resolution*, vol. 41, pp. 428–54.

Wallerstein, Immanuel (1979) *The Capitalist World Economy*, New York, Cambridge University Press.

Watson, Adam (1992) *The Evolution of International Society: A Comparative Historical Analysis*, London and New York, Routledge.

Weber, Max (1978) *Economy and Society: An Outline of Interpretive Sociology*, ed. by Guenther Roth and Claus Wittich, trans. by Ephraim Fischoff, Berkeley, CA, University of California Press.

Williamson, Jeffrey G. (1996) "Globalization, Convergence, and History", *Journal of Economic History*, vol. 56, pp. 277–306.

6 European civilization

Properties and challenges

Edgar Morin

From Europa to Europe

What was called Europe at the outset is not Europe at all. The Greeks applied the name to the unfamiliar continent north of their country in the seventh century BC, raising questions even then. Herodotus wondered that his compatriots gave the region the name of the young woman, daughter of the Phoenician king, whom Zeus had abducted to Crete. The Greeks, of course, turned their back on the continent and knew only the Mediterranean, which became the thriving center of trade and traffic in the Roman Empire. While Rome conquered maritime Spain, Portugal, Gaul and England, it collided vainly at the center of the continent with indomitable Germania.

Europe was a shapeless northern area beyond the known world of Antiquity. Although populated since ancient prehistoric times, the region had not yet entered history, at a time when the Roman Empire was already starting to decline. Europe would take part in the jumble of barbarian invasions that poured from east to west and from north to south, the hordes chasing one another, crowding together, fighting, overlapping, mixing, and finally causing the West Roman Empire to disintegrate (AD 476). A chaos of barbaric kingdoms would hold power from the fifth to the seventh centuries, the Eastern Empire aside, forming a large patchwork of populations, some arising from the tuff of prehistory, some Latinate, others Germanic, and some finally Asian.

It is from these peoples that a mosaic of innumerable ethnic groups, set in extraordinarily disparate territories, would gradually gel and diversify. Thus, the structure of Europe consisted from the start of an ethnic miscellany on which the centuries wove the shapes and figures of the continent's history; an ethnic miscellany that survives, and is even finding new life, despite the asphyxiating pressure of the modern states.

One cannot therefore define historical Europe by its geographic borders. And one cannot define geographical Europe by stable and closed historical borders. This, however, does not imply Europe's dilution in its environment. It means that Europe, like all important notions, is not defined by its borders, which are vague and unsettled, but rather through what organizes it and is responsible for its originality.

Europe not only lacks real borders, it also lacks internal geographic unity. One might then say that its originality lies in its very lack of unity: the inland part of the peninsula offers a great variety of landscapes, due jointly to the broken relief, the multifarious interlocking of land and sea, as well as to the diversity of climate. Nothing destined Europe to become a historical entity. Yet, it became one. In what way? When? How?

Europe originated from no initial founding principle. The Greek principle and the Latin principle arose from its periphery and antedate Europe; the Christian principle came from Asia and blossomed in Europe only at the end of its first millennium. All these principles would have to be agitated, shaken, mixed in the confusion of the invading and the invaded, of latinized, germanicized, and slavicized peoples, before associating or opposing one another. If one looks for Europe's essence, one discovers only an evanescent and antiseptic "European spirit". If one points to what seems an authentic feature, one obscures an opposite and no less European one. Thus, if Europe is law, it is also might; if it is democracy, it is also oppression; if it is spirituality, it is also materiality; if it is measure, it is also hubris, or excessiveness; if it is reason, it is also myth, persisting even within the idea of reason.

Europe is an uncertain notion, born of confusion, with vague borders, a shifting geometry, and subject to slippage, breaks and metamorphoses. What is therefore needed is to probe the idea of Europe precisely where it is uncertain, blurred, and contradictory so as to reveal its complex identity.

Europe's barbaric period was also the period when it became Christian. The missionizing of the barbarians marked its first success with the conversion of Clovis (496) and would spread through the interior of the continent to reach its full expansion in the seventh century. At that point, a European identity seems to emerge along with a Christian identity. However, Christianity is neither originally nor distinctively European. This religion, which came from Judaea, first spread throughout Asia Minor, then to both sides of the Mediterranean; only much later would it permeate Europe. It was the Arab conquest that, in Islamicizing the Near East and North Africa, would limit, partition, and hem in Christianity in Europe for centuries. We can thus say that in a first instance Islam *made* Europe by its containment of Christianity (seventh century), and that in a second instance Europe *made itself* against Islam by turning back Islam's might at Poitiers (732).

The concept of Europe enjoyed a fleeting boost in the immediate aftermath of Poitiers. Thirty years after the battle, Isidore the younger, a Spaniard, would write: "Leaving their houses in the morning, the Europeans could see the neatly aligned tents of the Arabs." And when Charlemagne was consecrated emperor in 800, he was called the venerable chief of Europe, and the "father of Europe". But after his death, the idea of Christianity absorbed the idea of Europe, and the factions within Christianity corroded it: the term seems to have disappeared until the fourteenth century.

Yet, Islam would goad and haunt Europe. The Islamic conquest, by driving Christianity out of Asia Minor and North Africa, would Europeanize

Christianity. And Islam's retreat, from Poitiers to the fall of Granada, permanently Christianized Europe. Furthermore, the establishment of Islam on the southern shore of the Mediterranean would isolate and turn Europe in on itself. A millennial path of communication for the world of Antiquity, the Mediterranean became for a decisive time the "liquid barrier" which, as Henri Pirenne (1958) emphasized perhaps excessively, would turn Europe inward on its continental mass. Though the short-term effect of being cut off at the Mediterranean was disastrous, even asphyxiating for the European economy, in the long term it allowed northwestern Europe to awaken and stimulated continental Europe to exchange and commerce. This removal from sea to land recalls the ocean's retreat during the Mesozoic, when fish were left stranded on the shores, at first gasping for air, but then, through the transformation of their breathing systems, adapting to terrestrial life. Likewise the European economy, formerly aquatic, became amphibious. An Arabic-Berber Spain had sprung up. It offered and even imposed on Catholic Spain a religious plurality that included Muslims, Jews and Christians. Was a multi-religious Europe possible? The Catholic kings, who were masters of all Spain after the fall of Granada (1492), would immediately expel unconverted Muslims and Jews from the country, for a long time imposing religious monolithism on Europe. Only the Jews would survive this, here and there, in constantly menaced small ghettos. Triumphant Christianity turned in arrogantly on itself, hounding out and eradicating all doubt and heresy. The Christian monopoly over belief and thought would hold sway in medieval Europe.

The Christian reconquest stopped at Gibraltar and did not extend beyond Europe. The crusades (1095–1270) had already failed in their attempt to reinstate Christianity in its land of origin. The crusaders were perceived – by themselves and also by the Byzantines and Muslims – as Franks, not Europeans. In actuality, the crusades do not represent Europe's first attempt at external colonization, but Christianity's refusal to be imprisoned within Europe, so far from its native soil. Then Europe had to abandon Byzantium and the Balkans to the Turkish conquest (fifteenth century). At that very moment, the onset of the Modern Era would disrupt the identity between Europe and Christianity, with the Americas opening to Christianity and Europe opening to secular thought. Thus only medieval Europe can be identified with Christianity.

There was of course extensive circulation at the capillary level between the Islamic world and Christian Europe, with the latter benefiting from the strong economic and cultural influence of the Islamic civilizations in the first flush of their greatness (ninth to eleventh centuries) (Lombard 1971).[1] Even during the crusades, clandestine cultural influences were at work, proceeding from the highly civilized Arabs to the rough-hewn Frankish knights. For several centuries, via Islamic Spain, medieval thought was irrigated by translations from the Greek and the works of Arab mathematicians, indispensable inputs to the flourishing of the modern era. But the legacy of this period was a closure of minds on either side between Europe and the Islamic world, reactivated in the fifteenth and sixteenth century as a fear of the Turks. In contemporary times, secularized

Europe and the Islamic world, building on the old closure, once more shut themselves off to each other, with Islam finding new energy in resisting the
Europeanization of its mores and the corruption of its Muslim identity.

Modern Europe shaped itself by losing the Old World (fall of Byzantium,
1453), by discovering the New World (1492), and by changing world views
(Copernicus, 1473–1543). Two centuries later, Europe would change the world.

European navigators from Henry the Navigator to Vasco da Gama and
Magellan reconnoitered the coasts of Africa and discovered the road to India via
the Cape of Good Hope (1498); the conquerors then explored and colonized
North and South America. The earth was truly round and the planetary era had
begun. Modern Europe appeared by metamorphosis, like a winged insect
emerging from its chrysalis and taking flight out into the world. What had been
gestating at the end of the Middle Ages took on new form and strength. There
now appeared monarchical states, the urban middle classes, and mercantile,
financial, and even industrial capitalism. Medieval Europe already harbored
breaks and ruptures within itself. Modern Europe caused Christianity to burst
and was in turn shaped in and through this bursting.

There was the bursting of the Reformation, which spread through Germany,
England, Switzerland, the United Provinces, and Scandinavia; whereas Spain,
Italy, Portugal, part of France, Bavaria, and Austria remained Catholic. There
was the gushing of speeches, ideas, and news in the swarm of printed pages
spewed in all directions by Gutenberg's invention (1440). There was the bursting
of the Renaissance, from the contact of Faith and Reason, of Religion and
Humanism. Thereafter, Judeo-Christiano-Latino-Greek culture ceased to form a
symbiotic unit, securely wrapped in a cocoon of theology: each of its
constituents became not just complementary but at odds with all the others.
There was the bursting on the economic, social, and cultural levels: the development of bourgeois civilization erected a new type of society by undermining the
archaic, rural, feudal, religious, customary, and communitarian foundations of
the old society. There was finally the bursting of Europe into national states,
each ruling over its constituent ethnic groups, the principal ones being Spain,
England, France, Austria, Sweden, and, before long, Russia. Thus a polycentric
Europe came into being, marked by the war of one against all.

These multiple burstings occurred in reaction to the pressure of anarchic
processes and in turn favored their growth. The mushrooming of cities, the
proliferation of trade, commercial and capitalist competition, and the development of sovereign states arose within and through the struggle of one against all.
Everything seems to have been chaos and conflict in the birth of the Modern
Era: the warring of the classes, the warring of nations, the warring of religions,
the warring of ideas. Antagonisms erupted everywhere, with their attendant
instability and reversals. War became the inevitable concomitant of the
nation–state. Economic crises swept Europe. The gold pouring in from America
brought prosperity, bankruptcy and delirium.

Thus modern Europe is the product of a metamorphosis, and it has
continued to live by metamorphoses: from a Europe of states to a Europe of

nation–states; from a balance-of-powers Europe to a Europe of chaos and violence; from a trading Europe to an industrial Europe; from an apogean Europe to an abyssal Europe; from a Europe mistress of all the world to a province Europe under guardianship. Thus, Europe's identity is to be defined not despite its metamorphoses, but *in* its metamorphoses. This metamorphic identity subsists in the accelerating change that, in a unique and prodigious way, characterizes European history from the fifteenth to the twentieth century, a time Europe experienced as a devastating cyclone. Modern Europe has never lived except in motion. Its being has never been other than as accelerated change.

Since the fifteenth century, Europe has been at the very center of history's whirlwind, a locus of intense political, military, economic, civilizational, and cultural activity. From that time on, one referred to "peace in Europe" or "war in Europe". With the spread of court etiquette, bourgeois morality, and eventually modern comfort and technological advances, there was more and more reference to "European civilization". As the rest of the world was better explored, the sense of belonging to Europe grew stronger. This sense of belonging is critically visible in the comparisons by eighteenth century philosophers between European brutality and depravity and the innocence of the Noble Savage or the wisdom of the Chinese mandarin. The Romantics may have looked nostalgically to the organic communities of the Middle Ages and of early Christianity, but in the nineteenth century, the sense of belonging to Europe was felt with greater and greater satisfaction. Toward 1800, the term "Europeanism" appears, referring to a taste for things that were particularly European. Then, toward 1830, came the verb "to Europeanize", voicing Europe's understanding that it brought the highest civilization to the rest of the world.

Europe's superiority complex over all other civilizations then arrogantly asserted itself. It is not only non-European civilizations that appeared backward, but non-European races were considered inferior as well. At the end of the nineteenth century, during its last spasms of colonization and its final moments of world hegemony, Europe believed it had been given the mission of bringing true civilization to the savages, barbarians, and primitive peoples of the world. And Europe entertained the Kiplingesque myth of the white man's superiority, the best of the best of whom was the tall blond Aryan. This racism, at first primarily Anglo-Saxon but later Germanic, dissolved all European solidarity at one stroke, as illustrated by the aggravated form nationalism then took and the unbridled rivalry that sprang up over colonies, markets, raw goods, and *Lebensraum*.

In contrast to the nationalism of European countries, a nationalism whose attendant belligerence was becoming increasingly clear, the dream of a United States of Europe – spectrally prefigured in the utopias of the seventeenth century (William Penn, the abbé de Saint-Pierre) and in Kant's "project for permanent peace" – now took on substance as a system of ideas in which were commingled the emancipation of nationalities, republican democracy, and a European federation. Victor Hugo prophesied in grandiose terms the advent of a United States of Europe, itself only a herald of the forthcoming reconciliation of humankind. Europeanism, federalism, cosmopolitanism, and internationalism would further weave this dream into the fabric of the late nineteenth century.[2]

At the beginning of the twentieth century, socialist internationalism and European fraternity even seemed sufficiently powerful to prevent a Franco-German war. But, in fact, the great French and German socialist parties joined their countries' sacred patriotic union during the summer of 1914. Lenin concluded in 1915 that the federation of Europe could never occur without a revolution. After 1918, the idea of a United States of Europe and the Bolshevik idea of internationalism went in different and opposing directions. All hope of confederating Europe went up in smoke in 1933 with Hitler's accession to power. The Second World War was preceded and accompanied by terrible confusion, resulting from the clash between an originally internationalist but now nationalist Soviet communism and Nazism, ever racist and pan-Germanic, but claiming after 1940 the mission of unifying Europe. In 1945, over Germany's corpse, two half-Europes saw the light of day.

Europe was a notion with vague territorial boundaries and changing historical borders. Today it is the boundaries of civilizations that are vague, since European civilization has flooded and continues to flood the rest of the world. Even when the cultures and religions of Asia or Africa try to resist Europe and combat its onslaught, they nonetheless borrow its formula for the nation–state and develop sciences, technology, and arms originating from Europe. In the end, it was not just the original fruits of the Whirlwind that spread throughout the world: now the Whirlwind itself has become planetary. Of course Europe is still caught and shaken in it but its center has moved elsewhere, where it has acquired a new scale and a new nature.

What is left of Europe? What remains of this multinuclear, polycentric, geohistorical, civilizational, and cultural complex which existed only through conflicts and communications, through resistance to political and cultural hegemony? There remains the very rich diversity of its transnational cultures (Germanic, Latin, Slavic) and of its national cultures, each marked by an original language. There also remains an extraordinary variety of micro-cultures, a fruit of the micro-ethnic texture of Europe after the last invasions – riches that survive because the project of national unity was never completed, even in such very ancient nations as France and England.

In comparison to the immense cultural spaces of the Asian or American world, Europe now appears like a system of small cultural compartments that are local, regional, provincial, and national in nature. True, taking the United States as an example, one cannot say that California is the same as New England, nor that Georgia is the same as Wisconsin, but in spite of the enormous geographic distances between them they share more common cultural substance than Brittany and Provence, than Flanders and Euzkadi, and of course than Portugal and Austria, than Italy and Sweden.

Are only diversity and plurality European? Might there not also be a foundation, a unity, a principle of order and organization that correspond to our needs of today? And yet the foundation of Europe is its loss of foundations (the

Empire, the Mediterranean, Christianity); Europe's order is the disorder of a tumultuous building site. Europe has never been itself except in self-organizing anarchy and has never existed as an organization superior to its constituents. Hence the staggering problem we now face, which is to search in the present and not in the past for Europe's organizing principle. But to do so we may draw on the historical principle that links Europe's identity to change and metamorphosis. And it would just be the vital necessity of rescuing its identity that calls Europe to a new metamorphosis.

The cultural whirlwind

European culture is rightly considered to be Judeo-Christiano-Greco-Latin. Jewish, Christian, Greek, and Latin sources appear to have come together to form a harmonious synthesis, which is at once the specific substrate of Europe and its common denominator. It is starting from this base that Europe has produced an original civilization, marked by spirituality, humanism, rationality, and democracy – virtues and values, that is, superior to those of any other civilization.

Such is the myth Europe entertains about itself. If the myth contains an indisputable truth, it is a mutilated truth, false by its very mutilation, amputated from an opposite and inseparable truth. Its nature is to color with euphoria and self-satisfaction a delusive truth. As Jean-Baptiste Duroselle very aptly wrote:

> When someone tells me that Europe is the land of the right and true, I think of all that is arbitrary; that it is the land of human dignity I think of racism; that it is the land of reason I think of the Romantic reverie. And I find justice in Pennsylvania, human dignity among Arab nationalists, reason everywhere in the universe, if it is true, as Descartes has said, that common sense is the most evenly divided thing in the world.
>
> (Duroselle 1965: 318)

I spoke of *culture* in invoking the Judeo-Christiano-Greco-Latin substrate and I spoke of *civilization* in invoking humanism, rationality, science, and freedom. These two terms, which often overlap in French, are clearly distinguished in German thought, where culture refers to what is singular and specific in a society, whereas civilization applies to what can be acquired and transmitted from one society to another. Culture, in the sense that it defines a genus, is generic, whereas civilization is generalizable; culture develops by returning to its roots and being loyal to its singular principles, civilization by accumulating what it has acquired, that is, by progressing.

I am forced here to straddle the two concepts. Thus, I will maintain the distinction between European culture, singular in its Judeo-Christiano-Greco-Latin texture and European civilization, whose humanism, science, and technology have spread outside Europe and become planted in utterly different cultural contexts. But – and here a complexity – humanism, rationalism, and science were, in their beginnings and early development, phenomena specific to European culture, only later becoming transmissible and universalizable phenomena of civilization, capable of being integrated by outside cultures, which the influence of the new civilization would in turn modify. Culture and civilization can, therefore, according to the situation, join and overlap to permute.

These two terms are typical products of European civilization/culture. The words came into use at the end of the eighteenth century, at first in the singular: civilization stands in opposition mainly to barbarism, while culture stands in opposition to nature. Culture and civilization define two polarities: the singularity, subjectivity, and individuality of the first contrast with the transmissibility, objectivity and universality of the second. The terms would be used in the plural during the second half of the nineteenth century, when cultures and civilizations other than our own came to be recognized. From the nineteenth to the beginning of the twentieth century, German thought put a premium on the term *culture*, which expresses the specific genius of a people, and French thought put a premium on the term *civilization*, a benefit that can be spread to all peoples because it derives from the universality of reason. Aware of the complex relations between these two terms, and because of the very nature of my proposals, I will not dwell on their contrasting aspects or, more particularly, on the demarcation between them. No terminological rigor is possible where no clear boundaries exist, or worse, where there is a likelihood of permutation between culture and civilization. So I will allow my vocabulary to float in these hazy zones and, according to the subconscious connotative pressures guiding my pen, will use now one and now the other term for the productions/products of European thought such as Humanism, Reason, and Science. However, I will retain the term *culture* for what relates specifically to ethnic groups, provinces and nations. This will help us understand at the end of the day that if the culture of Europe, in spreading throughout the world, has become Civilization, European cultures are today threatened by the very civilization that came from Europe (Delmas 1980).

Finally, I must return to the meaning of the term *dialogic*, essential for grasping the very identity of European culture, which both produces and is the product of the complementarity, competition, and antithesis between different ideas, theories, conceptions, and visions of the world. The state of conflict is inadequately expressed by the term *dialogue*. The term *dialectic* is inadequate to express the strong persistence of dualistic opposition within unity. The term *dialogic* is therefore essential to my theme but its constant repetition may lull the reader into insensibility rather than make him aware of what constitutes the originality of European culture.

While Western Europe in the Middle Ages was still divided into fiefdoms and was starting to be divided into states, Christianity nonetheless represented a cultural sphere in which trans-European artistic currents circulated: the Romanesque, for instance (eleventh century), and the Gothic (thirteenth century). Thus, as early as the eleventh century Europe nurtured an intense exchange of ideas.

Scholars communicated in Latin, the only recognized cultural language, which would remain in use in philosophy until the fifteenth century. Great centers of learning sprang to life in the eleventh century: the universities. First to be created was Bologna University, followed by other great centers of memory, of knowledge, of thought, and of debate in Valencia (1209), Oxford (1214), Paris (1215), Krakow (1347), Budapest (1383), Uppsala (1477), in short just about everywhere (Naples, Padua, Cambridge, Prague, Heidelberg, Aberdeen, etc.). This was medieval Christianity's original contribution to culture (though the university was host to excommunications and condemnations and, as early as the seventh century, thought, science, and research were more often pursued outside the University).

Thus was formed a polycentric cultural Europe that progressively reached the north and center of the continent. In the Renaissance, communications, exchanges, and debates multiplied and intensified, extending progressively beyond the theological sphere; and the development of national languages, some of which – French, English, Spanish – had also become cultural languages, did not curtail the flow of communication. French became the language of ideas from the eighteenth century to the beginning of the nineteenth; bilingualism and the mastering of several languages developed among the educated; translations multiplied (thus the *Tractatus Theologico-politicus* of Spinoza (1670) was translated into English and French less than ten years after its publication).

The thinkers of the Middle Ages peregrinated from monastery to university. Duns Scotus taught at Oxford, then at the University of Paris, and died in Cologne. The humanists of the Renaissance led cosmopolitan lives: Erasmus lived variously in the Netherlands, France, England, and Basle, with sojourns in Turin, Florence, Venice, and Rome. In the seventeenth century, Descartes worked in France and in Holland, then died in Sweden. The eighteenth century witnessed the formation of a quasi-international cadre of philosophers who were assured of addressing all humankind by addressing all Europeankind. Increasingly rich and diverse, Europe offered an undivided space for philosophy, science, political science, letters, poetry, novels, and music. The shared classical heritage was no longer restricted to the authors of Antiquity but also included the European heritage of Cervantes, Montaigne, Shakespeare, Molière, Galileo, Bacon, Descartes, Spinoza, and Leibniz.

From the Renaissance on, great waves of thought formed and traveled across Europe. First came the wave of the Humanist Renaissance, then that of the New Testament Renaissance. Science proliferated in the fifteenth century. The Rationalism of the Enlightenment radiated across Europe from Paris in the eighteenth century, just as Romanticism would shortly thereafter spread from Jena and Berlin. In the course of this history certain cities would for a time become privileged cauldrons of culture: Florence, Madrid, Amsterdam, Paris, and Vienna. European culture thus continued to cross and transcend individual nations, even though nationalist tendencies started to increase. Yet, European culture did not ignore the individual nations. National histories unfolded in the very midst of the European history of philosophy, literature, and art; there was osmosis between them, but each had its dominating characteristics or its spheres of excellence. Thus the Anglo-Saxon philosophical tradition has tended toward empiricism, the French toward rationalism, the German toward idealism, but each country admits powerful cross-currents, plural views, deviancies. Thus Russia has never left off harboring an inner dialogic between despotism and populism, between Slavophilism and Occidentalism; the ferment of the West has actively intervened in this dialogic even as the riches of the Slavic contribution have marked and impregnated Western European culture, notably with the works of Pushkin, Gogol, Tolstoy, Dostoyevsky, and Chekhov.

Europe therefore remained in all aspects a polycentric cultural reality. Those of us who attended secondary school, or who had an appetite for reading, for art, or for music have received or given ourselves, often without noticing it, an exposure to European culture. Calderon, Shakespeare, Molière, Dante, Erasmus, Cervantes, Montaigne, Pascal, Diderot, Rousseau, Goethe, Marx, Nietzsche, Kafka, Freud, Berdyayev, Croce, Gasset, Shelly, Büchner, Holderlin, Rimbaud, T.S. Eliot, Dickens, Tolstoy, Dostoyevsky, Mozart, Beethoven, Moussorgsky, Mahler, and Berg, among others, are at the heart of our identity.

During the Middle Ages, Christianity packed away the Judaic, Greek and Latin contents it had absorbed, but in the eleventh century it removed them from the deep-freeze: Christian thought took nourishment from Aristotelian ideas (via translations of Avicenna and Averroes), it returned to the early texts and consulted Roman law (thirteenth century). Henceforth, the New Testament, Greek, and Roman messages would ferment under the ecclesiastic cope, which contained them and prevented any outburst.

Any return to religious sources that pitted the Bible and the New Testament against the doctrines of the Catholic Church was denounced as heresy, excommunicated, reprehended, and crushed in the Middle Ages. However, within Christian thought a dialogue was broached between reason and faith. Reason does not oppose faith, it wants to be complementary, even necessary, to faith. In this way, Saint Anselm of Canterbury (1033–1109) sought to show that reason can understand and interpret the objects of Revelation and render God's existence understandable. Saint Albert the Great (1193–1308) asserted that nature, the work of God, is rational (*Natura est ratio*). Saint Thomas Aquinas (1228–1274) would work out a synthesis between faith and reason. Conversely, Duns Scotus (1265–1308) would insist on the limits of reason, which keep it from apprehending the Divine Providence and the Trinity on its own. Correlatively, the dispute over universals, constantly rekindled from the eleventh to the thirteenth century, concerned the possibilities and limits of the instruments of rational thought, notably classes and general concepts, for grasping reality. A self-critical rationality came into being with nominalism, notably that of William of Occam (1300–1344), which granted reality only to individual entities.

The Renaissance would draw out into the open what had previously been virtual conflicts between Christian, Judaic, Greek and Roman cultural contributions. A first, dissociation would arise strikingly between the message of the

Gospel, itself umbilically linked to the Old Testament, and Catholic dogma. A return to the sacred texts revitalized the messages of Paul and Jesus on the primacy of faith, awakened the majesty of the God of Abraham, and cast doubt on the Catholic deification of the Virgin. Medieval Catholicism had been able to inhibit and crush as heresy any return to evangelical roots. But the reactivation of New Testament and Judaic sources became irresistible in the fifteenth century, and, abetted by papal exactions, the Reformation broke out in Germany (1517), propagating in waves under a variety of forms throughout Europe. This precipitated the Wars of Religion, in turn provoking religious wars between Europe's states until a *modus vivendi* was much later reached – undermined in France by the Revocation of the Edict of Nantes (1685).

The Reformation, itself having become plural, introduced religious pluralism into Western Christianity. Thus did conflicts and rivalries take hold between variants of the same faith, definitively shattering the religious unity that marked the Christianity of the crusades and the cathedrals. Any dialogue between the Churches, which were now closed to each other, passed underground. The Reformation had a retroactive effect on the Roman Catholic Church, where a reformation occurred in the very midst of the Counter-reformation, and where faith to some extent took the ascendant over works. The real dialogic, though, would arise not within faith, but between faith and reason, belief and doubt, and finally between the new forms of philosophical and scientific thought. It is from the fifteenth century on, conjointly with the flowering of the Reformation, that Christian authority and Greek authority would begin to conflict and that the dialogue of reason and faith would become dialogical.

Just as modern Europe was born politically through ruptures and conflicts, it was born culturally through the outbreak of controversy between the Judaic, Christian, Greek and Latin authorities. The Renaissance, which emerged in the towns or principalities of Italy and the Netherlands before gaining all of Europe, was to open a dialogical process that would henceforth continue uninterruptedly, and which comprised mutual borrowings and incorporations, without bringing any end to the opposition of Greek, Roman, Judaic, and Christian cultural components. Europe's originality thus resides not only in its active complementarity, but also in the permanent conflict between its Hellenic heritage, its Roman heritage, and Judeo-Christian heritage. Starting with the Renaissance, the cultural dialogic would diversify and intensify in numerous different but interacting dialogics between faith, reason, doubt, and empiricism.

Within and through the Renaissance, therefore, European culture emerged as a permanent dialogic hotbed, inciting an uninterrupted outpouring of ideas, theories, aspirations, dreams, and forms that would intermingle as in a whirlwind. This cultural whirlwind arose from the very conditions that gave rise simultaneously to the political, social, and economic whirlwind that both carried off and made Europe. The cultural whirlwind is distinct from the historical whirlwind, though always interacting with it. And like the historical whirlwind, but without necessarily coinciding with it, its center moved constantly, flitting from Florence to Amsterdam, London, Paris, Jena, Berlin, Vienna. It was this whirlwind that swept Europe along culturally and shaped it. Just as the political, social, and economic history of Europe accelerated, and by this very acceleration produced what is original about Europe in contrast to other cultures, so the cultural history of Europe accelerated its transformation, until that transformation itself became the foundation, the key, the mystery, the fragility, the virtue, and perhaps the vice of Europe's culture.

Of humanity reconciled, and happiness on Earth

Humanism is an original and typical creation of European culture, whose ambiguities and complexities it reflects. Its foundation, which is man, is totally secular, but man became its foundation because of the mythic and religious substance poured into the concept of man, giving Humanism its radiant power and making it secrete its own myths, its primary religion (Progress), and its secondary religion (Salvation on Earth).

Humanism is also typically European because it has constantly been racked by the internal contradiction between its manifest principle, which is rational and secular, hence critical of myths and religions, and its occult principle, which is mythological and religious. This contradiction would grow stronger and stronger as developments in science reduced the importance and place of man in the universe and as determinism and scientific objectivity, denying all freedom and all human agency, would undermine the foundations of Humanism. Humanism would have to play a game of hide and seek with Science, considering it both as a truth about the world and as a tool of man's: scientific progress would bring about the higher sphere in which man as agent would master the world. When the theory of natural evolution was formulated, Humanism understood it not as representing the natural destiny of man and his kinship to the monkey, but rather his emancipation from nature and his superior place as *Homo Sapiens* and *Homo Faber*, the pinnacle and endpoint of the evolution of the world.

Humanism has also been racked by the contradiction between its universal principle, valid for all men, and its *de facto* Eurocentrism. It could escape this contradiction as long as it regarded the European as a full-fledged adult human, in contrast to the incomplete human of backward and primitive civilizations. Humanism could thus justify its colonial domination and regard the destruction of millennial cultures on every continent as the healthy eradication of errors, prejudices, and superstitions necessary to the introduction of true civilization.

European Humanism reached its pinnacle at the end of the last century. Imperialist Europe imposed its domination on the world, but cultural Europe believed it was bringing the world civilization and progress. This was the moment when the progress of civilization and the progress of science seemed unfailingly linked, where the triumph of reason and law were inscribed in the meaning of History. The pinnacle was shortly followed by crisis, eliciting soul-searching that further deepened the crisis. From the very heart of European culture it now became possible to perceive how blinding Eurocentrism was. Some Europeans would discover that their humanism had concealed and justified an appalling inhumanity. They would discover that their culture, which had seemed to be Culture, was in fact a culture that had generated contempt for other cultures and justified their extermination.

The ideas originating from humanism maintain their influence today in large parts of the world. But in Europe, at least, during the twentieth century, the progress of reason, the progress of science, and the progress of history entered into crisis, and this crisis would shake the foundations of Humanism.

Today we are starting to consider the adventure of European reason in all its ambivalence and complexity and to conceive the heterogeneous and sometimes contradictory multiplicity of interpretations contained in the word "reason". Thus we understand that rationality stands in contrast to rationalization, although they both have the same root. We have seen myth and religion insert themselves parasitically in reason and in the end sometimes take hold of it, just as reason believed that it was finally crushing them. We can therefore recognize that reason is not only the source of critical thought, but also a source of mythological thought. Unless one makes these distinctions and contrasts, one is forced to indict everything that bears the name of reason or else continue to sanctify the word at every instance.

Thankfully, critical reason has never been submerged by the self-mythology of reason, open reason has always been able to secrete the antidotes to rationalization, and emancipating hope, which is at the Greek and humanist sources of reason, has refused to be stifled by instrumental reason. Since the Greek Sophists, and, later, since Occam and Montaigne, reason has used its critical aptitude for self-examination and self-criticism to recognize the relativity and the limits of its power. Immanuel Kant's *Critique of Pure Reason* (1781) establishes a key date in European culture, because it marks the point when reason turned frontally on itself as a primary object of knowledge. Kant gave human reason full power to organize sense experience in the knowledge of phenomena, and he removed from it all power to know what lay beneath or beyond phenomena, that is, reality itself. By definitively linking the problem of the possibility of knowledge with the problem of its limits, Kant simultaneously brought out the all-powerful and all-helpless quality of human reason.

Reason was never fully triumphant in the history of European culture. It has always had to confront experience, or the existence of faith. Thus, rationalism never reigned over the sciences; what does reign is an often antagonistic dialogue between rationalism and empiricism. Rationalism has never been able to give man a *raison d'être* or give that which exists a reason for existing. On the contrary, it has provoked a reaction in the nineteenth and twentieth centuries, the existentialism of philosophers from Kierkegaard to Max Scheller and Heidegger. Finally, after having wanted to rid the world of its infamy, reason had to accept faith, just as faith had had to accept the autonomy of reason. Faith even became one of reason's key partners, incorporating much critical rationality in order to contest what was contesting it.

The European cultural identity

Since the Renaissance, European culture has been a tumultuous and disorganized building site which answers to no preconceived plan or program. Today still, science itself does not develop in conformity to an ordered program, but according to an inventive disorder made up of many rival or opposing research programs, intersecting with random initiatives and interactions. The *bouillon* [broth] of European culture has been and remains a *brouillon* [a mess].

The originality of European culture lies not only in its having been the offspring of Judeo-Christianity, the heir to Greek thought, the creator of modern science and reason, but in having ceaselessly been the producer and the product of a whirlwind made from the interaction and intersection between numerous dialogics that have joined and opposed: religion and reason; faith and doubt, mythical thought and critical thought; empiricism and rationalism; existence and idea; the particular and the universal; problematics and radical reform; philosophy and science; humanist culture and scientific culture; the old and the new; tradition and evolution; reaction and revolution; the individual and the collectivity; immanence and transcendence; Hamletism and Prometheanism; Quixotism and Sancho-Panzaism, etc.

The dialogical process admittedly occurs in all cultures, but in most cultures the dialogic is more or less hedged around with dogmas and prohibitions, and the process can be more or less slowed, arrested, or controlled. What is particular to European culture is mainly the continuity and intensity of its dialogical process, in which none of the constitutive authorities crush or exterminate the others nor even exert a massive hegemony for any length of time. This is what has made Europe a bubbling broth of cultures uninterruptedly from the fifteenth to the twentieth century. Conflict exists even within a single term of the dialogic. Thus, reason harbors internal opposition between its critical tendency and its systematic tendency, between open rationality and closed rationalization, and it must remain unremittingly self-critical if it is not to risk self-destruction. Likewise, European humanism suffers and generates a deep opposition between the belief in its universality, which conceals a dominating Eurocentrism, and its truly universalizing potential, open to all individuals and all cultures, which unmasks and criticizes Eurocentrism. The process allows for mutual contamination between the opposing partners: a great deal of critical rationality has thus entered into faith, certainly to work against reason itself, but also against the reasons of faith; and much faith has entered into reason and science. The process also harbors astonishing reversals, as for example when excessive doubt creates anxiety, which in turn leads back to faith; or when excessive rationalism creates a desiccation that brings on Romanticism; or when the anti-myth itself becomes a myth, as with reason and science. The process also contains crucial dialogical moments, in the exemplary oppositions of Pascal and Montaigne, Hobbes and Locke, Newton and Descartes, Rousseau and Voltaire, the Enlightenment and Romanticism, and Hegel and Kierkegaard. And finally the process admits crises for each of the terms of the dialectic, but none ever succumb, instead profiting from the crisis to become re-energized and renewed.

So it has been and so is it still with faith. European culture not only suffers these conflicts, oppositions, and crises but draws life from them. They are as much what produces European culture as the products of it.

What is important in European culture are not only the main ideas (Christianity, Humanism, Reason, Science), but the ideas together with their opposites. The genius of Europe resides not simply in plurality and change but in the dialogue between pluralities, which produces change. It is not in the creation of the new as such, but in the opposition of the old and the new (the new for the sake of the new declines into fashion, superficiality, snobbism, and conformity). In other words, what is significant in the ongoing life of European culture is the fecundating encounter between diverse, irreconcilable, rival, and complementary elements, that is, their dialogic. The dialogic is both the product and productive of the loop in the whirlwind whereby each element is at once the cause and the effect of the entire loop, which evolves in a nebulous spiral. *The dialogic is at the heart of European cultural identity*, and not one or another of its elements or moments.

European culture is not solely a culture whose most significant products – Humanism, reason, and science – are secular. It is more particularly a secular society in the sense that no idea has stayed sufficiently sacred or accursed to escape the whirlwind of debate, discussion, and polemics. The power of the cultural dialogic has dragged into discussion and debate those religious and political ideas that announced themselves as most Indisputable and Incontestable, and though they remained sacred to the faithful, they entered into the secular arena of debate. This *ipso facto* introduced pariah ideas into the discourse, ideas that had remained Untouchable as long as Irrecusable ideas held sway. Thus, the sacred could be publicly discussed and criticized by the profane, without being invaded or devastated by profanation.

Although written into the logic of the Renaissance from the start, secularization was a late development, one that has remained incomplete in certain countries and that has had to regress in this century because a sacredness of a new order was imposed on half of Europe. But in no other culture, including the Athenian, has secularization been so extensive. Not everything, however, was desecrated and made prosaic in the secular sphere. Quite otherwise, we have seen that myth and religion filtered into the very heart of anti-mythic and anti-religious ideas. But the myths of reason and the humanist religion are neo-myths and neo-religions, which, excepting the case of a Marxist-Leninist party in power, do not have at their disposal the established power of a Church or State. As myths and religions they must wear camouflage, and, where they have become parasitic, critical rationality parasitizes the parasites.

Thus, we should grant a special place at the heart of European culture to critical rationality, which is itself question-raising, concerned about objectivity, and apt at self-criticism and the criticism of its critics. This very rationality is the main vector of the principle of unity that nourished and was nourished by European culture. It is true that the God of Abraham was the God of the Universe, and it is also true that the Christian message was addressed to all men;

but for centuries and centuries only the faithful benefited from Christ's charity. It is true that Greek democracy recognized the dignity of man as citizen; but Greece excluded the slave and the barbarian. It is true that the Germans and the Franks were free men; but they never conceived of freedom for others than themselves.

It was critical rationality that pushed European humanism – threatened then as now by Eurocentrism – to concretize its universality by recognizing the full humanity of every man, independently of his race, continent, or culture. However, the love of humankind comes not from rationality but from the quasi-religious mysticism behind Humanism. European universalism consists not only of rationality, objectivity, and scientism, but also of faith and fervor, and in that sense is the heir to Christianity. The universal is a powerful entity in all thought and all culture. But no other culture had put the universal as the driving force of its particular culture. And it is precisely because the universal worked against individual selfishness and egocentrism of the nation or the culture that it was always circumvented, diverted, and betrayed in the very European culture that conceived it.

In the midst of the dialogical whirlwind, ideas constantly negate one another: a whirlwind of negativity bears modern European culture aloft. Born of the negation of medieval truths, modern European culture continually applies negation to every idea, every system, and every theory. The Faustian desire for absolute knowledge makes the "ever-denying spirit" appear: Mephistopheles. But negativity is diabolic only toward what it negates. It is also, as Hegel said of the skepticism of the sophists, the spirit's energy, and it is it precisely what has animated the whirlwind.

Negativity could take the aspect of doubt, irony, contestation, and revolt. European doubt is all the more energizing in that it allies skepticism to something that in turn denies skepticism. Thus, doubt is not only right at the core of Montaigne's meditations, it is at the core of Descartes's method, of Pascal's faith, and of Hume's empiricism. In considering the real heroes of European literature, who are all anti-hero heroes, great by virtue of their very weakness, can we not say that doubt is at the heart of Hamlet's sacred duty, of Oblomov's impervious sluggishness, of Ivan Karamazov's tragedy, and of Stavrogin's distress?

Today, Milan Kundera can retrospectively recognize Don Quixote, Faust, and Don Juan as typically European heroes because they are heroes of failure and derision in the pursuit of the sublime and the absolute (Kundera 1988). Each in his own fashion refused to accept finitude, believed in boundlessness, and ignored the reality principle just when reality came to confront him. And this at the very time when the capitalist, bourgeois, and scientific world was achieving the most phenomenal successes by obeying every realist principle. But we know today that capitalism, science, and Europe itself were obeying deep urges to deny finitude, believe in boundlessness, and forget the reality principle. European literature has always carried within it the invisible negative, made up of suffering and failure, of the euphoric image of infinite progress and world conquest.

Was there not finally some secret and permanent connection between the negativity inherent to European culture and the ultimately self-destructive process that dragged Europe to its ruin? There is no ready answer. Here also the problematics must be examined.

The inclination to problematics is the hallmark of European culture. Let us not forget that the Renaissance gave rise to generalized problematizing: questions were raised about God, the cosmos, nature, and man. Later there were instances when European culture believed that one thought, one principle, one fact had finally brought it absolute certainty. Humanism believed that man, the measure of all things, could be the foundation of all things. Reason believed that it had founded the truth of its discourse in logic, Science that it had founded the certainty of its theories in the certainty of its experiments. But these principles, thoughts, facts, and foundations were put in question each time within a generation, and problematics each time resumed its hold of European culture. From this perspective, the ongoing evolution of European culture was nothing more than the effect of ongoing problematizing, which led to the widespread and radical problematizing of today. Europe plunged all things – men, life, the cosmos – into a process of change and evolution, problematizing everything. For a long time, it seemed that change, history, and progress were immune to problematics because they themselves raised the problems. They have now entered the realm of questioning, and have even been swallowed up by it. They are problematic and will always be so. As Jan Patocka has said: "The problem of history cannot be resolved. It must remain" (1982).

A generalized problematics took root in Europe. From now on "Europe can only take root in problematics, because such is its inheritance" (Chenavier 1987: 12–19). We are the heirs of problematics; we must now become its shepherds.

Europe and global challenges

We live henceforth in the planetary era. Since the discovery of America, the world has become increasingly connected at all points. The uninterrupted inter(retro)actions between three or four billion human beings constitute a common fabric and a *de facto* solidarity. Any event at any point on the planet, not only in Moscow, Peking, or Washington, but also in Iran, Iraq, Israel, Lebanon, Brazil, Mexico, Nicaragua, or Chile has almost immediate repercussions for the rest of the world.

The AIDS virus, traveling at jet speed, is spreading meteorically across the globe. Humanity, while maintaining its extraordinary diversity of cultures, has united under the aegis of a technology that enables and assures all imaginable intercommunication. Humanity constitutes *one* geo-ecological entity, within one biosphere, on which it relies and which in turn relies on human actions. Humanity recognized its planetary habitat in the blue orange, lost in a black sky, transmitted via televised image from the moon. Humanity has learned that the human species, despite the diversity of its races, ethnic groups, and its individuals, is genetically and intellectually one. Everything is therefore converging so that Humanity can become aware of its common destiny, to which all other common destinies, including the European community, are subordinately linked. We are part of the planet and the planet is part of us, just as the whole of a hologram is inscribed in each of its points. Thus, the coffee beans I drink each morning come from the high plateaux of Central America or Abyssinia; the tea brewing in my cup was picked in faraway Yunnan, my fruit juice was pressed from Floridian or Israeli grapefruits. My shirts of Indian cotton were manufactured in Taiwan or Macao. I blow my nose into handkerchiefs of Egyptian thread or Kleenex tissue from the Canadian forests. I listen to the news on my Japanese transistor radio, write the rough draft of this European book with a fountain pen nib of Siberian or South-African gold, type it on my Japanese Canon while awaiting delivery of my American Macintosh. At meals, my glass is reserved for France, but South America, Asia, and America are invited onto my plate. Already the fabric of our lives contains a large share of planetary texture. We are unquestionably in the planetary era, since the planet is in us.

Europe has shrunk. It is now no more than a fragment of the West, where four centuries ago the West itself was a fragment of Europe. It is no longer at the center of the world but pushed back to the margins of History. Europe has become provincial in relation to the gigantic empires now extant, and it has become a province, not only within the Western world but also within the planetary era. And yet, Europe can only assume its provinciality if it stops being parceled up and split into states, each of which enjoys absolute sovereignty. It is the fact of Europe's provincial nature, paradoxically, that makes it necessary for Europe to overstep its constituent nations to preserve them and declare itself a Law above the level of the states.

Thus, the new situation requires much more than bare acceptance and adaptation; it forces two conversions that, while apparently contradictory, are in fact complementary: one that has us go beyond the Nation, and the other that reduces us to a Province. It is necessary to join together the act of regenerating into Province-Europe and the act of assuming the destiny of the planet, that is, to reassume the Universal in a new and concrete fashion, a concept developed by our own culture. Europe must metamorphose at once into a province and a meta-nation.

European identity, just like any other identity, can only be a component within a set of identities. We live in the illusion that identity is one and indivisible, whereas it is always an *unitas multiplex*. We are all individuals with multiple identities, in the sense that we bring together a family identity, a local identity, a regional identity, a national identity, a transnational identity (Slavic, Germanic, Latin), and possibly a religious or doctrinal identity. A conflict between identities has often ended in tragedy, as in the first half of the twentieth century when a child had a German father and a French mother. But there can also be happiness in reconciling the blessings of two conflicting identities – as I was forced to do myself with my numerous "motherlands" and as the young of Algerian-French descent will do once they have transformed what is for them a contradiction into complexity.

Actually, there is no more possible conflict between the national identity of a European and his European identity. The problem is that awareness of this European identity is still underdeveloped, as we have pointed out, in relation to the real developments of the community of shared destiny. One has to be severed from Europe to feel one's European identity acutely, as were the Czech intellectual refugees in New York in the wake of 1968 who, when leaving on vacation, some to France and others to Italy, said: "We are going home." We are not all emigrés, fortunately, and we must decompartmentalize Europe from the inside and open Europe up to itself. We need an immediate instrument of linguistic communication in the new province. It would be easy, as the example of Switzerland shows, for every European to speak two European languages besides his own. Europe runs no risk to its culture from having English become the common language. Did it not become the *lingua franca* for the various cultures and ethnic groups of India without corrupting them or devaluating the regional languages, or imposing an English identity on the Indian? The use of English, in addition to a knowledge of two other European languages, would also have the advantage of facilitating communications with the rest of the planet.

European identity has no choice but to integrate with a fully human identity, the consciousness of which is favored by our planetary era, but is opposed by regressions, ruptures, and conflicts appropriate to the Iron Age. The European identity and the planetary identity are both underdeveloped, but they in no way contradict each other; there are rather strictly linked in the insight that binds the idea of the Meta-nation to the idea of Province Europe.

While a marginal province – indeed, because a marginal province – Europe can have a central awareness of planetary problems. Europe is certainly not the only place where a planetary awareness exists or an acute awareness of the crises of technology, science, and the industrialized society. But it is the only place where there is a sufficiently general awareness of false solutions and false messiahs. It is the only place where, in the past forty years, government paranoia and the religion of the Nation have slumbered, where the hearth of imperialism has gone out, where the myth of earthly salvation has exposed its lie even to its most fervent believers.

Europe may then take on the vocation of becoming a Foundation, in the sense given this term by Isaac Asimov in his science fiction epic of the same name: at a time when galactic civilization was at its pinnacle, a few sages foresaw its inevitable decline and its return to barbarism and chaos; they decided to gather on a remote planet all the knowledge needed for civilization to flourish again in the coming millennia, a planet known as the Foundation (Asimov 1951). The idea of the Foundation brings together the conservation and preservation of cultural and civilizational goods from the past (not European goods alone) and the preparation for future transformations.

The past has to be saved in order to preserve the future. But we must also sow the seeds for a future that will pull humanity out of the planetary Iron Age. Europe's stake in this matches that of the planet. Europe has two "foundational" vocations, one cultural, the other political. We must imagine a "second

Renaissance" in Europe that would link these two dimensions. The first dimension, starting from the experience of nihilism and generalized problematics, should open the European dialogic to outside cultural contributions and dedicate the second Renaissance to civilizing barbarian ideas by opening them to complexity, to thinking the hidden principles that govern human thought invisibly, and to attempting, in short, to graduate the human spirit from its prehistory. The second dimension, starting from the consciousness of the planetary Iron Age, should assign Europe the mission, at once altruistic and selfish, of protecting, regenerating, refreshing, developing, and reincarnating democracy.

We must take root again in Europe in order to open ourselves up to the world, just as we must open to the world in order to take root in Europe. Opening up to the world is not the same as adapting to the world. It is also adapting the contributions of the world to one's own uses. One must assimilate anew in order to experience a new expansion. If the Renaissance was an opening up of Europe during which the assimilation of ideas, far from proving corrosive, enabled Europe to construct its unique and original character, then why not envisage a second Renaissance? If the Renaissance was the demolition and reconstruction of thought, why not envisage, taking nihilism and the loss of foundations as a point of departure, the re-beginning of thought? The Europe we should opt for is the Europe that was able to elaborate meta-European viewpoints. This is the Europe that would be able to integrate non-European viewpoints into its dialogic.

Once again openness and regeneration are linked. The Japanese have shown themselves able to assimilate Western civilization "with a Japanese soul" (*wakon-yosai*). For us it is a question of assimilating non-European thoughts "with a European soul", that is, of introducing them as new partners in the European cultural dialogic. An encounter with a strong foreign civilization or culture raises the alternative: assimilate or be assimilated. The capacity for assimilating supposes a certain cultural vitality, which supposes certain economic and social conditions.

European culture remained somewhat open to the world it had dominated, if only because it had discovered and explored this world. Whereas one strand of European thought took strength from comparing itself with the world, believing in the superiority of the Western white male, another nourished its humanism and its critical thought on the knowledge of the diversity of men and cultures. As early as Montaigne, travel and travel accounts had inoculated our beliefs and ideas with relativity. In the sixteenth century, the apparently naive theme of the Noble Savage helped us to conceptualize the vice and the corruption of our civilization. And as early as Montesquieu, Europeans put themselves in the shoes of an imaginative Persian in order to examine our culture from the outside in a quasi-ethnographic way.

Moreover, through the mythico-real notion of the Noble Savage, European culture, undergoing rapid transition, was able to consider the problem of its growing distance from a natural art of living. Through the mythico-real notion of the Wise Mandarin, Europe raised the problem of a wisdom that has become impractical within a history that has turned into a whirlwind. Then Romanticism expressed the diffuse, vast, and inexpressible needs of the soul in the midst of a civilization dedicated to technical precision and numerical calculation. Today, the original arts of living that arose from European cultures, particularly the Mediterranean, have tended to decline into consumerism and to disintegrate through haste, acceleration, time slotting, and bureaucratization. If there is one problem raised and imposed by Europe's trajectory at the close of the scientifico-technological civilization, it is the problem of the art of living. Now that Europe has been pushed back to the margins of history, it can envisage the problem concretely. Europe ought not to seek the art of living in other cultures, but raise its own questions on the art of living by questioning the cultures of the world, including archaic and dead cultures, "with a European soul".

Our mission is not only to stop the "culturecides" initiated by us, but also to recognize the treasures of experience, wisdom, and subtlety in the cultures we are annihilating. What contemporary European anthropologists have experienced among certain tribes in Amazonia, Africa, and Oceania is not simply the strangeness of the mores and rites but also the sense of a peaceful fabric of existence with better relations between individuals, in short, a genuine art of living. What I felt on Machu Picchu was not solely the emotion of a tourist, but the sudden realization that the life of a monk dedicated to the Sun God Inti had as much or as little meaning as the life of a European deputy, or sociologist, or philosopher. In my journeys to Latin America, Asia, and Africa, I learned that the arts of living had flourished everywhere. Here again the European spirit's inner quest necessitates an opening onto the outside world.

We can already observe in Europe and America the extensive spread of different forms of yoga and zazen, which bring something to our utilitarian and consumer-oriented universe beyond their value for relaxation or gymnastics: they are also methods for achieving inner peace. Obviously we make use of the practical and consumable forms of these oriental practices only – that is, degraded forms – and we are not capable of introducing to our mental universe the philosophies or mystical beliefs that subtend these practices. We, nonetheless confusedly, perceive that yoga and zazen invite us to meditate. And we sense that there are several forms of meditation, from those that cultivate an inner void to those that are slow, long, and in-depth reflections on a perception, a word, an idea, or a show of nature.

We must learn (anew) to meditate. In Europe, meditation had been reserved for the piety of monks, in isolation from the world, and for the reflection of philosophers grappling with a problem. Yet, it could well become an antidote to one of the main poisons of our civilization, which exteriorizes, dismantles, divides, and accelerates everything it touches. Meditation could possibly become more than an antidote: a necessary means to return inside ourselves and inside our real problems, a means of acceding to the contemplation of the amazing world that science reveals to us, a means of communicating with the mystery of what we call the Real.

Furthermore, we may well ask ourselves, as S.C. Kolm (1982) suggests, whether the Gautama Buddha's message does not also concern our European civilization. I say "message" and not "religion", although Buddhism in its pure form is a religion without religion. Here again I do not claim that we should integrate the message as it stands: we cannot wish to annihilate within our lifetime a "me" that is at the heart of our individualist culture, and we cannot wish to escape reincarnations we do not believe in. But what we can draw from Prince Gautama's message is the invitation not to turn away from nothingness and suffering. Although the salvation religions have terrified us overly with its threat, we are indeed today called on to confront a terrifying nothingness. As Europeans, we must confront it because we have been driven to the doors of Nihilism by our philosophy and to the threshold of destruction by our science.

The demise of a promised earthly happiness confronts us with the intensification of human suffering. The latter does not just come from hunger, poverty, slavery and war. The abolition of these scourges would eliminate immense suffering but would not resolve the problem of despair. Where we now have affluence and prosperity, new forms of suffering have cropped up: loneliness, torment, misunderstanding, anxiety, distress, and grief.

The Buddah's message tells us that pain is the problem above all other problems and asks us to consider it with infinite respect and emotion. This means that pain does not just pertain to anaesthetists, Sisters of Theresa, psychoanalysts, tranquilizers, or prescriptions reimbursable by social security but calls instead for a cultural and civilizational reform that will deepen and revolutionize the meaning of what Christianity called *charity* and what Humanism termed *humanitarianism*.

Bastardizations and syncretism are no doubt to be feared when cultures mix and decline. But we must also remember that there is no pure culture, and that they are all of them, starting with our own, of mixed blood. Turning to Buddhism should not be understood as a substitute for Christian salvation or psychotropic drugs, designed to rid contemporary life of anxiety and torment. I would say that on the contrary, our European culture – dialogical as it is – could not and must not escape contradiction and conflict. It bears anxiety and torment within it not only as gnawing ills but also as virtues of conscience and elucidation. European culture could not renounce them without debasing itself. But it could also not avoid questioning the message of peace and deliverance. European culture can summon them and absorb them in her dialogical process.

The first Renaissance was open to all the horizons of its world. The second Renaissance cannot help but be open to all horizons of the World.

Conclusion: a new crisis of European civilization?

Europe fully participated in globalization on its ambivalent journey in this process. It reacted within the process and tried to adapt to globalization in a number of different European countries in a number of ways, notably through privatization of businesses. Aware that it could totally dismantle some of her social conquests, Europe tried to avoid phenomena caused by economic liberalism. If one can claim that the global era began in Europe with enslavements and colonizations, the most lethal of remedies, which inflicted disastrous effects on the dominated countries, stemmed from European ideas. To understand these remedies, one should start with Bartolomeo de las Casas, the priest who persuaded the Spanish episcopate that the Indians were vested with a soul enjoying full humanity. One can begin with Montaigne, who believed that each civilization had its merits and virtues and for whom there was no monopoly from Europe. One can begin with Montesquieu who looked at France with a Persian gaze. One must begin with the Rights of Men, one must begin with democratic ideas. All of these ideas transform into global ideas when they are grasped by emancipating people. Born in Europe, the idea of modern state was appropriated by the people who were dominated or colonized for the best (emancipated) or the worst. Even today one perceives that the women's rights problem is a world problem but whose epicenter is Europe. One notes that many solidarity movements directed toward countries oppressed by globalization stem from Europe.

Europe is therefore both the poison and the antidote. It is the problem of the "Pharmacon", a word that indicates both the former and the latter. Thus what produces evil also produces the remedy to evil. Anti-globalization is very much discussed although it in fact relates to the second globalization emanating from the aforementioned European emancipation ideas involving awareness that the world is not merchandise. The European role in this movement is undoubtedly present and incarnated by the Roquefort cheese producer Jose Bové's symbolic role. Attac is another illustration of the movement, originally a French idea that subsequently globalized. As far as I am concerned, I believe that we are in a gestation epoch for the *second globalization* and we obviously do not yet know who will prevail. I believe Europe to be very present in this movement but she is not alone.

Originally, Europe's intentions (EU) were political. A small political elite of Christian-democrats and Socialists embodied the European project. The obstacles obstructing this political idea were great, but the economy benefited from the favorable economic boom of the 1950s and practically set up the constitution of the European economic unity. This is manifested today by the Euro. But the political institutions have remained dwarves. Europe was a political dwarf as well and likewise a military dwarf. And yet, it is obvious that it is to exist politically. Indifferently of a federal or a confederate system, what matters is to invent, not to imitate. I am personally not a partisan of a single European state. I am a partisan of supranational instances having executive power on fundamental problems: military, political, ecological, economic and others. National states should remain. I think one has opposed native countries to a Supranational Europe through a schematic vision of Europe. *There must be a Europe of native lands in a supranational Europe*. Patriotic entities as such are not condemned, but absolute national sovereignty ought to be transcended when vital and fundamental problems of a collective and global nature are involved. This is what ought to be brought about by a new organization.

I regret the abandonment of the word *Community*, but we now have to institutionalize this Union through what is called a charter. I think one should multiply the symbols. The Euro in fact is just as much a political and psychological symbol as it is a currency. Just as the European passport constantly confirms a European identity, the Euro contributes to this identity. Like any other identity, Europe must develop it from membership symbols. Logic, even economics, must lead to harmonized taxing systems, social protection, etc. For now, the problem is that Europe has great challenges to face and difficulties to surmount. It has already overcome some in the past, but we now find ourselves confronting several very serious and important crises: an evolutionary crisis of institutions related to the admission of new countries into the European Union. A crisis related to the disappearance of a whole generation of great Europeans from the public scene, spirits who had distinguished themselves during WWII and who held the European ideal in their souls. We experience today a pragmatic era, of day-to-day politics. Political life has undergone an amazing shrinking process. You have a crisis of the *European spirit* and a crisis of *European mythology* concomitant with the crisis of political thought. Politicians themselves live narrowly; for them politics are in tow to economics. They do not seem to be aware of the fact that the great cultural and intellectual problems can be a hindrance for the Second Renaissance of Europe.

I am totally unsure about the future. The reason why I am not optimistic. I would rather be *voluntarist*. I am afraid Europe will actually stall, even dissolve, because my assumption is *that what does not regenerate degenerates*. If Europe does not regenerate, she will degenerate. The possibility of virulent neo-nationalisms is one of the existing degeneration factors. To what extent these neo-nationalists' manifestations eventually prevail, in different European countries, remains unknown. As you all know, the most rational and reasonable of predictions never expected that the insignificantly small and hysterical Hitlerian party (having never obtained more than 10 percent popularity) would be pushed to power in 1929. The crushing economic crisis as well as the renewed surge of national frustration provoked by the defeat of WWI made it somehow possible. Reasonable predictions today exclude the return of past fascism to power, but forms of neo-dictatorships, neo-fascisms, post-fascisms, etc. cannot be excluded. One cannot exclude an intermediary neo-authoritarian system in Russia which, thanks to a pluralistic party government, cannot be totalitarian any more. However, with very complex political networks initiated under Putin with the help of the press, with freedom, etc. everything is possible. The future is in no way determined, no one possesses the future, the world is in a state of chaos, crisis. Were Europe to be carried out, not only would it be a great opportunity for Europe, but perhaps also for the whole world.

The greatest of all mistakes is to believe that everything that exists today is eternal. We have a historical example: the practice of torture had disappeared from all European countries in the nineteenth century. However, in the twentieth century, torture returned to Nazi Germany, as well as in Russia, and the French practiced it during the Algerian War. What was thought to be abolished, that is torture, had reappeared. Nothing is politically irreversible. There is nothing established, and I would even declare that a democracy must constantly regenerate itself. Having democratic institutions is not enough. In Switzerland there is a marvelous local democracy. One can vote in the public square. But if the citizens do not move to the public square, what is left of democracy? *Democracy is an institution powered by a democratic vitality.*

One can argue that it will be very arduous to impose democracy on a European scale. Why? It has already proved extremely difficult, and took centuries, to install democracy on the scale of the national states. Originally, democracy was a City phenomenon. It appeared in ancient Greece, reappeared in Tuscany in the Middle Ages, and finally in the small towns of the Netherlands. A very long historical process was necessary for England to attain national democracy. A long historical process was also necessary for France. In short, a general historical European process proved necessary. Today, there would be extremely thorny problems building a European democracy. Trans-European political parties would have to be established, syndicates, cooperatives and trans-European employers should be organized. A public-spirited European mentality must come into existence. One should be able to install a European "Présidence de la République" accepted by a majority of Europeans. Thus, it is a long process towards unity within diversity; we are involved in a long haul whose goal is to save what exists of democracy.

I stand for the extension of the European Union. The political problem is the true problem. The problems raised by the integration of new nations in the EU would be the questions of executive power and the right to veto. This entails that the extension of the EU, meaning the increased membership of the EU, must be expressed through a modification of executive powers. That is to say through a simple majority in some cases, two-thirds in others and vetoes in extreme cases.

This is where we sense the need for a charter, which is moreover necessary to reaffirm the first and fundamental intentions of the European fathers. Europe was born to put an end to wars and fratricides and it was born with a requirement of democracy, as demonstrated by how far back it goes. Europe can only live democratically, and I trust that in the meantime the need for a European tribunal imposes itself to breach the gap until the international tribunal becomes operational. It is quite obvious that if Europe is to be democratic, each offense against democracy and each attempt to establish a dictatorship falls under the jurisdiction of a European tribunal.

Finally, the European Renaissance can only be carried out with the help of a deep reform of thought, of ways of thought. These should from now on enable nations to confront the complexities of world problems, in order to return to fundamental problems, and to rediscover the sense of the global problems. A tremendous effort is necessary, bearing in mind that the future is undecided.

Notes

1   In contrast to Henri Pirenne, Lombard believes that the influence of Islamic civilization has a fecundating effect on barbarian Europe. These two contradictory theses could be successively true.
2   On the idea of Europe in history, see Duroselle (1965), Voyenne (1964), Rougemont (1961).

References

Asimov, Isaac (1951) *Foundation*, New York, Gnome Press.
Chenavier, Robert (1987) "Sortir du XXe siècle", in *Lettre internationale*, vol. 12, Spring, pp. 12–19.
Delmas, Claude (1980) *La Civilisation européenne*, Paris, Presses Universitaires de France, Que sais-je?
Duroselle, Jean-Baptiste (1965) *L'idée d'Europe dans l'Histoire*, Paris, Denoël.
Kolm, Serge Christophe (1982) *Le bonheur-liberté: boudhisme profond et modernité*, Paris, Presses Universitaires de France.
Kundera, Milan (1988) *The Art of the Novel*, trans. Linda Asher, New York, Grove Press.
Lombard, Maurice (1971) *L'Islam dans sa première grandeur*, Paris, Flammarion.
Patocka, Jan (1982) *Essais hérétiques sur la philosophie de l'histoire*, Paris, Verdier.
Pirenne, Henri (1958) *Histoire de l'Europe des invasions au XVIe siècle*, Brussels, La Renaissance du Livre.
Rougemont, Denis de (1961) *Vingt-huit siècles d'Europe, La conscience européenne à travers les textes, d'Hésiode à nos jours*, Paris, Payot.
Voyenne, Bernard (1964) *Histoire de l'idée européenne*, Paris, Payot.

7   The crisis of European civilization

An inter-war diagnosis

Jan Ifversen

The mental response to WWI in Europe was an increased feeling of crisis. In all the European countries, quantities of books and articles detecting a crisis in Europe appeared in the 1920s. Titles such as *The Crisis of Our Civilization*, *Untergang des Abendlandes*, *La decadenza dell'Europa*, *La crise de l'esprit*, *Världskatastrofer*, *Een diagnose van het geestelijk lijden van onzen tijd* flourished. In all these diagnoses, the crisis was not seen as a phenomenon limited to specific political, economic or military areas, or to a specific event, but rather as something that touched the heart of European life. It seemed to be a common idea that WWI had been the catastrophe releasing the crisis. But the causes of the crisis itself were typically located in the deep structures of European life. This location was emphasized by the use of the term *civilization* that referred to an important semantic field for conceptualizations of European coexistence. In order to stress the fundamental character of the crisis, many intellectuals chose to talk of a *crisis of civilization*.

This contribution to the discussion of the concept of civilization aims at focusing on the different ways in which the feeling of crisis gained force in European self-reflections of the 1920s by being lifted up to the level of civilization, and furthermore, at discussing the different ideas of European culture involved in the diagnoses of crisis. I am interested in analyzing the discursive and conceptual frames within which European intellectuals and politicians could express their ideas on Europe. These frames were held together by the conceptual triangle around the concepts of crisis, civilization and Europe. By moving inside this triangle, the texts could combine different semantic fields and different discourses and thereby produce the general themes that dominated the reflections on Europe in the years after 1918. One central theme turned around the idea of a fundamental decline within modern civilization, which expressed itself through the dominance of technology and the loss of world hegemony. Linked to this theme was another one about the cultural and historical boundaries of European civilization. These two themes could be combined through the concept of civilization. I shall try to show that the concept of civilization came to function as a pivotal point by which a cultural discourse on Europe could meet a more general discourse on modernity.

It is furthermore my contention that the whole notion of crisis in the years following WWI revealed a mental and intellectual condition marked by a general loss of orientation which, in some ways, resembles our actual condition. Today, solid notions of civilization, nation and culture are under heavy fire from all kinds of global talk involving new conceptualizations such as globalization and postmodernity. After 1989, we have been witnessing a flow of texts trying to grasp all sorts of phenomena within a framework of globalization and post-modernity. Although we, Europeans, today cannot refer to a catastrophe of the same magnitude as WWI, there is certainly no lack of "smaller" calamities. And, as far as I can detect, there is an effort to combine these calamities into an image, if not of crisis, then certainly of general uncertainty. Descriptions of the current uncertainty often make use of what I would call a language of civiliza-tion. Thus, even though the Europeans invent new terms such as postmodernity and globalization in order to grasp the new condition, they are still under the spell of civilization.[1]

The crisis is launched

In April and May 1919, the French author Paul Valéry published an article with the title "The Crisis of the Mind" which first appeared in the British review *Atheneum*. Valéry was among the first to launch the idea of a crisis of European civilization, and his article was soon to become a key reference in the ongoing European reflections on crisis in the 1920s. It opened with a famous statement on the mortality of "our" civilization: "We later civilizations ... we too know that we are mortal" (Valéry 1962: 23). By this opening statement, the reader is imme-diately included in a European "we". The scene is set for a discussion among Europeans of the actual state of their civilization. Valéry goes on to construct a European point of view. Throughout the article, any talk of national differences is deliberately omitted. The statement also indicates that "we" have "now" lost an illusion.[2] The reader would, of course, immediately know that this present refers to the end of the world war and the terrible experience of mortality. We are thus introduced to a rupture between the past and the present. In the present, the Europeans have gained the knowledge that their civilization is frail or even historical.

From the beginning, Valéry situates Europe within two established meanings of civilization: on the one hand, the idea of civilizations developing through a historical life cycle, on the other, that it contains an idea of universality. But he makes a distinction between these two meanings. The first belongs to the present reality, the other to a past illusion. Furthermore, he implies that reality had to be revealed to Europe "by accident" (ibid.: 24). The accident was the world war which produced a feeling of loss: "She [Europe] felt in every nucleus of her mind that she was no longer the same. That she was about to lose consciousness" (ibid.). The rupture that Europe experiences is described by Valéry as paradox-ical: on the one hand, a loss of universality which reveals its historicity, and on the other hand a loss of its past which created a feeling of " no longer (being) the same". The result was "a disorder of mind", an "intellectual crisis", "the death agony of the European soul", i.e. a general "crisis of the mind".

The reference to crisis is abundant in Valéry's diagnosis of the post-war condition of Europe. The crisis is fundamental. What is at stake is the whole idea of a European culture. Valéry uses the concept of crisis to signal an end for Europe. Jacques Derrida, in his essay on Europe, demonstrates how the use of the term within the tradition of modernity in Europe refers to

> the moment when the limits and contours, the *eidos*, the ends and confines, the finitude are beginning to emerge; that is to say, when the capital of infinity and universality, which is to be found in reserve within the idiom of these limits, finds itself encroached upon or in danger.
>
> (1992: 32)

The term highlights the presence of the rupture. Europe is not the same as it was, and without any sense of direction. This lack of sense is emphasized by Valéry when while looking at Europe after the war he "sees nothing" (Valéry 1962: 27), or when he deliberately inverses a Hegelian philosophy of history by letting Europe lose its mind (*esprit*). As we shall see, the idea of a lack of sense and direction reverberates in many reflections on the crisis. Derrida indirectly points to the tension at play in the meaning of civilization between the potentials for universality and the limit which will always exist when the concept is linked to a European culture. As a culture, Europe has its limits. As a civilization it has an engagement with history.[3] In the latter perspective, a rupture becomes fatal because no fulfillment can be envisaged.

One way of coming out of the crisis could be to deliberately limit Europe by asserting its original culture. This solution was chosen by many of the post-war participants in the debate over the European crisis. Valéry, however, does not go for this option. For him, the essence of Europe is its universal quality, its status as "the elect portion of the terrestrial globe, the pearl of the sphere, the brain of a vast body" (ibid.: 31). This view of universality is clearly Eurocentric. The ground on which such a claim rests is a conception of the world as consisting of unequal parts. Only Europe has, due to the quality of its people, acquired a status of dominance in the world. Although Europe is viewed as one among several civilizations, it is also "the brain" of the world, i.e. the part which directs the world. This is what gives it a universal vocation. Valéry, however, does not fully endorse the typical Eurocentrist position. The crisis is precisely a feeling of doubt about the actual potentials of Europe. In the actual situation, the question is whether Europe will "become *what it is in reality* – i.e. a little promontory (*cap*) on the continent of Asia? Or will it remain *what it seems* – i.e. the elect portion of the terrestial globe?" (ibid.). The geographical "reality" of Europe as an appendix to Asia points in the direction of a geopolitical discourse of *Realpolitik*, while the "appearance" of Europe as a leading civilization points toward culture. Only the culture of Europe can explain its universal potentials. But the contradiction between geopolitical "reality" and cultural "appearance" shall be one of the problems any discourse on Europe will have to cope with. When Count Coudenhove-Kalergi, in the book *Paneuropa* from 1923, launched his pan-European movement, he presented a double view on Europe: on the one hand, Europe, due to its size, was about to become dominated by the world powers, on the other, it could turn to its common culture for salvation.

Valéry sees the world war as a moment of revelation for Europe. The crisis, however, has deep roots in European civilization itself. Following a certain tradition of modernity, Valéry detects a potential self-destructing effect within civilization. He locates this effect in a specific epoch of European history, the modern epoch or modernism. Modernism is characterized by a disordered level of plurality, by "the free coexistence … of the most dissimilar ideas, the most contradictory principles of life and learning" (ibid.: 27). Referring to a common metaphor of modern civilization, he describes this modernism as "the insane displays of light in the capitals" (ibid.: 28), or again hinting at appearance, modernism is described as "a carnival". Modernism has its roots in a European culture based on "an intellectual light" of "incompatible colors" (ibid.: 25). Heterogeneity thus seems to characterize the essence of Europe. But if heterogeneity is the dominant feature of European culture and of modernism, its contours tend to become blurred. This is further emphasized when Valéry points to "the most intense power of radiation" and "the equally intense power of assimilation" (ibid.: 31) as characterizing the singularity of European culture. Valéry hesitates between two solutions to this problem. A distinction can be made between culture and (modern) civilization. As we shall see in a moment, this is the solution favored by the antimodernist responses to the European crisis. Heterogeneity can thus be viewed as the reason for the singular European creativity, the "folly" of Europe (ibid.: 29). "Folly", however, can turn into "insanity". In order to safeguard European culture, civilization thus has to be detached from culture. Valéry describes this detachment as taking form by a separation of science from artistic creativity. Having lost its artistic counterpart, science will instrumentalize, quantify and standardize all values. Values are then turned into commodities and means of power exportable to the whole world. The result is that the global "inequality" to which Europe owed its singularity will disappear, and that Europe itself will be absorbed by the world. A negative image of European modernism is thus linked to a process of cultural standardization through technology, capitalism and world politics, which we may – anachronistically – call globalization. This link between modern civilization and globalization will be a recurring theme in the different descriptions of the European crisis.

In his article, Valéry tries hard to save European culture from modern civilization. But, contrary to his own later attempts to solidly anchor European culture within a traditional historical narrative, his problems of separating the two are manifest in 1919. In a lecture from 1922, Valéry provided the European essence with a history in the form of the traditional axis of Greece, Rome and Christianity. Consequently, according to Valéry, "every race and every land that has been successively Romanized, Christianized and, as regards the mind, disciplined by the Greeks, is absolutely European" (ibid.: 322). In his 1919 article, he does not display the same comfort. Here, the misfortunes of Europe are seen as

produced "by its own reaction" (*par ses propres effets*) (ibid.: 34). If modern civilization cannot be separated from European culture, it becomes difficult to envisage
a way out of the crisis. Or, maybe, the crisis is fostered by this impasse. At one
point, Valéry seems to end at the insanity of civilization.[4] When he lets "the
European Hamlet" overlook the battlefields of Europe and watch "millions of
ghosts (*spectres*)" – European culture turned into ghosts (*fantômes*) (ibid.: 29) – he
situates insanity within European culture.[5] The reality behind this nightmare
would then be the reduction of Europe, its *deminutio capitis*, through democracy,
capitalist exploitation and technology.[6] But, at the end, Valéry puts his trust in
the cultivated European mind (*esprit*) which is able to recreate heterogeneity. By
this celebration of the cultivated mind, Valéry can select one meaning of civilization; namely the one associated with *l'esprit cultivé*, and let this spirit loose. The
civilized Europe that comes out of this intellectual construction resembles the
eighteenth-century idea of a European *république des lettres*.

This hasty glance at Valéry's dense text reveals some of the central themes
that will come to dominate the post-war debate on the crisis of European civilization. First of all there is the idea that a certain modern development is
destroying Europe. Modernity can be placed in a specific period of European
history related to phenomena such as technology, mass society and democracy.
As we shall see in a moment, this is precisely what Oswald Spengler does in his
diagnosis of the decline of the West. Linked to this theme of destructive modernity is another, more spatial theme of what Arnold Toynbee called the dwarfing
of Europe where European modernity turns into a globalization that again is
seen as a diminishing of Europe's power in the world. Very often, what I here
call globalization is viewed in geopolitical and cultural terms as a play between
continental civilizations. An image of Europe is produced to counter the destructive forces of modernity and globalization. Related to the production of this
image is a whole theme around the true values of Europe involving history,
culture and space. The crucial question concerning Europe is how to free it from
the modernity that produced its crisis. Several strategies can be observed in
answering this question. Some will look for rescue in a European past, others in
a solid concept of culture, and others again in an image of the metaphysical
tranquility of the Orient. The theme of Europe is typically linked to an anti-
modernist and culturalist ideology offering the eminent possibilities of
conceptually fixing borderlines. Of course, "Europe" can also find room in more
politically and practically oriented settings as a political project for the future.[7]
But even these pragmatic and technical projects will ultimately contain an idea
of European culture. This is certainly true for the best known of these projects
Coudenhove-Kalergi's pan-Europe which is based on a traditional, historical
perception of a European culture.

It would be wrong to claim that the whole debate on the crisis of European
civilization took place within a culturalist discourse. Since its appearance in the
eighteenth century the concept of civilization has involved a strong universalist
component. A more truly universalist response is certainly present in crisis
debate. In his book, *From Plato to Nato*, David Gress demonstrates how universalist

claims are revived both through the new communist idea and through an American-dominated narrative of Western civilization.[8] With the spread of communism, a universalist image of the world based on a Marxist interpretation of civilization becomes dominant among intellectuals on the left. The communist version of civilization certainly involves a notion of crisis and of rupture. But, contrary to Valéry's description of the crisis, due to the sturdy philosophy of history in communism, there is no loss of orientation or feeling of decline. If decline there is, it can only concern "capitalist civilization".[9] Less universal is the narrative of Western civilization that mainly works through a rewriting of European history in the light of liberalism. This Eurocentric view of universalism can also be found in nineteenth-century post-Enlightenment treatments of civilization, such as François Guizot's *The History of Civilization in Europe* of 1828. In this liberalist narrative of civilization, universal civilization is made to coincide with European culture without any problems. As Valéry forcefully stated, it is precisely this coincidence which becomes difficult to uphold after 1918. In my overview of the crisis debate, I will leave out both of these two forms of universalism and only, hastily, consider some examples of universalism represented as cosmopolitan thoughts on world government.

Anti-modernist responses

Anti-modernism is the central matrix for the crisis debate. Already in the eighteenth century, the concept of civilization was used in a criticism of modern European life. Mirabeau who was the first to use the word in 1756, spoke of the masque of civilization.[10] One of the favored topoi of *les philosophes* was the noble savage, which permitted them to stage a critical counterpart from where modern civilization could be judged. This tension around the concept of civilization between an optimistic belief in modern progress and a pessimistic criticism of modern life was strengthened in the nineteenth-century dichotomy of civilization and culture. Pessimism and anti-modernism found a forceful expression through the romantic concept of culture. Civilization could thus be attacked from this new stronghold.

Oswald Spengler, more than everybody else, produced the conceptual framework for the crisis debate. Although partly written during the war,[11] his monumental *Decline of the West* first gained importance as the main reference point for any – anti-universalist – contribution to the post-war crisis debate. His work immediately triggered a heated debate among German intellectuals and was soon to be known in the rest of Europe.[12] The influence of Spengler's thoughts was so overwhelming that almost any reflection on the actual situation of Europe had to engage with it. In a striking way, he seemed able to pick up the existing post-war moods and views and insert them in a vast synthesis of world history.[13] When we look at his work several reasons to this can be found.

First, he offered a total world history of decline into which the actual crisis could be inserted and thereby contained. Through his world history, Spengler was able to explain the crisis as an almost natural phenomenon. Since the history of the different "high cultures" could be viewed as a life process with a normal rhythm of birth, youth, maturity and death, nothing became unusual. The main purpose of Spengler's grand scheme of world history – its morphology, as he called it – was to eliminate every form of accident from history. Contrary to Valéry, any talk of the war as an accident would be impossible. What the war revealed was not a moment of disorientation and disorder but, on the contrary, the orderly life process of Western culture. For Spengler, the war could only be a symptom of the end of Western culture, its phase of civilization. In a way, it had to come because "(t)he civilization is the inevitable *destiny* of culture" (Spengler 1926: 31). The fundamental determinism of Spengler's philosophy of history could thus serve as a means to close the debate on the European crisis. Whereas Valéry struggled to find in the European spirit an opening for the future, Spengler would set the scene for the ultimate end, and for a radically new beginning. There was no need to search for salvation in European history. The whole of history could be bypassed by his idea of a new beginning. There is no doubt that this solution appealed to and gave form to the radical longings of many Europeans.[14] By turning the crisis into a moment of catharsis which would open up for a new future completely leaving civilization behind, disorder could be transformed to order. Valéry's vacillation between a European bygone past and an impossible future, between illusion and reality, could thus be replaced by a determinate march toward a new order.[15] Here we clearly see the difference between the conservative criticism of modernism expounded by people like Valéry and Spengler's radical anti-modernism. In the first case, we detect an effort to revive the old Hamlet, in the second nothing in European culture is left untouched.[16]

The idea of decline was certainly not new. Spengler only rehearsed a theme that was well established in European thinking. But he forcefully linked it to the concept of civilization, and to the critique of modernity which this concept pointed to. Actually, he got most of his ammunition from the specifically German way of setting the authentic culture up against the artificial and uncultural civilization.[17] The originality of Spengler was due to the fact that he created the most complete catalogue of the destructive forces of civilization and linked these together in an impressive image of decadence which he finally placed at the end of history. Civilizations were to be seen as "the most external and artificial states of which a species of developed humanity is capable" (ibid.: 31). The civilization was this terminal period of any culture. In Spengler's totalizing perspective, everything modern could be described in the language of artificiality that was connected to a dominant view of civilization. At the same time, civilization could be identified as "a higher form" which any culture would develop. But, as in any critique of civilization, this form was described as a continuous process of alienation and distancing from the truth. For Spengler this truth was to be found in the being of culture.[18] Probably, the main reason for his success was that he systematically collected all the different anti-modernist statements and melted them into a solid image of civilization. Every alleged calamity could be located in civilization: Metropoles, science, machines, cosmopolitanism, democracy, rights, individualism, spirit, reason, masses, world wars, imperialism, capitalism, materialism, goods, sport, and so on. The globalization that blocked Valéry's view of Europe could thus be encapsulated within civilization. The technological elimination of physical distances which was (and still is) taken as the prime symptom of the emergence of a new supra-European world was treated by Spengler as "the passion of our civilization" (ibid.: 337). Civilization was everywhere ... within each culture. Spengler spent a lot of imagination locating these modern phenomena in the civilizations of other, older cultures.[19]

All the marks of civilization expressed the same essential lack of form which according to Spengler was the fundamental feature of civilization. By referring to one of the traditional meanings of civilization, the life in the city, Spengler used the metropole – the "formless" and "petrified" mass with no limits – as the basic metaphor for civilization.[20] Spengler concentrated the whole of civilization in the metaphor of the city. In the city all the aspects of civilization – money, rationalism, democracy, spirit – were gathered. With civilization, the city became the world, "the city-as-world" (Spengler 1928: 94) blurring all cultural differences. What a forceful and surprisingly modern view on globalization![21] But Spengler reversed the traditional opposition between the civilized city life and the barbaric life outside of the city and populated the metropoles with all sorts of "intellectual nomad(s)" (ibid.: 100). In this way, civilized man could be posited as a modern barbarian, and the traditional primitive in European thinking, man outside the city, could be set as the true bearer of culture. Furthermore, the rescue from civilization would come from the primitive and barbaric forces – the "animal advantage" (ibid.: 49), "the powers of the blood, unbroken bodily forces" (ibid.: 432) which contained the seeds for a new culture.

Valéry conceived of the actual crisis as a loss of orientation, a loss of sense. True to his general approach, Spengler had no difficulties in making this loss the general condition of civilization. Turning the famous dictum by Nietzsche into "the formula" of civilization, he wrote: "Transvaluation of all values is the most fundamental character of *every* civilization" (ibid.: 31). Civilization is thus described as a form of pure relativism. To support this view, Spengler could lean on the fundamental relativism at play in his world history. He vehemently denounced any idea of a universal sense of history. History has no sense, he continually reiterated. The prime target of his denunciations was the universalist and humanist tradition in European thought. In Spengler's history, humanism is just a sign of fatigue of Western civilization: "European weariness covers its flight from the struggle for existence under catchwords of world-peace, humanity and brotherhood of man" (ibid.: 357). Is it the same fatigue that also seems to overtake Valéry's European Hamlet when he exclaims: "Have I not exhausted my desires for radical experiment?" (Valéry 1962: 30). At least, they agree on the exhaustion of Europe.

Spengler's relativism is based on his perception of hermetically closed and self-containing cultures which allowed him to depict several independent "high cultures" in world history, and not least a European or rather Western culture – since he demands that "(t)he word 'Europe 'ought to be struck out of history" (ibid.: 16). In his construction of a Western culture based on a specific essence, we can detect a third reason for the importance of the Spenglerian framework. By incorporating European history into a very essentialist pseudo-biological concept of culture[22] which, as in the case of civilization, assembles all the traditional signs – blood, soul, land, nature, peasant, race, religion, emotions, and so on – into one totalizing image, he can unveil the essential West freed both from civilization and from the different Oriental and classical cultures. In his effort to isolate the West, he breaks with the traditional narrative of European history based on the succession from Greece, Rome and Christianity. Spengler fiercely rejects any idea of a cultural heritage from antiquity. The same goes for Christianity which, according to him, did not form Western culture. On the contrary, Western culture formed Christianity (ibid.). The purpose of these separations is to create a proper Western past not contaminated by Oriental influences. In order to denounce any sort of intercultural influences, Spengler even invents a new term for the destructive mixtures. He speaks of these as "historic pseudomorphoses" which arises when "an older alien culture" occupies the place of the original culture and prevents it from expressing its own soul (Spengler 1928: 189). The Arabic culture and the Russia of Peter the Great are given as examples of such destructive hybrids. Mixtures are invalidating because basically "(c)onnotations are not transferable" (ibid.: 57). This sturdy cultural relativism creates problems for the image of a Western culture, however, when applied to the concept of nations. Since Europe consists of nations that "(e)ach understands merely as a self-created picture of the other" (ibid.: 171), it becomes difficult to perceive of a common Western culture. This inconsistency between a unitary concept of the West and the different nations stemmed directly from the inherent nationalism within the relativist logic. Therefore, all the more nationalistic expressions of European culture would run into trouble handling the unity in diversity.

Spengler found the proper Western past in the "gothic" Middle Ages. In his language, the Faustian soul gives the West its form. This soul is synonymous with energy, direction, will power, expansion and intensity. It is this soul that makes a difference to antiquity's Apollonian soul and to the magic soul of the Oriental cultures. It is, however, also this soul that produces the end of the West. Thus, Spengler is faced with another problem: how to save the West from itself, or how to divide between the good Western culture and the bad Western civilization.

Whereas Spengler took the full consequence of the crisis metaphor by framing the crisis as a decline that could only be solved through a complete catharsis, others tried to defend the West from its enemies. Henri Massis, a French ultranationalist thinker, wrote a book in 1925 called *Défense de l'Occident*. In a way, Massis' text can be viewed as an effort to save the West from Spengler and the Germans. Although he agreed that the "terrible crisis" and "mental disorder" (Massis 1956: 65) that Europe had experienced after 1918 were caused by a more far-reaching process of decline within Europe, he did not sentence Western culture to death, first of all because the threats to the West could be exorcised. Contrary to the Spenglerian construction, Massis was able to separate the negative civilization of democracy and homogeneity from culture (which, in his language, amounted to true civilization) by revealing its stable core values. According to Massis these were "personality, unity, stability, authority and continuity" (ibid.: 69), the opposite of negative civilization.

The strategy of Massis leads in two directions. On the one hand, he constructs an image of Western culture, and, on the other, he refers the negative and threatening aspects to a non-Western world. A traditional way of doing both at the same time was to revive Christianity as the essence of the West. Christianity, and more specifically Catholicism, being the fulfillment of the "Greco-Latin culture", could be made to embody the core values of Western culture: "the idea of personal liberty and autonomy, of order, of authority and of jurisdiction" (ibid.: 149). What Massis and many others here did was to focus solely on the Christian dimension in the traditional historical axis of European culture. The Christian focus lead directly to "the old, stable medieval civilization" as it was termed by Hilaire Belloc, another anti-modernist Christian thinker. The Middle Ages became a period before the modern fall of Man. The ideal of the Middle Ages was opposed to modern civilization. It was seen as an ideal of unity and perfection opposed to the modern ideal of false progress and division (Massis 1956: 162). This return to the ideal Middle Ages became one way of escaping Spengler's pessimism.

The Russian émigré writer Nicolay Berdyayev published a widely successful book in 1923 entitled *The New Middle Ages* (*Novoje Srednevekovje*) which made this period a slogan for the nostalgic utopia of a certain reactionary discourse. Like Spengler, Berdyayev combined all the miseries of modernity – "individualization, the atomization of culture, the limitless desire, the growth of populations and needs, the decline of faith, and the growing sterility of spiritual life" (Berdyayev 1937: 19) – into an image of decline, the escape from which would mean a radical break with the present. For Berdyayev, such an escape would herald the coming of a new middle age. "The way to the Middle Ages goes through decline", he claimed (ibid.: 18). Although he follows Spengler's radical idea of a catharsis, he is much closer to Massis in his construction of a future based on Christian values. Medieval Christianity offered itself as a suitable image of an anti-modern West. Christianity could be set as universalist and unitary contrary to the particularist and dispersive aspects of modern civilization. Berdyayev specifically pointed to the anti-nationalist elements of Christianity. From this unitary view of Christianity the path was cleared to a unitary view of the West.

The idea of the essential Christian values of the West had a certain flexibility attached to it. Berdyayev's whole project was to use Christianity to separate the new medieval man from the still modern man. In this general view, the true Western values should transgress borders and become universal, and true Europe should acknowledge its universal mission, i.e. "renounce its monopoly of culture" (ibid.: 22). For Berdyayev, this would ultimately mean that Europe should meet with the Russians because they were the most universal of all people. Massis and Belloc, on the other hand, wanted to Westernize Christianity thereby enforcing the separation between West and East. Belloc made a clear distinction between true Christians and the Germans and those of Slav blood who were "semi-barbaric, though Christian" (Belloc 1937: 123). In-between these two strategies we find Spengler who would oppose both Berdyayev's fusing of the West and the East, and the Christianization of the West which is so important for the Christian thinkers. Massis' and Belloc's Christianity is Catholic because they want to strengthen the Latin dimension of the West. The main danger in their view of the crisis is not modern civilization as such, but its alliance with the barbaric Orient. Massis can thus describe the Orient through the traditional catalogue of Orientalism as the uncivilized *par excellence*: the unlimited Asian plains, the formless masses of the conquering Asian hoards, the degrading customs of the Oriental despots, etc. This alliance of "the barbarism that smells of machine" and "the barbarism that smells of forest" (Massis 1956: 128) he sees epitomized in the Russian Revolution. For Belloc it was this alliance between capitalism with its globalizing consequences and communism, "this hostile younger brother of capitalism" (Belloc 1937: 179) which put "the whole structure of our life in peril of immediate ruin" (ibid.: 132). Massis' text is not only orientalizing modern civilization. It is also orientalizing Germany. Making two moves simultaneously it opposes "Lutheran egocentrism" to Catholic values and relates the former to the materialism of modern civilization. Germany is at the same time modern and non-Western, which means Oriental.

Massis inserts the national confrontation between Germany and France into a construction of the West as Catholic. Germany fills out the role of the dangerous Orient – "the India of Europe", as Massis says (1956.: 135), radically different from the West. "Germanism" and "Slavism" can thus be aligned side by side: "Germanism and Slavism, they are sources from where all that revolts against the West supply themselves" (ibid.: 110). And German philosophy can be the location of all the negative forces from mysticism ("Hindu metaphysics", ibid.: 136) to materialism and nationalism.[23] Massis is thus capable of disguising his own nationalism as a critique of nationalism!

The search for a European spirit

Another way of westernizing and latinizing Germany is evident in the work of the German Romanist Ernst Robert Curtius. In his case, "the Latin civilization" that constitutes the European soul is completely different from the religious image of Europe represented by Massis, Belloc and other antimodernists. Not religion, but democracy is the moral core of this soul, according to Curtius. And not the Middle Ages, but the Renaissance and the Enlightenment are the high times of this civilization. Like others, Curtius strives to produce an image of a modern European civilization filled with positive values such as rationalism and humanism. The ideal is the eighteenth-century *république des lettres*. As claimed by the French author Georges Duhamel, who like Curtius is searching for "a European spirit". The eighteenth-century ideal of Europe as " a superior father-land" (Duhamel 1928: 24) is still to be found: "cette Europe-là n'est pas anéantie.

Il existe encore, dans les grandes villes d'Occident, une société où l'on est à peu près d'accord sinon sur les idées, du moins sur les termes qui servent à exprimer les idées" (ibid.: 25). Contrary to the anti-modernist image, this Europe is intellectualist, spiritual, urban and modern. The intention of reconstructing Europe as a new *république des lettres* lay behind the 1933 meeting in Paris of leading European intellectuals. The theme of the meeting was "the future of the European spirit" (Entretiens 1934). The general tendency in the many contributions at the meeting was to emphasize the intellectual character of Europe as its spirit, and to oppose this European spirit to the negative, "anti-spiritual" elements of modernity. By combining the eighteenth-century understanding of civilization as a process of cultivating and of educating the spirit with the idea of a specifically European place for this spirit, the participants in the meeting could revive the idea of a European mission and a European responsibility towards the whole of mankind, as Count Keyserling formulated it in his opening speech (ibid.: 27). And as the foremost "representatives of the spirit" he appointed the intellectual elite. Only this elite could "create a model for the future civilization by attaching it to the values of the past" (ibid.: 26).

But although Curtius, Duhamel and the other intellectuals tried to counter the anti-modernist image of civilization, the feeling of crisis also haunted them. Curtius feared the threats to the European spirit (*Geist*) from its own civilization and from external forces. The internal crisis stemmed from the modern character of the spirit which tended to make everything fluid. It was this "fluidization" (*Verflüssigung*), as Curtius named it, of traditional European thinking that Valéry lamented and Spengler hailed as the final stage of civilization. For Curtius, though, this state of fluidization had a positive side, since "it (was) the general psychological condition for the change and renewal of the European cultural spirit (*Kulturgeist*)" (ibid.: 262). Curtius' argument was that fluidization made it possible to combine elements in new ways, and that the whole of European spirit was based on this capacity for "synthesis". Contrary to Valéry and Spengler, who only saw the destructive potentials in the "reversal of all values", Curtius turned this alleged condition into something constructive and dynamic. As we shall see, the idea of a "synthetic" Europe would become one of the main strategies in the search for a European spirit.

Curtius' positive view of the condition of disorientation was tempered by his pessimist description of the external threats to Europe. Like most other thinkers he feared the barbaric effects of civilization in the form of "American mechanization" and the global "cultural standardization" (*der Prozess des Kulturausgleichs*), on the one hand, and the barbarism of "the newly awakened forces of Asia", on the other (Curtius 1925: 306). He placed the crisis within the same general framework of barbarism and civilization as Spengler. Barbarism referred to the unconscious, to the instinctive and to chaos, while civilization meant reflection, reason and harmony (ibid.: 231). But like many of his fellow thinkers among European intellectuals, he opted for the positive elements of civilization which could be found in the European soul: "Wenn wir aber den Aufstieg wollen, dann müssen wir vor allem diese zerrissene europäische Seele reinigen und heilen. Wir müssen sie zur Harmonie stimmen, wir müssen ihre Einheit neu errichten" (ibid.: 306). Julien Benda, another of the worried intellectuals, opposed the universalist and spiritualist sentiments of civilization to the nationalist particularism which he saw as the most present threat. For Benda, the intellectuals, as the traditional spiritual guides, were about to betray their civilizational mission by endorsing these new "political passions". He drew up an image of a crisis which linked massification, new forms of communication and "the reversing of all values" to nationalism (and to democracy). Nationalism could thus be placed on the side of the irrational, the relativist and the passionate, i.e. the barbaric. Benda's universalization of civilization did not stop with Europe. He spoke of a "humanitarianism" that "holds in honor the abstract quality of what is human" and opposed it to internationalism and cosmopolitanism both of which were based on interests (Benda 1955: 62–3). But although he attached this civilization to a loosely described European humanism and to a development of a higher order than the national one, it mainly served to produce a counter-image to the barbaric tendencies of the present "*clercs*". Most interestingly in Benda's view of the crisis is his fierce denunciation of "the systematic nationalization of the mind" (*esprit*) (ibid.: 46).

Although thinkers like Curtius and Duhamel imagined a European civilization very different from the medieval and Catholic nostalgia constructed by the reactionary thinkers, they could neither escape the framework of civilization and barbarism, nor the feeling of a deep crisis. In his book *Das Spektrum Europas* from 1928, the Latvian Count Hermann Keyserling painted a gloomy picture of a world in which Europe "(a)s contrasted with the new world has become very weak, very small" (Keyserling 1928: 378–472). This dwarfing of Europe is mainly explained by an ongoing globalization: "Today space, as a significant factor, has been conquered" (ibid.: 354–441). According to Keyserling, globalization introduces a new age where Europe will have to find its place. In one of his telling formulations – which almost anticipates actual definitions of globalization – he views this new age as "a synthesis of extreme universalism and of equally extreme particularism" (ibid.: 367–459). The Europe of Keyserling is squeezed between these two poles. On the one hand, Europe has to overcome nationalism which is seen as a main reason for its "attempt at suicide" (ibid.: 370–463) in the world war. It has, in the words of Keyserling, to let "the supranational … triumph over the national" (ibid.: 367–458). On the other hand, "the consciousness of difference" which is specific for Europe – and which, according to Keyserling, make the Balkans a European "prototype" (ibid.: 363–453) – must be kept alive. In his understanding, supranationalism is thus different from the globalizing forces of the international. Keyserling sees a heightened consciousness of European supranationality as a possible escape from the negative forces of globalization and civilization. The latter are to be found in America and in Russia. In his diagnosis of the crisis, America functions as the embodiment of all the negative forces of modernity such as standardization and instrumentalization.[24] On the other hand, Bolshevik Russia "still barbaric, with the instinct of the primal herd" (ibid.: 388–485) fulfills the role of the barbaric counterpart to civilization.

Keyserling foresees a convergence of these two negative locations that will challenge the true European values of diversity, individualism and spirituality
inherited from classical antiquity.

Contrary to the reactionary, Spenglerian image of the West, Keyserling is
forging a Europe of the peoples. Europe has to be seen in its diversity, as "a spectrum" in much the same way as the German writer Hans Magnus Enzensberger
would write about it in his book *Ach Europa!* almost sixty years later.[25] Diversity
could thus be seen as an asset and not as a particularist threat to civilization.
Perhaps it could be seen as the main feature that had formed the European spirit
and its dynamic, as the Hungarian Count Teleki told the participants at the 1933
Paris meeting (Entretiens 1934: 93). The diversity in unity was later to become a
catchword for any effort to describe Europe.[26] But it already played an important
role in the efforts to save the European civilization from the many alleged
dangers. The obvious problem with this catchword was (and is) how to describe a
European unity. As we have seen, this could best be done within the vocabulary
of civilization. In Coudenhove-Kalergi's vision of a pan-Europe which was one
of the most advanced attempts to cope with both unity and diversity in Europe,
civilization is the only way of evoking the idea of a European unity. He closely
links the geographical (the small continent) and political (the loss of world hegemony) descriptions of Europe to a cultural definition of civilization. Europe is
one of the four great civilizations (*Kulturkreise*). Relying on the standard repertoire, he constructs a European civilization whose essence is activism, rationality
and science, precisely those features that makes this civilization the most civilized. The menace to the European civilization partly comes from the integrative
forces of technology that makes the world "shrink", partly from the "dissolving"
tendencies within Europe itself (Coudenhove-Kalergi 1926: 16, 19). These latter
tendencies can be explained by the split-up (*Zertrümmerung*) of Europe after the
world war, but they are also due to the fundamental make-up of European civilization. Coudenhove-Kalergi alleges that Europe is made up of national
cultures, although he energetically tries to reverse the relation between diversity
and unity by emphasizing that the national is part of a unitary European culture:
"alle Kulturen Europas (sind) eng und unentwirtbar zusammenhängende
Bestandteile einer grossen und einhetlichen europäischen Kultur" (ibid.: 131).
He even goes so far as to talk about a European nation based on the same
cultural heritage and the same way of life (ibid.: 132). In order to safeguard the
idea of diversity in unity, he has to explain the actual division of Europe as a
result of a negative nationalism which induces "the mistake of perspective" to
see one's own culture as greater than others only because it is closer (ibid.: 129).
Another, surprisingly modern option for Coudenhove-Kalergi is to advocate a
separation of nation and state which would limit the former to the private sphere
of the individual (ibid.: 136).[27] His strategy for conserving diversity in unity thus
involves three elements. First, he introduces a concept of national culture not
coinciding with state borders. Nations are "empires of the spirit" without clear
borders, he claims (ibid.). Second, he leans on a strong concept of a European
unity formed by culture which coincides with the geography of Europe. Whereas

this cultural Europe can be precisely delimited (by geography), the national cultures are defined as fluid entities which make it possible to let them become integrated into one European culture. Third, Europe becomes a civilization when viewed in a global perspective. The test case for the boundaries of European civilization is "the Russian question", i.e. the question of whether Russia is part of European culture or not. Coudenhove-Kalergi's answer to this question does not deviate from the dominant view that Russia was not truly European. Although he admits that Russia at times has seemed European and therefore refuses the dominant "Asiatic" option of anchoring it in barbaric Asia, he still claims that the European character of Russia is something external (*äusserlich*). If anything, Russia is a mixture of European and Asiatic elements.[28] This negative view of cultural mixture serves to delimit European culture. But, at the same time, this view does not seem to fit in with the idea of European diversity, and certainly not with the claim that "Alle Völker Europas sind Mischvölker" (ibid.: 123). It is true that Coudenhove-Kalergi here argues against any idea of racial purity, but even from his own viewpoint the problem of cultural mixture in Europe seems difficult to escape, as long as any idea of national differences is recognized.[29] His solution to the problem differs from Keyserling's. Whereas the latter stressed the more particularist vision of the Balkanized Europe, Coudenhove-Kalergi chooses the unitary vision of a cultural Europe. The culturalization of European civilization involves a delimitation from other cultures whether barbaric or not. Certainly, Coudenhove-Kalergi does not endorse any cultural relativism, but stands firmly within the framework of civilization. He seems, however, to tone down the barbarism of the other cultures. On the other hand, he has to accentuate the internal force of the European culture, since he does not accept the idea favored by Keyserling and others that diversity is the reason for the dynamics of Europe. The dynamic (and civilized) character of Europe can only be explained by the core elements of this culture.[30] Consequently, this strategy must entail a deculturalization of precisely those modern aspects of civilization which threatens Europe. But, again, Coudenhove-Kalergi is ambivalent. On the one hand, the shrinking of the world is not described as caused by a European civilization, but seems rather a general effect of communication technology. On the other, this development is seen as deriving from elements of European culture. Coudenhove-Kalergi thus speaks of "Americanism" as one of the dynamic varieties (*Spielarten*) of European culture and as the one that dominates the industrial centres of the world (ibid.: 33). In much the same way, he sees the actual development in the non-Western world as formed by a double process of "cultural Europeanization" and "political de-Europeanization" (ibid.: 157). In this description, European culture detaches itself from the fixedness of the political and geographical borders and spreads out in the world, just to return as a menace to itself. The problem for Coudenhove-Kalergi is that he does not rely on some stable elements in the culture which would have allowed him to draw up a difference to the modern civilization. He dismisses the different solutions such as the organic elements of Spengler's Western culture, the medieval values of the Christian antimodernists and the humanist values of the *république des lettres*. But he also refuses to draw any cosmopolitan conclusions. In his view, cosmopolitanism only obscures the hopes for a pan-European unity because it demands the impossible. The only solution left for Coudenhove-Kalergi is to shift the focus from culture to politics and see pan-Europe as a strictly political project. However, although he certainly recommends political actions, he stays caught up with the idea of a European culture and therefore cannot escape the view that the actual crisis is caused by it.[31]

Unity in diversity is also what another leading European intellectual, Ortega y Gasset, propagates in his famous book, *The Revolt of the Masses* of 1929. However, Ortega y Gasset is in several respects a far more radical European than Keyserling and Coudenhove-Kalergi. His description of the European crisis as "a depressed state" resulting from the revolt of the barbaric masses against the true principles of civilization is seemingly much closer to a Spenglerian framework.[32] Also Ortega y Gasset's barbarian, primitive mass man, is a product of civilization: "this man full of uncivilized tendencies, this newest of the barbarians, is an automatic product of modern civilization" (Ortega y Gasset 1964: 101). And as a true barbarian, he is pure nature, devoid of any civilized character: "a *Naturmensch* rising up in the midst of a civilised world" (ibid.: 82). Just as in the antimodernist language, civilization is here contrasted to the primitive and barbaric by its "artificial character" (ibid.). But when it comes to the judgment on civilization, Ortega departs from the anti-modernist matrix. The problem is not civilization, which, in the eyes of Ortega y Gasset, is something valuable, but the uncivilized threat to it. In one of his dense formulations, Ortega y Gasset links the artificial character of civilization to the need for the artist to uphold it (ibid.: 88). Civilization is thus not something superficial and formless produced by the technical, but a phenomenon related to art and creativity. Following the traditional meaning of civilization, Ortega y Gasset sees it as "the will to live in common", i.e. as the possibility of *civitas* (ibid.: 76). This will is fulfilled in the doctrine of liberal democracy which is based on "the supreme form of generosity" (ibid.).

I will not try to summarize Ortega's description of the primitive mass man destroying European civilization. In many ways, he reiterates the themes of what had by the time he was writing his book become the standard narrative of all the evils of modernity, such as hyperdemocracy, technicism, standardization, the dwarfing of Europe, etc. But, as mentioned, he significantly departs from Spengler's matrix. Nor does he directly follow the more moderate proponents of European culture as diversity when he uncompromisingly condemns nationalism as the cause of decline (ibid.: 149). In his view, nationalism has to be understood in two ways: it is a barbarism on a large scale where mass man leads to an idea of "mass-peoples" (ibid.: 134): and it is a barbaric reaction against the feeling of crisis unleashed by the disjunction between man and his civilization. Therefore, nationalism is precisely what has to be overcome in order to save Europe. As he claims, the nationalist response to the actual crisis leads to "an exaggerated and artificial intensification of the very principle which had led to decay" (ibid.: 183). His project – far more radical than Keyserling's and even more daring than

Coudenhove-Kalergi's – is the creation of a European nation–state based on "the common European stock" which, as he claims, has always superseded the limitations of the nations (ibid.: 180). This stock is what designates the true value of European civilization. Surprisingly, Ortega does not find the common stock in the Middle Ages, nor with the Greeks and Romans or the Enlightenment, but in a nineteenth-century liberalism:

> the most reactionary of Europeans know, in the depths of his conscience, that the effort made by Europe in the last century, under the name of liberalism, is, in the last resort, something inevitable, inexorable; something that Western man today is, whether he likes it or not.
>
> (ibid.: 103)

Mass man, mass democracy and nationalism are thus opposed to European values in the form of liberalism which fills out the double role of being both an element of cultivated civilization, of the spirit, that is, and of European culture.[33]

The forming of a European response to the crisis, in many ways, rested on the general post-war narrative of European and civilizational decline. But instead of following the decline to its logical end, these descriptions searched for a positive and future-oriented answer in the European spirit. Like the reactionary Catholic thinkers they had to provide an image of a Europe free from the evils of modern civilization. Unlike these, though, they did not invent a nostalgic utopia to arise out of the ashes of modernity. Keyserling set up a European culture based on a dynamic principle of diversity producing "the amazing Hellenic intellectuality" (Keyserling 1928: 372–466). Coudenhove-Kalergi sought rescue from the European nationalisms and geopolitical complexes of inferiority in culture. Ortega y Gasset found the vitality of Europe in nineteenth-century liberalism. Both Ortega y Gasset and Keyserling approached the pan-European projects for a united Europe. But, although these projects included practical, economic and political elements, the glue that kept them together was made up of the European spirit and its cultural foundations. The spirit and the culture were the remedies that could free Europe from the malaise of modern civilization. Ortega y Gasset was more political and more Western than Keyserling. His Europe would be based on "a will to coexistence" led by France, Britain and Germany, whereas Keyserling's Europe was a more moderate call for unity among the diverse cultures. Coudenhove-Kalergi was a more practical man whose Europe was based on the creation of Franco-German understanding.[34]

The Orientalists' utopia

Among the different voices in the crisis debate, we can also detect a certain Oriental point of view. For some, not least in Germany, the Orient functioned as a critical position from where modern Western civilization could be castigated.

The effort to construct an Oriental position resembled the role played by the classical figure of the noble savage. But in the post-war years, the Oriental seemed more suited for forming a critical position than the savage. Leaning on an established discourse of Orientalism, these contributions to the debate could easily set up a dichotomy between the Orient and the Occident. One such contribution was a book entitled *Orient et Occident* written in 1930 by a French Orientalist, René Guénon. Armed with the conceptual tools of the civilization discourse, he undertook to severely criticize the civilization of the West. His point of departure was the common idea of the decline of the West. He spoke of the "bankruptcy" of Western civilization (Guénon 1947: 10) and went on to paint a picture of this civilization as threatened by its own defects. Though mainly stressing the intellectual shortcomings of its science – its hyperrationalism, materialism, positivism, and agnosticism – he combined these with the classical themes of the antimodernist narrative. Among these he included the Western "spirit of conquest" (ibid.: 99) and the Western aptitude for absorbing everything strange. He could thus conclude that the West had degenerated to "a civilization permanently on the move, without neither tradition nor profound principles" (ibid.: 100). The main reason for this degeneration he found in a destruction of metaphysical thinking that began in the Renaissance.

Against the self-destruction of the West he posits the Orient. The Orient functions solely as a contrast to the negative modernity of Western civilization. It has all the metaphysical and spiritual values that the modern West lacks. The Oriental position allows Guénon to reverse the language of civilization, since Western civilization from the Oriental point of view must appear as barbarism (ibid.: 37). The whole structure of his text is based on this asymmetrical relation between an Oriental position capable of revealing the West ("The Orientals have no difficulties in penetrating into and understanding the special knowledge of the West", ibid.) – and a self-centered Western position incapable of any understanding of others. By "orientalizing" the West in this way, modern Western civilization can be bypassed and a road to a metaphysical West cleared. In Guénon's words, "the understanding of Oriental civilizations could eventually lead the West back to the traditional paths which it inconsiderately has deviated from" (ibid.: 116). The Orient, then, becomes just another way of imagining an anti-modern West. And when Guénon is talking of the Orient, he only has what he calls "the real Orientals" (ibid.: 113) in mind. The traditionally negative markers – the Muslims and the Russians – are left out. The former belong neither to the West nor to the Orient, while the latter are part of modern Western civilization.

The cosmopolitans

The concept of civilization carries with it a universal potential which often takes the form of Eurocentrism. A Eurocentrist universalism is based on the contention that European values are universal *per se*. But universalism can also be viewed as a standard which does not automatically coincide with the European values. In the latter case, a universalist claim demands an effort to establish an abstract position from where all cultures can be viewed and judged. Euro-centrist universalism was clearly dominant in the post-war years, either in the form of Wilsonian idealism or as the so-called standard of civilization which played an important role in the institutionalization of a legal framework for international politics.[35] It is therefore not surprising that universalism was an option in the crisis debate.

In his book *The Salvaging of Civilization* from 1921, the British author H.G. Wells gave a spectacular answer to what he saw as "the actual smashing and breaking down of modern civilization" (1921: 46). Wells related this breaking down of civilization to the catastrophe of the war. But the war was only the climax of a development that had taken place since the eighteenth century. Wells describes this development as a growth in technological means that augmented the destructive forces of mankind. The crisis unleashed by the war is described in the negative language of decline and barbarism. Wells speaks of "a new phase of disorder, conflict, and social disorder" (ibid.: 6), of "decadence" and "barbarism" (ibid.) and even of "a degenerative process towards extinction" (ibid.: 12). Through his description of development as a technological process producing a global world, he can situate the crisis on the level of mankind. Since "the world has been brought into one community" (ibid.: 11), as he claims, mankind needs to recognize this fact. The causes of the current crisis can be explained by the gap between a global reality and a retarded view of the world based on nationalism and imperialism (ibid.: 32). Wells' solution to the crisis is the creation of a world state. In his flowery language, this state could become "a universal palace (making) the whole globe our garden and play ground" (ibid.: 33). Wells has no difficulties in marrying his world state to a European point of view. By focusing on the "unifying ideas" of the Roman Empire and of Christendom he can create an image of a Europe prepared for the world state. However, the earlier efforts of uniting Europe did not continue because technology at that time did not match the unifying ambitions. Instead, the result was a Europe split into nations.[36] Like those searching for a European spirit, Wells placed the responsibility for the actual crisis in the nationalism which emprisoned Europe and hindered a match of the globalizing tendencies of modern civilization. But unlike the proponents of European values, Wells only treats the unification of Europe as a first step on the road to a world state. By referring to modern civilization as an inevitable globalization, he is able to establish a disjunction between a traditional and lethal Europe of the nations and a world becoming more and more one civilization in a positive sense. Civilization is thus presented as both a modern condition following a technological determinism and as an ideal for a world community. This latter understanding of civilization is stressed even further by another cosmopolitan thinker, the socialist political scientist Harold Laski for whom civilization as such can only be "the civitas maxima of mankind" (Laski 1932: 21). In this more radical cosmopolitanism there is no room for specifically European values not even as stepping stones to world civilization. The true values are only to be found at the level of world civilization. Consistent with his more internationalist outlook, Laski eliminates Europe as a positive position from where the universal values become visible. Wells' more European (and Eurocentric) point of view is demonstrated by the connection he makes between a set of positive European values in the form of the unifying, i.e. antinationalist ideas and the world civilization which can be built on these ideas.[37]

For both Wells and Laski, the step to the universal follows a logic of globalization, or as elegantly put by Laski: the "tremendous syllogism" where "(m)odern science means a world-market; a world-market means world-interdependence; world-interdependence means world-government" (Laski 1932: 25). Although they are both located within a discourse of modern civilization as globalization, they do not see globalization and modernity as negative forces that have to be circumvented in order to save Europe. Modern civilization is seen rather as the inevitable condition or "the reality" which Europe will have to cope with. In their view, nationalism and the imperialist and martial logic that follows from it cause the misery. Nationalism thus comes to mean the opposite of civilization: it is non-modern and it is uncivilized.

The historian Arnold Toynbee coined the expression "The Dwarfing of Europe" in a lecture held in 1926. Toynbee described the situation in 1918 as paradoxical: at the same time as the world was witnessing a radical Westernization due to the spread of Western civilization, Europe was losing its supremacy in the world. By adopting Western values, the non-European civilizations, and specifically Russia, had become capable of threatening Western civilization. Toynbee presents a gloomy picture of a Europe overrun by its own civilization. In Toynbee's case, globalization originates in the dynamic forces of industrialism and democracy in the Western civilization. But because of "the dead-weight of (its) tradition" (Toynbee 1958: 113), Europe cannot keep pace with its own forces. The result is the dwarfing of Europe. And for Toynbee this European dwarf does not have much to hope for. Euthanasia seems the only possible solution.

If one takes Toynbee's grand scheme of world history which he later developed in his monumental work *A Study of History* into consideration, there is nothing abnormal in the dying away of Western civilization since many civilizations has disintegrated in the past.[38] Although Toynbee clearly adopts a non-universal position in his splitting up of world history into the history of twenty-one different civilizations, I have chosen to include him among the cosmopolitans because he eliminates any position from where the universal can be challenged. But his universalism does not have the optimist and moral coloring of Wells' and Laski's world state. It is a universalism reduced to the negative effects of globalization.

Conclusion

By way of concluding, we may ask whether the crisis debate of the inter-war years has any relevance for current treatments of Europe. There are certainly similarities. Actual developments are perhaps not represented in a language of crisis, but we may at least detect a lack of conceptual orientation characterized by the widespread use of terms signifying an end such as postmodern, post-national etc. These terms are typically connected to *globalization* which, apparently, has become the key concept in the diagnosing of our general situation today. Globalization is often used in criticism of our present modernity which recall the use of civilization in the inter-war years. This is certainly the case in Benjamin Barber's pessimist description of globalization – or McWorld in his fanciful expression – conquering the different national states. Barber's immensely popular book, *Jihad vs. McWorld* of 1995, is part of a whole new genre of world descriptions under the heading of globalization.[39] McWorld designates a technologically driven process which homogenizes all cultures in the world and thereby destroys the national basis for democracy. Barber's dichotomy between a global, technological modernity and the different national societies serves to exorcise the negative components of modernity from these societies, in much the same way as in the anti-modernist strategy of the 1920s. One difference being, however, that Barber does not recur to the pseudo-biological language of Spengler and others, but to a more modernized, communitarian version of culture.

Many pessimist judgments on globalization tend to be formed in narratives of decline. Another way of responding to the actual uncertainty is to turn to European or Western culture. This is manifest in the setting up of an opposition between Islam and the West that plays a crucial role in current neo-nationalist discourses in Europe. But the turn to Europe can also be found within scholarly works such as Samuel Huntington's *The Clash of Civilizations* of 1996 where a cultural description of the West (including the United States) is inserted into an analysis of developments within international politics. Like the earlier proponents of a unified European culture, Huntington must provide an image of the true European values based on the axis of Greece, Rome and Christianity, and like his predecessors he has to draw up the borders of the West. Huntington's velvet curtain that expels orthodox Christianity from the West resembles earlier efforts of exorcising the Oriental specter.

The modern debate of the global situation also shows examples of a universalist approach. Francis Fukuyama's paradigm of the end of history reintroduced a classical enlightenment version of universal civilization into the debate (Fukuyama 1992). In his slightly modernized version, universalism revealed itself in the progressive march towards democracy. Although he did not forecast the coming of a world state, his idea of democracy as an end point in the rational development of mankind certainly has affinities with it. And his smooth dissolution of an originally Western set of practices into a world civilization (of democracy) reminds one of Toynbee's ideas of a Westernization of the world, although the latter, contrary to Fukuyama, saw this happening at the expense of the West itself.[40] We could, of course, point to other examples of pronounced universalist expressions in the actual debate. One can only think of the current efforts to introduce a humanitarian vocabulary into discourses of international politics.

But what about postmodernism? This is clearly a conceptual frame that did not exist in the debate of the 1920s. But if we broadly define postmodernism as a skeptical and deconstructive attitude to the traditional master narratives of Western civilization (and among other things, the concept of civilization itself) we may find some points of resemblance. Paul Valéry, who launched the crisis debate in 1919, described the situation as an intellectual crisis characterized by a loss of existing points of orientation. In the same vein, Curtius spoke of "the fluidization of traditional European ways of thinking as the psychological precondition for a change in the European cultural spirit" (Curtius 1925: 262). We may therefore spot a certain deconstructive mood, although, contrary to postmodernism, this mood was related to a feeling of decline. In this respect, postmodernism is of a second order, since it claims to be a condition we have to live in. Postmodernism, of course, locates itself at the opposite end of modernity than that of anti-modernism. But in its effort to deconstruct modernity, post-modernism has something in common with the earlier anti-modernist efforts to exorcise the negative elements of modern civilization. Both approaches try to establish an external point of view from where modern civilization can be exposed.

A certain version of postmodernism can even be said to acknowledge the dwarfing of Europe. The British sociologist Mike Featherstone, who links post-modernism to globalization, argues that globalization leads to a dismantling of Western cultural hegemony including its master narratives. Postmodernism should then be the theoretical answer to this situation. In that sense, it can be argued, he claims, "that globalization produces postmodernism" (Featherstone 1955: 114). This claim is not a very far cry from Valéry's bemoaning of standardization as the cause for the loss of illusions. When Featherstone, furthermore, contends that "it may well be that what we consider to be the substantive cultural responses and experiences of modernity likewise can be relativized to the Western particularity", is he then not celebrating that dwarfing of Europe which was lamented by so many in the 1920s and 1930s?

Resemblances do not make it up for influences. Is it possible to claim that the crisis debate of the inter-war years has had a direct influence on the actual debate? This question cannot be answered in a simple way. But insofar as this debate can be seen as the first general revaluation of all the major themes and concepts attached to the concept of civilization, it left a space open for the continuing rehearsal of a civilizational vocabulary in the debate over Europe.

Notes

1 According to René Dagorn, the word *globalization* was introduced in the English language "at the end of the 1950s" (1999: 189). The Merriam-Webster's Collegiate Dictionary dates the first occurrence of the word *postmodern* to 1949.
2 In the French version, Valéry refers to a "now": "Nous autres, civilisation, nous savons maintenant que nous sommes mortelles" (1919: 11).
3 The conceptual link between civilization and a universalist view on history can be traced back to the eighteenth-century use of the term civilization by authors such as Turgot and Ferguson, see Ifversen (1998).

4 To imagine the ultimate end – be it insanity or destruction – is obviously a radical conclusion to any description of a crisis.

5 It is worth noticing that Valéry instead of the traditional Faust chooses Hamlet as icon of Europe. While Faust sells his soul to the devil, a significant other, Hamlet sees ghosts. The problem is perhaps within Hamlet himself.

6 In Valéry's sophisticated play with words, democracy and homogenization result in a *deminutio capitis* of Europe. After the French Revolution, every anti-modernist would know about democracy's decapitating consequences!

7 For an almost complete overview of the political projects for a united Europe in the 1920s, see Pegg (1983).

8 Among the different ways of defining Western identity in the inter-war years, Gress lists communism and "the grand narrative" of Western civilization produced in USA. Both of these ways propagated an optimism which contradicted with the dominant version in Europe, see Gress (1998: 29–58, 347–405).

9 For a standard description of the decline of capitalist civilization, see Webb and Webb 1927. Not even Marxists like the Webb couple, however, can escape the dichotomy of the civilized and the barbaric related to the semantics of civilization: thus only "the cultivated races" are ready for socialism (Webb and Webb 1927: 13).

10 For the conceptual history of civilization, see Ifversen (2000a), Moras (1930), Fisch (1993).

11 The first volume was written during the war and appeared in April 1918. The second volume, mostly written after the war, appeared in May 1922 (Koktanek 1968: 149, 252).

12 For an overview of the German debate, see Schroeter (1922) and Merlio (1982).

13 Robert Musil explained Spengler's success by his ability to mirror the *Zeitgeist*: "Wenn man Spengler angreifft, greift man die Zeit an, der er entspringt und gefällt, denn seine Fehler sind ihre." (*Geist und Erfahrung. Anmerkung für Leser, Welche dem Untergang des Abendlandes entronnen sind*, 1921, quoted in Merlio 1982: 14).

14 The many works on radicalism in post-war Europe attest to this. Spengler is typically viewed as one of the leading ideologists of so-called radical conservatism. For this view, see among others Sontheimer (1962). A recurring topic in the debate over Spengler has been his relation to Nazism.

15 Determination has a twofold meaning in Spengler's depiction of civilization. It indicates the fundamental determinism of history, and also the pure will to power that characterizes the formlessness, "the barbarism" of the end phase of civilization (Spengler 1972 : 1102–7).

16 Gress rightly stresses the difference between the nihilists and the revivalists who refused to accept the radical consequences of Spengler, see Gress (1998: 348–9).

17 The German opposition between civilization and culture is treated in Bénéton (1975); Pflaum (1967). As I have showed elsewhere, this opposition can be traced back to the first appearance of the concept of civilization, Ifversen (2000a).

18 Spengler's analysis of culture is an uncovering of the being (*Dasein*), of the fundamental symbols (*Ursymbole*) in every phenomenon within a delimited cultural space.

19 This brings him to make fascinating, but also hazardous comparisons between the time of Hyksos in the Egyptian culture around 1675 AD, the Hellenistic period around 200 AD, the sultan dynasties in the Arabic culture of the ninth and tenth centuries and twentieth-century Western culture.

20 In European thinking, the life in the city is probably the oldest and most persistent image of the civilized life as opposed to the wild, irrational and disorganized life outside, see White (1972).

21 The metropolis or the world city plays an important role in the present efforts to conceptualize globalization, see Sassen (1991).

22 Gilbert Merlio demonstrates that Spengler's concept of culture is influenced by a nationalist historicism as well as a vulgarized version of life philosophy (Merlio 1982: 117–22).

23 Massis argues that the Lutheran identification of God with state created an all sovereign collectivity which is the condition for a nationalist ideology, see Massis (1956: 154–5).

24 For an analysis of the dominant image of America as the locus of the bad elements of modern civilization, see Kroes (1996: 1–43).

25 Keyserling describes eleven different locations in Europe, while Enzensberger writes about seven countries, Enzensberger (1987).

26 For the development of this catchword after 1945, see Wæver (1993).

27 Coudenhove-Kalergi's advocacy of a decoupling of nation and state and the 'privatization' of the nation is not a very far cry from Habermas' idea of the postnational constitution as the separation of the shared political culture from "the levels of subcultures and prepolitical identities" (Habermas 1996: 289).

28 The same view was put forward by Spengler who saw the Russian culture as a "historical pseudomorphosis".

29 To argue that Coudenhove-Karlergi was "a convinced multiculturalist" as Michael Heffernan does (Heffernan 1998: 127), is first of all to disregard the difficulties he had with how to recognize what he called "the veneration for the national idea" within a European culture (Coudenhove-Kalergi 1926: 128); and, second, to minimize his unitary view of European culture. In that respect, Keyserling was much more of a multiculturalist, although I would contend that the modern idea of multiculturalism did not make much sense in a Europe so completely dominated by a nationalist horizon.

30 The most convincing way of explaining European culture was to provide it with a history. Several histories of European culture were written in the inter-war years. Widely popular was the Austrian author Egon Friedell's *Kulturgeschichte der Neuzeit* published from 1927 to 1932. Friedell analyzes the decline of European (mostly high) culture within a Spenglerian framework. The eight volumes on *European Civilization* edited by Edward Eyre and published between 1934 and 1939 represent another more traditional example.

31 One way of simply avoiding any idea of a European culture when talking about the crisis is to reduce *Europe* to an international and geopolitical scene where the different leading nations confront each other. In the Italian ex-premier Francesco Nitti's warning against the decline of Europe (due to what he saw as the disastrous peace settlement), *Europe* is merely a scene for economic and political exchanges among states. Although he refers to a language of civilization when claiming that Europe had reached the highest level of culture, he does not say anything about the content of this culture (apart from it being made up of nations), see Nitti (1922: 208).

32 Ortega y Gasset even introduces a second-order view on the crisis where the ongoing discourse on crisis and decadence is taken as a symptom of the crisis (1964: 144).

33 Actually, Ortega y Gasset is leaning much more towards the spirit and the language of civilization than towards that of culture. There is hardly any mentioning of cultural traits in his handling of Europe.

34 For an almost complete overview of the practical projects for a united Europe in the 1920s, see Pegg (1983). These projects were mainly formulated within the terms of international security where the Franco-German relation became the main axis around which a united Europe could be conceived of. As already noted, many contributions to the discussion of the crisis were set within a cultural battle between French civilization and German culture, cf. Bénéton (1975: 85–99); Curtius (1925: 217–89).

35 For the development of the standard of civilization within international politics and jurisprudence, see Gong (1984).

36 As many other antinationalists, Wells does not really explain why Europe became divided up into nations.

37 Very much in line with Ortega y Gasset, Laski derives his vision of a world community from an idea of a non-sovereign statehood, thereby implying that state and nation rest on different values and can be separated.
38 The impact of industrialism and democracy is discussed in Toynbee (1939) which treats the breakdown of civilizations.
39 Barber (1995). For a discussion of the different meanings of civilization, see Ifversen (2000b).
40 The idea of a process of Westernization somehow detaching itself from the West is formulated in a significant way by the French economist Serge Latouche, see Latouche (1996). As many other postcolonial critics, Latouche wants to insist on the unmistakably Western character of globalization.

References

Barber, Benjamin (1995) *Jihad vs. McWorld: How Globalism and Tribalism are Reshaping the World*, New York, Ballantine Books.

Belloc, Hilaire (1937) *The Crisis of Our Civilization*, London, Cassel and Company.

Benda, Julien (1927) *La Trahisson des clercs*, Paris, Grasset.

Benda, Julien (1955) *The Betrayal of the Intellectuals*, Boston, Beacon Press.

Bénéton, Philippe (1975) *Historie de mots: culture et civilisation*, Paris, Presses de la Fondation Nationale des Sciences Politiques.

Berdyayev, Nikolay (1937) Den nye middelalder (1923) in N. Berdyayev, *Tidsskifte*, København, Europa-bøgerne, pp.11–35.

Coudenhove-Kalergi, Richard N. (1926) *Paneuropa*, Vienna, Paneuropa–Verlag.

Curtius, Ernst Robert (1925) *Französischer Geist im neuen Europa*, Stuttgart, Deutsche Verlags–Anstalt.

Dagorn, René (1999) Une brève histoire du mot "mondialisation", in GEMDEV, *Mondialisation: Les mots et les choses*, Paris, Karthala, pp.187–206.

Derrida, Jacques (1992) *The Other Heading: Reflections on Today's Europe*, Bloomington, Indiana University Press.

Duhamel, Georges (1928): *Entretien sur l'esprit européen*, Paris, Cahiers Libres.

Entretiens (1934) *L'avenir de l'esprit européen*, Paris, Société des Nations.

Enzensberger, Hans Magnus (1987) *Ach Europa! Wahrnehmungen aus sieben Ländern*, Frankfurt a.M., Suhrkamp.

Featherstone, Mike (1995) *Ondoing Culture: Globalization, Postmodernism and Identity*, London, Sage.

Fisch, Jörg (1993) "Zivilisation, Kultur", in O. Brunner, W. Conze, R. Koselleck (eds) *Geschichtliche Grundbegriffe, vol. VII*, Stuttgart, Ernst Klett Verlag, pp. 679–774.

Fukuyama, Francis (1992), *The End of History and the Last Man*, London, Hamish Hamilton.

Gong, Gerrit (1984) *The Standard of "Civilization" in International Society*, Oxford, Clarendon Press.

Guénon, René ([1930] 1947) *Orient et Occident*, Paris, Les Éditions Vega.

Gress, David (1998) *From Plato to NATO: The Idea of the West and Its Opponents*, New York, The Free Press.

Habermas, Jürgen (1996) "The European Nation–state – Its Achievements and Its Limits", in G. Balakrishnan (ed.) *Mapping the Nation*, London, Verso.

Heffernan, Michael (1998) *The Meaning of Europe*, London, Arnold.

Huntington, Samuel P. (1996) *The Clash of Civilizations and the Remaking of World Order*, New York, Simon & Schuster.

Ifversen, Jan (1998) "The Meaning of European Civilization A Historical–Conceptual Approach", *European Studies Newsletter*, vol. I, no. 2, pp. 20–38.

—— (2000a) "Begreber, diskurser og tekster omkring civilisation", in T.B. Dyrberg, J. Torfing and A.D. Hansen (eds), *Diskursanalysen på arbejde*, Copenhagen, Samfundslitteratur, Roskilde Universitetsforlag, pp. 189–220.

—— (2000b) "Globalization – A Catch-all Concept for the End of the Millennium", in I. Johansen (ed.) *Fins de Siècle/New beginnings*, *The Dolphin*, vol. 31, 2000, pp. 215–39.

Keyserling, Graf Hermann (1928) *Das Spektrum Europas*, Heidelberg, Niels Kampmann Verlag.

Keyserling, Count Hermann (1928) *Europe*, New York Harcourt, Brace & Company.

Koktanek, Anton Mirko (1968) *Oswald Spengler in seiner Zeit*, München, C.H. Beck.

Koselleck, Reinhart und Paul Widmer (eds) (1980) *Niedergang: Studien zu einem Geschichtlichen Thema*, Stuttgart, Klett–Cotta.

Kroes, Rob (1996) *If You've Seen One You've Seen the Mall: Europeans and American Mass Culture*, Chicago, University of Illinois Press.

Laski, Harold J. (1932) *Nationalism and the Future of Civilization*, London, Watts & Co.

Latouche, Serge (1996) *The Westernization of the World*, Oxford, Polity Press.

Massis, Henri (1956) Défense de l'Occident (1925) in H. Massis, *l'Occident et son destin*, Paris, Bernard, pp. 61–167.

Merlio, Gilbert (1982) *Oswald Spengler: Témoin de son temps*, vol. I–II, Stuttgart, Akademischer Verlag Hans–Dieter Heinz.

Moras, Joachim (1930) *Ursprung und Entwicklung des Begriffs der Zivilisation in Frankreich (1756–1830)*, Hamburg, Hamburger Studien zur Volkstum und Kultur der Romanen.

Nitti, Francesco (1922) *Der Niedergang Europas: Die Wege zum Wiederaufbau*, Frankfurt a.M., Frankfurter Societäts–Druckerei.

Ortega y Gasset, José ([1929] 1964) *The Revolt of the Masses*, New York, W.W. Norton.

Pegg, Carl H. (1983) *Evolution of the European Idea, 1914–1932*, Chapel Hill, NC, The University of North Carolina Press.

Pflaum, Michael (1967) "Die *Kultur–Zivilisations–Antithese* im Deutschen", in Sprachwissensshaffentlichen Colloquium (ed.) *Europäische Schlüsselwörter*, vol. III, Kultur und Zivilisation, München, Hueber, pp. 288–361.

Sassen, Saskia (1991) *The Global City: New York, London, Tokyo*, Princeton, NJ, Princeton University Press.

Schroeter, Manfred (1922) *Der Streit um Spengler: Kritik seiner Kritiker*, München, C.H. Beck-'sche Verlagsbuchhandlung.

Sontheimer, Kurt (1962) *Antidemokratisches Denken in der Weimarer Republik*, München, Nymphenburger Verlagshandlung.

Spengler, Oswald (1926) *The Decline of the West: Form and Actuality*, vol. I, New York, Alfred A. Knopf.

—— (1928) *The Decline of the West: Perspectives of World History*, vol. II, New York, Alfred A. Knopf.

—— (1972) *Der Untergang des Abendlandes: Umrisse einer Morphologie der Weltgeschichte*, München, Deutscher Taschenbuch Verlag.

Toynbee, Arnold (1939) *A Study of History*, vol. IV: The Breakdown of Civilizations, Oxford, Oxford University Press.

—— (1958) "The Dwarfing of the West", in A. Toynbee, *Civilization on Trial*, New York, New American Library.

Valéry, Paul (1919) "La crise de l'esprit", in P. Valéry, *Variété I*, Paris, NRF 1924, pp. 11–32.

—— (1922) Note. Extrait d'une conférence donnée à l'Université de Zurich le 15 novembre 1922, in Valéry, *Varieté I*, Paris, NRF 1924, pp. 33–49.

—— (1962) *History and Politics*, New York, Pantheon Books.

Wæver, Ole (1993) "Europe Since 1945: Crisis to Renewal", in Jan van der Dussen and Kevin Wilson (eds), *The History of the Idea of Europe*, Milton Keynes, The Open University, pp. 151–215.

Webb, Sydney and Webb, Beatrice (1927) *Den kapitalistiske civilisationens förfall*, Stockholm, Tidens Förlag.

Wells, H.G. (1921) *The Salvaging of Civilization*, London, Cassel and Company.

White, Hayden (1972) "The Forms of Wilderness: Archeology of an Idea", in E. Dudley and M.E. Novak (eds) *The Wild Man Within*, Pittsburgh, University of Pittsburgh Press, pp. 3–38.

8 The Eastern perception of the West

Djamshid Behnam

> I felt the Eastern presence, but I doubt if anyone can describe this sensation. Besides, is it necessary to describe something that all of us have felt deeply?
>
> (Borges 1985: 5)

Introduction

There is no evidence on our maps of the twelfth-century Iranian philosopher Sohravardi's concept of the East. To him, the term neither represents a geographic nor an ethnic meaning. It denotes, instead, a metaphysical signifi-cance which reflects the spiritual world of the wider East from where rises the clear and brilliant sun (Corbin 1977: 45).

But when we speak of Eastern and Western destinies, the words take on their common and ordinary meanings. For Europeans, the word "East" signifies a Levantine area which stretches around the eastern banks of the Mediterranean: Turkey, Greece, Syria, Palestine, Egypt, with Constantinople as its center. Until the end of WWI, it remained a mixed Islamic-Christian area filled with conflicting features and an object of constant fascination.

The East was never the East, it came to be so only together and in contact with the West. As the subject invents the object, it is the West which constructed the East.

The subject, observing the object from a distance called it "the East". Thus, the East is thought of as being within and viewed from the subject's modern Western system (Hoodastian 1998: 73).

On the other hand, from the point of view of Easterners, the West remained an unknown and imaginary continent for a long time. Travel accounts were appreciated, even if they were written by travelers whose knowledge was limited to describe the rarities and exotic curiosities they had seen. For decades, Europe presented itself as the synonym of progress and power, the struggle against despotism, the search for freedom, and science. But this perception of the West soon changed. The Europe of freedom also became the Europe of domination. The question is in fact the following: is the West a geographical entity, a group of colonizing states, or on the contrary, an idea, a concept indicating a certain "modernity", law and liberty?

Everyone is aware that, between the West and the East, it is not a question of plain divergence of views but a hierarchy built up by ethnocentrism, driven by a basic feeling of difference between types of humanity. Moreover, this difference was linked to a geopolitical confrontation of unequal powers, which began well before the century of conquests, during which colonialism was nothing but an historical moment. Contrary to what Rudyard Kipling and many others proclaimed during the colonization period, the West and the East met long before. Although saying when and where would be naive. Friedrich Nietzsche was right: "The East and the West are the circles of chalk we paint under our eyes to hide our shyness" (Assayag and Bénéï 2000: 15).

In this chapter, we will attempt to describe the following: first, the diversity of perceptions and the complicated relationships which existed and still exist between the West and the East, within the Middle Eastern cultural region, and more precisely, in Iran and Turkey. Situated between the East and the West, crossroads between Europe, Asia and Africa, the Middle Eastern region and North Africa constitute a cultural area based on the belief in Islam, on the struggle against the climate's aridity (the reason behind nomadism and the ingenious techniques of irrigation), on an ancient city life, and finally, on a common historical destiny. This region was home to the oldest civilizations of humanity: Mesopotamian (Babylonian, Chaldean, Assyrian), Persian, Egyptian, Phoenician; as well as the great religions of Mithraism, Zoroastrianism, Judaism, Christianism, and Islam. It has absorbed influences from the Chinese and Indian civilizations and has known Hellenic, Roman and Islamic periods. However, there are three distinct cultural areas within this region: the Iranian, the Arab, and the Turkish areas.

Second, the modernization process (the transfer of Western modernity to other regions) took place in two distinct "situations". First, the "colonial situation" which consisted of territorial occupation, foreign administration, colonial appointments, and direct economic exploitation. Second, the "national situation of dependence", meaning the condition of the countries on which the "quasi-voluntary" transfer of European modernity was practiced. These politically independent but economically exploited countries could take their choice from the various European models available.

The obligation which required their opening up to the West was often transformed into a voluntary search for new techniques by governments keen to catch up for lost time, by innovative ministers and modernist elites, who extolled and recommended Western technology and know-how. Iran and Turkey were examples of this situation where countries hoped to be in touch with the West as partners and even as equals.

Diversity of perceptions

The will to modernize, which emerged at the end of the eighteenth century in the Ottoman Empire and at the beginning of the nineteenth in Iran, was the result of an observation of stagnation and decadence in relation to Europe.

Thus, it was not a spontaneous movement, attributable to the impossibility of reconciling internal conflicts in society, but a comparison with the outside world, with "the other". The outcome was the acknowledgment of an historical "backwardness" and a desire to "catch up".

It was not a question of transforming society at the outset, but rather to provide the authorities with more efficient means to help it preserve its values, and to defend itself from foreign aggression. This change was based on defense security rather than on actual transformation (Djalili 1989: 209).

Consequently, from the outset, the justifications underpinning the process of modernization were different. The traditional authority – Muslim, Iranian, or other – is convinced of the superiority of the respective values (to which they adhere); the only thing they conceded to the West was a certain technological and material advance, hence, their recognition of a need to fill the gap in know-how and other tools.

The second stage of modernization based on the need to transform society, to change its mentality, and to include new values and establish new political structures originated with the intellectuals who, in their effort to transform their own society, sought guidance from the experience of others. There were various reactions among the intellectuals towards the West, ranging from idealization to demonization. These phases of fascination, criticism, rejection and negation alternated and sometimes manifested in cycles.

The temptation of the West

In the eighteenth century, the two great Ottoman and Iranian Empires shared the Middle Eastern cultural region, following the impact of military defeat. Conscious of their backwardness in comparison to the West, they set out in search of modernity.

Faced with the intrusion and the growing economic, cultural, and political domination of the European powers, the responses were fundamentally inspired by a resolve on renewal in the Ottoman Empire as well as in the Qadjar Monarchy in Iran. The reforms at the end of the nineteenth century, known as the Tanzimat reforms in the Ottoman Empire and the Islahat reforms in Iran, prepared the ground for the nationalist and constitutionalist movements and a complete disruption of the region.

For historical and geographical reasons, the Ottoman Empire was the first one to establish links with Europe whereas Iran, because of her geographical isolation, experienced a delay in her *rendez-vous* with Western civilization.

The Qadjar government, or more precisely, a handful of enlightened men in this government, tried to establish direct connections with Europe (visits from European scientists, students sent out to European institutions of higher education, imports of machinery, etc.) but they were obliged to abandon this strategy and follow the Tanzimat model which they considered more accessible. In this way, they managed to provide themselves with European institutions through the example of the Ottoman Empire.

Apart from colonialism, voluntary Westernization should be taken into account. The intellectual elites of countries which were not directly colonized but under Western influence felt a true fascination for the European civilization. In the eyes of these intellectuals, Europe represented an image of unlimited progress and the only way out of underdevelopment and poverty. Some Middle Eastern countries showed their keen interest in the disrupting events in the West by sending students to Western countries to draw inspiration from the philosophical and revolutionary thinkers of the time. Through their political and social ideas these students were responsible for the first struggles against the ruling classes. The Western culture swiftly became the synonym of "government by law", and consequently paved the way for the constitutional revolution in these countries. The intellectuals pondered the reasons for their underdevelopment and the backwardness of their societies. Some of them were persuaded that religion was the main obstacle to development and recommended reforms in this sphere. In contrast, others explained their backwardness through scientific, technical and social underdevelopment and did not consider anything outside Western culture worthy of interest. Faith in the almighty power of God, in the supremacy of the spirit and in the brotherhood of believers were replaced by the ideals of sovereignty of the State, supremacy of the nation, transcendence of popular will, and the equality of citizens.

Nevertheless, a common aspect came to light: that of progress, and this irrespective of cultural identity. While the idea of progress conveyed different and alternating significations of liberty and of social or economic progress, the idea of the need to Westernize was implicit. At the time, the intellectual circles reflected on the reasons for the Western progress, the stagnation of non-industrialized countries, and the means to remedy the situation. These intellectual discussions had important consequences which led to the emergence of three movements:

1   a cultural and secular movement which allowed the translations of literary essays, an increase in the number of newspapers, and sending out a growing number of students to Europe;
2   an Islamic revival movement, spreading from Egypt to India and from Central Asia to Turkey and Iran;
3   a movement to combat despotism, thus paving the way for the establishment of constitutional governments.

The *Nahda*, evocative of "rebirth" or "awakening", referred to an intellectual and political movement which unfolded at the end of the nineteenth century in the Nile valley. This "awakening" should be a "return to one's roots" (*salafiyya*), and at the same time a "rebirth" (*Nahda*). Many thinkers, statesmen, social reformers and religious personages consecrated their names to these two objectives. They tried to set up a movement towards the return of the spiritual values of Islam, and to create the precondition for opening to the modern spirit from the healthy intelligence of "*salaf*" .

Towards the middle of the nineteenth century, this movement became widespread and took the dimensions and characteristics of what history would retain under the name of *Nahda*. For a while, Lebanon took the lead by opening its large windows to the West, thus welcoming various foreign "religious missions". Their preoccupation with disseminating their ideas urged them to develop their teaching in Arabic, and hence translate a host of European works, and multiply their organizations and schools and colleges. In the second half of the century, the center of all intellectual ferment was set in Egypt, and this intellectual activity, which was strictly and incessantly focused on cultural problems and religious concerns, took a more pronounced political orientation. After the period of translators/popularizers such as Tahtawi (1801–1873), followed a period of thinkers, who were philosophers and fighters at the same time, more resolutely committed to the defense, the teaching, and illustration of Islam.

The Ottoman modernization efforts which started towards the close of the eighteenth century under two sultan reformers, Sélim III (1789–1806) and ... II (1000–39), continued throughout the nineteenth century with the ... at period (1839–76) and the promulgation of the first Ottoman Constitution (1876).

The most famous writers were Ibrahim Sinasi (1826–71), Ziya Pasha (1825–80) and most of all Namik Kemal (1840–88). Their works were read by the rising bourgeoisie: civil servants, military officers, jurists, and journalists, in Istanbul and in the Ottoman Empire or by Iranian political exiles.

The radical positions held by Sinasi and the eclectic stance of Namik Kemal quite faithfully reflected the fundamental difference between the fanatics of civilization and the others, meaning those who were in search of a synthesis; an always highly spirited controversy.

Among the exiled ideologists, an important figure to remember is Ahmed Rida (1859–1930). The thoughts of Ahmed Rida initially addressed the reasons behind the backwardness which affected the Ottoman Empire. In the articles he wrote in his newspaper and in a positivist journal, he supported the idea that it was not necessary to be Christian to embrace morality, civilization and progress. In this sense, Rida changed the young Ottomans' wording of the problem which was a search for the possibility of integrating progress in the static world of Islam.

Iranian intellectuals who were prisoners of the Iranian cultural isolation and suffered from the despotic system of state control and the obscurantism of religion, sought solutions, among which was the use of external intermediaries in certain large cities where Iranian communities already existed on its periphery. They attempted to get in touch with and listen to the news of hope which arrived from Europe through relay centers in Istanbul, Tiflis, Cairo, Calcutta, Bakou. These towns, where a certain impact of European civilization was already increasingly perceived, lived in the ferment of the three movements of intellectual, cultural and political renewal.

Between 1880 and 1900, the works of an Iranian generation born between 1830 and 1840 appeared in Tehran, Istanbul, Tiflis, Cairo and Calcutta. These publications were the works of statesmen, intellectuals, and even of enlightened businessmen. They brought up the subject of despotism, economic backwardness and the intervention of foreign powers, as well as the grounds for, and the factors in the progress of European countries. Some became defenders of a non-theocratic legislation, and others recommended above all the establishment of a constitutional government, while nobody found the Muslim unity and religious reforms to be the way to a solution. Practically everyone, implicitly or explicitly, suggested adopting the European model with some adjustments of course. The advocates of modernization were Malkum (1815–1908), Jamâl al-Dîn al-Afghâni (1839–97), Tâlebûf (1833–99), Aqâ Khân Kirmâni (1854–96) and Akhûndzâdeh (1811–78).

This handful of men belonged to a small but important group. They wrote articles on aspects of social life and political pamphlets which were secretly passed around. They took part in political meetings of the opposition and traveled between Tehran, Cairo, Istanbul, Tiflis, and Calcutta, from where the external relay points transmitted Western ideas and concepts to Iran. These activities were dangerous and many of the involved persons were exiled or executed.

The Iranian reformist elite propagated progressive European philosophical and social ideas, and the growing bourgeoisie which was essentially composed of businessmen, took interest in the ideas. Accepting the necessity of industrialization but fearing a blind imitation of the West, they sought the basis and the principles of the European civilization and not its appearance. The Iranians, who were profoundly nationalists, were not afraid of losing their identity and believed instead in the possibility of a synthesis. They questioned the sociopolitical situation in Iran and demanded reforms. The West was thought of as an example but not as a goal. This liberal elite denied all intellectual backwardness and only recognized social and economic underdevelopment.

Their works addressed despotism, economic underdevelopment, the intervention of foreign powers in Iran as well as the grounds for and the factors underlying the progress of European countries. From the comparisons followed the search for solutions. Some talked about the necessity of Westernization, provided it was adapted to the Iranian culture.

Some placed emphasis on the economy and tried to create a national industry. They addressed, for the first time, the creation of a railway system, the need for savings, investments and banks. Strange as it may seem, it was at this stage when the economic dependence of Iran started, following the concessions granted to Russia and England for the establishment of banks, the fishing industry in the North, the customs administration, and oil extraction.

The last decades of the nineteenth century were marked by a reawakening of the Muslim world. This phenomenon, at once political and religious, came as a result of two currents of thought: one of religious inspiration based on the reformist ideology taking shape in the Muslim world since the end of the eighteenth century; and the other, of purely profane origin and of modernist orientation (modernity having chiefly a European connotation at that time).

While the efforts under the theme of *Nahda* tried to make up for the socio-cultural underdevelopment of the Islamic world, the search inspired by religious motivations aimed to create a process of renewal and reform (in Arabic: *Islâh*), with a view towards harmonization of traditional realities and the facts of modern life.

Three names in particular illustrated this movement: Jamâl al-Din al-Afghâni (died, 1897), Muhammad Abduh (died, 1905), and the Pakistani thinker Muhammad Iqbal (died, 1938) who, with a deeper analysis, undertook the "reconstruction of the religious thought of Islam" and the "building of new foundations of Islamic thought in terms of modern philosophical categories". The ideas developed by Muhammad Abduh, which summed up the reformist doctrine in its entirety were focused on a certain number of fundamental points whose main features were: the purification of Islam from the corrupting influences and practices inherited from decadent times.

It was not until the second half of the nineteenth century, through the medium of the relay points such as Turkey, India, and Russia, that Iran received the forerunner themes of the philosophy of Enlightenment and the French Revolution. Owing to the courage of intellectuals who clashed with religious resistance and the monarchy, these ideas were passed on thus contributing to the success of the constitutional movement at the end of the nineteenth century.

The period was marked by the radical challenge of the structures of power by the modernist elites who were able, at the same time, to mobilize certain social strata while associating some of the traditional elites to their cause. This movement would lead to the constitutional revolution which truly marked the advent of modernity. This revolution introduced important notions such as popular sovereignty, freedom of speech and mind, civil rights, the separation of powers, government responsibility, etc. The introduction of these ideas would go beyond the initial objectives of the movements, on which a certain consensus had been agreed upon between the laity and the radical clergy, implying the limitation of the powers of the king, and the establishment of a judiciary. Despite certain analyses, which would subsequently attempt to minimize the importance of the constitutional movement, the revolutionary magnitude of this event seems to us unquestionable in so far as it introduced entirely new notions into the Iranian political spheres. It was fundamental concepts such as the state, the nation, political legitimacy, the participation of the people in the life of the nation, and the majority/minority dialectic.

Fascination for the West

After the decline of the Ottoman Empire (1918) and the fall of the Qadjar Empire in Iran (1925), the decade 1920–30 marked the constitution of nation–states and the attainment of power of Atatürk in Turkey and Reza Shah in Iran. While the rest of the Islamic world were languishing in a more or less direct form of European domination, Atatürk and Reza Shah, both passionate nationalists, nevertheless chose to radically Westernize the institutions and practices of their countries. In both cases, national recovery was obtained through an undoubtedly enlightened and forcibly modernizing despotism.

The national pride of the two leaders was toned down because of their boundless admiration of European nations' "Progress", which they wanted their countries to have at any cost. Iran's and Turkey's reformist ideologies were guided by contempt for the recent past and the "decadence" of Islamic societies, unrestrained fascination for "modern civilization", the wish to rediscover in the nation's ancient past the grounds for comparisons with the Western models.

The most profound revolutionary aspect of Kemalism did not manifest itself in political institutions, economic organization, or in social stratification, but rather on a cultural level. The Kemalist policy reflected an extremely rigid concept of the interdependence of social realities. He conceived what he would call "the civilization" which had to be accepted as an entity. To remain an independent nation, Turkey had to become a modern political and economic state; and to this end, the way of life and system of values of the Turkish people had to be Europeanized.

To understand this policy, it has to be placed in the ideological context of the time, which was very different from that which prevailed in the Third World after WWII. For the modernizing elites of the Middle East, in Turkey and in Persia, no doubt less so in the Arab countries which were under direct European colonization, the West not only represented a technical model, but also, in a large measure, a moral ideal. Public-spiritedness, rejection of corruption, professional conscience, self-respect, were considered appealing values in themselves and the secret of European success (Derriennic 1980: 65).

The unification of the territorial foundation of the State, the establishment of a central power capable of affirming the authority of the government throughout the country, and the strengthening of national cohesion by developing the means of communication, were the first objectives of Reza Shah's project. These were followed by attempts at homogenization and the merging of disparate communities through the institution of national military services, state education, abolition of privileges held by certain social groups, or the impetus given to the emancipation of women. Finally, there was an economic development outline based on industrialization, the establishment of a state-controlled economic sector intended as a driving force, and on the rehabilitation of public finances which was a real scourge during the Qadjar period.

Following the Kemalist example, Reza Shah adopted at the same time in Iran, commercial, penal and civil codes of the European type, created a judicial system inspired by the European model, and regulated the religious tribunals. Dress codes were imposed on the population; a language reform was undertaken in order to exclude words of Arab or Turkish origin from the vocabulary; and the use of the patronymic was made compulsory. Admittedly, unlike Turkey, the republic and the "secular" State were not officially announced and the social power of the Shiite clergy, which was both economic and moral, remained basically intact.

The introduction of Western culture always came hand in hand with nationalism and a certain historical awareness. Indeed, Western superiority was recognized in scientific and technical fields but not in the sphere of cultural values. The modernization efforts of Atatürk and Reza Shah were continued, often with the same zeal and determination by their successors, notably by Ismet Inönü who relied, on the one hand, on support from the Republican Party of the People (the only party for a long time) and the army, and on the other, on Mohammad Reza Shah until the end of the 1970s. In both countries, the modernization process was authoritarian; albeit more radical in Turkey than in Iran.

In the 1920s, germanophilia prevailed and the Iranian elites, who were fascinated by the West, accepted it without calling the proposed model into question. In 1922, Taqizadeh, statesman and writer, inaugurated a new series of the magazine *Kâveh* (published in Persian in Berlin) which summed up his aim in a formula that Iranian intellectuals will remember:

> first the unconditional adoption and promotion of the European civilization, a total submission to Europe, cultural assimilation of habits and customs, of organization, of the sciences and the arts, of European life and its life styles as a whole, with the sole exception of language, and the rejection of any kind of self-satisfaction, any objection which may originate from any misplaced or false feeling of patriotism ... Iran has to become Europeanized in appearance and in reality, body and soul, that's all.
>
> (*Kâveh* 1920, no. 36)

In the magazine *Iranshahr*, also published in Berlin, Kazemzadeh, writer and philosopher, developed his ideas regarding a spiritual revolution whose core would be the secularization of society. This should liberate society from the religious control of the Ulama. To achieve this, Kazemzadeh argued it would be necessary to purify religion of superstitions, to separate the spiritual from the temporal (the categorical rejection of clericalism and theocracy), and to adapt religious principles to modern world conditions.

According to this new concept, religion as the principal factor of social cohesion should give way to the nation. This would solve the problem of the clash between Islamic identity and the Westernization process since the new national identity intended to make Islam a personal matter.

In Turkey, the official ideologist of the Young Turk Regime, Zia Gökalp, who was a sociologist and a disciple of Durkheim, proposed in 1916 that Islam should become a personal matter with no control whatsoever on the conduct of society based on the frame formed by a nation and the Turkish culture, and the scientific and technical civilization of the West.

Gökalp thought that, exactly like the Protestant religion, the Muslim religion should be nationalized through the language. Thus, the Koran should be translated into Turkish; the language in which the prayers and the *Ezan* (call to pray) would be recited. The most interesting of his projects of reform remains "Westernization". He distinguished culture from civilization, and this distinction was understood in a materialistic sense. The Turkish people had to Westernize and adopt the Western culture. This new idea should allow the Turkish people to assert: "I am of Turkish nationality, of Muslim religion, and of Western civilization."

More than anyone, Zia Gökalp had grasped that the clash between the Muslims, the Turks, and the Westernizers, representing the three main trends of Turkish life, was mistaken. He carefully tried to dissociate the Ottomans which allowed him to propose his formula: "Turkeyfication", "Islamization", "Westernization", as a "magic" formula.

The ideology of the Young Turks was not monolithic. Most of them favored Westernization; but there was also a pro-Islamic group. The first group, according to Abdullah Cevdet, one of their master thinkers, argued that "there is no such thing as a second civilization. The term civilization signifies Western civilization and it is imported with its roses and its thorns" (Kazancigil 1994: 57).

Kemalism would be more radical than other Western trends, (New Ottomans, Young Turks) because of another Gökalpian link of an inverted nature: it would reject the dualism of Zia Gökalp and his dichotomy: *hars* (culture) and *medeniyet* (civilization – technology).

Gökalp believed that the second term is "international" and could be adopted whereas the first one could not be imported since it was "national" by nature. The elites would go to the people to absorb its culture and to introduce them to Western culture. For Atatürk, these two concepts would be difficult to separate. In reality, he wanted to be given a free rein in approaching the West. His radical approach would prove to have a much deeper impact on society.

Under Atatürk, the term *batililasma* (Westernization) was the synonym for *muasir medeniyet* (modern civilization). "We would like to become a modern society. All our efforts aim at establishing a modern government, i.e. Westernized, in this country. In wishing to attain civilization which nation would not choose the West?"

WWII induced great changes in the relations between Western, African and Asian cultures. With the invasion of Western technology, new forms of dependencies appeared. Industrialization fever swept through the Third World countries. They chose to benefit from the quantitative aspects of development, which took greater and greater importance, at the expense of the cultural dimension. Once the technocrats came to power, industrialization became the synonym of Westernization, i.e. of modernity; the internal dynamism of national cultures was neglected straight out. These cultures have given way to a kind of Western culture which spreads in a breathtaking speed among the young by the means of mass communication. In the Third World countries, a majority prefers economic and social development at the risk of loosing their cultural identity. From 1950 to 1952, the presence of nationalist movements under the leadership of Mosaddegh led to the nationalization of the oil industry and the departure of British staff from the south of Iran. Imperialism was taken over by the bourgeoisie. With the fall of Mosaddegh and the return of the king, a new period was established until the events of 1980.

These events had been the source of disillusionment and later of hatred for the imperialist West. At the beginning of the 1950s, Iranian elites were drawn to the Third World movement which replaced those of Marxist inspiration.

Criticism and rejection of the West

From the 1960s onwards, Western evolution brought about changes which complicated the sociological situation. The original experiments in Japan and China were followed closely. In general, the Third World intellectuals became aware of the value of their respective cultures and started worrying about their future. Finally, the rise of the young generation's discontent is observed in the East as well as in the West.

Weary of society's superficiality and extravagance, the young have chosen a new lifestyle which challenges the existing society. We are witnessing new practices in the sphere of family life, in the man–woman relationship, and in the role of women in society. The East has been "rediscovered" and intellectuals have refused to live, as Jacques Berque (1986) would say, "in a history separate from the rest of the world".

A deeper knowledge of the West, original experiments taking place in non-Western countries, as well as a re-evaluation of national culture, have prompted the true Third World elite's desire to return to their roots and enhance the national culture. This return to one's origins was not a simple rejection of the West; when considering all sides of the question, it is most of all, characterized by a will to keep the identity, while at the same time remaining open to the outside world which is no longer limited to the West.

Accepting the need for development in its broadest meaning does not in the slightest imply imitating or importing the Western industrial culture born out of the specific environment of the nineteenth-century industrialization and the first half of the twentieth in certain geographic situations in Europe and North America. Was Europe not the first to question the "industrial culture"?

The 1960s and the 1970s were periods of rapid economic growth which, unfortunately, did not take into account the cultural and political dimensions of development. The initial reactions to authoritarian modernization were fraught with confusion and extremism. The rejection of its political dimension served as a pretext for the systematic rejection of everything new. The submissive and initial fascination for the West has assimilated modernization to Westernization, making modernity the synonym of the loss of social and cultural identity. The choice, therefore, was a defensive withdrawal into the well-known petrified traditions on the one hand, and the denial of one's roots, on the other.

Exacerbated by violent repression, the political protest was reinforced by a cultural resistance searching for original answers. It took half a century for the intellectuals to formulate original answers which came to be ideological catalysts for the revolutionary movement. Two of the intellectuals of that time particularly marked the movement by their analyses of the West, modernity, social change, and the interrelation with cultural identity. They were Jalal Al-e Ahmad (1923–69) and Ali Shariati (1935–77).

It was in the early 1960s that Jalal Al-e Ahmad (writer, essayist) published his book entitled *Gharbzadegii* and described this term as an "epidemic" which he saw spreading under the effect of Western domination in the Iranian society. '*Occidentalité*', "*occidentalose*", "*ouest-toxification*" are possible translations of the Persian term *gharbzadegi* composed of the term *gharb*, "the West" and the suffix *zadegi* which describes an action which has a violent physical effect: "to strike", "to defeat", "to possess". By its semantic composition, this construction identifies the West as the enemy of man (disease, virus, plague, cholera, snake, scorpion, evil spirit, natural calamity, earthquake, floods, etc.) and represents the Iranian as its victim.

Gharbzadegi was presented as a cultural disease attacking the individual and the societies of countries dominated by the West in terms of appearance (dress style, language of gestures, inclinations), but also in conduct (behavior, attitudes, practices) and in spirit (representation, perception, judgments, values, images, etc.). In short, "being Western" is losing yourself to the foreigner, the "other" (Yaveri 1991: 87). It was the Iranian version of the same phenomenon analyzed by the Martinicians Franz Fanon and Aimé Césaire, and by the Tunisian Albert Memmi.

This term which was adopted by all thinkers and ideologists no longer described a simple socio-cultural and political phenomenon; it became a true debate on identity issues, interpreting the recent evolution of society in terms of successive attacks on cultural identity as a result of the Westernization process launched by the Pahlavi dynasty.

The ideology of Shariati is a syncretism of Marxism and leftist ideologies of the 1960s (Fanon, Sartre) in which a revolutionary and anti-democratic vision prevailed. Shariati's ideal of a classless society conforms with the divine Unity. He exerted a predominant influence over the revolutionary youth. Intellectuals such as Jalal Al-e Ahmad and clerics such as Murtaza Motahhari (assasinated in 1979), also exercised influence; albeit to a limited degree.

During Shariati's studies in France in the 1960s, the confrontation intensified in Iran between the tyrannical authorities and the nationalists of religious orientation to which he belonged. He would become one of the most influential in the Iranian intellectual movement, putting his militant thoughts at the service of readers in his country. His open mind to Western culture did not divert him from his original problem of identity. He was not satisfied with asking "who am I?", but like all theorists, he added: "What is to be done?" To the question "What is to be done now?," Shariati answers:

We should therefore understand how the West has deprived us of our cultural and spiritual resources, how they made us, Easterners, a generation incapable of exploiting these immense mines overflowing with spiritual wealth, thoughts, morality, culture – in a broad sense – incapable of transforming this abundant intellectual reserve. We have to recognize the course it has followed, the methods it has practiced, the tricks and cunning it has used to achieve its goals. We have to understand how this East that had shone brightly in its culture and spirit, that one considered as the origin of the world's culture and the cradle of civilization, has become today a synonym of savagery, of decline, and of decadence. It is this Western success which we have to study; how did it make its way into the East, how do we follow its tracks and retrace the course it has followed.

(Shariati 1982: 110)

On the eve of the revolution in 1979, the proposed solutions against rapid Westernization in Iran were no longer "the enhancing of the past" or " a search for a synthesis of Western and Eastern values", but rather a categorical rejection of the West and "the return to one's roots and to Islam in its entirety".

Demonization of the West

The period from 1925 to 1979 were years of an authoritarian modernization divided into two stages: from 1925 to 1952 (nationalization of the oil industry) and from 1952 to 1979 (accelerated economic development and the growth of oil revenues). However, since 1979 until today, the Iranian government has been searching for an "Islamic way of development" which has led to a glaring failure.

Since the emergence of Islamism as a puritan movement of disenchantment which is the consequence of the forced marriage of religion and politics, we have witnessed the arrival in civil society of resistance supported by post-Islamic intellectuals, who led a big protest campaign while the conflict raged between the conservatives and the reformers. A society in search for an identity will give birth to a new culture.

The term "Western cultural invasion" used by the authorities, tries to hide this social reality. Loaded with traumatizing connotations, it expresses a deep feeling of discomfort and the deadlock of the authorities as an attempt to divert the population's attention by putting the blame outside the country to explain the reasons behind the crisis they are experiencing.

According to an article which appeared in the magazine *Kyân* published by modernist religious intellectuals, "the Western cultural invasion" serves as a pretext to oppose demands for freedom of speech and mind, improvement of the economic situation, and a less gloomy social environment. The author of the article adds that the authorities (political and religious) who invented (the term of) cultural invasion, put the cause of the problem outside the country, when in reality, Westernization of the population emanates from internal harassment. The author finds cultural progress and freedom to be strongly linked, and specifies that the state monopoly of cultural activities and attempts at introducing censorship have hindered cultural creation, hence favoring the expansion of Western culture notably among the youth (Kian 1995: 73–81).

In as much as the public sphere remains closed and under surveillance by the secret police, the private sphere is the only area of free expression where the individual is able to reconstruct an identity and acquire an identity of one's own through consumption safe from state control. Opposing the ideological supervision and the cultural surveillance by the Islamic regime, the educated and modern middle class became the precursor of Western culture which is considered to form an integral part of its identity.

For a few years now, Iran has experienced the new trend of post-Islamic intellectuals who differ from the group of Islamic intellectuals on a number of points. The most outstanding difference is the renunciation of a close link between Islam and politics. This is to preserve the religion from the damaging effects of politicization. The group of post-Islamic intellectuals is not a homogenous movement. Based on an Islamic exegesis, some of them reject the Islamic claim to the political power, whereas others are non-religious intellectuals who, in the name of a technocratic vision of society, seek to promote the need for non-religious rationalization.

Another argument concerns the relation between Islamic religion and democracy. The Islamic argument claims democracy to be a Western creation and, as such, should be prohibited in the Islamic world. A scholastic version of this rejection argues that democracy is the idolatry of number (the cult of the rule of majority), whereas on the basis of the Islamic doctrine, issues are settled according to its precepts that embody the absolute. This way it indicated an incompatibility between Islam and Western democracy. Abdulkarim Soroush and his partisans seek to prove that in principle there is no incompatibility between the two ideologies (Khosrokhavar 1996: 53).

Sorouch argues that the West does not constitute an integral whole and that it should not be perceived as such. Sorouch refuses to employ grandiose concepts such as Western philosophy, Western art, Western culture, Western essence, Western destiny, and Western spirit. He insists on the fact that the West does not constitute a homogenous whole with well-defined intellectual and cultural limits. Non-Western societies should not believe that they are confronting the West, but rather that they are confronting individual thoughts coming from the West. Furthermore, he maintains that what comes from the West is not necessarily contaminated, and that Western thoughts, politics, and technology may be accepted without fear. From his point of view, the issue is not of submission or denunciation, but rather of analysis and training. Having said this, Sorouch strongly believes in cultural exchange and the dialogue between religions (Sorouch 1999: 9).

The emergence of Islamism in political debates in Turkey is the result of the autonomization of civil society and the strengthening of pluralism. At present, the Kemalist state elites are playing a defensive role as guardians of republican values and the integrity of the state, in the face of a serious disorder which puts their existence at risk. But it is no longer the exclusive source of modernity in Turkey. The old schema which is rejected by progressive Kemalists, and the modernity version of which reactionary Islamics resist, have not completely disappeared. But from this point on, it falls within a wider debate revolving around modernity and democracy, cultural identity, and an open-minded humanism, and Islamic morality. Basically, this debate is public, and here state elites are but one of the many protagonists. Despite the control on official Islam which the secular state exercises through its take-over of the running of the religious hierarchy and religious education, these two forms of Islam constitute the breeding ground for Islamic movements today (Kazancigil 1990).

To sum up, in spite of the setbacks (revolution and war), Iran continues the modernization process and aspires to modernity. It is a long-drawn-out underground modernization process taking place behind the scenes, but nonetheless a decisive movement (the emergence of civil society; the claim for democracy; women's movement, etc.).

According to G. Balandier, modernity is shaped and understood as resulting from what is carried out "in depth", in the "fundamental movement" of a society and culture. The fundamental movement is that which relates to modernity and the surface movement is that which corresponds to modernization (Balandier 1985: 132).

Globalization – another version of Westernization?

Modernity is a European historical experience. A kind of forced globalization of this model of modernity was brought about by the great colonial waves of the nineteenth century which were mostly carried out by military conquest. The scientific and technological part of this model is now considered a valuable asset. Whatever their ideology, all states in the world try to attain it. Much of it is about economics. Everyone tries to conform to the market economy. However, some parts of the model are causing problems: the construction of a national, legislating, secular state; subsequently ethics; and finally, the aesthetic values. These three aspects clash with the traditional societies' mode of representation which are forced to evolve too fast, provoking, as a consequence, an intellectual break-down and a crisis of reference.

The crisis is aggravated by a clear awareness of a development failure, and sometimes provokes a collective anger as well as a categorical rejection of the source of the model, i.e. the West, and of the "carriers," i.e. the state, the Western elites, and the media. The reaction is always against the West and the Westernized native. This rejection can take brutal forms; hence the hostility of religious radicalism to the strongest symbols of modernity: the state and women.

Today, the world is faced with economic and cultural globalization and the emergence of a postmodern debate. We need to formulate new questions and reformulate old ones. In the near future, our problem will no longer be the relation between the East and the West or the choice among different development models. We will be faced with an unprecedented event: globalization taking over Westernization. There will no longer be an Eastern–Western dialectic nor colonization in its old form, but rather a global system and a myriad of cultures and nations struggling for survival in a global economy in full transformation towards a global culture. In other words, the organizations of the system of production will move from companies linked to nation–states to supranational companies.

Moreover, multinationals in full expansion increasingly determine the work we do, not to mention the place where we live, our lifestyle, and even the type of information disseminated by the media, and the education systems. Gradually, the goods of universal consumption become the foundation of our new global culture.

The slide towards universal tastes and styles goes hand in hand with the growing uniformity of technology and consumption (with monocultures based on a small number of products where most basic foods will be derived), and will put an unusual pressure on the natural environment. Indigenous and traditional cultures depending on specific ecologies for survival will be gradually eliminated and with them will go a wealth of knowledge; not to mention the secondary effects.

Globalization can be defined as the process of the extension of planetary interdependence. Under the influence of technical progress and of the expected return on investments, companies and markets organize a tightly interwoven network spread around the planet. This principle of transnational network essentially contradicts the territorial principle which is the driving force of states, consequently weakening the traditional regulatory role of states. This calls two things into question. First, the separation of internal and external affairs according to clearly defined boundaries and, second, the dividing line drawn between the private and the public sphere. Big companies usually escape from national state control. Globally, they anticipate the rules of the game for a global society which is still uncertain.

Qualitatively different from the classic internationalization where nation–states were the principal actors, the globalization process is already so well ahead in certain sectors of activity that it could be qualified as globalized since they form a whole and are treated as a set of interrelated activities. In view of these events, the reach of which seems irreversible, the apparent ascendancy of market economy leads us to speak of the "end of history" following the "brilliant victory of liberal economics and politics". Even if this victory first appeared in the field of ideas and awareness and is still incomplete in the real world, Fukuyama maintains that there are strong reasons to believe that it is the ideal which will govern the real world in the long run.

Fukuyama's thesis is simple:

> Of the different types of regimes that emerged in the course of human history, from monarchies and aristocracies, to religious theocracies, to the fascist and communist dictatorships of this century, the only form of government that survived intact to the end of the twentieth century has been liberal democracy.
>
> (1992: 45)

According to Fukuyama, "there is a fundamental process at work that dictates a common evolutionary pattern for *all* human societies. In short, something like a Universal History of mankind in the direction of liberal democracy" (ibid: 48).

Despite Fukuyama's optimism, this triumph, however, is not universal because the world is going to be divided into two large contrasted areas. There will be a "post-historical" sub-group (a free world with a market economy) on the one hand, and the mass of countries which are still "prisoners of history", on the other.

The nation–state has become too small in the eyes of big entities and too large in the eyes of small ones. Associated with "modern times" and for a long time considered an impassable fact, the nation–state is sometimes challenged today on two conflicting processes which are profoundly linked. One is an internal dispute due to extreme fragmentation of identities, and another is an external dispute by a growing globalization of economic and cultural structures. Inextricably linked to the nation–state, the ideas of democracy, territory, and social cohesion are suddenly being challenged.

The big problem today is that we risk having a world cut into two between the globalization of economic exchange and the fragmentation of cultural identities. New management models at national and global levels are necessary to take into consideration the rise in the aspirations of the individual and the constant decline of the nation–state.

There are two conflicting theses facing globalization. First, the disappearance of national frontiers and the emergence of a world where all economies are interconnected will be a mortal blow on regional and national cultures, traditions, customs, beliefs and models of behavior determining the cultural identity of each community or country. Because of their powerlessness in the face of invading cultural products coming from developed countries (or more precisely from the superpower, the USA) following the expansion of big multinationals, the North American culture (arrogantly considered a "sub-culture") will succeed in imposing itself, standardizing the entire planet, and wiping out the rich flowering of its numerous cultures.

Second, cultures need freedom to live as well as a continuous contact with the outside world for renewal and enrichment to gain strength. The notion of cultural identity is dangerous: from a social point of view, it represents a set-up with a doubtful intellectual validity. From a political point of view, it threatens the most precious human conquest: freedom. I am not claiming that a group of individuals who speaks the same language, who were born and live in the same territory, who face the same problems, and practice the same religion and the same customs would have the same common characteristics. But this common denominator cannot be used to define each of them and relegate the specific qualities of each group member to a level of second importance.

In theory, for a country to maintain its cultural identity, following the example of certain lost tribes in deep Africa, or in Amazonia, it would be necessary to decide to live in total isolation, without any contact with other nations; i.e. in autarky. The cultural identity, which will be preserved at this cost, will eventually bring society back to the living standards of prehistoric man (Llosa 2000: 505).

With regard to the globalization process, further thought needs to be given to the problem of cultural fragmentation or unification. A strong philosophical and historical tradition has made the existence of distinct and lasting civilizations one of the foundations in the understanding of human history. An equally strong philosophical and sociological tradition, going back to the Enlightenment, through Hegel, Marx and Weber, has made Western modernity and its attributes a universalism destined to spread to everyone.

These theoretical traditions shape the basis of four big, complicated but distinct debates covering the social sciences: is there a standardization of culture through economic globalization, through a generalization of cultural industries and the spread of Western products? Do the values and practices of modernity (secularization, democracy, individualism, etc.) have the vocation to spread globally? How does one articulate the claims and resistance of ethnic, political, and religious communities? What are the principles, the forms of action, and the justification of numerous identical strategies? Today these issues are common to all disciplines examining the subjects of cultures and their transformations.

It should be noted that if everyone agrees to face the realities of globalization, there will be conflicting opinions as to the effects of this world homogenization. If some see the future, as Huntington does, in the form of an increased frequency of "culture shocks", others, on the other hand, place emphasis on the growing blending of these same cultures.

Conclusion: a multilevel modernity?

How should we put the question of modernity in the Middle Eastern world? What answers may we give: closure or openness, confinement or a turn-around? Going beyond the temptation to imitate (the other) or to withdraw (into oneself), is there a way towards modernity which does not lead nowhere?

In fact, is there a single or several kinds of modernity? Is there a universal model which tends to stand out as a reference model, or, on the contrary, are the unusual paths being established able to shape a new form of modernity? Is it possible to avoid the influence of economic, political, and cultural globalization without getting marginalized and falling behind the times in the process?

There are two conflicting theses. First, there is but a single modernity; there are many kinds of modernizations. Modernity belongs to everyone while each modernization belongs to a culture or a type of society.

What is modernity? In the language of sociologists, it is achievement; the action that society exerts on itself. It is investment, creation, self-transformation and as some sociologists say, autoproduction of society. It is rationalization since the only reason for its universalism is strength unscathed by criticism, transformation, and movement.

No stages of economic growth are found everywhere, and Walt Rostow is one of the authors who have exerted the most negative influence on the social science line of thinking. The world is not a caravan of camels where each animal puts its feet in the tracks of the camel in front, as if the richest, the best-fed, and the fastest camels are in front, and the camels of such and such backward countries are lagging behind. That is absurd. On the one hand, there is modernity, and on the other, a plurality of economic growth paths (Touraine 1998: 589).

Second, as a matter of fact, there is not an absolute, universal and planetary modernity, but rather a number of different modernities from one epoch to another and from one place to another. In other words, modernity is an historic phenomenon, and, as such, remains conditioned by the circumstances wherein it manifests, and is confined within the space–time limits which determine what it will become in the course of history. Modernity should therefore depend on each historical experience: European modernity is different from Chinese or Japanese modernity (Al-Jabri 1995: 25).

For a better understanding of the two hypotheses, it is necessary to distinguish modernity from modernization. The second is within a non-Western society, imposed by visible and identifiable means, while the first penetrates society and settles in invisibly with an unrecognizable introductory shock. The Army, the factory, television as well as school, university, the publishing house and the identity card are considered evidence of modernization in non-modern countries. Thus, establishing such amenities is often a conscious action and can easily be dated.

Modernity, however, is imperceptible but lies within the framework of these objective elements. It affects the soul, attitudes, and points of view. It affects social relationships and most of all people's vision of the world. These processes are difficult to identify, a beginning without a date, and without an end. It moves with know-how, economy, and the modern school, but it is neither know-how nor economy; it is what ensues from it.

Western modernity established itself as a reference model. It became globalized but strong challenges to this hegemony which have sought to repeat the Western version of progress and values developed during this century.

At the end of a long journey, from the nostalgia of the Enlightenment to postmodern disenchantment, Middle Eastern societies are today facing these issues. Will globalization be the synonym of globalization of Western modernity? Or rather, can other types of modernity emerge in cultures different from those of the West and find their place in the process of globalization?

Without being able to provide the definitive answer, we join Al-Jabri, a Moroccan philosopher, in considering that:

> Modernity is not about rejecting traditions, nor a break with the past, but rather an enhancement of the manner of coming to terms with our links with tradition, at the level of what we would call "contemporaneousness", which should mean, for us, rejoining the march of progress that is now taking place at the planetary level.
>
> (Al-Jabri 1995: 24)

References

Al-Jabri, M.A. (1995) *Introduction à la critique de la raison arabe*, Paris, La Découverte.
Assayag, J. and Bénéï, V. (2000) "A demeure en diaspora", *L'Homme*, no. 156.
Balandier, G. (1985) *Détour*, Paris, Fayard.

Berque, Jacques (1986) *L'enjeu culturel du développement*, Rapports, Section Politiques Culturelles, CC86/WS. 30, Paris, UNESCO.

Borges, J.L. (1985) *Conférences*, Paris, Gallimard.

Corbin, H. (1977) *Philosophie iranienne et philosophie comparée*, Paris and Tehran, Buchet–Chastel.

Derriennic, J.P. (1980) *Le Moyen-Orient au XXe siècle*, Paris, Armand Colin.

Djalili, M.R. (1989) "Modernité politique en Iran", in *Iran-Nameh*, vol. XI, no. 2, Washington, (in Persian).

Fukuyama, F. (1992) *The End of History and the Last Man*, London, Hamish Hamilton.

Hoodastian, A. (1998) *Mondialisation de la modernité*, PhD thesis, Université Paris VIII.

Kâveh (1920) Iranian Review, Berlin, no. 36.

Kazancigil, A. (1990) "De la modernisation octroyée par l'Etat", *Cemoti*, Paris, no. 4.

—— (1994) *Atatürk*, Paris, Masson.

Khosrokhavar, F. (1996) "Les intellectuels post-islamistes en Iran", *Le Trimestre du Monde*, 1er trimestre, pp. 53–7.

Kian, A. (1995) "L'invasion culturelle occidentale", *Cahiers d'études sur la méditerranée orientale et le monde turco-iranien*, Paris, no. 20.

Llosa, M.V. (2000) "Cultures locales et mondialisation", *Commentaire*, no. 91, pp. 505–8.

Shariati, A. (1982) *Histoire et Destinée*, Paris, Sindbad.

Soroush, A.K. (1999) "Qui sommes-nous?", *EurOrient*, no. 3.

Touraine, A. (1998) "Modernité et spécificités culturelles", *Revue Internationale de Sciences Sociales*, Paris, UNESCO, no. 118.

Yaveri, N. (1991) "Identité et Modernité", in S. Vaner (ed.) *Modernisation autoritaire en Turquie et en Iran*, Paris, L'Harmattan.

9 Islamic civilization between Medina and Athena

Mehdi Mozaffari

> There were the Mahometans (Moors of Spain) who transmitted sciences to the Occident; since then, they have never wished to take benefit of what they had given us.
>
> (Montesquieu [1949]: 1569)

Arnold Toynbee believes that a civilization may emerge through (1) the *spontaneous mutation* of a pre-civilizational society; (2) *stimulation* of a pre-civilizational society to develop into a civilization by the influence of an already existent civilization; or (3) *disintegration* of one or more civilizations of older generation and the transformation of some of their elements into a new configuration (Toynbee 1995: 85). Following this classification, Islam in its origin was a civilization of the second category. Muhammad, the Prophet of Islam, explicitly claimed being the true successor of the Abrahamian monotheist tradition in which Islam – as a religion – is but a modern and revived version of Judaism and Christianity. It is to say that even at the heart of its religion, therefore, Islam renewed itself by borrowing from ancient Eastern and Mediterranean civilizations (Braudel 1995: 73; Khamenei 1998). However, when Muhammad moved to Yathrib, an anonymous city north of Mecca, established his government, drafted a constitution and changed the name of Yathrib to *Medina*, it was already clear that he had greater ambitions than merely establishing a new state among others. The choice of *Medina*/city from which the term *tamaddun*/civilization is derived, was a good indicator of the real intentions of the New Apostolate. Another significant indication was the multi-ethnical character of his disciples composed of a clear majority of Arabs, but also Persians (*Salman Pârsi*) and Ethiopians (*Balâl Habashi*) were represented. Mohammad aimed at achieving a universal religion through a universal message. In Medina, Muhammad founded a government with a leadership, an army, a taxation system and a new social order. The leadership was composed by a chief (Muhammad himself) surrounded by a Council of Ten (*Ashara Mubashshara*) representing the most powerful tribes and fractions. The crucial decisions concerning war and peace in particular were taken in consultation (*mashvara*) with members of the Council. The army was composed of all members of the community which at that time was quite limited. Muhammad, in the capacity of prophet and leader, was also the supreme commander of the

army and participated himself in most of the battles (*ghazavât*). The new administration and army were mainly financed by two sources: taxation (*zakât*) and
donation (*sadaqât*), and booty (*qanima*). The social order was based on equality
(*musavât*) between members of the *Umma*/community. However, equality was
rather a formal principle. A well-defined hierarchical system regulated the range
and status of each group: the early Believers (*Sahâba*), which had its own hierarchical order (the Emigrants/*Muhâjirûn* and the Auxiliaries/*Ansâr*), the Believers
(*Mu'minûn*), the Adherents (*Muslimûn*) and so on and so forth (Mozaffari 1987:
19–29). The entire system was cemented by a message determining the world
vision of the new Community. The message, revealed by fragments, was codified
under the caliphate of Othman (assassinated in 656 AD) and called the Koran.
After the death of Muhammad, a new leadership system called Caliphate
(*Khalâfat*), which literally means vicariate, was established. The first Caliphate,
known by Muslims as the "Rightful", began in 632 and ended in 661 AD.

After the Formative Age, the Islamic system turned into a kingdom
(*mulk*/*saltanat*), abolishing the cooptive caliphate system, replacing it by a
heritage system. The great civilizations are imperial. Accordingly, the Islamic
civilization also became an empire. With the *Umayyads*, the first Islamic Empire
emerged in 661 and ended in 750 AD. Should the creation of Umayyads be
considered the beginning of an Islamic civilization? In territorial terms, there is
no doubt that during the Umayyad period Islam did extend considerably; and
the first pillars of a civilization were built upon. It was a clear and powerful
centralized political system, based in Damascus, assisted by a new bureaucracy,
recruited especially among Persians. With the Umayyads began a modeling of a
new way of life and a new set of administrative, cultural and social relations.
Simultaneously, the Arab grammar was structured by two Persians (Sibawayh
and Zamakhshari). However, according to Fernand Braudel, "Muslim civilization began only when Islamic schools spread throughout the *Umma* or
community of the faithful, from the Atlantic to the Pamirrs" (1995: 73). This
was the beginning of the Axial Age.

During the Axial Age, Islam became a world religion, and, as such, "it can
perhaps be thought of as the first globalized world religion" (Held *et al.* 2000: 415).
As a "globalized world religion", Islam became both integrative and dynamic. It
was integrative in the sense that it easily integrated within itself not only different
races, ethnicities, territories, but also and especially the cultural, philosophical and
scientific baggage which the new arrivals brought along. It was dynamic in the
sense that it was able to absorb the alien ideas and concepts, having enough
capacity to transform them into Islamic vocabulary and express them through
Islamic terminology. From this epoch until the thirteenth century, Islamic civilization became increasingly *cosmopolitan* and even *secular*. It was in such a way that
"the creative minority – philosophers and scientists in particular – viewed religious
as a conventional matrix of social norms and communal behavior" (Kraemer
1986: 14). In the time of the great philosopher and political scientist Al-Fârâbi
(827–950), philosophers saluted the banner of religion in deference to political
and social responsibility. The prevalent political philosophy, inspired by Al-Fârâbi

held religious truths to be symbolic representations of the truth. The true and the good were determined autonomously, not on a religious background, and these criteria became the measure and standard for religion. Philosophy was viewed as independent of, not as auxiliary to, faith and theology (Kraemer 1986: 15).

It was also in the same period that Islamic civilization became *cosmopolitan* and *tolerant*, where Muslims were prepared to discuss religious issues with others on a fair basis without threat of retribution (ibid.: 29). In fact, during this period, "most Arabic-writing *faylasûfs*/philosophers were either Christian, Jews, or Muslims; they all acknowledged the pagan Greek sages, especially Plato and Aristotle" (Hodgson 1974: 430 "I"). Kraemer attributes the open-minded character of Islamic civilization, during the Axial Age, to the emergence of an affluent and influential middle class, which, having the desire and means to acquire knowledge and social status, contributed to the cultivation and diffusion of ancient culture (Kraemer 1986: 4).

The Islamic civilization reached its zenith under the caliphate of Al-Ma'mûn (813–33) whose "intellectual curiosity was far-reaching, and his works are collections of rare and interesting knowledge concerning the human and natural world: countries, animals, the oddness of human beings" (Hourani 1991: 52). Al-Ma'mûn was the first Islamic ruler who created an official forum for free debates for intellectuals and scientists. This forum was called the "House of Wisdom"/*bayt al-hikma*.

Al-Ma'mûn opened his court to all kinds of intellectual tendencies, also to those philosophers and moralists whose ideas were banished by the orthodox Ulama. His personal preference was undoubtedly rationalism and especially the *Mu'tazili* movement which at that time was the dominant school of thought in both Basra and Baghdad. There is evidence that some prominent *Mu'tazili* figures such as Bishr Ibn al-Mu'tamir and Tumamam Ben Ashras had free access to the Caliph's court. Other *Mu'tazili* (e.g. Bishr al-Marisi) played the role of mentor for Al-Ma'mûn. Josef Van Ess, who has studied Mu'tazilism extensively, thinks that it is very plausible that Al-Ma'mûn's inclination for rationalism stems from the period of his residence in Khorasan, where Hellenism was dominant from the epoch of Alexander the Great. Furthermore, it is also possible that Al-Ma'mûn created the "House of Wisdom" under Hellenistic inspiration, the *Academy* (Van Ess 1984: 27).

Hellenism survived a few centuries more in Islamic life, producing a group of philosophers, moralists and writers such as Al-Khwârazmi (780–850), Al-Râzi (865–923/932), Al-Fârâbi (872–950), who tried to reconcile Hellenism with Islam, Avicenna (980–1037), and Averroes (1126–1198) who still shine in the memory of Muslims. They disappeared gradually and gave way to the dogmatics and theologians. Jurists such as Al-Ghazâli (1058–1111) and Ibn Taymiyya (1263–1328) belong to this group.

In short, this epoch was characterized by two trends. The Islamic Empire reached its peak of power, conquest, and prosperity. The Abbasid Empire represented at that time the most powerful state in the world. The second predominant trend was deep infiltration of Hellenistic ideas and cosmology which contributed to an opening of dialogue. After the end of this period, the Islamic intellectual vitality changed place, moving slowly from Baghdad, Basra, Damascus and Cairo to Southern Spain, and Andalusia, which represents the second Islamic intellectual, glorious epoch.

Andalusia evokes to Muslims a splendid epoch, intellectually and scientifically. Politically, however, the Muslim situation at that particular time was almost chaotic and full of confusion. In political terms, Andalusia was in clear opposition to Al-Ma'mûn's epoch. At this time, the central authority in Baghdad began to weaken and faced new and serious challenges. Consequently, some relatively small dynasties began to establish themselves as autonomous or independent in different parts of the immense Abbasid Empire. One of these Empires was founded in Southern Spain by Umayyad "princes" who had escaped from the Abbasids' yoke. The Andalusian adventure, in the most positive meaning of the word, began with the Cordou Caliphate (929–1031) and continued for three centuries. This Caliphate was a successor of an Emirate which was established by the emigrants who came to North Africa and then to Southern Spain because of the Abbasid repression. During these centuries, there was great political and religious tolerance in the area. This was a necessary condition for close collaboration between the scientists of different races, religion, and political convictions. Juan Vernet's (1978/85) great book on *La cultura hispanoàrabe en Oriente y Occidente* and the two volumes edited by Salma Khadra Jayyusi (1994) entitled *The Legacy of Muslim Spain* perfectly describe the rise and fall of the Andalusian epoch. All the disciplines of the arts, music, botany, mathematics, medicine, astrology, astronomy, physics, chemistry, and many other branches were represented at that time in Andalusia. The extraordinary vitality of culture and science in this period was so great and of such variety that it is difficult to choose specific examples.

The Andalusian experience accomplished at least two main objectives: first, it created a cosmopolitan forum for different scholars of different disciplines. This extraordinary task could not have been accomplished without creating a hospitable environment. The result was overwhelming and greatly benefited Europe. As Margarita Lopes Gómez put it:

> The flood of translations centered around the preferred fields of mathematics and science. It is to Islamic culture that we owe our knowledge of numbers, including the zero, of Indian origin but transmitted by a Muslim from Persia named Al-Khwârizmî, and Muslims also developed geometry, demonstrated the position and movements of the planets and made many other scientific and medical discoveries, such as the discovery of the minor circulation of the blood, in the seventh–thirteenth century, by the Arab doctor Ibn-al-Nafîs.
>
> (in Jayyusi 1994: 1060)

Second, and actually the result of the first, is the transfer of Hellenistic knowledge to medieval Europe. This transfer was undoubtedly crucial to the beginning of the Renaissance in Europe. Montesquieu affirms that "there were the Mahometans

(Moors of Spain) who transmitted sciences to Occident; since then, they have never wished to take benefit of what they had given us" (Montesquieu [1949]: 1569).

The glorious epoch of rationalism and Hellenism reached its end when *dogmatism* and *jurisprudence* became dominant again in Islam. Montesquieu believes that the destruction of the Caliphate led to the destruction of sciences for Mahometans (ibid.). In fact, Al-Ghazâli (1058–1111) was perhaps the first, or at least the most reputed, theologian who introduced Islam to dogmatism. Later, in the fourteenth century, Ibn Khaldun (1332–1406) tried to reintroduce rationalism in Islamic culture by founding the sociological school and his famous *Prologomena (Al-Muqaddimah)*. Unfortunately, he was too late because the people of Islam were already in a deep crisis which finally led them to several centuries of decadence.

The Ma'mûnian and the Andalusian examples showed that the free dialogue and exchange of views and experiences were possible in two different contexts. When the central authority of the Islamic Empire was strong enough and confident – e.g. the Abbasids under Al-Ma'mûn – it could afford and neutralize any attempt at subversion. But when the central authority disintegrated into a variety of small emirates, sultanates and caliphates in Andalusia and North Africa, the opposite was the case.

The fall of Baghdad in 1258 and the end of the Abbasid Empire by Hulâku, the grandson of Genghis Khan, also marked the beginning of further political division of the Islamic Empire. The Empire was divided among a variety of large and small *emirates, sultanates, khanates,* etc.

The question now is how and under what circumstances did this brilliant, cosmopolitan, tolerant, integrative and dynamic civilization decline? And when did the decline of the Islamic civilization begin? All authors agree that Islam had created a civilization. They also agree that the Islamic civilization reached its peak between the ninth and the second half of the tenth century continuing *circa* three centuries ahead. Fernand Braudel even specifies two dates: one for the beginning and the other for the end of the Islamic civilization. According to him, the golden age lasted from 813, the year of Al-Ma'mûn's caliphate and ended with the death of Averroes – the Cordoba physician and commentator on the works of Aristotle – in Marrakesh in 1198 (Braudel 1995: 73). In this way, Braudel rightly included the Andalusian epoch – at least partly – within the golden age of Islam. Whatever the exact period of the Islamic golden age, we have to understand the causes of its decline. On this question, different responses have been provided. For the task of clarification, they should be listed as follows: (1) philosophical-intellectual; (2) geo-strategic; (3) technological-scientific; and (4) the unification of the world theory.

Philosophical–intellectual explanation

Those who are in favor of this thesis offer two major arguments. First, there is the question of quality and intellectual aspiration of Islamic philosophy. Muslims knew very well of both Plato and Aristotle. Thus, despite the fact that Aristotelian thinking dominated their logical investigation and their reflections on ethics, their political thinking was fundamentally Platonic (Kraemer 1986: 6). Moreover, their approach to philosophy was more literal and textual than critical. The knowledge was used rather for the purpose of refinement and urbanity (*adab/âdâb*) than as a commitment to a specific philosophical system. Braudel attributes this fact to the force exercised by religion on philosophers. He says "as admirers of Aristotle, the Arab philosophers were forced into an interminable debate between prophetic revelation, that of the Koran, and a human philosophical explanation" (Braudel 1995: 83). Second, general stagnation of Islamic civilization was due to the spring of a powerful Islamic dogmatism in the twelfth century which aimed at eradicating *philosophy* as a compatible discipline with Islam as religion. This movement was led by theologians such as Al-Ghazâli[1] and Ibn Taymiyya. The rise of dogmatism put an end to the tolerant, integrative, cosmopolitan and dynamic character which were the dominant trends of the golden age.

Geo-strategic explanation

Following this explanation, the decline began when power was taken over by barbarian soldier slaves (*Seljuqs/Saljuks*) in almost all of the Muslim territories. Parallel to this, a dramatic circumstance with long and substantial consequences ensued: after the twelfth century, Islam "lost the control of the sea" (Braudel 1995: 87). When Islam conquered the Mediterranean Sea by the end of the seventh century, it was a fatal blow to the Byzantine Empire dividing the unity of the European *Mare Nostrum*[2] and establishing, until our time even, a "barrage liquide" in Henri Pirenne's jargon. When Islam lost control of the Mediterranean, it became permanently handicapped, unable to expand and ill-equipped for daily life (Braudel 1995: 87). The loss of the sea was not limited to the Mediterranean; in time the loss became global. Toynbee believes that the epoch rupture happened in 1498, when Frankish ships arrived in India, by Muslims considered as "water-gypsies" which could not even capture the attention of Babur, the Emperor of India. Nevertheless, the West European seafarers' voyages of discovery were an epoch-making historical event (Toynbee 1948: 62). From this moment, Islam became an exclusively *territorial* power deprived of the modern means of communication, which held the necessary and efficient instruments for political, economic, and cultural power.

Technological–scientific explanation

The Galileo and the Copernican revolutions fundamentally changed the human view on the world and on itself. These revolutions transformed the *mentality* of the population which resulted in the Renaissance and the birth of European civilization. The point is that the Islamic civilization remained untouched and uninformed. It continued its traditional way which at the time was equivalent to stagnation and further disintegration. The emerging technological rationality was characterized by three elements: (1) the progressive conquest of all areas of knowledge by mathematics; (2) the application of scientific knowledge through associated technology; and (3) the appearance of an impersonal bureaucracy (Shayegan 1997: 85). None of these elements were present in the Islamic world. Furthermore, the technological revolution demanded a secular scientific rationalism. Islam, after having experienced a dose of rationality, secularity and cosmopolitan culture during three or four centuries (ninth–thirteenth), did actually return to dogmatism and the revivification of theological sciences (*fiqh* and *kalâm*).[3] In short, the technological backwardness of Islamic civilization at that time was enhanced by a gradual intellectual and mental backwardness. And this was the cause of its decline.

Unification of the world

This explanation is a sort of combination of various elements causing the decline of Islamic civilization. It is to say that the loss of the sea, the return to dogmatism, and technological backwardness made the Islamic civilization incapable of being dynamic and integrative. Essentially, the reason was that the sense and orientation of encounters changed. The revolutionary Western invention was the substitution of the ocean for the steppe as the principal medium of world communication (Toynbee 1948: 70). The world became unified and divided at the same time. Unified by the new Western system of communication, and divided by the end of encounters within non-Western civilizations. Shayegan illustrates very well the depth of the new gap. He writes:

> The decline of these Asian civilizations brought their mutual cross-fertilizations to an end. The era of the great translations leading to fruitful encounters between India and China, Iran and India, China and Japan, came to an end. These great civilizations turned away from each other and towards the West. They withdraw from history, entered a phase of passivity, stopped renewing themselves and lived increasingly on their accumulated fat. They were like rich aristocratic families overtaken by events, ruined by a shift in economic reality, who keep up appearances for a time by selling off their inheritance bit by bit: jewelry, paintings, carpets, silver, everything, until the bitter day comes when there is nothing left.
>
> (Shayegan 1997: 44)

The "unification of the world" did not come about through the introduction of modern communications and transportation facilities only. The most substantial change occurred in the field of economy. "For the first time in human history, an instance of a world-economy survived its 'fragility' and consolidates itself as a capitalist system" (Wallerstein 1992: 223). Without going into further discussion about the rise of capitalism, it should be noted that this was a qualitative change in world history which had (and still has) a huge impact on all civilizations, including the Islamic.

Continuing its fall, the Islamic civilization completely lost the characteristic drive and will of the golden age. The decline was so striking that some authors asked whether a Muslim civilization still existed (Braudel 1995: 111). As we will see later on, the doubt about the existence of a Muslim civilization was not only Western. Muslims themselves (even the fundamentalists) asked the same question. What about the Ottoman Empire which was Islamic and survived for several centuries and was dissolved only in 1923? It is true that the Ottoman Empire was Islamic, but this was rather by name than by essence. In reality, the Ottoman Empire was almost a culturally inert construction contributing little to the development of Islamic civilization.

Up to this point, I have been concentrating on the explanations provided by non-Muslim authors. The reason is that as paradoxical as it may appear, there were not many Muslim thinkers (except for Ibn Khaldun) who, in the medieval period, which is concurrent with the beginning of the Islamic decline, were interested in the study of the decline of Islamic civilization. In fact, Muslim consciousness about their own stagnation and fall only arose after the Napoleonic invasion of Egypt in 1798. During the French occupation of Egypt, the Muslims became aware of their own backwardness in social, political, technological and intellectual terms. Thanks to Al-Jabarti who with an extraordinary precision and accuracy described this encounter (Al-Jabarti 1995). This event had tremendous repercussions on Muslim awareness starting in the nineteenth century and continuing in the twenty-first. Thinkers and leaders such as Al-Afghâni (1839–97), Muhammad Abduh (1849–1905), Al-Tahtawi (1801–73) and many others tried to reform Islam and the Muslim way of life by observing the progress of Europe. The important thing is that from this period all Muslims admitted the decline of Islam in terms of civilization and the necessity for reform. As described by a Muslim leading thinker of the twentieth century: "During the last century, we became aware that we – Muslims – need a deep rooted and correct reform in our religious approach. We need to revive Islam by returning to the limpid source from which we have been lost during fourteen centuries" (Shariati 1973: 2–3; author's translation). This citation illustrates a genuine Muslim discourse capturing the essence of all discourses (reformist and fundamentalist under their different etiquette) from the past century until the present time. The genuine discourse attests to the progress of the Western world and the backwardness of the Islamic; although two incontestable facts, the solution proposed is not the logical result or consequence of the observed facts. Instead of looking forward, trying to combine the idea and the path of *progress*, it proposes *regression* and looks backward by rhetorical statements such as "returning to the limpid source from which we have been lost during fourteen centuries". Muhammad Khatami also acknowledged the non-existence of an Islamic civilization in our time. He made a useful and correct distinction between Islam as a *religion* and Islam as a *civilization*. He wrote: "if the sun of Islamic civilization ... declined and its time passed; this was [only] the end of a [specific] interpretation of Islam, and not the end of religion" (Khatami 1997a:183).

In short, all Muslims acknowledged the decline of the Islamic civilization. They have interiorized this fact at the same time as they are avoiding drawing the necessary conclusion in accordance with the already observed and accepted fact.

While Muslims agree on the decline of Islamic civilization, they are significantly divided on the ways of reconstructing it. Is reconstruction possible? Is there any empirical evidence? Reconstruction differs from reproduction in the sense that the former does not aim at reproducing something identical to something else. On the contrary, reproduction is, in a way, aiming for reincarnation. One thing is a photograph, another is a painting. Reproduction is mechanic and reconstruction intellectual. The process of reconstruction takes place at two stages: first "civilization" which is subjected to revision and renewal must be deconstructed. Without deconstruction, the concept of "civilization" will remain vague and a-historic. The proposed deconstruction model is based on a specification of the elements of a civilization, which, in a condensed form, is composed by two elements: a *world vision* and a *historical formation*. Subsequent to this acknowledgment follows the second phase: the *reconstruction* stage. As we know, civilizations are generally long-lived extending over many centuries. When talking about the reconstruction of a specific civilization, we do not mean that the target civilization must be reconstructed in its entire life. We have a selected momentum, as well as certain values, ideas, concepts, organizing principles etc.; all of which relate to this specific civilization. By reconstruction, I mean that a civilization is a great civilization only when the *world vision* and the *historical formation* meet in a coherent and fertile manner. Thus, the Islamic civilization, which is our case of study, did not necessarily exist for fourteen centuries; probably just for three or four centuries where the above mentioned elements constitute one integrated system. The advantage of such a method stems from its empirical verifiability since we know when and in which specific periods the junction occurred. In this connection, the best and perhaps most unique example for a successful reconstruction of a declined civilization is the Renaissance. The Renaissance was a reconstruction of the Greek and Roman heritage all together. Athens represented the main source of inspiration, the "idea" and the "spirit" while Rome stood for the "body", a form of organizing power based on law and prosperity. Apart from these two basic elements from which sprang the European civilization, Christianity added itself to it as an *ad hoc* element; subsequently the rising capitalism completed the construction. The Renaissance model exemplifies the course and the mechanism to apply for a successful reconstruction.

Following the above discussion, we have to investigate the possibilities, opportunities, and the Muslim view on the subject.

Three main currents

Different authors have presented different classifications of Muslim tendencies towards the revival of Islam. In this connection, Fred Halliday identified four distinct responses or themes from within an Islamic discourse.

> The approaches they adopt are classifiable as: *assimilation, appropriation, particularism, confrontation*, to which may be added a fifth approach, present within

Islamic societies and the non-Muslim world and falling outside an Islamic discourse. This fifth could be described as the *incompatibility* thesis.

(Halliday 1995: 135–6)

Toynbee, already in 1948, long before the rise of the Islamic fundamentalism and Islamic revolution in Iran, made a broader and, in a sense, a prophetic classification of Muslims by dividing them into Zealots[4] and Herodians.[5] Muslim leading figures have their own classification. Personalities such as Sayyed Qub (executed in 1966), Al-Mawdudi (died 1979), Shariati (died 1977), Khomeini (died 1989), Soroush,[6] and Khatami have almost the same classification. They divide Muslims into three categories: the Traditionalist–Conservatives, the True–Revolutionaries, and the Corrupt (e.g. the Shah of Iran, President Sadat of Egypt, and the Saudi royal family). Each of these groups of course holds different views on the revival problematic. In this study, for the purpose of a better clarification, I divide Muslim options adopted *vis-à-vis* the renewal of Islam into three paths or three main currents:[7] *reproductivism, communalism* and *universalism*.

Reproductivism

Reproductivism is animated by an *idée fixe* and is an attempt at reincarnating an ossified body. What must be reincarnated is the Medina model at the time of Mohammad (*Madinat ul-Nabî*), and to some extent the period succeeding the death of Muhammad (632 AD), the epoch of the Rightful Caliphs (632–61). This approach has at least the advantage of clarity and accuracy. It refers to a specific *time, space* within which an explicit *world vision* did create a *historical formation*. All these elements are empirically verifiable. The time is limited to 622 until 632 or 661. The space is geographically located in Medina, and secondarily in other parts of the Arabian Peninsula. The world vision is represented by the message embodied in the Koran and, the historical formation is illustrated by the government of Muhammad and his four immediate successors. The Medina with its fixed set of values (unchanged forever) is perceived as the perfect city, the sublime form of human organization and the unique valid model for humankind. What is important to know is that the Medina model is not considered the point of *departure* or a source of aspiration in itself. It is, indeed, the *arrival* and the final point; the harbor, not the voyage. Consequently, the task of Muslims, today as at any time in history, consists in recreating the Medina model as close as possible to the original version. Leaders and thinkers such as Khomeini, Sayyed Qutb, Mawdudi and many others who share this view do not, however, reject science and technology. In this respect, it is interesting to observe how Ayatollah Khomeini admits new technology and his opinion on Western civilization. In his *Political Testament*, he writes:

> If civilization means innovations, inventions and advanced technology, neither Islam nor any other monist religion opposes. But if civilization and

modernization (*tajaddud*) implies – as the professional intellectuals put it – freedom in all illicit (prostitution, even homosexuality) and other such things, these things are in contradiction with all religions since they are in contradiction with scientists and rationalists.

(Khomeini 1990: 178; author's translation)

Mawdudi, another reproductivist, explains the reason why Muslims – without concern – may apply modern science. It is because "the modern science was not based on any particular philosophical perspective, nor did it promote a set of values or require an attitude from Muslims that could interfere with their faith" (quoted by Nasr, 1996: 53). As for what they accept, there are some techniques which "can be exchanged and diffused fairly easily in isolation". As for what they reject, there is "a certain scientific vision of the world in conjunction with a certain perception of reality"; they reject any new set of values, any thought which could disturb the koranic immutable set of values.[8] Hasan al-Turâbi, the influential Sudanese Islamic fundamentalist leader, represents another example of this tendency. In his point of view, revival was required by the need for a "total revival in all aspects". Revival here is not to be understood as modernization along Western lines. Revival is seen as a means toward the establishment of a new society where *shari'a* is applied. Furthermore, Turâbi, in our days, claims what Al-Ghazâli claimed in the eleventh and twelfth centuries: renewing the fundamentals of religion (Abu Khalil 1995: 435). Turâbi's arguing is circular indeed: we have to revive Islam, in all aspects with the purpose of returning to *shari'a*. The claimed values here are static, because the reproductivists do not recognize the autonomy and authority of the human being. On this question, a scholar, criticizing the fundamentalist approach, writes that man "is everything because he is the jewel of creation, distinct from the other created beings in that he incarnates the divine Logos; but he is nothing, because he is not a founding authority" (Shayegan 1997: 34). Another important characteristic of this approach stems from their belief in the absolute supremacy of Islamic civilization over all others in the past as well as in the future. In fact, they believe in the existence of a single civilization: the Islamic. All others are either thought of as corrupt or unjust and considered *jâhiliyya/*ignorant. Consequently, in the contemporary world where the Western civilization is dominant, Muslims must opt for an antagonistic attitude *vis-à-vis* the West as did Muslims in the formative period of Islam towards Persian, Byzantine, and other civilizations and empires. They could also "wait for the West to destroy itself and then take the place of the West in the world leadership". This confrontation mentality is ignoring the reality that "if the West destroys itself, either physically or morally, it will hardly perish alone" (Hodgson 1974: 430 "III").

Communalism

Communalism refers to a group of individual Muslim thinkers who have not yet formulated a coherent discourse; thus they are all aware of the weakness and inaccuracy of the reproduction theses and try to reconcile certain aspects of

Islam with certain aspects of modernity. They may be called *half and half*: half-zealot and half-herodian; half-traditionalist and half-modernist; half-democrat and half-theocrat. Their main reference model remains Medina;[9] "the limpid source", however, not as an immutable model, nor in order to return and stay in the past – which is pure regression – but rather to discover the essence of Muslim identity and its refinement in the mentalities and habits as well as to achieve a rational criticism of the past in order to find the proper support for today to reach a future grander than the past.

They distinguish between religion and ideology, arguing also for a further distinction between society and Islam which is eternal and unchanging on the one side and, the "human understanding of Islam" which is changing on the other (Shariati and Soroush). They believe in a religious society hence rendering the government religious; a society that remains open to criticism and where nobody is above criticism.

The above view was shared by e.g. Afghâni (died 1897) and Abduh (died 1905) in the nineteenth century and, by Shariati, Bazargan,[10] Arkoun,[11] Hassan Hanafi,[12] Soroush and Khatami in the twentieth to the twenty-first century. In their opinion, Medina remains the original source, thus not as an immutable one. They advocate a new interpretation of Islam in which "reason" must play a key role. In a sense, they represent the *New Mu'tazili* of Islam. Some of them (e.g. Arkoun, Hanafi, Bazargan) are more rationalist than others. Apparently, their favored historical reference to Islamic civilization is essentially Al-Ma'mûn's epoch where Islam was tolerant, rational, cosmopolitan, and powerful. This group is fully aware of the decline of the Islamic civilization, but they believe that a *new* one can/must be reconstructed. Assuming it is true that the glory (historical formation) of Islam belongs to the past, the religion (world vision) is still alive in their view, and "religion is broader than a single civilization". They accept "the positive aspects of Western civilization rejecting only the Western vision on freedom and on the human being which is wrong, narrow and unidimensional" (Khatami 1997a: 183–91; author's translation). The fact that they do not reject *in toto* Western civilization as does the Reproductionists, and that they pay respect to "reason", indicates that implicitly they accept the multiplicity of civilizations. It is in this spirit that the Organization of the Islamic Conference (OIC) embracing all Muslim countries chaired (1997–2000) by Iran, launched the idea of organizing a "world dialogue among civilizations". On 4 November 1998, the UN General Assembly proclaimed the year 2001 as the UN Year of Dialogue among civilizations. This resolution was initially proposed by President Khatami of Iran. Such initiatives from these quarters are positive, and also appear to be the appropriate solution for a reconstruction of Islamic civilization. The problem lies in the ambivalence and the contradictory character of this type of reconstructive project. It is not clear which part of the past is likely to be included in the reconstructed civilization and, which part will be rejected. Along the same lines, how much of Western civilization is likely to be integrated into the "New Islamic Civilization"? Will the partial integration of the Western civilization be limited to the technological rationality, or will it also comprise scientific mentality, critical spirit, the idea of freedom and human rights? How to combine individual freedom with a religious government? Democracy, theocracy or theo-democracy? How can a monotheistic conscience, which evolved in an agrarian context, and a pre-da Gama world vision possibly be transformed into a modern, prosperous and powerful civilization? The most significant element of the Islamic heritage now is religion and religious conscience. Is it possible or likely to create – in our time – a new civilization on the basis of the same religion or on religion in general? These questions need answers, or at least to be offered the clarification which is still lacking in communalism. It should be noted, however, that some of the communalist thinkers (e.g. Khatami) do provide clarifications; these clarifications consist in the rejection of principles such as "freedom" which constitute the pillar of Western civilization. Therefore, to claim that they represent the communitarian thesis is not an exaggeration. In the best case, this will lead to a neo-Shar'î communalist revival.

Universalism

From this point of view, the reconstruction of a declined civilization is directly conditioned by the *world-time* where the new civilization will emerge. In the old world, living civilizations interacted. In that world, a particular civilization could be renewed itself having gone through a process of weakness and decay. One reason for the existence of a possible renewal was that the cumulative process consisting of perpetual learning and accumulating experiences proceeded almost internally, within the civilization's own universe. This situation enabled various civilizations to live in separate spaces, side by side, at the same time. In our time, under the pressure of the world system represented essentially by what Braudel called the world economy, and combined with a progressive tendency towards globalization, the very existence of different civilizations – each preserving their own set of values, world vision, ethics and political organizing principle, and operating with their own parochial economic system (world economy) is hardly plausible. How can different civilizations continue to live together in a world governed by global capitalism and by increasingly standardized civilization and human rights? In such a world, different *cultures* can easily live together and mutually enrich. However, *civilization* in my definition can hardly be more than one. Furthermore, if we recognize that "the need, even the urgency, for 'universal references' has never been so strong as in our time" (Bourricauld 1987: 21), we have no other alternative than to admit the existence of such "references". Where should we search for "universal references" today? Some may suggest the Internet. Actually, this is not a bad guess. But, more seriously, it seems obvious that the majority of these references are to be found in the Western civilization. Here, we have to distinguish Western *civilization* from *Westernization*. These two concepts have often been confused, hence creating further confusion, misunderstanding, and an opportunity to exercise manipulation of the people and to justify the authoritarian political regimes in Muslim countries. The distinction consists in the former concept referring to a set of values and concepts embodied in a world vision which is materialized in a specific historical formation generally referred to as Western civilization. Ideas such as belief in progress, freedom of speech and mind, equality, justice, democracy, and secularity are representative basic concepts of this civilization. Having said this, the objectionable side of the West expressed by colonialism, domination, exploitation, and war should not be ignored. The point is that the objectionable side is not the whole story of the West, and to reduce the West only to its non-civilized side would be incorrect. Furthermore, these elements are far from being specifically Western; all other empires and civilizations have been expansionist, conducting war and committing crimes against humanity, including a succession of Islamic empires (e.g. the Umayyad, the Abbasid, and the Ottoman Empires). However, none of those were based on the trilogy *liberté, égalité, fraternité* or on other related ideas. In addition, none of those created an economic system (capitalism) which is applicable world wide for good and for bad. The "Westernization" is a mimetic and mechanical adoption of some superficial and trivial aspects of the way of life in Western societies. Doing the things in a way that has no relation with the quality or state of being real. To allow import of goods with the sole purpose of emphasizing the consumer's distance from their indigenous environment. This is a kind of alienation, a "plague".[13] This is one of the main reasons why, in Muslim societies, the West is often perceived as trivial, morally decadent, luxurious, dominant, arrogant all together, at the same time. In this imaginary world, Westerners are caricatured as a bunch of immoral exploiters who, by stealing Muslim natural resources, do not have to work and may spend their time drinking alcohol and practicing free and bizarre sex.

Faced with "Westernization", the Muslim universalists deny this reductionist and superficial picture of Western civilization. They do not consider Western civilization as a civilization belonging only to the West. As Toynbee puts it: "The West is not just the West's own parochial concern but is *their* past history too" (1948: 83). A West the basic set of values of which – if not universal – are certainly *universalisable* (Morin 1987); although a civilization with the potential of being "universal." The reason is that its basic set of values is broader than those of all other existing civilizations taken separately.

The reconstruction project of Muslim universalists consists in: (1) considering the existing Western civilization as the necessary basis for a universal civilization; (2) qualitative transformation of Muslims to actors and contributors to universality, instead of challenging it and being ultimately submitted to it; (3) preserving cultural and Muslim identities. How can this be concretized? The first step consists of "mental migration" from a parochial and communitarian orthodox mentality to a forward looking mentality by joining a broader value system with gender equality, religious equality, freedom of speech and mind, social justice, etc.; leaving also aside a permanent suspicion towards the West concerning an illusionary mysterious international plot against Islam and Muslims. This purely imaginary perception results in needless frustration causing unproductive cultural and political depression. As already mentioned, in the globalizing process that the world is currently experiencing not only Islam is challenged; globalization challenges every religion, ideology, culture, including those of the West.

Along these lines, we have to recognize that Islam represents a high culture. Islam poses a message to humanity. The concept of *Umma*/community, the Islamic notion of brotherhood, recognition of differences between people, principles concerning human moral and physical integrity are among many others which could be transmitted to the universal civilization. However, a reinterpretation of these concepts is called for. *Umma* is easily "universalisable". In a period of globalization where people are becoming citizens of the global village, sharing the same destiny, facing similar problems (environment, health, the Internet, CNN, disaster, etc.), they are in reality members of the same community: the *Umma*. Thus, the *Umma* of Islam (*Ummat al-Islâmiyya*) may be extended to the *Umma* of humankind (*Ummat al-Insâniyya*). Another fact is that Islam is *alien* to racism, preaching universality and equality among human beings. In reality, these elements constitute powerful pillars of Islam's strength, and are highly qualified to contribute largely to the improvement of "Western" civilization. Furthermore, Islam's particular focus on justice/ *'adâla* could bring new blood to a civilization suffering from lack of justice. The virtue of compassion/ *sabr* and the quality of solidarity/ *ta'âwûn* are necessary for an improvement of the dominant capitalist system. There is quite a long list of components which Islam may contribute with. Other elements must be set aside for use in the reconstruction task. Considering the world power system today, it is undeniable that

> something of the leadership … for all mankind is likely to come from the West. But moral vision cannot be left to the West alone. Muslims must face their share of the tasks. There is much in their heritage itself that should help them find the relevance of that heritage to Modern mankind.
>
> (Hodgson 1974: 436 "III")

What is also necessary is a "heroic act, maybe; Promethean audacity, perhaps; rebellion against established truths, undoubtedly" (Shayegan 1997: 34). The problem is that these "Herodians", who are called to audacity and rebellion, are absolute minorities in Muslim societies. Muslim thinkers and intellectuals who firmly believe in a universal civilization, with Islamic contribution and participation, are generally quite reluctant to express their ideas explicitly. Maybe to avoid reactions (sometimes violent); they are also liable to allegations labeling them "Western agents". In general, they try to attract public attention to their ideas through the translation of classical works of thinkers such as John Locke, Jean-Jacques Rousseau, Voltaire, Hobbes and contemporary authors such as Karl Popper, Bertrand Russell, and Jürgen Habermas. Nevertheless, taking the current situation in Iran as an example, it is astonishing that, in recent times, some groups of especially young men and women have slowly emerged from the very heart of a fundamentalist culture and regime. One of them, among the most active and open-minded, is composed of people who joined forces around the newspaper *Jâmi'a* (Society). In the issue of 1 July 1998, one could read the following lines: "In the matter of History and Civilization, we [Muslims, Iranians?] are plying the role of radical critics. Criticizing [Western civilization] is, of course, much easier than participating in its improvement" [author's translation]. In a democratic–pluralist society, such a statement sounds normal, maybe too normal, even a commonplace remark. But considering that it was published in today's Teheran, where Western civilization is still perceived as "satanic", the statement takes on a different dimension.

On 27 July 1998, *Jâmi'a* ceased its publication in accordance with an order from a jurisdictional trial.

Conclusion: Islam and the new Hellenism

Islam created a great civilization. That civilization is no longer alive. What we have today are agglomerations of Muslim people organized within a variety of states. Others live in states (e.g. India, Russia, USA, and European countries) which are not Muslim. The Muslim world is not the only one to be challenged by globalization. Globalization challenges every civilization, every ideology, and every society. In addition, what complicates the process of connecting Islam to the modern and globalizing world must essentially be found in the special character of Muslim-European relations. While there was no noticeable *religious* war between European Christianity and other religions (Judaism, Buddhism, Hinduism, Confucianism, etc.), there were bloody, religious wars between Islam and European Christianity (e.g. the Crusades). Furthermore, while there were no genuine wars (of non-religious character) between European powers and non-European powers within Europe, there were multiple wars between Muslim and European powers. In Poitiers (732), in Constantinople (1453), in Granada (1492), in Vienna (1529 and 1683), etc. This means that during history, Muslims and Europeans have been in direct physical contact within Europe. Therefore, from a European point of view, Islam represents a unique case. And Muslims have a different perception of Europe and the West compared to other colonized and dominated people (Chinese, Hindu, Indians, etc.). Those people were colonized by Europe but they were physically remote. In contrast, some Muslims were in a sense Europeans (e.g. the Umayyads in Spain and the Ottomans in large parts of Europe). The historical factor alone does not sufficiently explain the entire problematic of Islam and globalization; it explains, however, an important part. Other parts are common as well for Muslims as for other colonized and dominated people of the world.

Many Muslims dream of a revival of Islam. This dream took flight once they discovered and acknowledged the decline of the Islamic civilization. Since the nineteenth century, the Muslim dream has taken different shapes and proportions. The real struggle is going on between those who believe that a reconstruction of Islamic civilization can only be realized through new patterns. In contrast to this view, there are those who struggle (sometimes violently) for ideas and projects which call for a reproduction of the original model. The idea of modernity is rejected, and some Muslim utopians even advocate the creation of an Islamic global world. However, the success of a reconstruction depends – in the first place on the extent to which it is connected with reality, i.e. the present time. An overwhelming number of facts and reasons indicate that the world is moving towards a broader construction rather than a pure narrow religious construction. The trend of neo-religious communities are, in fact, reactions to universality, or at least to globalization, rather than being independent factors. I argued that Islam as a civilization is unlikely to be reproduced. At the same time, I argued that Islam holds a valuable set of values and visions which are highly likely to be incorporated into the new world system. The notion of *Umma*, *'Adâla*, even *'Asabiya* are needed for the improvement of Civilization. Robert Cox provides us with a redefinition of *'Asabiya* by putting it in a world system context. *'Asabiya* as a supra-intersubjectivity, a new "global *Mahdî*"/saviour which could take the form of a collectivity rather than an individual. This "supra-intersubjectivity would have to embody principles of coexistence without necessarily reconciling differences in goals. It would have to allow for a degree of harmonization of trajectories of different macro-societies" (Cox 1996: 168).

Twice, Islam has missed the opportunity of conciliation with Hellenism: the first time due to a massive dogmatic influence during the twelfth and thirteenth centuries, and the second time, with the end of the brilliant Andalusian experience: a sort of "Islamic Silicon Valley". For some Muslims, globalization, especially in its intellectual significance, represents a New Hellenism. From this point of view, Muslims must not miss this new opportunity. They have to proceed to achieve a religious reformation. This would pave the way to modernity, democracy and intellectual liberalism. For others, the Medina remains – forever – the true and valid model. Along these lines, "salvation" will be realized only by a return to the Medina model. The outcome of the inter-Muslim struggle will ultimately determine the Muslim response to globalization.

Notes

1 On Gazâli, see particularly Henri Laoust, *La Politique de Ghazâli* (1970).
2 In a sense, this event did contribute to the rise of European civilization which will progressively dominate the world. As Henri Pirenne puts it:

> L'Occident est embouteillé et forcé de vivre sur lui-même, en vase clos. Pour la première fois depuis toujours, l'axe de la vie historique est repoussé de la Méditerranée vers le Nord. La décadence où tombe à la suite de cela le royaume mérovingien fait apparaître une nouvelle dynastie, originaire des régions germaniques du nord, la Carolingienne.
>
> (Pirenne 1937: 187)

3 It is astonishing that Al-Ghazâli, the most prominent figure of dogmatism, named his monumental work "Revivification/*Ihyâ*" which is a clear indication of the dominant trend of his time. In fact, the revivification was a dogmatic renaissance; a rupture with philosophy and Hellenism and a return to theology.

4

The 'Zealot' is a man who takes refuge from the unknown in the familiar, and when he joins battle with a stranger who practises superior tactics and employs formidable newfangled weapons, and finds himself getting the worst of the encounter, he responds by practising his own traditional art of war with abnormally scrupulous exactitude.

(Toynbee 1948: 188)

The North African Sanusis and the Central Arabian Wahhabis (Saudi Arabia) are used as examples.

5

The 'Herodian' is a man who acts on the principle that the most effective way to guard against the danger of the unknown is to master its secret; and, when he finds himself in the predicament of being confronted by a more highly skilled and better armed opponent, he responds by discarding his traditional art of war and learning to fight his enemy with the enemy's own tactics and own weapons.

(Toynbee, 1948: 193–4)

As an example of a Herodian, he mentions Mustafa Atatürk.

6 Abdulkarim Soroush (alias Hossein Dabbagh) studied pharmacology in Iran and history and philosophy of science in England. After the Revolution of 1979, he became one of the most influential ideologists of the Islamic revolution and was a member of the Committee of the Cultural Revolution until 1987 where he resigned. Soroush is the author of many books and articles such as *Theoretical Contraction and Expansion of the Shari'a* (1991/96) (in Persian) and *Reason, Freedom, and Democracy in Islam* (2000). For a short review of his ideas, see Valla Vakili (1996).

7 "Muslims" here are both the Muslim believers and those who were merely *cultural* or *secular* Muslims.

8 On this point, Mawdudi declares that "We aspire for an Islamic renaissance on the basis of the Qur'an. To use the Qur'anic spirit and Islamic tenets are immutable, but the application of this spirit in the realm of practical life must always vary with the change of conditions and increase of knowledge" (quoted in Nasr, 1996: 51).

9 Khatami's statement on Medina is insightful. He says that: "The civil society we have in mind has its origin from a historical and theoretical point of view", in *Madinat ul-Nabî* which "remains our eternal moral abode" (Khatami 1997b).

10 Mehdi Bazargan was a French-educated engineer who became Professor at Tehran University and the leader of the Liberation movement of Iran. After the Islamic revolution in Iran in 1979, he became the first Prime Minister of the revolutionary regime, but resigned in November 1979 after the occupation of the US embassy in Teheran and the "hostage affair". He is the author of a number of books and articles through which he tried to reconcile Islam with modern science. He died in 1995.

11 Mohammed Arkoun was Professor at the Sorbonne in Paris and is the author of books on Islam. Among his best work is *Pour une Critique de la Raison islamique*, Paris, Maisonneuve & Larose (1984).

12 Hassan Hanafi is Professor at Cairo University and one of the front figures of the Islamic revivalists. One of his works is *Istighrâb/Occidentalism* (in Arabic) which is a reply to Orientalism. See also his article, "An Islamic Approach to Multilateralism" (1997).

13 Jalal Al-e Ahmad, an Iranian author whose writings have had a decisive influence on the decline of the Shah's regime described – not without exaggeration – the impact of westernization on the Iranian society. See his book, *Plagued by the West/Gharbzadegi* (1982).

References

Abu Khalil, As'ad (1995) "Revival and Renewal", in John L. Esposito, *The Oxford Encyclopedia of the Modern Islamic World*, vol. 3, Oxford: Oxford University Press.

Al-e Ahmad, Jalal (1982) *Plagued by the West*, trans. by Paul Sprachman, New York, Caravan Books.

Al-Jabarti, Abdd al Rahman (1995) *Napoleon in Egypt* (Tarikh Muddat Al-Faransis Bi-Misr), translated by Shmuel Moreh, Princeton & New York, Markus Wiener Publishing.

Arkoun, Mohammed (1984) *Pour une Critique de la Raison islamique*, Paris, Maisonneuvee & Larousse.

Bourricauld, François (1987) "Modernity, Universal References and the Process of Modernization", in S.N. Eisenstadt (ed.), *Patterns of Modernity*, vol. I, New York, New York University Press.

Braudel, Fernand (1995) *A History of Civilizations*, New York, Penguin Books.

Cox, Robert W. with Sinclair Timothy J. (1996) *Approaches to World Order*, Cambridge, Cambridge University Press.

Halliday, Fred (1995) *Islam and the Myth of Confrontation*, London, I.B. Tauris.

Hanafi, Hassan (1991) *'Ilm ul- Istighrâb* [Occidentalism], Cairo, Dâr ul-Fanniyyah, (in Arabic).

—— (1997) "An Islamic Approach to Multilateralism", in Robert Cox (ed.), *The New Realism*, Tokyo, Macmillan.

Held, David *et al.* (2000) *Global Transformation*, Cambridge, Polity Press.

Hodgson, Marshall G.S. (1974) *The Venture of Islam*, Chicago, The University of Chicago Press, (I, II and III).

Hourani, Albert (1991) *A History of the Arab Peoples*, London, Faber & Faber.

Ibn Khaldun, Abdelrahman (1968) *The Muqaddimah*, trans. by Franz Rosenthal, 3 vols, London, Routledge & Kegan Paul.

Jayyusi, Salma Khadra (ed.) (1994) *The Legacy of Muslim Spain*, Leiden, E.J. Brill.

Khamenei, Sayyed Ali (Supreme Leader of Iran) (1998) "Today, the World Needs the True Islam", in *Ettela'at*, 9 July, (in Persian).

Khatami, Sayyed Muhammad (1997a) *Bîm-é Mowj* [Fear of the Wave], Tehran, Simây-e Javân, (in Persian).

—— (1997b) "Statement to the 8th Session of the Islamic Conference Summit Conference", Teheran, 9 December.

Khomeini, Ayatollah (1990) "Political Testament", in *Sahifay-e Nur* [Light's Scriptures], Tehran, Soroush, (in Persian).

Kraemer, Joel L. (1986) *Humanism in The Renaissance of Islam*, Leiden, E.J. Brill.

Laoust, Henri (1970) *La Politique de Ghazali*, Paris, Paul Gauthner.

Montesquieu, Charles-Louis de ([1569] 1949) "Considérations sur les causes de la grandeur des Romains et de leur decadence", in *Oeuvres Complètes*, vol. I, Paris, Gallimard.

Morin, Edgar (1987) *Penser l'Europe*, Paris, Gallimard.

Mozaffari, Mehdi (1987) *Authority in Islam: From Muhammad to Khomeini*, New York, M.E. Sharpe.

Nasr, Seyyed Vali Reza (1996) *Mawardi and the Making of Islamic Revivalism*, New York, Oxford University Press.

Pirenne, Henri (1937/1961) *Mahomet et Charlemagne*, Paris, Club du Meilleur Livre.

Shariati, Ali (1352/1973) "Tamaddun va Tajaddud/ Civilization and Modernization", speech (10 Dey 1352/31 December 1973).

Shayegan, Dariush (1997) *Cultural Schizophrenia: Islamic Societies Confronting the West*, Syracuse, Syracuse University Press.

Soroush, Abdulkarim (1991/1996) *Qabz wa Bast-e Teoritik-e Shari'at* [Theoretical Contraction and Expansion of the Shari'a], Tehran, Sarat, (in Persian).

—— (2000) *Reason, Freedom, and Democracy in Islam*, trans. by Mahmoud and Ahmad Sadri, Oxford, Oxford University Press.

Toynbee, Arnold (1948) *Civilization on Trial*, New York, Oxford University Press.

—— (1995) *A Study of History*, London, Oxford University Press.

Vakili, Valla (1996) *Debating Religion and Politics in Iran: The Political Thought of Abdulkarim Soroush*, New York, Council of Foreign Relations.

Van Ess, Josef (1984) *Une lecture à rebours de l'histoire du Mu'tazilism*, Paris, Geutner.

Vernet, Juan (1978/85) *Ce que la culture doit aux Arabes d'Espagne* [original title: La Cultura hispanoárabe en Oriente y Occidente], Paris, Sindbad.

Wallerstein, Immanuel (1992) *Geopolitics and Geoculture*, Cambridge, Cambridge University Press.

10 What is "Chinese" about Chinese civilization?

Culture, institutions and globalization

Xiaoming Huang

I start this chapter with a friendly warning: if the reader expects to find some classical arguments here as how uniquely wonderful Chinese civilization is and why others should understand and respect it, or better yet, why a revitalization of Chinese civilization is a solution to the problems of globalization, then s/he might be disappointed. The basic arguments of this chapter are straightforward: first, civilization is a system of homogenous human activity confined by a set of prevalent rules, habits and tools developed over a considerable period of time. Civilizations in this sense are attempts to solve the problem of human order in a given setting, national or otherwise.

Second, Chinese civilization, dominated by Confucian traditions, is a moral approach to the human order problem and has proved to be ineffective in meeting the challenge of modern conditions. These modern conditions have moved societies once dominated by Confucian traditions away in search of more effective solutions.

Third, in contrast to the moral approach of Chinese civilization, and the coercive approach prevalent in the early times of human history, modern civilization, with the principles of efficiency and fairness at its core, is an institutional approach to the human order problem. Globalization, in essence, is a global expansion of the modern civilization. This global expansion has led to the spread of modern civilization in *individual countries* and, hopefully, to its growth at the global level, eventually.

The aim of this chapter is to substantiate these arguments, and in doing so, to make a case for the challenge of globalization for Chinese civilization. The chapter will first take a close look at the organizing concepts for a framework in support of the arguments I have just laid out above. The focus will be on the notions of culture, institutions, and their dynamic interaction as the defining elements of a civilization. This framework will then be applied to (re)interpreting Chinese civilization. With Confucianism at its core, the reinterpretation will concentrate on locating Confucianism in the range of competing solutions to the problem of human order upon which the Chinese civilization has evolved. Third, the problem of globalization will be examined in some detail to explain what globalization means for civilizations in general and for Chinese civilization

in particular. But before we do that, an overview of the debate regarding globalization and civilization is in order.

The debate

The problem of civilizations in the age of globalization has been an interesting
issue to many, especially to those who either have profound knowledge about
themselves or are part of the civilizations that have survived thousands of years.
As civilizations have long been seen as a primary framework for our understanding of the structure of the world and the dynamism of its evolution,[1] the
forces of globalization, which seem to be eroding the defining elements of many
long-lasting civilizations,[2] would naturally compel us to seriously re-examine
many of our fundamental assumptions about human history and its dynamics.

The debate on the globalization–civilization problem so far, however, is
fought mainly between those who see the increasing irrelevance of the notion of
civilizations, along with those of cultures, nation–states, national economies, on
the one hand, and those who see the further strengthening of diverse civilizations as a solution to the problems brought on by the global expansion of the
dominant political and economic institutions (Scott 1997; Jameson and Miyoshi
1998; Thesis Eleven 2000). As civilizations are just one kind of the "old boundaries", in fact a relatively weak and insignificant one if compared to, for
example, the nation–state, that globalization is to crush, the problem of civilizations does not feature well in the argument for globalization's "creative
destruction" (Schumpeter 1975: 81). Instead, much of the debate has been
generated by those on the civilization/culture side, assuming that there is a
natural consensus that globalization will overcome civilizations.

Standing out among the civilizationalists, if I may call them that way, are
those associated with the theory of *civilizational dynamics* (Jaspers 1953; *Daedalus*
1975; Eisenstadt 1986a). The theory is built upon the notion of axial-age civilizations, namely, Greek, Hebrew, Persian, Indian and Chinese civilizations,
which experienced profound change within a very short period from 800 to 200
BC, thus the Axial Age, resulting in "major spiritual, moral and intellectual
breakthroughs" (Schwartz 1975a: 1). These breakthroughs led to the formation
of the spiritual, moral and intellectual cores in each of the axial-age civilizations,
which have transcended "the superstructures we have erected and go on
erecting" (Weil 1975: 21) and kept the civilizations "alive".

The civilizational theory, apart from bringing "exotic fields" into more meaningful relationships with others in the 1970s, can be quite relevant to the
globalization–civilization debate of today. While many theories of globalization
foresee the eventuality of "homogenization" (Holton 2000: 140) of the world on
the basis of technological advances and the most efficient and effective forms of
production, distribution, and social organization, the civilizational theory finds in
retrospect the self-perpetuating power of these "higher civilizations", manifest
over the last two millennia since their axial-age breakthroughs. Indeed, if the
civilization theory could have gone one step further from simply recognizing the

breakthroughs to explaining why these breakthroughs came about in the first place, we probably would have a very different view of the globalization–civilization debate.

For the purposes of this chapter, however, the civilizational theory has other and perhaps even more significant difficulties, which make its answers to the globalization challenge weak. The notion of civilization entertained in the theory is vague and mysterious at the best. One reading would suggest that a civilization is the totality of human life at a particular historic point. Therefore, civilizations would have existed *before* the Axial Age. During the Axial Age, these higher civilizations had breakthroughs and became *axial-age* civilizations. Another reading, however, would lead us to think that the real civilizations for them are the new religious, moral and intellectual cores born out of the breakthroughs. One could reason that there were no civilizations before the Axial Age.[3] With the latter claim – in contrast to globalization theories that make their claims on a solid basis of human nature and rationality and the consequent dynamics of political economy – axial-age civilizations became mysterious products of the "imaginary significations" (Arnason 2001), mostly of the intellectuals, in the form of religious beliefs, moral principles and intellectual inspirations.

The claims

I am not in a position to assess how successful this civilizational theory could be in explaining other civilizations, but the theory would certainly have difficulties with regard to Chinese civilization. The key question, one that has even created a great debate among China scholars themselves lately,[4] is whether China had such breakthroughs in the Axial Age. In his original essay on the case of China as an axial civilization, Benjamin I. Schwartz carefully documented the "transcendent turn" that occurred during the Axial Age, which he believes provided "a basic *Problematik* of the whole subsequent age" and "established a range of thought that was to shape all future developments without predetermining them" (Schwartz 1975b: 68).

This claim cannot easily survive a careful scrutiny. As Samuel Eisenstadt himself recognized in introducing a collection of follow-up investigations by noted China scholars on the subject, the Chinese case presents a paradox for the civilization theory. According to its advocates, the breakthroughs for an axial-age civilization are essentially the emergence of a transcendental vision. The transcendental vision represents independent human consciousness rising above the "mundane world" in seeking "salvation" from God. As such, the theory expects in the breakthroughs a religious signification of the "mundane orders" and a "strong chasm between the transcendental vision and the mundane world" (Eisenstadt 1986b: 291–2). There is no evidence of either of them in the early evolution of Chinese civilization, even to the extent that Schwartz finds "transcendence *inward* in Confucianism" (1975: 63). Confucianism calls for self-cultivation and awakening to one's own nature as a solution to the worldly problems. This "this worldly" conception of "salvation" (Eisenstadt 1986b: 291) has little to do with God of any kind; and because of the "this worldly nature" of the Confucian "vision", there is no chasm of the kind that can be found in the Confucian world. In the end, Mark Elvin doubted whether there was a transcendental breakthrough in China after all (Elvin 1986).

If my brief critique of the civilizational theory is valid, and if there occurred no axial breakthroughs in Chinese civilization, then what provided the "basic *Problematik*" for the long-lasting Chinese civilization? What were the range of imperatives that were to "shape all future developments"? What were the foundations upon which we have kept erecting "superstructures"? If these are the same set of dynamics that have shaped human history in India, China, Greece, as the civilizational theory suggests, then is there anything mistaken in the theory about the basic *Problematik*, imperatives, foundations in other "Axial Age civilizations" as well? Above all, what is the thing called civilization in the first place?

My contention is that the civilization theory is unable to recognize the importance of human nature and human interest as the "original substance", and thus cultural patterns and institutional dynamics in the making of civilization. Consequently, the historical phenomenon it observed, however accurate it might be, has been left largely unexplained, and its challenge to the visions of globalization has been mainly ineffective. *Civilization*, in this author's view, is a system of homogenous human activity confined by a set of effective rules, prevalent habits, and necessary tools developed over a considerably long period of time. Habits as a whole constitute a pattern of behavior which is often called *culture*. Rules are formed by, of, and for uniquely related individuals, which are often referred to as *institutions*. Tools are the extensions of human capability, with the aid of technological advances, for the better satisfaction of human interests.

At the level of human nature and human interests, we are all the same, whether we are Chinese, Hebrew, or Russian. Our desires as humans to satisfy our interests and our instincts to respond to changing conditions are also the same. What have made humans different over time, whether in terms of civilization, culture, ethnicity, or political economic and social status, are the function of the following. First, the *initial conditions* effective on the group of people. Second, the *responses* of concerned individuals and their associations complicated by their rational calculations and incidental factors which trigger a unique path of dependent events.[5] Third, *rules* that are developed to promote and protect privileges and benefits, and to eliminate or reduce costs, risks, or uncertainty regarding the privileges and benefits. Finally, *habits* that are formed under the effective conditions and rules. Over time, the established habits and rules would themselves become part of the *existing conditions*.

Civilization thus defined is dynamic, as human beings constantly assess their existing conditions and respond to their changing environment. It is progressive, as there is always a tension between human interests and existing conditions, and consequently there is always a need to find a (better) way to revolve the tensions. The basic *Problematik* in this reading of civilization is not so much how to bridge the chasm as envisioned in the civilization theory, but how to bridge the gap between human interests and their existing conditions. The foundations upon which we have erected and continue erecting superstructures are the basic human interests. These superstructures are the rules for a particular political, economic and social order.

While the exact nature of the birth of humankind on the earth is a matter of debate, civilizations have evolved in various geographic locations, mostly in isolation early on. Given that peoples in these various locations all shared the same human nature, civilizations that evolved there would have been essentially the same. People wanted to have exclusive control over the limited resources available to them (tribes, nation–states, sovereignty, ownership, etc.); to have a better use of these resources (production, technology, efficiency, etc); to have some order for distribution of privileges and benefits (politics, legal system, taxation, welfare provisions, etc.); and to expand to the extent possible the boundaries of the exclusive control and ownership (colonialism, capitalism, international law, wars, multinational corporations, etc.). At this basic level of civilizational dynamics, there is no difference between Chinese civilization and Japanese civilization, or between Islamic civilization and Anglo-Saxon civilization. What is Chinese about Chinese civilization is not so much of a *Chinese* imaginary signification, a *Chinese* breakthrough, a *Chinese* religion, or a *Chinese* vision. What has made Chinese civilization *Chinese* is the habits formed among the Chinese and the rules effective on them that have accumulated over time in response to their initial and subsequent conditions.

Like any other major civilizations which have survived from ancient times, China is considered a unit of civilization, because within *China*, habits, rules and conditions have evolved in a distinctive level of homogeneity through intensive interaction among residents. The boundaries of this *China* have been constantly defined and redefined with the aid of tools in communication, transportation, production and coercive power available at the times. In other words, defining the unit of a civilization is an art of ascertaining the relative level of homogeneity and that of intensity of dynamic interaction in a given communal area. One could argue, for example, northern and southern China represent two different kinds of civilizations. By the same token, a case can be made that Japan, China, Korea, Taiwan and Singapore belong to the same civilization.

This leads us to the problem of globalization. Globalization can mean different things for different people. For the economists, for example, globalization is a process of expansion in production and distribution on a global basis (O'Rourke and Williamson 1999). For those of cultural interests, globalization is the expansion of modern culture on a global scale (Robertson 1992). There are of course globalizations of politics (Luard 1990; Baylis and Smith 1997), governance (Pieterse 2000), democracy (McGrew 1997), information (IFID 1998), social movements (Lindberg and Sverrison 1997), or even religion (Beyer 1994). From the perspective of civilization defined here, globalization is a process of the emergence of a level of homogeneity among residents on the globe in habits, rules, and human conditions, generated by their dynamic interactions of growing intensity. What allows globalization to cause alarm to many, understandably, is the fact that the global expansion of one civilization, namely the modern civilization, while it may bring some forms of solution to the problems of fairness and efficiency as seen in many limited scale civilizations (the modern civilization included), will further intensify the tension between civilizations at different levels and those of less compatible systems of habits, rules, and human conditions. This fact reflects the working of an innate logic of the civilizational dynamism that operates on the principle of exclusiveness and homogeneity, which also led to similar tensions and often their violent solutions among earlier civilizations. With this general framework set up, let us turn to the case we have set for this chapter.

What is civilization?: Human nature, institutions, and culture

Let me start with three concepts: human nature, culture and institution, which in this author's view form the basis for a civilization. Human nature is the essential qualities that make a human different from nonhumans. Conscious of the fact that the issue of what constitutes human nature has been a subject of constant debate from the times of Plato, Confucius, Mencius, Aquinas, Bentham, Hobbes, Rousseau,[6] I will argue that human interest in biological, psychological and intellectual satisfaction largely defines human nature. Such satisfaction tends to seek its maximization and perpetuation.

There are two conditions that make institutions necessary and culture inherent in human activity in seeking such satisfaction. First, there are limited satisfying materials available for distribution in a community of a given scale. Consequently, an internal order and external sovereignty are needed to create a system of controlled access and thus maintain a system of orderly satisfaction. Human relations defined by such an internal order and external sovereignty can be as simple as a marriage of two people and as complex as the nation–state. At the same time, individuals can also enhance their levels of satisfaction by expanding the material basis itself through production and exchange, with the help of new tools. Since activities of these sorts are generally impractical, if not impossible, for each individual to perform on his own, a form of cooperation among individuals is often desirable. Tribe, village, family, factory, trade union, etc. are all forms of cooperation in achieving collaborative effects of this nature.

This leads to the second condition which is more closely related to human nature. The above forms of cooperation are mostly voluntary. However, there is often a high level of uncertainty about the costs, benefits, risks as well as additional opportunities involved in a given set of relationships, and the effects of one party's action on the rest of the relationship and on the individual himself are therefore contingent. From each individual's point of view, they will pursue the course most favorable to their own interests based on their best calculations. For the group as a whole, this is a challenge as well as an opportunity. It is a challenge because each individual's best option may not be the best one for the group. Therefore cooperation tends to fail under natural conditions. This overall situation is what is often referred to as the collective action problem (Olson 1965; Axelrod 1984), or what I will call the problem of human order.

Nevertheless, uncertainty can be reduced by clearly stated and enforceable rules and procedures. The forms of cooperation we mentioned above, tribe, village, family, factory, marriage, nation–state, which are often referred to as institutions, are the embodiments of the rules designed or developed to achieve a level of certainty. An institution thus is a set of coherent arrangements that secure exclusive privileges and benefits and demand necessary obligations for the involved parties. Institutions are necessary for an orderly satisfaction of human interests, a process complicated profoundly by limited satisfying materials, the necessity for cooperation, and the natural difficulties in achieving that. An institution involves calculated activities of the parties, reflects their interests and varied capacities in shaping the arrangements, and has certain purposes and performs certain functions. In this sense, for example, the state is an institution as it has certain purposeful functions pursued by individuals and their associations. Whereas a social structure (a hierarchical structure, for example) is not an institution, as it involves no intentional arrangements, no enforceable rules, and no clear membership. It is simply a pattern of relations among people.

This, interestingly enough, leads us to the concept of culture. Culture could be a very different thing for different people. For our purposes, culture is a pattern of habitual behaviors among a group of people. Culture so defined does not involve purposeful arrangements or calculative decisions. It is mainly of *habitual behaviors*. Individuals act on or react to their conditions, following the rules and exemplars established within the group. A habit in this context is not necessarily to act without thinking or rational calculation, but rather, to act as part of a *repetitive experience* that no longer needs calculation and decision each and every time. Past experiences within the group have established exact scenarios for alternative actions. The benefits and costs of a certain course of action are apparent to all members. The cumulative effects of these habitual behaviors will lead to the emergence of a stable set of relations among members. There is a substantial level of certainty about the likely directions and consequences of these members' actions and reactions.

What is more significant for our discussion is the dynamic relationship and perhaps the blurred boundary between institutions and culture. Institutions have effects on people's behaviors, and consequently would result in a pattern of behavior and stable relations. The Federal and State Government in the United States, for example, designed new welfare programs that would encourage welfare recipients to move from "welfare to work". Party system reforms in Japan may change the way how the Prime Minister is decided, allow more voters' say in the process, and thus encourage voters to be more closely involved in the substantive political and policy process. We are certainly too familiar with the attempts of institutional reform and restructuring in China, Russia, and many other former socialist countries to change the behaviors of the millions who developed a whole set of behavioral habits under the socialist system.

On the other hand, culture has an impact on human purposes and efforts in pursuit of these purposes. Such an impact, however, does not necessarily lead to, and often could become an obstacle to the advancement of these purposes and efforts. The function of institutions, whether they are created independently, have resulted from the modification of an existing institution, or evolved from their early form, would add new elements of incentives and punishments to the original matrix of calculations taken for granted by people at the cultural level and compel them to recalculate their options for action, which, if the designer of the institution were right, is expected to go in the direction desired by the designer.

Two related mechanisms of the institution-cultural interaction need to be discussed at this point. First, if the elements brought on by the new institutions are not significant enough to impose a new basis for behavioral recalculation, or the resistance by concerned parties is strong enough to offset the power of the new institutions, culture will still prevail and one will probably see a mixture of institutional efforts and cultural habits in that particular issue area. If the new institutions are significant and strong enough, a new pattern of habitual behaviors will evolve after a period of adjustment and adaptation. When that happens, the impacting institutions themselves would eventually become part of the cultural and social conditions which are to be taken for granted by members in their daily actions and reactions, until new institutional demands occur. The communist system in China in the 1950s was a typical example of the aggressive power of new institutions. The new pattern of political deference and "iron rice bowl" work attitude among the Chinese in the 1960s and 1970s were good examples of institutionally induced new cultural habits. Here, institutions are constantly evolving, through institutional innovations, reforms and restructuring, to shape and reshape cultural and social conditions for certain effects and will eventually be either overcome by the cultural traditions or integrated into the renewed culture. We might call this the *creative function* of institutions.

Institutions also have a *preserving function*. Culture is driven by habitual behaviors. While there is a level of certainty embedded in habitual behaviors, there is no guarantee of their likely direction, much less of their endurance over a long period. To perpetuate the cultural and social conditions with some form of enforceability and therefore a greater reliability, those which benefited most from the existing conditions will incline to turn these conditions into intentional arrangements capable of being enforced, independent of the circumstances of the individual members. Decision-making by the government during Mao's era, for example, involved a wide range of *ad hoc* practices which went back to as far as the Yanan years. The enlarged Politburo conferences were one of the practices. They were not an established institution under the Communist Party's constitution, but often used by Mao as a way of by-passing the majority of the Politburo who might vote against Mao's policies and programs. It was eventually "institutionalized" as an integral part of the Party's decision-making system. Here, cultural and social conditions demand the support of institutions for their ensured effects.

From this perspective, civilization is the totality of the dynamic institution–culture interaction. Civilization does have its institutional side. The evolution of a civilization, in a fundamental way, can be seen as the evolution of the rules, such as those regarding the legitimacy and boundaries of possessions and authority, and production and distribution of satisfying materials. Civilization also has its cultural side. The interaction between human interests, effective conditions, and prevalent rules would effect a distinct pattern of social relations and behaviors. Because of the dynamic nature of institutions and culture, civilization is also dynamic even though that can be best observed only over a long historical period.

Moreover, civilizations so defined is about the *mode* rather than *location* of human activity. Civilizations in the latter sense are concerned with human activity developed in a general geographic area or with a particular group of people. Thus we have Chinese, Persian, Indian, Egyptian, European, or Japanese civilizations. Civilizations in the first sense, however, involve human activity evolved around a key set of human interests. Capitalism as a civilization, for example, represents both the rules regulating profit-seeking activity and the behavioral properties manifest in the activity. In many cases, a civilization can be distinctive in both senses. Capitalism is about the mode of human activity, but also originated as a principal form in Western Europe. Confucianism is about the mode of human activity, but originated as a principal form in Northeast Asia.

What is Chinese civilization?: The Chinaman, the Confucian man and the Singaporean

What is *Chinese* civilization then? We perhaps should start with the problem of Confucianism, as many would see Confucianism as a defining core of Chinese civilization. I myself though take a rather broader view on this, not only because Confucianism was only one of the schools of thought shaping Chinese civilization in its formative age, but also that Confucianism can be seen as one of major attempts in human history to solve the problem of human order. With regard to the latter point, there are various "visions" about the nature of the problem and its desirable solution: Hobbes's idea of natural order, Confucius' idea of moral order, Bentham's idea of utilitarian order, and Aquinas' idea of Christian order. Hobbes's idea, even though never popular in Chinese intellectual traditions, depicts a human order derived from the interplay of undisciplined coercive powers, a state of human affairs that dominated much of the pre-modern and early modern history and perhaps still in the domain of international relations. The idea of external salvation appealed to the Chinese in a very subtle way. The Ideal Man of Confucianism has never really gone beyond Northeast Asia except echoed in a corner of France by Rousseau. The idea of Rational Man with utilitarian purposes, however, has become a key foundation for a range of modern institutions for production, distribution, and governance at various levels.

In this broad context, Confucianism is uniquely significant. Confucius' inspiration for the Ideal Man reflected his desire for a kind of individual that would be willing and capable of contributing to the public good which was deemed terribly missing in the Eastern Zhou China of his time (551–479 BC). But the "Confucianization" of the uncultivated Chinese was not able to solve the "human order problem" in traditional Chinese society. Rather, it led to the stratification of Chinese society between what can be called "low culture" (the uncultivated Chinese) and "high culture" (of the Confucian Men).

Moreover, Confucianism was adopted and transformed into a state ideology for the purposes of helping maintain the political and economic order. As a moral solution, Confucianism urges individuals to surrender their own genuine interests for the sake of the collectivity's well-being, whether that is the family or the state. While the disciplinary power of the moral order combined with state coercion may have proved to be effective under the system of an agrarian economy, a centralized state and centripetal society, it was fundamentally incompatible with the modern conditions where unsuppressed human interests emerged as the driving force for a social order. With the lack of effective institutional mechanisms regulating human activity and the gap between the high moral ground and genuine human interests, a typical Confucian society of the modern times tended to be ineffective in regulating human relations.

The ugly Chinaman

It would not be too difficult for anyone who has been to a town in China to report that China towns are dirty, chaotic, noisy, etc. For those who are interested in Chinese films, it is likely that they would end up with one featuring Chinese gangs and their fighting skills. These are all part of the phenomenon of what Bo Yang (柏杨), a well-received writer from Taiwan, calls the "Ugly Chinaman" (Bo 1992). In his book, Bo tries to identify some "genetic" cultural traits of the Chinese as the critical cause of the problems long associated with Chinese society: poverty, illiteracy, bloody internal fights. The Chinese, according to Bo, are "crass, arrogant, noisy, uncivilized, uncooperative, boastful, dirty, unforgiving", passive, bragging, exaggerating, telling lies, slandering other people, dishonest (Bo 1992: 30–31).

Bo is not the only one who sees the deep-rooted bad habits of the Chinese. Another writer in 1930s' China with a much higher status in modern China's intellectual history, Lu Xun (鲁迅), is also of a similar view. For Lu, however, it was Confucianism that was fully responsible for the decay of Chinese society. In his account, the Chinese were hypocritical, morally insensitive, and even tragically sarcastic about their life and fate under the oppressing Confucian social and political structure (see, for examples, Lu 1971 and 1973). Indeed, Lu's relentless attack on Confucian traditions was part of a large New Cultural Movement in early twentieth-century China when high-profile intellectuals, from Hu Shi (胡适) to Liang Qichao (梁启超), from Chen Duxiu (陈独秀) to Mao Zedong (毛泽东), were eager to find an explanation for the long process of decay of the Chinese society and the decline of national power at the time when the European powers came to confront the Chinese empire, with not only new materials and products, but also different ideas and ways of life. While these leading opinion-makers differed in desirable solutions, they seemed to share the view that Confucianism that penetrated deep into Chinese society and state institutions was the fundamental cause of the problems in modern Chinese society. As the result of the prevalence of Mao's Communist Revolution in the mid-twentieth century over other options for social and cultural change, Confucianism was completely discredited as a social ideal and a system of standards for social behavior. What followed since then, however, was not a solution in any sense to the Chinaman problem as the New Cultural Movement had hoped, but an even more rampant manifestation of the cultural habits.

In this author's view, the pioneers of the New Cultural Movement detected signs of the problem, but failed to understand the nature of the problem. Blaming Confucianism seems to have missed a larger issue of the original Chinaman problem, and how exactly Confucianism related to it. Some of the problems identified by New Cultural advocates were the very same problems found in the Chinaman by Bo Yang, and indeed in the outside-court coun-trymen by Confucius two thousand years ago. Others were the consequences of the Confucianist efforts in dealing with the original Chinaman problem.

The Confucian man

To understand how Confucianism relates to the original Chinaman problem and to other subsequent and competing attempts to deal with the problem, and thus how Confucianism relates to Chinese civilization or East Asian civilizations, we have to go back to the days of Confucius.

It would perhaps be an over-statement to say that Chinamen before Confucius were all "ugly". We do not have enough evidence of that. What we do know is that Confucius' life was occupied by a constant tension within himself between, on the one hand, the noble traditions he inherited from his family and found well preserved in his native state, *Lu* (鲁), in the early Zhou (周) period (1027–771 BC), and on the other, the increasing decay of court governance and civic life: corrupt government, collapsed morals, and fighting states, in the late Zhou period (770–221) when he lived. More fundamentally perhaps from a contemporary observer's point of view, Confucius looked at the masses of society from the position of the noble in the court. Wu-chi Liu provides a vivid descrip-tion of the social life in *Lu* around the year of 551 BC when Confucius was born (Liu 1955). On the one hand, there was the feudal hierarchy where the feudal prince was the center of the local state and his "miniature court imitative of the royal pattern" (ibid.: 6) formed the feudal court. This feudal court was a cluster of governors, warriors, bureaucrats, hereditary intellectuals, men of arts, headed by the feudal prince. Confucius was from the circle of hereditary intellectuals whose main function was to ensure the intellectual enlightenment of the feudal prince beginning from his childhood and the ethical order of the feudal court.

On the other hand, there was what Liu called the "landless class", the other side of the social scale where the "little fellow", "common man", or the "ugly Chinaman", if you will, were located. The overwhelming majority of this class were farmers. They were tied to the land that they did not own under the lord–vassal arrangements and later the well-field system. For this part of the population, noble standards were less important, perhaps irrelevant. "According to a prevailing view of the time, it was the duty of those who toiled with their bodies to feed those who worked only with their minds" (ibid.: 16).

There were two critical factors that complicated this clearly stratified social order and made Confucianism not only desirable in his times, but also increasingly necessary in subsequent dynasties in Chinese history. First, "as the feudatory grew in lands, power, and wealth, the government machinery became complicated", more of those from the landless class moved into towns to become part of the aristocracy working for the feudal court, or became service men working for themselves between different trades and between farmers and the government. A consequence of the expansion of court and town activities was the increasing complicity in sustaining the noble order over the feudal court. Those newly appointed court bureaucrats and traders needed to be properly educated and taught to behave in accepted manners, follow proper rules, respect existing relations, and be a "perfect gentleman" as the system required.

Second, as the "sort of family relationship and communal life" under the feudal system yielded to a more sophisticated social structure, and the reach of the expended government penetrated into the life and activity outside the feudal court, a social system took shape that required a unified ethical order covering both court and civic life. Confucius' teachings, which were delivered mainly as royal advice, from an hereditary intellectual to the ruling feudal princes, on how to become "princely man" (Kaizuka 1956) and how to run the government and win over the warring states in a more "civilized" way, were extended to become the principles of moral authority symbolized by the life of ruling aristocracy and applied primarily to the masses in society. It is no surprise that the feudal princes of the warring states, where Confucius took extra pains to travel, and was eager to find a royal ear for his advice, did not take him seriously. His royal encounters were largely unproductive, and his dream of moral teachings to become the foundation of the government unfulfilled.

Over a thousand years after his death, however, his teachings were collected, promoted and established, not so much as the basis for a moral order within the government and for the ruling classes themselves, but as moral guidelines for society as a whole, which were aimed mainly at those often unruly, uneducated, uncultivated farmers and other low classes in urban areas, in short, those "ugly Chinamen".

This immediately reminds us of Hobbes and Machiavelli. Both had the personal experiences and ambitions similar to Confucius' and set a similar role for themselves as a royal adviser to the prince to help the royal court steer at the times of fundamental social changes (Goldsmith 1966; Viroli 1998). But there was a critical difference between the Chinese adviser and the European advisers, one that perhaps lies at the heart of the differences between China and Europe in their modern development. In a sense, the problems that faced Confucius, and Hobbes and Machiavelli were essentially the same. In a social setting where the feudal system built on simple lord–vassal relationships collapsed and more sophisticated forms of production, distribution and social organization emerged and where authority relations within the system became more complicated and ambiguous, individual compliance became the key to the effective execution of any meaningful social agenda which would require the cooperation of the population. Yes, this is the same collective action problem or the problem of human order we have discussed earlier.

But the Chinese and European approaches differed fundamentally to the problem of human order. The European one, as evolved from the teachings of Hobbes and Bentham, is what I call an *institutional approach*; and the Chinese approach, as envisioned in Confucius' teachings, a *moral approach*.[7] The institutional approach in essence seeks a setting of rules that incorporates the individual's decision capacity and the manipulative power of the neutral public authority into the process of formation of a social order. It does so with clearly defined rules, an effective enforcing authority, and predictable benefits and costs for a range of courses of action for the individuals. The independent state authority in the eyes of Hobbes was a necessary first step in building such a "social order" out of natural order (Hobbes 1988). Max Weber went to great lengths to make the case that the modern bureaucratic state would be indeed impartial and efficient (Weber 1947).

The moral approach, on the other hand, also wants to influence people's behavior. But it differs profoundly from the institutional approach in several aspects. First, the disciplinary power of a moral order comes from within each individual himself, while that of an institutional order comes from a neutral third party of strong imposing authority. Second, an institutional order relies on the individual's rational decision for his course of action, while a moral order makes the calculations for individuals. Third, a moral order seeks the compliance of the individuals to the established standards and therefore tends to be more "conservative". The credibility of these moral standards depends to a great extent on their sustainability. An institutional order, however, allows the individual's utilitarian interests to determine their course of action and thus tends to be more "liberal", with less constraint by existing rules and arrangements. Confucianism as a moral solution to the human order problem lacks the interests of the individuals at its foundation, an effective disciplinary power behind its moral appeal, and the mechanisms that are necessary to make the system viable under ever-changing conditions and human interests.

The Japanese turn

The Confucian problem was first picked up and seriously dealt with in Japan.[8] The Meiji Restoration of the late nineteenth century was carried out in the name of restoring the power of the Emperor, realizing that the system dominated by Confucian principles lacked the necessary institutional effectiveness for the increasingly feudalizing state. The reforms introduced a wide range of modern institutions of non-Chinese origins. This, combined with the process of "de-Confucianization" of the Samurai and the emergence of neo-Confucianism several hundreds of years leading to the Meiji Restoration, laid the foundations for the rise of modern Japan.

While Confucianism was upheld in China as a moral solution, it was received mainly as an institutional ideal for the warring feudal kingdoms in Japan in the sixth century, which very much resembled the China of Confucius' times, as well as a cultural fashion for the Japanese in a much later stage. The Confucianism adopted in Japan was primarily institutional for two reasons. First, over the successive dynasties, the moral substance of the original Confucian teachings had been increasingly overshadowed by more systematic arrangements of institutional manipulation exercised by the government for the same purpose and still in the name of Confucianism. In addition to rituals, music, letters, paintings, education, what the Japanese adopted was, first and foremost, a system of government and social management.

Second, even Confucianism in China itself underwent significant change. What was eventually established in Japan is, what is called, neo-Confucianism that emerged from the reinterpretation of Confucianism by Zhu Xi (朱熹) and Cheng Hao (程颢) of the Song Dynasty, and Wang Yang-ming (王阳明) of the Ming Dynasty. Zhu and Wang reshaped Confucianism to incorporate elements of practical learning into the system of moral principles.[9]

On the subject of the adoption of Confucianism in Japan, John H. Gubbings, for example, focuses much of the discussion on the Great Reform introduced in 645 AD in Japan where it was "the new form of government", that is, a centralized bureaucracy, official hierarchy and feudal system that was first established, "in imitation of changes made under the T'ang dynasty in China" (Gubbings 1973: 18–20). Warren W. Smith, on the other hand, traces the introduction of Confucianism in Japan and notes that Confucianism began to be really understood and utilized in Japan "when Prince Shotoku (572–621) promulgated the famous so-called 'Seventeen Article Constitution' in 604". But if one looks at how Confucianism was understood then, it is clear that

> Prince Shotoku seems to have considered Confucianism as having an important role to play in buttressing the position of the central government, and the main emphasis of the "Seventeen Article Constitution" was on the duties of people towards their sovereign and the need for harmony among inferiors and superiors.
>
> (Smith 1959: 6–7; Collcutt 1991: 115)

This perception and practice of Confucianism were very much in tone with the Confucianism of the Han Dynasty which "was quite different from earlier Confucianism of the time of Confucius" (Smith 1959: 2). This institutional character was well kept until the Tokugawa period (1603–1868) when Confucianism "flourished most widely" (ibid.: vi).

While Confucianism "flourished" during the Tokukawa period, Western learning also grew in Japan. Confucianism was widely promoted as a form of organizing and managing Tokukawa Japan under the siege of feudal warriors. But it could not prepare Japan for the even greater challenge of developing a modern society, a modern economy and a modern government. Western learning became increasingly popular at the expense of Confucianism which was gradually reduced to guidelines for the moral side of society. The decline of Confucianism and the simultaneous rise of Western learning in the late Tokukawa and early Meiji era were a clear indication that Confucianism was inadequate as an institutional framework for the modern social, economic and political conditions. Smith observes that Confucianism of the Tokugawa period

> was no longer adequate to deal with the problems caging the nation in the years immediately preceding the Meiji Restoration ... With the advent of the Meiji Restoration, there was relatively little difficulty in putting aside all vestiges of institutionalized Confucianism which the Tokugawa had maintained.
>
> (ibid.: 232–3)

Let us take a look at a particular example of how Confucian traditions yielded to modern institutions in the grand social transformation culminating at the Meiji,[10] one that is concerned with the rise of the class of capitalist entrepreneurs. The traditional Japanese society was no less rigid, static and hierarchical than its Asian neighbors. Indeed the pre-Meiji society was by and large a replica of the Chinese imperial system where prestige was enjoyed by the *samurais* and *daimyos*, and merchant and trade activities were considered the business of the lower classes. In particular, the *samurai* were mainly warrior turned Confucian scholars who were retainers of the *daimyos* or local governors. Generally, they lived on a government salary but did not involve any of what today would be called "value-adding" economic activities. Towards the end of the Tokukawa reign, the *samurai* had become increasingly a burden on the government and their prestigious existence continued to marginalize the lower classes and therefore suppress productive activity in society.

The government determined to change the situation. On the one hand, neo-Confucianism was introduced in which the pure moral self-cultivation, as the core of the Confucian traditions supposedly practiced by the *samurai*, was no longer considered sufficient or even appropriate. One's virtues and knowledge had to be acquired in practical doing and attested in reality. On the other hand, the *samurai* were forced to give up their retainership as the government no longer provided living for the *samurai*, and with a one-time lump sum payment to seek new, independent life outside government support. Consequently, these *samurais* started a new life as craftsmen, merchants, property owners, or traders, and gradually formed a new entrepreneurial class that prepared for the rise of modern capitalism in Japan.

It was the perceived failure of Confucianism as a solution to the challenge of organizing society and production in the modern times that led to the rise of Western learning and the decline of Confucianism. By early last century, modern institutions were already in place which included universal education, a credible legal system, a constitution providing an uncontestable basis for legitimate national government, and those promoting and protecting individual property rights and production and trading activity. And the transformation from a Confucian society to a modern nation was effectively accomplished.

The Singaporean turn

If Japan was a good example of opting for a more effective institutional approach, Singapore has pushed the idea further. Because of the closer connection of Singaporean society to Confucianism, its experience was more significant. In short, many believe that Singapore's successful economic and social development was an instance of the working of a genuine Confucian society (Tai 1989; Mahathir and Ishihara 1995). Careful scrutiny will show that it was the *de-Confucianization* of the Singapore society during much of the early decades of the new republic that led to the rise of a modern Singapore. The modern Singaporean has been shaped by a system of strict and sophisticated rules and regulations, more than the appeal of Confucian moral principles, or the old habits of the Chinamen.

Singapore at the time of its establishment in the early 1960s consisted of three major ethnic groups: Chinese, Malays and Indians. The three groups spoke different languages, practiced different religions, lived in different local communities, and dominated in different domains of society. There was literally no nation, nor state as we know it, only three ethnic groups that happened to be in a geographical area and tried to survive one way or another. When an independent nation became the only option after 1965, a way had to be found for the three groups to live within one political structure and for the structure to be able to survive with the challenges from the Malay mainland, Indonesia, and from Indochina where Communism was spreading rapidly.

For Lee Kuan Yew, then the Prime Minister, the real challenge was from within, and more precisely from the Chinese community. Among the three ethnic groups, the Chinese community was the largest and most influential. Like their compatriots in other Southeast Asian countries, they controlled much of the nation's businesses. In addition, the Chinese community could well be linked to the Communist movement in the region. But subtly and more fundamentally for a political leader trained in Oxford with a vision of a society ruled by modern laws and civility, it was the original qualities of the Chinese that could be the ultimate obstacle to the rise of Singapore as a viable nation–state and a competitive economy in the long run. The qualities of the Chinaman we discussed earlier found their revived and even enhanced forms among the Chinese in Southeast Asia who moved there from China over the past hundred years. These qualities seemed to fall far below the standards the Oxford-trained politician envisioned for a modern Singapore.

The initial campaign to erase the "Chineseness" was to ban Chinese language in the first place, along with Chinese language schools and newspapers. Leaders of the Chinese community were put in jail. The government used the Emergency Act to suppress any opposition forces, mainly those of Chinese background. The suppression of the Chinese influence was not followed by the privileging of other ethnic groups as seen in other countries. Instead, English was upheld as the official national language. In the place of parochial interests, especially those of ethnic nature, laws and rules have been forcefully promoted. Citizens were urged to abide by the laws and not to opportunistically play between laws and communal rules. Indeed, incentives and punishment were clearly stipulated to shape people's behavior. More important, citizens were called upon to identify with Singapore as a nation over a particular ethnic group. People in Singapore have been nurtured to see themselves first and foremost as a Singaporean rather than Chinese or Indians.[11]

The making of the Singaporean has been not only through legal enforcement and political coercion, but more significantly through public policies. The government, for example, used its housing subsidy policy to make sure that people of different ethnic make-ups mixed with each other in residence, which in the long run helped forge local communities with less ethnic underpinnings (White and Goodman 1998: 201).

Forty years later, with a series of political campaigns, legal enforcement and policy manipulation, there has emerged a new generation of Singaporeans who are reputed for their law-abiding nature, being highly educated and skilled, and having a strong sense of citizenship and national identity, very different from either the Chinese, Malay or Indians forty years ago. This grand transformation has prepared the human and social conditions for Singapore's growth, a remarkable process that led to a modern, prosperous, harmonious society; a clean and effective government; and a competitive and dynamic economy.

Back to the homeland: the rise of Asian capitalist

The successful stories of transforming Chinaman and Confucian Man in Japan and Singapore have not occurred to the same extent in Taiwan, Hong Kong or China. In fact, expectations of a moral solution to the Chinaman problem embedded in the Confucian tradition have remained high in these societies. Certainly, the Chinese, Taiwanese, Hong Kongers today are certainly not the same Chinese, Taiwanese, Hong Kongers of twenty or forty years ago. They are no longer those of the Chinaman, nor those of the Confucian man. In the 1980s Professor Tu compared the prosperous "China peripheries" (Hong Kong, Taiwan as well as Korea and Singapore) and stagnant China proper and concluded that there was something new in the Confucianism in China peripheries (Tu 1994).

If there has been successful industrialization in these societies, it was certainly not a successful story of Confucianism as many believe.[12] Neo-Confucianism of the twentieth century in these former Confucian societies was more than the neo-Confucianism of the seventeenth and eighteenth centuries in China proper (Mettzger 1977; Tu 1989). Practical learning and social action as new additions to Confucianism in the seventeenth and eighteenth centuries have become even more important in the twentieth century as modern industrialization required the individual to possess these qualities. Since the early twentieth century, movements to promote new learning, that is, learning of science and technology, have swept across the greater China area. Old learning, i.e. learning of Confucian classics and self-cultivation, has gradually been marginalized.

Completely new to the neo-Confucianism of the post-war Taiwan and Korea and post-Mao China has been the rise of entrepreneurism. Confucianism looked down upon merchants, traders, craftsmen in its moral order. Those pledging faithful to Confucian teachings were urged to improve themselves through self-negation and re-cultivation. In a Confucian society, one's self and self-interests needed to be suppressed for him to be morally noble. On the other hand, modern society, and modern capitalism in particular, is built upon individuals' self-interests. The rise of entrepreneurism reflected an adaptation of the Confucian society to the requirements of modern capitalism (Redding 1988). This would not be possible, however, without the establishment first of a high-percentage of private ownership in society. This has been much clearer in China than in Taiwan or Hong Kong. Before Deng's reform, China was 100 percent state-owned. Without private ownership, there was no basis for entrepreneurship. The ice was broken first in rural communes in the late 1970s where peasants were allowed to work for themselves. Soon state lands were also reallocated for private use and then allowed to be sold by the farmers. By the late 1980s, forms of private ownership had been well re-established in rural areas. The problem of ownership in state-owned enterprises has not been completely solved yet. But newly established private enterprises have already dominated the Chinese economy and are on their way to significantly marginalize the SOEs (Naughton 1996).

More than Japan or Singapore, entrepreneurialism grew in Hong Kong, Taiwan, China *along* with their Chinaman and Confucian traditions. Indeed, entrepreneurialism has not led to a systemic transformation of the cultural and social character of these societies. Rather, there has been a level of opportunism, with regard to existing institutions, norms and rules. In many ways, entrepreneurial efforts were often attempts to test the bottom line of the existing conditions and dominant institutions, and locate a favorable balance between potential profits and benefits, on the one hand, and risks and costs, on the other.

Consequently, the new capitalist in these societies is not completely new. If the making of the modern Japanese and the Singaporean has been the result of a relatively successful transformation of the Chinaman and, to a less extent, of the Confucian Man, then, the making of the new Asian capitalist in China, Taiwan and Hong Kong is a much less thorough transformation of either the Chinaman or the Confucian Man. In all these cases, however, elements of the modern civilization have been solidly established. These new elements have demonstrated a much stronger capacity in effecting people's behavior than the Confucian moral order.

In summary, Confucianism rose as a response to the initial Chinaman problem. As a moral solution, however, it has been largely ineffective in tackling the problem, much less the challenge of modern conditions. This ineffectiveness has led to various attempts in Confucian societies at alternative solutions. The Japanese and Singaporean stories of modern transformation and more recent change and adaptation in the greater China area suggest that the dual problem of the Chinaman and Confucian Man in Chinese civilization has to be tackled from outside the system.

Chinese (or any) civilization under globalization

Now let us look at the problem of globalization and what it means for Chinese civilization, and in fact, for any civilizations. Earlier in this chapter, I defined civilization as a system of homogenous human activity confined by a set of habits, rules, and tools developed over a considerable period of time. Civilization thus is the totality of dominant rules and habitual behaviors with a distinctive level of homogeneity. Modern civilization, therefore, is such a system dominated by rules and habits of profit-seeking activities. Needless to say, modern civilization is accompanied by a set of revolutionary tools and methods of production, distribution and social organization, made possible by technological advances. Originating in Western Europe, modern civilization, like Chinese or Indian civilization, is a limited scale civilization.

From this perspective, globalization is a global expansion of the modern civilization. It is driven by the same dynamics that have shaped the modern institutions and it carries on the process of seeking the most efficient forms of production, distribution and organization on a largest possible scale. On the other hand, it is indeed the construction of a civilization on a global scale which is significantly different from those at a limited scale, modern civilization itself included. For one thing, many of the conditions that have made globalization possible as well as necessary are not found in the initial conditions for the rise of modern civilization. For another, globalization will inevitably create friction and fusion with limited scale civilizations, as a *global* civilization will have to form *over* limited scale civilizations.

Second, unlike many early attempts at large-scale expansion, globalization expands at the time when expansion with force and at the expense of the physical existence of others is no longer accepted as a legitimate form of boundary alternation. To a great extent, coercive power is not even necessary. Moreover, globalization is not a movement in pursuit of moral high grounds, but rather the highest possible levels of efficiency and profit. Globalization, by definition as an extension of the modern civilization, is an approach of neither coercive power nor moral appeal, but one of institutional rationality to the problem of human order.

Third, unlike the expansion of many civilizations in the past, the expansion of modern civilization is incomplete. Indeed, globalization, at least so far, is the development of the modern civilization in *individual countries*. The traditional boundaries among countries may be eroding, but the real boundaries for the emergent civilization are still very much *national*, in terms of the ultimate powers of making and enforcing rules, and effective mechanisms of the orderly satisfaction of human interests. Globalization may be able to synchronize national systems along the lines of efficiency and fairness, but it is constrained within a structure that operates against turning global governance into a civilization of both efficiency *and* fairness.

To put it differently, there has been an accelerating process of the spread of the modern civilization from one country to another in the past several decades. But there has been a very slow and often frustrating process of such civilization spreading vertically from the level of the nation–states to that of the globe. To the extent that there is a degree of vertical spread, it is mainly on the side of efficiency. The world as a whole is still very much defined by a set of rules and habits fundamentally different from those of modern civilization. In global affairs, elite countries still rule and power politics is still the rule. Ironically, those who champion the rules of modern civilization most enthusiastically at the national level are often those that are most reluctant at the global level. The logic seems to be that those different rules at the global level are in fact necessary for the spread and consolidation of the rules of the modern civilization at the national level.

Now, the question of Chinese civilization. The challenge of globalization for Chinese civilization is threefold: derived from the three defining aspects of globalization and the corresponding qualities of Chinese civilization we discussed earlier. First, Chinese civilization is a limited scale civilization. As such, there will be more friction and fusion, as there has been already in the past, between Chinese civilization and the global expansion of the modern civilization. Given that the conditions for the prevalence of the modern civilization (resource scarcity, necessity of orderly satisfaction of human interests, and human nature itself) would not fundamentally change in the foreseeable future, the friction/fusion balance for Chinese civilization will tilt more toward the fusion side.

Second, Confucianism-centered Chinese civilization is a moral approach to the problem of human order. Certainly, a moral approach is more "civilized" than one of coercive power. But as I have shown, Chinese civilization as a moral approach is ineffective in meeting the challenge of modern conditions. Not only those societies once influenced and dominated by Confucian traditions have largely moved away in search of more effective forms, but the Chinese themselves also seem to be moving in that direction as well. If the current trend continues, we will see further erosion of the distinct character of Chinese civilization.

Third, the question of sustainability of the human conditions and that of the possibility of a genuine global civilization. This more philosophical question has two aspects. On the one hand, if further advances in technology could fundamentally change the conditions upon which the modern civilization has excelled or if they could even lead to changes that might affect human nature itself to some extent as Fukuyama (1999) suggests, then there could be some new elements that might fall outside the parameters of modern civilization. More realistically, on the other hand, if efficiency of scale reaches its final limits on the earth, and the problem of fairness cannot be satisfactorily solved within a global modern civilization, then there might be some role for a moral approach to play. Such a moral approach though does not necessarily have to be the Chinese one. All of these, however, involve contingent factors and thus how they would affect Chinese civilization and its relation with a global modern civilization is unclear.

Conclusion

Now what is *"Chinese"* about Chinese civilization, and what has globalization to do with Chinese civilization? These questions can be answered at three levels. First, in terms of its relation to civilizations in general, Chinese civilization is one major approach to the problem of human order and one that relies on high moral standards in shaping human behavior, in contrast to those that rely on coercive power and institutional rationality.

Second, in terms of its relation to those societies once influenced and dominated by Chinese civilization which have since been moving away in search of alternatives, Chinese civilization is a system of rules and habits dictated by Confucian principles. Chinese civilization of today, though, is no longer the one of pure Confucianism: not only Confucianism has undergone fundamentally changes over time, China itself has already gone beyond the system in search of more effective forms of production, distribution and social organization.

Finally, the meeting of Chinese civilization and the global expansion of the modern civilization has created both friction and fusion at the same time. However, as the latest revitalization in Chinese civilization is more of the working of elements of the modern civilization, fusion between Chinese civilization and the modern civilization has been a dominant trend.

Notes

1 Arnold Toynbee being one of such framers of the early years (Toynbee 1963), and Samuel Huntington, one of more recent years (Huntington 1996).
2 There are two aspects of the eroding processes that need to be distinguished. On the one hand, even globalization is considered the expansion of modern civilization, there is a process of transforming the limited-scale modern civilization into a global one. This process is destructive (as well as constructive) for modern civilization itself. There is a large volume of literature dealing with this aspect which mostly focus on the problem of the nation–state and related issues (McGrew 1992, 1997; Baylis and Smith 1997; Gill 1997; Holton 1998; O'Rourke and Williamson 1999; Ferledger and Mandle 2000; Pieterse 2000). On the other hand, globalization is inviting even more profound change in "peripheral" (Hannerz 1991) civilizations and, as we will show, such changes have more to do with the basic organizing rules themselves than the scale on which the rules are applied (King 1991; Le Heron and Park 1995; Appadurai 1998; Jameson and Miyoshi 1998; Haynes 1999).
3 One of the key writers of the theory, Eric Weil, noted "the existence of an axial time... it was then that our intellectual, moral, and religious civilization was born and that the foundations were laid on which we continue to build" (Weil 1975: 21).
4 See, for example, 「軸心文明與二十一世紀I」 and 「軸心文明與二十一世紀II (Axial-Age Civilizations and the twenty-first Century I and II), 香港《二十一世紀》(*The Twentieth-First Century* (Hong Kong), vols. 57 and 58 (2000) and also Liu (1998).

5 Dependent events in the sense that the qualities or even the occurrence of a subsequent event are affected by those of the prior one.
6 The debate has been raised to a new level lately when Fukuyama cast his "second thoughts" on his end-of-history thesis (Fukuyama 1999).
7 I have to add immediately that there were those of the moral approach also in Europe (*à la* Rousseau, for example) and those of the institutional approach in China (*à la* Li Si, for example), although the moral approach in Europe and the institutional approach in China were marginalized in their respective settings.
8 For a more systematic treatment of the spread of Confucianism in Japan and the rest of East Asia, see Rozman (1991); de Bary (1988); Tu (1994); and Pye (1985).
9 For more on the subject, see Tu (1976 and 1989).
10 For more on this subject, see Pyle (1978), particularly, Chapter 3, "Growth of Tokugawa Society": 23–33. Also Cook (1998); and Moore (1970).
11 For more on this, see Quah (1990); Clammer (1998).
12 A notable example is Tai (1989).

References

Appadurai, Arjun (1998) *Modernity at Large: Cultural Dimensions of Globalization*, Minneapolis, University of Minnesota Press.

Arnason, Johann P. (2001) "Imaginary Significations and Historical Civilizations", unpublished manuscript.

Axelrod, Robert (1984) *The Evolution of Cooperation*, New York, Basic Books.

Baylis, John and Smith, Steve (1997) *The Globalization of World Politics*, New York/Oxford, Oxford University Press.

Beyer, Peter (1994) *Religion and Globalization*, London, Sage.

Bo, Yang (1992) *The Ugly Chinaman and the Crisis of Chinese Culture*, North Sydney, Allen & Unwin.

Clammer, John R. (1998) *Race and State in Independent Singapore, 1965–1990: The Cultural Politics of Pluralism in a Multiethnic Society*, Brookfield, Ashgate.

Collcutt, Martin (1991) "The Legacy of Confucianism in Japan", in Gillbert Rozman (ed.), *The East Asian Region: Confucian Heritage and Its Modern Adaptation*, Princeton, NJ, Princeton University Press, pp. 111–56.

Cook, Harry (1998) *Samurai: The Story of a Warrior Tradition*, New York, Sterling Publishers.

Daedalus (1975) "Wisdom, Revelation and Doubt: Perspectives on the First Millennium B.C". *Daedalus*, vol. 104, no. 2.

de Bary, Wm. Theodore (1988) *East Asian Civilizations: A Dialogue in Five Stages*, Cambridge, MA, Harvard University Pres.

Eisenstadt, Samuel N. (1986a) *The Origins and Diversity of Axial Age Civilizations*, New York, State University of New York Press.

—— (1986b) "The Axial Age Breakthrough in China and India", in S. N. Eisenstadt (ed.), *The Origins and Diversity of Axial Age Civilizations*, New York, State University of New York Press, pp. 291–305.

Elvin, Mark (1986) "Was There a Transcendental Breakthrough in China?", in Samuel N. Eisenstadt (ed.), *The Origins and Diversity of Axial Age Civilizations*, New York, State University of New York Press, pp. 325–59.

Ferledger, Louis and Mandle, Jay R. (2000) *Dimensions of Globalization*, Thousand Oaks, CA, Sage.

Fukuyama, Francis (1999) "Second Thoughts: The Last Man in a Bottle", *The National Interest*, vol. 56, pp. 16–26.

Gill, Stephen (1997) *Globalization, Democratization and Multilateralism*, London, Macmillan.

Goldsmith, Maurice M. (1966) *Hobbes's Science of Politics*, New York, Columbia University Press.

Gubbings, John H. (1973) *The Making of Modern Japan*, Wilmington, Scholarly Resources Inc.

Hannerz, Ulf (1991) "Scenarios for Peripheral Cultures", in Anthony D. King (ed.) *Culture, Globalization and the World-System: Contemporary Conditions for the Presentation of Identity*, London, Macmillan, pp 107–28.

Haynes, Jeff (1999) *Religion, Globalization and Political Culture in the Third World*, New York and London, St Martin's Press and Macmillan.

Hobbes, Thomas (1988) *The Leviathan*, New York, Prometheus Books.

Holton, Robert J. (1998) *Globalization and the Nation-state*, New York and London, St. Martin's Press and Macmillan.

——. (2000) "Globalization's Cultural Consequences", in Louis Ferledger and Jay R. Mandle, *Dimensions of Globalization*, Thousand Oaks, CA, Sage, pp. 140–52.

Huntington, Samuel P. (1996) *The Clash of Civilizations and the Remaking of World Order*, New York, Simon & Schuster.

IFID (1998) *Globalization of Information: The Networking Information Society*, The Hague, Netherlands, International Federation for Information and Documentation.

Jameson, Fredric and Miyoshi, Masao (1998) *The Cultures of Globalization*, Durham, NC, Duke University Press.

Jaspers, Karl (1953) *The Origin and Goal of History*, London, Routledge & Kegan Paul.

Kaizuka, Shigeki (1956) *Confucius*, London, Allen and Unwin.

King, Anthony D. (1991) *Culture, Globalization and the World-System: Contemporary Conditions for the Presentation of Identity*, London, Macmillan.

Le Heron, Richard and Ock Park, Sam (1995) *The Asian-Pacific Rim and Globalization: Enterprises, Governance and Territoriality*, Avebury, Atheneum Press.

Lindberg, Staffan and Sverrisson, Arni (1997) *Social Movements in Development: The Challenges of Globalization and Democratization*, Basingstoke, Macmillan.

Liu, Gang (1998). "Is There an Alternative to (Capitalist) Globalization? The Debate about Modernity in China", in Fredric Jameson and Masao Miyoshi (eds) *The Cultures of Globalization*, Durham, NC, Duke University Press, pp. 164–90.

Liu, Wu-chi (1955) *Confucius: His Life and Time*, New York, Philosophical Library.

Lu, Xun (1971) *Ah Q and Others: Selected Stories of Lusin*, Freeport, Books for Libraries Press.

—— (1973) *Silent China; Selected Writings of Lu Xun*, London, Oxford University Press.

Luard, Evan (1990) *The Globalization of Politics: Changed Focused of Political Action in the Modern World*, New York, New York University Press.

Mahathir, Mohamad and Ishihara, Shintero (1995) *The Voice of Asia*, Tokyo, Kodansha International.

McGrew, Antony G. (1992) "Conceptualizing Global Politics", in Antony G. McGrew (ed.), *Global Politics: Globalization and the Nation-state*, Cambridge, Polity Press, pp. 1–28.

—— (1997) *The Transformation of Democracy: Globalization and Territorial Democracy*, Cambridge, Polity Press/Open University Press.

Mettzger, Thomas A. (1977) *Escape from Predicament: Neo-Confucianism and China's Evolving Political Culture*, New York, Columbia University Press.

Moore, Ray A. (1970) "Adoption and Samurai Mobility in Tokugawa Japan" *Journal of Asian Studies*, vol. 29, pp. 617–32.

Naughton, Barry (1996) *Growing Out of the Plan*, London, Cambridge University Press.

Olson, Mancur (1965) *The Logic of Collective Action: Public Goods and the Theory of Groups*, Cambridge, MA, Harvard University Press.

O'Rourke, Kevin H. and Williamson, Jeffre G. (1999) *Globalization and History: The Evolution of a Nineteenth-Century Atlantic Economy*, Cambridge, MA, MIT Press.

Pieterse, Jan N. (2000) *Global Cultures: Shaping Globalization*, London and New York, Zed Books.

Pye, Lucian W. (1985) *Asian Power and Politics: The Cultural Dimensions of Authority*, Cambridge, MA, Harvard University Press.

Pyle, Kenneth B. (1978) *The Making of Modern Japan*, Lexington, MA., Heath and Co.

Quah, Jon S.T. (1990) "National Values and Nation-building: Defining the Problem", in Jon S.T. Quah (ed.), *In Search of Singapore's National Values*, Singapore, Time Academic Press.

Redding, S. G. (1988) "The Role of the Entrepreneur in the New Asian Capitalism", in Peter L. Berger and Hsin-huang. Hsiao (eds), *In Search of An East Asian Development Model*, New Brunswick, Transaction Books, pp. 99–111.

Robertson, Roland (1992) *Globalization: Social Theory and Global Culture*, Thousand Oaks, CA, Sage.

Rozman, Gillbert (1991) *The East Asian Region: Confucian Heritage and Its Modern Adaptation*, Princeton, NJ, Princeton University Press.

Schumpeter, Joseph (1975) *Capitalism, Socialism and Democracy*, New York, Harper.

Schwartz, Benjamin I. (1975a) "The Age of Transcendence", *Daedalus*, vol. 104, no. 2, pp. 1–7.

—— (1975b) "Transcendence in Ancient China" *Daedalus*, vol. 104, no. 2, pp. 57–68.

Scott, Alan (1997) *The Limits of Globalization: Cases and Arguments*, London, Routledge.

Smith, Warren W. (1959) *Confucianism in Modern Japan*, Tokyo, The Hokuseido Press.

Tai, Hung-chao (1989) *Confucianism and Economic Development: An Oriental Alternative?*, Washington, DC, Washington Institute Press.

Thesis Eleven, (2000) "Civilizations", *Thesis Eleven*, 62.

Toynbee, Arnold J. (1963) *A Study of History*, New York, Oxford University Press.

Tu, Wei-ming (1976) *Neo-Confucian Thought in Action*, Berkeley, CA, University California Press.

—— (1989) *Confucianism in an Historical Perspective*, Occasional Paper and Monograph Series, Singapore, Institute of East Asian Philosophies.

—— (1994) "Cultural China", in Wei-ming Tu (ed.), *The Living Tree*, Stanford, CA, Stanford University Press, pp. 1–34.

Viroli, Maurizio (1998) *Machiavelli*, Oxford, Oxford University Press.

Weber, Max (1947) *The Theory of Social and Economic Organization*, Glencoe, IL, Free Press.

Weil, Eric (1975) "What is a Breakthrough in History?", *Daedalus*, vol. 104, no. 2, pp. 21–36.

White, Gordon and Goodman, Roger (1998) "The Politics of Welfare in East Asia", in Richard Maidment, David Goldblatt and Jeremy Mitchell (eds), *Governance in the Asia-Pacific*, London, Routledge, pp. 195–220.

11 Globalization and Indian civilization

Questionable continuities

Niels Brimnes

> Ram's birthplace is not a quarrel about a small piece of land. It is a question of national integrity. The Hindu is not fighting for a temple of brick and stone. He is fighting for the preservation of a civilization, for his Indianness, for national consciousness, for the recognition of his true nature.
>
> (Sadhvi Rithambhra, quoted in Khilnani 1998: 187)

In the 1990s, India has opened to the economic and cultural forces of globalization. American soft drinks, Korean cars and German white goods are visible everywhere. On television, *CNN*, *BBC World* and *STAR News* compete with numerous national and regional channels to deliver a wide range of news stretching from municipal politics to global affairs, while *MTV India* offers a peculiar and endless mixture of Western and Hindi pop music. Yet, the most significant political development in India over the last decade is the rise of Hindu nationalism; an assertion of *Hindutva* – "Hinduness" – which has produced an ambivalent attitude towards the Western world and a forthright hostility towards Muslims. The rise of Hindu nationalism began in the 1980s, took off with the demolition of the *Babri Masjid* in Ayodhya in December 1992, and ultimately led to the formation of two successive governments led by the *Bharatiya Janata Party* (BJP) from 1998.

This development seems to fit all too well, as one scholar has recently remarked, into an understanding of the world as made up of a number of distinct and essentially different "civilizations" (Hansen 1999: 11). At the same time, however, the rise of Hindu nationalism challenges established and widespread notions of the Indian civilization as particularly peaceful, syncretic and tolerant. While the nature of the Indian civilization is contested in the cultural politics of modern India, we must also ask to what extent and in what way the concept "civilization" can be usefully employed in analyses of current events in Indian society and politics. In this chapter, I investigate the concept of an Indian civilization from two related, historically informed perspectives. First, I try to assess how useful it is as an analytical tool for the present-day historian aiming to create a sense of order in the multifaceted history of the Indian subcontinent. Second, I will analyze how the notion of an Indian civilization has been constructed by influential writers over the last two centuries; in Western attempts to come to terms with an unfamiliar society as well as in Indian attempts to formulate an identity in the modern world. Finally, I present two recent analyses of Hindu nationalism and use them to speculate about the relation between Hindu nationalism and the concept of a distinct Indian civilization. Before I turn to the more detailed investigation, I shall, however, briefly consider a few general aspects of the concept of civilization, particularly as it has been employed in the scholarly debate of the 1990s.

De-essentializing civilization

Although "civilization" appeared in the eighteenth century as a universal expressing intellectual, cultural and moral refinement, it became relativized during the nineteenth century and increasingly came to designate the distinct and complex whole of a given society (Fisch 1972). Prasenjit Duara has recently suggested that the relativist concept of civilization triumphed at the end of WWI and linked this triumph to the spread of nationalism to the colonized areas (Duara 2001: 100, 103). Civilization understood in the relativist sense is closely related to the concepts of "culture" and "nation". These overlapping concepts all aim to order mankind into identifiable entities based on common properties and to demarcate both internal homogeneity and external difference between societies appearing in space and time. Civilization, however, does this on the most extensive scale. Unlike cultures – which seem to exist in an endless variety – and nations – that are numerous – the number of civilizations is limited to a few. Civilization is also the most exclusive concept. We are familiar with multicultural societies and states comprising more than one nation, but find it difficult to express this phenomenon through the concept of civilization.[1] While cultures mix and nations coexist, civilizations seem to clash. Finally, although civilizations are not necessarily seen as unchanging and eternal, they must at least be stable, durable and possess a distinct history of their own. In short, using the concept of civilization in explanations of current affairs is an argument of both distinctiveness and historical continuity.

The major problem inherent in the concept of civilization is the essentialism, which it – like the related concepts of culture and nation – seems to imply. Understood in the relativist sense a civilization is normally assumed to have a "core" or "nucleus", which demarcates it from what is outside. This essence expresses the inherent properties and defining features of a social entity – its inner being. Moreover, essences stand above history. The capacity of making history is denied historical agents and transferred to ahistorical and substantialized essences – in the case of India typically "the caste system" or "the Indian mind" (Inden 1990; Prakash 1992). In consequence of essentialism, history is organized into a number of distinct and homogeneous entities. No longer a conjuncture of heterogeneous and contingent processes, history instead becomes the manifestation of essences. We may well ask ourselves whether this is a useful way of understanding history.

In the last two decades, the discipline of history has been occupied with the deconstruction of essentializing concepts. Most notably the "nation" has been dismissed as the hypostasized agent of historical change and the subject of history. Instead, the nation has been viewed as a relatively recent product of contingent conjunctures (Anderson 1983; Duara 1995: 6–16). For similar reasons, historians have also become uneasy about the way in which they employ the concept of civilization. An interesting example of this process is William H. McNeill, who organized his seminal book *The Rise of the West* from 1963 around the concept of civilization. Although McNeill sees the rise of civilization (in the singular) as a process of diffusion from a single source in Mesopotamia, he quickly identifies "unique styles of civilized life" (in the plural) in separate locations, characterized by what he terms as "master social institutions". By 500 BC, both Greece and India had developed their master institutions: *polis* and caste (McNeill 1963: 63, 68, 168). The castes of India were not, however, entirely separate entities, because that would make the existence of an Indian civilization impossible, and – McNeill insists – "there *is* an Indian civilization, and what holds it together and gives it unity is religion". The emphasis on religion enables McNeill to define the essence that marked off India from contemporary civilizations as: "a spiritual resolution of the worldly frustration" (ibid.: 177, 183). Moreover, the Indian civilization found its basic and enduring form early on:

> In other words, Indian civilization in the fifth century BC was a living growing thing with a long history ahead of it. Yet the directions of growth and some of its limits had been defined by the time Buddha died. The master institution of caste and the major outlines of the religious world view which were to govern all subsequent Indian history down to the present had emerged. Indian civilization, in short, had achieved its distinctiveness.
>
> (ibid.: 187)

While this passage emphasizes both distinctiveness and historical continuity, McNeill took a somewhat different view twenty-five years later. In the inaugural article in *Journal of World History*, McNeill reassessed the arguments of *The Rise of the West*, and he was now skeptical of explaining macro-history with primary reference to autonomous and separate civilizations. Inspired by Immanuel Wallerstein's concept of a world-system, McNeill prefers to pay much more attention to "the trans-civilizational process" and to heterogeneous systems with shifting centers and boundaries (McNeill 1990: 7–8, 13, 19).

In the work of the sociologist Shmuel N. Eisenstadt, a related reappraisal seems to be under way. Eisenstadt was a major figure in the investigation of the so-called Axial-age civilizations in the 1980s. Building on the insights of Max Weber and Karl Jaspers, Eisenstadt argued that the major civilizations of the world found their enduring form in an axial age through the resolution of the tension between "the transcendental and mundane orders" (Eisenstadt 1982: 294). Although this basic tension was common to all societies, it was

resolved in specific ways within each civilization and this had profound consequences for their future "basic contours". In India this resolution was
instrumental in creating two far-reaching "other-worldly" civilizations: the
Buddhist and the Hinduist (Eisenstadt 1986: 25, 291). This line of argument is
similar to what McNeill argued in 1963, but in a recent article written by
Eisenstadt and Wolfgang Schluchter this position has been modified. In a
discussion of the concept of early modernity, which was always intimately
connected to Western civilization, they suggest that the term might be relevant
in a broader trans-civilizational perspective. Eisenstadt and Schluchter are,
however, keen to avoid the pitfalls of euro-centrism and reject the assumption
of modernization theory that all societies converge towards the same point.
They accordingly suggest that instead of one early modernity, there might be a
number of related early modernities. Playing down both homogeneity and
distinctiveness, each civilization is now seen as "multicentered and heterogeneous". Although they generate their own internal dynamics, these dynamics
are related and they all have a share in the broader development of modernity
(Eisenstadt and Schluchter 1998).

The recent formulations of McNeill and Eisenstadt indicate that scholars are
currently seeking to make the concept of civilization more open and flexible.
Yet, the most resounding recent employment of civilization as an analytical tool
came in 1993 with Samuel P. Huntington's influential article "The Clash of
Civilizations?" Huntington utilizes civilization – in a thoroughly relativist and
essentialist sense – to understand the world after the Cold War: "as the post-Cold
War world evolves, civilization commonality ... is replacing political ideology
and traditional balance of power considerations as the principal basis for cooperation and coalitions" (Huntington 1993: 35). This is, however, an
understanding with deep historical implications.

To Huntington, civilization is "a cultural entity" and it is defined through a
number of elements, which constitute its core or essence: language, history, religion, customs and institutions. To these "objective" elements he adds the
subjective self-identification with a civilization (ibid.: 23–24). According to
Huntington, differences between civilizations are "the product of centuries" and
thus more fundamental and "real" than differences between the political ideologies of the Cold War. While Huntington's analysis might be an adequate
description of the pattern of conflict in the twenty-first century, he does not see
this as a new pattern contingent on specific historical developments, but as the
re-emergence of an older and more fundamental pattern (ibid.: 25, 30). One
must, however, inevitably ask about the importance of differences between civilizations before 1989. How could political ideologies such as communism and
liberalism outdo – if only temporarily – these deep and enduring differences?
One of Huntington's critics, Fouad Ajami, has aptly caricatured Huntington's
use of the concept of civilization in the following way:

> Huntington has found his Civilizations whole and intact, watertight under
> an eternal sky. Buried alive, as it were, during the years of the Cold War,

these civilizations ... rose as soon as the stone was rolled off, dusted themselves off, and proceeded to claim the loyalty of their adherents.

(Ajami 1993: 2)

Huntington regards the "hinduization" of India as an example of the new
world order (1993: 26). According to his general line of argument, the growing
Hindu nationalism should be interpreted as the realization of an age-old essence
after decades of false flirtation with Western ideologies. In this perspective
Hindu nationalism is not a contingent product of recent history, but the embodiment of the hypostatized and ahistorical agent that moves India toward her
destiny.

Huntington further elaborates on his ideas in the book *The Clash of Civilizations
and the Remaking of World Order*. The basic line of argument is unaltered and the
historically privileged nature of the civilizational approach to recent world
history is stated with exemplary clarity: "The twentieth-century conflict between
liberal democracy and Marxist-Leninism is only a fleeting and superficial historical phenomenon compared to the continuing and deeply conflictual relation
between Islam and Christianity". He further argues that the animosity between
Muslims and Christians should not be explained with "transitory phenomena",
but with the deeper nature of the two religions. Ahistorical essences clearly
prevail over specific historical developments (Huntington 1997: 209–10).

Despite this commitment to deep historical continuities, there are elements
which point in the other direction. Given the long periods of peaceful coexistence between Islam and Christianity, Huntington acknowledges that historical
constants cannot alone account for the recent intensification of the conflict
between the two civilizations. Instead, Huntington points to shifting demographic balances, breakdown of identities in multinational states – such as the
Soviet Union and Yugoslavia – and modern electoral politics; all explanations
rooted in recent and specific historical developments, or "transitory phenomena"
if you like (1997: 259–62). Similarly, the resurgence of religion – the primary
element in civilizational identity – is interpreted as an answer to "the social,
economic, and cultural modernization that swept across the world in the second
half of the twentieth century". Consequently, the "hinduization" of India now
seems to be the construction of a *new* Hindu identity, rather than the resurrec-
tion of an old civilizational essence (ibid.: 97–8). This interpretation conforms, as
I shall demonstrate in the last section of this chapter, much better to the
prevailing scholarly opinion.

One important consequence of the de-essentialization of the concept of civilization is that claims to deep historical continuities become highly questionable.
In the case of India this leads to reservations against invocations of an ancient
integrated Hindu civilization in current Hindu nationalist rhetoric as well as
against claims that Indian civilization was always peaceful and tolerant. Ancient
India does not provide any legitimacy for the vision of an exclusive, homogeneous Hindu nation (Thapar 2000). But neither do Ashoka's 12th rock edict
about religious tolerance serve as the "ontological base" for the secular Indian

state, as claimed recently by Satish Chandra. References to Ashoka's rule provides no guarantee that India will retain what Chandra labels "its historical vision of a world based on cultural multipolarity and toleration between different sects, beliefs and ways of life" (1997: 125, 139). Indeed, the history of the Indian subcontinent is much too complex to champion any essentialist reading of it. This is what I hope to demonstrate in the next section.

Searching for an Indian civilization

If we take Huntington's "objective" criteria for what may constitute a civilization – language, history, religion, customs and institutions – as our point of departure, it is easy to realize that an Indian civilization cannot be defined as a homogeneous linguistic entity. Even if the Dravidian South is excluded, the major linguistic bloc of the North – the Hindi–Urdu belt – collides with another of Huntington's constitutive elements: religion. It is more debatable whether a distinct Indian civilization was formed by a common history. Needless to say, an Indian civilization cannot be limited to the present-day Indian Union: a recent geo-political construct with frontiers that from a historical point of view are arbitrary. Alternatively, one might point to South Asia as the broader region, which fostered a civilization of its own. This, too, is questionable. Historically, Tamil Nadu and Sri Lanka have stronger connections with South East Asia than with the Punjab, while the area which today is Pakistan has been closely connected to Central Asia. One ought, as Sanjay Subrahmanyam has recently pointed out, to be cautious about insisting on the unity and homogeneity of regions defined by the recent institution of "area studies"; regions which are supposedly defined by "multimillennial 'civilization constants'" (1997: 742).

Even common political structures on the Indian subcontinent are hard to locate. Political fragmentation has been the normal state of affairs in Indian history, interrupted by relatively short-lived attempts to unify large parts of the subcontinent under imperial rule (Kulke and Rothermund 1998: 210; Khilnani 1998: 157). As ancient empires were limited to North India, and as it seems paradoxical – although in a certain sense not entirely besides the point – to recognize the British empire as the midwife of the Indian civilization, the Mughal state appears as the most likely creator of a distinct Indian civilization born out of a common historical experience. This also enables us to envisage the Indian civilization as an entity shaped by the encounter between a Muslim warrior aristocracy and a predominantly Hindu population.

There is a long tradition of defining the Mughal State as a highly centralized political structure. This is still advocated by influential writers. To J. F. Richards, the Mughal empire was "an intrusive centralizing system which unified the subcontinent" (Richards 1993: 1), and he has coined the term "autocratic centralism" to characterize its political structures. Richards emphasizes centralism because it has been attacked in recent writings. Studies of power-relations in the periphery of the empire suggest that, rather than being a highly centralized revenue-extracting polity, the Mughal State was forced to make flexible compromises with the local elite (Perlin 1985; Wink 1986). Although the debate on the nature of the Mughal polity is by no means concluded, it can be argued that the coherent and unifying Mughal "system" dissolves as it comes under closer scrutiny. Sanjay Subrahmanyam has identified the "excessive preoccupation with identifying an essential structure" supposedly underlying Mughal history as a major historiographic obstacle for further insight into this period of Indian history (1992: 320).

For obvious reasons, the definition of an Indian civilization through religion is problematic. The problem is often avoided by labeling the Indian civilization a "Hindu civilization". But this eliminates millions of Muslims, which it is unfounded to separate from the majority of Hindus on the Indian subcontinent. Moreover, the concept of "Hinduism" is itself problematic. Although Hinduism today is often represented as a coherent proper religion comparable to Islam and Christianity, there are indications that the Hinduism discovered by the British in the eighteenth century was more like a loosely integrated collection of sects (Metcalf 1994: 134, Thapar 2000: 77). It seems, however, possible to identify two major varieties within the multitude of religious practice defined as Hinduism. On the one hand, there was a Brahman-dominated high Hinduism emphasizing ritual purity and vegetarianism. On the other hand, a popular religious practice, which incorporated features of high Hinduism but combined it with elements of a very different character. Susan Bayly has revealed how not only vegetarian gods and local "blood and power" divinities; but also Muslim saints and Christian beliefs coexisted in a number of syncretic forms in pre-colonial South India (Bayly 1989: 40–4).

In their attempt to reach a deeper understanding of the bewildering social fabric of Indian society from the late eighteenth century, the British naturally sought stable and fixed features. To the British, Brahmanic Hinduism presented itself as an obvious way of coming to terms with an alien and complex society, and in the last decades of the eighteenth century they attributed a hitherto unknown coherence to Hinduism. As Christianity had the Bible and Islam the Koran, the British Orientalists discovered the Hindu equivalent: the classical Sanskrit texts (Metcalf 1994: 11, 134; Marshall 1970). Having created the category of Hinduism, it could be established, for instance, that Hindus should be judged according to Hindu standards, as they appeared in the classical texts. The colonial power and the Brahmans had common interests: the British read into Indian society a comprehensible order, while the Brahmans assumed for themselves the role as authorities on religious, cultural and social features among the Indians. They knew the sacred texts and thus possessed the key to true knowledge about Indian society. Thomas Metcalf concludes: "In the end, indeed, one can only see the 'constructed' Hinduism of the early colonial era as a joint product of British scholars and Brahmin pandits" (Metcalf 1994: 12; Bayly 1988: 155–8). Following recent trends within the discipline of history, it seems that Hinduism can be fruitfully analyzed as both an "imagined community" and an "invented tradition" (Anderson 1983; Hobsbawn and Ranger 1983).

For North India – and increasingly for the Indian State as a whole – the paramount religious issue is of course violent communal conflict. Proponents of an ancient and integrated Hindu-nation would obviously like to see communal tensions stretching right back to the advent of Muslims on the subcontinent, while secular nationalists since the 1930s have accused the British of fostering "false" communal identities (Pandey 1990: 251). Today, most scholars tend to see abstract communal identities as a comparatively recent phenomenon. Sandria Freitag, for instance, has described how the abstract identities as Hindu and Muslim gained ground in the late nineteenth century, while more local forms of identity prevailed earlier (1989: 127, 146). The reason why abstract *communal* identities prevailed in India was that the colonial state – by contrast to the nation–state in Europe – abstained from providing integrative *national* rituals (Freitag 1989: 192–6). In order to modify this view, C.A. Bayly has stressed the existence of Hindu–Muslim riots in the pre-colonial and early colonial period. Instead of dating the emergence of communalism further back, however, Bayly suggests that riots between Hindus and Muslims both before and after the late nineteenth century can be explained by local processes of change in political, social or economic structures. This preference for explanations rooted in specific and localized histories leads Bayly to conclude: "Indeed, one may very well doubt whether there was ever an identifiable 'Muslim', 'Hindu' or 'Sikh' identity which could be abstracted from the particular circumstances of individual events or specific societies" (1985: 202). Gyanendra Pandey has offered a third perspective on communalism in nineteenth-century India. His focus is on the decontextualization of specific events, which took place in the generation of knowledge about sectarian conflicts in the colonial administration. Pandey demonstrates how specific conflicts were made to fit into a "common structure of the colonial argument on the history of Indian society". All conflicts seemed to follow a master narrative of two incompatible religiously defined communities, which made any two serious riots interchangeable and which enabled the emergence of abstract politically powerful notions of community. Communalism, Pandey argues, is a form of colonialist knowledge (Pandey 1990: 6, 57–65). Despite their differences, Freitag, Bayly and Pandey all reject essentialist readings of communalism. Communalism is not the natural relation between exclusive religious communities, but conflicts expressed through religious idioms were not absent before colonial rule.

The argument that Indian civilization is constituted by a common set of customs and social institutions leads us directly to the issue of caste. Caste occupies a central position in most conceptualizations of India; at once the symbol of Indian society as a whole and the feature that makes India entirely different from other societies (Dirks 1992: 56). Signifying both totality and uniqueness, caste enables us to envisage Indian society as a whole and it seems to offer an outstanding opportunity to grasp the essence of the Indian civilization. Caste has, indeed, been given a pivotal position in almost every conceptualization of Indian society since the early nineteenth century. As with Hinduism, however, recent studies suggest that caste is not an age-old essence but an institution which has been constantly reshaped through history and which underwent particularly important transformations in the nineteenth century, partly as a result of the alliance between the colonial power and its Brahmanic advisers.

The concept of caste has a number of connotations. The two most important are its supposed unchangeability and its religious character. These connotations construct India as the West's fundamental opposite, employing binary oppositions between the static and the dynamic and between the religious and the secular. The argument of many recent writings is that although the description of caste as a static and religious system, might bear some relevance to the social order of the nineteenth century, it is inadequate for earlier periods. The existence of caste is not denied, but it is seen as a much more dynamic, conflict-ridden and competitive institution, in which the identities and positions of social groups were fluid and malleable. Nor was caste a purely religious system separated from power and statecraft. On the contrary, caste was a highly politicized institution (Bayly 1999).

One of the most important contributions to this revision of our understanding of caste is Nicholas Dirks' monograph *The Hollow Crown*. Dirks' analysis of the small South Indian princely state Pudukkottai reveals a social order centered not on the Brahman priest, but on the local kingly ruler. The status of caste is determined in the relations they enjoy with the king, and these relations are constantly challenged and negotiated. Dirks places caste in a dynamic social order, in which the Brahmans played a limited role and status was always contested. It was not until the nineteenth century, when indigenous political authorities disappeared, that "the caste system" froze in the form by which we recognize it today: a static, religious and Brahman-dominated hierarchy. Later historians and anthropologists have mistakenly reified and essentialized what was in fact a result of specific historical developments and thus contributed to the vision of a unique and timeless Indian civilization (Dirks 1987). My own work on the so-called "right-" and "left-hand" caste divisions in early colonial South India tends to support Dirks' model of caste. These divisions were competing factions of castes, organized in patron–client networks. In the port cities the divisions were headed by powerful commercial castes, not by the Brahmans. The two divisions frequently clashed in violent disputes over economic resources, social position and ritual prestige. In other words, the right- and left-hand caste divisions were part of a social order, which was not predominantly religious, in constant change and where Brahmanic conceptions of purity and pollution were relatively unimportant (Brimnes 1999: 26–35). There is no point in denying that caste is a peculiar feature of the Indian subcontinent, but before its nineteenth-century reification it might not have been so fundamentally different from other types of social stratification and identity as we normally suppose. If this is the case, caste is perhaps not so evident as the "master institution" that constitutes the unique essence of a distinct Indian civilization.

Similar arguments can be fielded regarding the so-called *jajmani* system. *Jajmani* designates the system of exchange relations, which in the absence of the market was supposed to govern the economy in the Indian villages and it is intimately connected to the idea of the isolated self-sufficient "village republic". *Jajmani* is supposed to be an age-old institution found throughout the entire subcontinent. Louis Dumont has described the *jajmani* system as "the system corresponding to the prestations and counterprestations by which the castes as a whole are bound together in the village, and which is more or less universal in India" (1980: 97). Similarly, the *Cambridge Economic History of India*, in a chapter dealing with the Mughal period, presents *jajmani* as the foundation for village production over the entire subcontinent (Raychaudhuri and Habib 1982: 279–80). Again, the connotations are important; *jajmani* signals static relations, the absence of a proper economy and lack of individualist aspirations. Represented through the *jajmani* system, India once again appears as the negation of the West. And again, much indicates that the *jajmani*-system is yet another "invented tradition". Peter Mayer has delivered a highly readable critique of the conventional picture of *jajmani*. Through a systematic reading of references to *jajmani*, he concludes that it appears as a label for a certain type of exchange-relations found in parts of North India in the late nineteenth century. Moreover, Mayer explains the appearance of *jajmani* relations with two specific developments: an individualization of rights in land and lack of artisans in the villages (Mayer 1993: 378–85). It is beyond my competence to comment on the details of Mayer's analysis, but I am sympathetic to his attempt to explain social features with reference to specific historical processes.

If Mayer is correct, the *jajmani* system was a specific, regional feature, which has been taken out of its social, geographic and historical context and transformed into an *a priori* starting point for any consideration of the Indian village. Arguably, this process of essentialization is strongly influenced by the missionary-anthropologist William H. Wiser (Mayer 1993: 357, 359). Together with his wife, Charlotte, he published in 1932 a popular study of the village Karimpur and although the term *jajmani* is not explicitly used, the village is described in terms well suited to function as the framework for *jajmani* relations: "Every member of village society has his special function and the proper maintenance of the group depends on the proper functioning of each member: No one can be carried along, who does not contribute" (Wiser and Wiser 1932: 16). Four years later followed the book *The Hindu Jajmani System*, in which William Wiser provides a systematic interpretation of village exchange-relations and which became an anthropological classic (Wiser 1936).

In relation to both "the caste system" and "the *jajmani* system", it seems that if we go beyond the essentialization of these institutions, they dissolve into something much more heterogeneous and changeable. Even if the essentialized representations of caste and *jajmani* has functioned as reasonable adequate descriptions of Indian society, this is only the case for a relatively recent period, and can hardly be seen as constitutive elements for a timeless and unchanging Indian civilization. Indian civilization, in short, is highly complex, heterogeneous and hybrid, and historical scrutiny reveals how difficult it is to reduce it to something simple and easily comprehensible. This should not induce us to give up all notions of order and social or cultural coherence on the Indian subcontinent, but it should induce us to formulate such coherence in less certain forms. Recently, Sunil Khilnani has suggested that shared narrative structures and religious motifs constitute a "civilizational bond" throughout India. This formulation is useful if we understand such bonds not as the religious essence of India, but as a reservoir of powerful images, which can be effectively reinvigorated in later and entirely different contexts (Khilnani 1998: 155). Modern research suggests that this is in fact what the Hindu nationalist movement has cleverly done.

Constructing Indian civilization

Indian civilization is no stereotype, but numerous attempts have been made to stereotype it. Above, I have indicated how general theories of civilization have employed essentialist notions of Indian civilization and how complex institutional structures like caste or *jajmani* has been systematized into abstract social principles. In this section, I shall analyze a few of the most influential formulations of the Indian civilization over the last two centuries. Ranging from the British attempt to construct Indian society as a comprehensible "other" in the late eighteenth century to Jawaharlal Nehru's grand attempt to formulate a modern identity for an independent India.

Known as the "father" of Indology, founder of the "Asiatick Society" (in 1784) and the most prominent representative of the late eighteenth-century British Orientalists, William Jones is an obvious point of departure for this analysis. Although Jones did not himself explicitly use the concept civilization in his writings, his approach to the study of Indian society has left later writers in little doubt that he discovered – or constructed – the Indian civilization. In his standard biography of Jones, S. N. Mukherjee concludes: "It was Jones and his society which he founded who discovered that India had produced a civilization equal to any other in the ancient world" (Mukherjee 1968: 140). While Mukherjee refers to the Indian civilization as one among several ancient civilizations, Jones himself occupies an interesting position in the development of the relativist concept of civilization. Although the Indian civilization was treated as a distinct entity, it formed an important element in Jones' general project: writing a universal history of mankind. As a Christian, Jones was convinced that such a history had to be written within the framework of biblical chronology. Jones was deeply affected by the claims of Hindu mythology to stretch far longer back in time than the Bible would allow. Thus, he sought to shorten the Indian chronology and – more interestingly in the present context – he sought to connect Indian mythology to the mythology of ancient Greece and Rome. In the essay "On the Gods of Greece, Italy and India", Jones argued that Indian mythology so closely resembled the Greek–Roman that they had to have a common offspring (Jones 1807, III: 391). This insight led Jones to his grand theory of the early development of mankind. He suggested present-day Iran as the place from where mankind after the deluge had spread over the globe in three families: the Arabic, the Tartarian, and the Indo-European (ibid., III: 201).

Emphasizing the common offspring of the ancient civilizations (in the plural) and the similarities between them as well as relating them to a universal history, Jones was far from simply anticipating later relativist notions of civilization.

Contrasted with the imperialist and racist ideologies of the nineteenth century, Jones has been famed for his sympathetic attitude towards Indian society. It is, however, symptomatic that this sympathy was primarily directed towards ancient India. More than anyone else, Jones established the notion of India's remote golden age – a notion which in the nineteenth and twentieth centuries would become one of the pillars of romantic visions of India. Jones invested a lot of time and energy in translating the ancient text known as *The Laws of Manu* because he thought the text useful for the contemporary British administration in Bengal. As *The Laws of Manu* expressed the timeless custom and accumulated wisdom of Indian society – its essence – their application could help restoring the golden age. Despite the degeneration and the many absurdities, which Jones found around him, he was convinced that "in some early age [the Indians] were splendid in arts and arms, happy in government, wise in legislation and eminent in various knowledge" (ibid., III: 32). Although not using the concept explicitly, this seems to be a description of the intellectual, cultural and moral refinements of an ancient civilization. This civilization had distinct features, but it was not understood within the general universe of cultural relativism.

In the first half of the nineteenth century, James Mill was arguably the most influential writer on India in Europe. His monumental *History of British India*, published in 1818, was the authoritative interpretation of Indian history and society throughout much of the century. By contrast to Jones, the concept of civilization was explicitly at the center of Mill's understanding of India. The history of India was adapted to the framework of a universal history. This framework resembled the stage theories of the eighteenth century, according to which all societies would eventually pass through identical stages of evolution towards the ultimate goal of history: societies modeled on contemporary north-western Europe. A central concept was the *scale of civilization*, and Mill's formulation in that respect comes close to a definition of civilization and thus worth quoting at length:

> It is not easy to describe the characteristics of the different stages of social progress … It is from a joint view of all great circumstances taken together, that their progress can be ascertained; and it is from an accurate comparison, grounded on these general views that a *scale of civilisation* can be formed, on which the relative position of nations may be accurately marked.
> (Mill 1826, II: 139; emphasis mine)

Note that Mill proposed to identify the position of "nations" in relation to each other, and that it is "nation" not "civilization" which appears in the plural. Civilization was the universal yardstick measuring progress in any society, something to be possessed in smaller or greater degree. Mill ranked India – which for Mill meant the Hindus – low on the scale of civilization; just above tribal societies: "The Hindus were so far advanced in civilization ... as to have improved in some degree upon the manners of savage tribes" (ibid., II: 391). The employment of civilization as a universal concept enabled Mill to compare the degree of civilization in societies across time and space. With regard to revenue systems, India was placed on a par with "the rude parts of Africa", Egypt, the Ottoman Empire, Persia, Indonesia, China and even Wales in the ninth century (ibid., I: 258–60). Mill further claimed that Indians and Chinese were equals with regard to science and art, but the Chinese more civilized in governance and legislation (ibid., II: 192–3). Obviously, comparisons of this sort would not make sense within the relativist concept of civilization.

As mentioned above, Mill's vision of history comes close to the universal stage theories of the enlightenment. There is, however, one major difference. Whereas the stage theories took it for granted that societies would eventually pass through the stages of development, Mill denied India the capacity to progress without the intervention of the West. This was due to a single institution: *caste*. According to Mill, India reached the first stages of civilization quickly, and the institution of caste developed in reaction to the challenges posed by a more advanced state of society. But caste led India into a blind alley, from where progress was no longer possible. Caste is presented simply as a more "effective barrier against the welfare of human nature, than any other institution which the workings of caprice and of selfishness have ever produced" (ibid., II: 429–30). The interpretation of India as a society that – due to the institution of caste – was trapped in the early stages of progress transcends, however, the universal concept of civilization. As caste was seen as a uniquely Indian phenomenon, Mill's interpretation actually pointed towards the notion of India as a distinct civilization, defined more than anything else by the institution of caste. In Mill's account of Indian history, we encounter the seeds of the later so powerful idea that caste constitutes the essence of India.[2]

The notion of an Indian civilization acquired a new significance in the late nineteenth century when nationalist writers sought to establish an Indian identity in the modern world. Building on romantic notions of the authentic cultural nation, Indian intellectuals like Swami Vivekananda and Bal Gangadhar Tilak began to formulate ideas about a particularly spiritual Indian – and often specifically Hindu – civilization, opposed to the materialism of the West (Veer 1994: 68–9; Hansen 1999: 40, 69, 75–6). These writers also adopted the historicism of romantic nationalism in Europe and – with obvious inspiration from eighteenth-century Orientalists like William Jones – dated the birth of the Indian civilization to a remote golden age. From this early zenith, the rest of Indian history was decline. Consequently, the indigenous narratives of Indian civilization became narratives of future revitalization (Veer 1994: 20).

These writers in turn inspired Gandhi, who adopted ideas of Indian spirituality and tolerance developed in the nineteenth century. Gandhi was most explicit about the notion of civilization in *Hind Swaraj*, originally published in Gujarati in 1909. His text was, however, more a rejection of Western civilization – which he equated with "modern civilization" or just "civilization" (in the singular) – than it was a positive definition of a distinct Indian civilization. Unfolding his anti-modernism Gandhi called Western civilization a "civilization only in name" as it took note of neither morality nor religion: "This civilization is such that one has only to be patient and it will be self-destroyed" (Gandhi 1963: 18–21). The strength – and beauty – of Indian civilization were, on the other hand, its unchangeability. All civilizations will face tests, Gandhi argued, and "That civilization which is permanent outlives it. Because the sons of India were found wanting, its civilization has been placed in jeopardy. But its strength is to be seen in its ability to survive the chock" (ibid.: 36–7, 39). Gandhi's Indian civilization was "traditional" India, composed of village communities and governed by essentialized and beneficial versions of caste and *jajmani* (Chatterjee 1986: 92). Partha Chatterjee has argued that Gandhi rejected the historicist mode of thinking: Indian civilization should not be understood historically as a process of decline from a golden age, but as the manifestation of a superior and permanent moral truth (ibid.: 94–7). It is, however, clear that Gandhi ascribed particular value to the ancientness of Indian civilization: he wanted the ancient schools and courts back and saw the ultimate task as the restoration of India "to its pristine condition" (Gandhi 1963: 57, 61). This was, perhaps, not so much a vision of the Indian civilization unfolding itself in history, as it was a return to an uncorrupted historical original.

If Gandhi was ambivalent towards historicism, the conceptualization of Indian civilization returned firmly to the historicist mould in the writings of Jawaharlal Nehru. His book *The Discovery of India* is really the discovery of an identity for the modern Indian State envisaged in one form or another by most observers in the decade preceding 1947. Invoking the theme of "the continuity of a cultural tradition through five thousand years of history", Nehru wrote that British rule was nothing but an unhappy interlude in India's long, continuous history and that "she would find herself again" (Nehru 1947: 32). To Nehru, India was a woman with a body and a lost – but recoverable – soul, and his national project was in certain ways a project of restoration and revitalization.

Yet, it was an inherently ambiguous project. On the one hand, Nehru argued that an independent India was capable of following the West into modernity and industrialization; on the other hand, India was to retain her distinctiveness – her soul – in that process (Chatterjee 1986: 2). At the same time as Nehru was searching for the fundamental and distinctive qualities of Indian society, he maintained that modernity was not alien to or incompatible with those qualities (ibid.: 133–8). The extent to which Nehru managed to solve the contradiction between "modernity" and "distinctiveness" is not to be considered here. Instead, I shall concentrate on Nehru's attempt to define India's distinctiveness. In this attempt, Nehru utilized the concept of civilization to its full extent, and it happened in an interesting conjunction with Jones' concept of India's golden age, a Hegelian philosophy of history, and cultural relativism. First, Nehru was searching for the Indian civilization in the remote past; the key to understanding India was "ancient India". Second, civilizations were portrayed as something, which arise, culminate and fall. The inspiration from Hegel is obvious, when

Nehru asked whether the light of civilization had left India: "Have we had our day and are we now living in the late afternoon or evening of our existence, just carrying on after the manner of the aged, quiescent, devitalized, uncreative; desiring peace and sleep above all else?" (Nehru 1947: 34). Third, civilization was unmistakably in plural: "Ancient India, like ancient China, was a world in itself, a culture and a civilization which gave shape to all things" (ibid.: 40). Civilization was now a specific world, which "in itself" influenced "all things". As the "culture" of modern anthropology, civilization was for Nehru a *circum-scribed totality*.

On the face of it, the Indian civilization is full of differences. Most important – and embarrassing – at the time of writing was the communal differences between Hindus and Muslims, which Nehru preferred to explain with reference to economic and social factors. Communalism also served Nehru's historicist perspective as an expression of conservative feudal interests. This, of course was a denial of the importance of religious identity in a modernizing nation:

> The real conflict had, therefore, nothing to do with religion, though religion often masked the issue, but was essentially between those who stood for a nationalist – democratic – socially revolutionary policy and those who were concerned with preserving the relics of a feudal régime.
>
> (Nehru 1947: 335; see also Pandey 1990: 240–1)

Behind these differences, however, we may discover the essence of India. Thus, Nehru wrote that all the Indian people despite their peculiar characteristics have remained "distinctively Indian, with the same national heritage and the same set of moral and mental qualities" (Nehru 1947: 40). We begin to discern the outlines of Huntington's concept of civilization: the core that unites a number of different elements in a civilization is here "a set of moral and mental qualities". If we dig a little deeper, we find that Nehru provided a number of suggestions as to what more precisely constituted these essentially Indian moral and mental qualities. One suggestion was the idea of "some kind of penance", which he found "inherent in Indian thought, both among the thinkers at the top and the unread masses below. It is present today as it was present some thousand of years ago" (ibid.: 68). Nehru also emphasized the goodness and self-sacrificing nature of the Indian mind and found the Indian habit of mind "essentially one of quietism" (ibid.: 76, 306). Finally, Nehru touched upon the stability of the Indian civilization:

> The civilization that was built up here was *essentially* based on stability and security and from this point of view it was far more successful than any that arose in the West. The social structure, based on the caste system and joint families served this purpose and was successful in providing social security for the group and a kind of insurance for the individual who by reason of age, infirmity or any other incapacity was unable to provide for himself.
>
> (ibid.: 111; emphasis mine)

This passage indicates that Nehru's vision of the Indian civilization in this respect was an inverted version of James Mill's: whereas Mill saw a society trapped on the lowest scale of civilization, Nehru saw a civilization displaying the virtues of stability and security. Both of them, however, saw a civilization defined by the institution of caste. This inversion of the Western discourse on India was a general feature in Indian nationalist historiography. In the words of Gyan Prakash:

> While affirming the concept of an India essentialized in relation to Europe, the nationalist transformed it from passive to active, from dependent to sovereign, capable of relating to history and reason. Nationalist historiographers accepted the patterns set for them by British scholarship. They accepted the periodization of Indian history into Hindu, Muslim, and British periods ... and reiterated the long and unchanging existence of a Sanskritic Indic civilization.
>
> (1992: 358)

The last writer to be discussed here is Louis Dumont, author of the highly influential book *Homo Hierarchicus*, which has defined much of the debate on the features of Indian society during the last three decades. As in the case of William Jones, we are dealing with an author who does not employ the concept of civilization. We might note that Dumont is author of another book entitled *La civilisation indienne et nous. Esquisse de sociologie comparée* and that India in *Homo Hierarchicus* occasionally is portrayed as the bearer of a great civilization (Dumont 1980: xxiv, 2), but the concept is not employed as a systematic analytical tool. Being a consequent structuralist interpretation of the "caste system", *Homo Hierarchicus* has, nevertheless, powerfully reinforced the notion of India as a distinct and homogeneous entity. Indian society is presented as an ordered totality, based on a single fundamental principle: *hierarchy*. Hierarchy is based on the religious opposition between pure and impure, and caste is the social manifestation of this opposition. Indian society is, therefore, fundamentally religious and the king in principle subordinated to the authority of the Brahman priest (ibid.: 3, 72–9). As a structuralist, Dumont was less interested in the specific and always confusing empirical appearances of the caste system – the multitude of *jatis* and sub-*jatis* – and concentrated on identifying the underlying well-ordered whole: "it is the whole who govern the parts, and this whole is very rigorously conceived as based on an opposition" (ibid.: 43–4). Once again Indian society is seen as a circumscribed totality: a "whole" clearly distinct from other "wholes" by its defining principle. Whether we identify this principle as the institution of caste, the opposition between pure and impure or simply as hierarchy, is of no great importance, because they are all manifestations of the same essence. If the views held by James Mill contained the seeds of the notion that India was defined by caste, Dumont marks the culmination of this notion (Prakash 1992: 364). In the last two centuries, Indian society has often been contrasted to the West through simple dichotomies; the most far-reaching probably being the contested conceptual pair of "modernity" and "tradition". A number of such dichotomies are implicitly or explicitly present in Dumont's account of Indian society, where they are incorporated into his fundamental opposition: the principle of equality versus the principle of hierarchy. Indeed, the binarism inherent in Western conceptualizations of India reaches a climax in Dumont's definition of the Indian as a *homo hierarchicus* which is fundamentally opposed to the Westerner: *homo aequalis*.

It is hardly necessary to add that Dumont's view is profoundly ahistorical. The principle of hierarchy – and its institutional manifestation through the caste system – have paralyzed Indian society since time immemorial and prevented any kind of qualitative change. This view can be traced back not only to Mill but also to Marx, who could see neither development of the forces of production nor dialectical movements in India if it was left untouched by European intervention. Dumont could not see any changes in the abstract principle governing society, and referred the historian to look for the "fundamental constants in Indian civilization" (1980: 195). It is telling that Dumont – to the extent he used the concept of civilization at all – thought of it as an entity containing "fundamental constants".

Hindu nationalism and Indian civilization

Continuity with an ancient and distinct Hindu civilization is a central theme in modern Hindu nationalist ideology. As I have illustrated above, the search for civilizational constants throughout the history of the Indian subcontinent was also central to colonial historiography, to secular nationalist writers, as well as to important strains of modern anthropology. I have also questioned a variety of notions of continuity in Indian history. My argument here builds on a major current in modern scholarship, which rejects the essentialization of India into an easily comprehensible "other". In this final section, I shall present two accounts of Hindu nationalism, which attempt to analyze it without recourse to essentialism and employment of basic civilizational constants.

In 1994, Peter van der Veer published *Religious Nationalism: Hindus and Muslims in India*, which he presents as an attempt to make a problem of the essentializing of "the Hindu" and "the Muslim". Veer does not, however, accept that religious nationalisms in South Asia – of which Hindu nationalism is the most powerful – are merely recent constructions. Religious identities must rather be viewed as being in a constant process of transformation (Veer 1994: xii–xiv, 29). Veer pays particular importance to the transformation of religious identities taking place under colonialism. It was in this period that reified categories of "caste" and "community" gained ground and the British constructed a "master narrative" of two incompatible communities. This conceptualization of Indian society was successful partly because these categories were employed by the colonial administration, partly because they were adopted by indigenous religious reform movements; but also – and notably – because they had a basis in pre-colonial society (ibid.: 18–21, 151). The essentializing of community might be colonial, but the "raw-material" was pre-colonial.

An illustrative example of the way in which pre-colonial features became important for later developments is Veer's treatment of pilgrimage. Since pre-colonial times, pilgrimage has provided a sense of a "sacred geography" and a notion of trans-local religious community to Indians. In the 1980s the Hindu nationalist organization *Vishwa Hindu Parisad* (VHP) began to conduct modern pilgrimages (*yatras*) throughout India to promote the Hindu nationalist message, including campaigns for the demolition of the *Babri Masjid* in Ayodhya. According to Veer these *yatras* suggested the geographical unity of India as a sacred area of the Hindus and in this way "pilgrimage was effectively transformed into a ritual of national integration". An existing ritual practice with rich connotations in Indian society was thus cleverly refashioned to suit modern politics (ibid.: 124, 126). Despite the emphasis on the pre-colonial roots of Hindu nationalism, Veer explicitly defines it as deeply involved with modernity: "what the VHP tries to do is to formulate a modern Hinduism that can serve as the basis of a Hindu Nation". He adds, however, that in this process they employ a *ritual repertoire*, which is based on pre-colonial as well as colonial forms of identity (ibid.: 133–6). In his attempt to understand Hindu nationalism Veer has exchanged historical continuity for a recently developed ritual repertoire building on elements from both the pre-colonial and colonial past. The Hindu nationalists do not represent an essentialized Indian civilization, but they do work cleverly with themes drawn from the loose civilizational bonds of the Indian subcontinent.

In 1999, Thomas Blom Hansen published his interpretation of Hindu Nationalism as *The Saffron Wave: Democracy and Hindu Nationalism in Modern India*. Hansen and Veer share basic assumptions about the impact of colonial rule on the construction of communal identities in late colonial India, but Hansen is even more focused on recent developments. He sets out to explore "the conditions of possibility in terms of political discourse" that made the recent enunciation of the Hindu nation so successful. Rejecting the concept of "a single Hindu culture" as a fiction, Hansen understands recent notions of "Hinduness" as produced historically "at a particular juncture in the development of democracy and modern governance in India" (1999: 11, 19).

Although it has roots back to the early decades of the twentieth century, the breakthrough for Hindu nationalism came in the 1980s when the Congress disintegrated as a consequence of the religious populism pursued by Indira and Rajiv Gandhi.[3] The 1980s also witnessed an incipient process of liberalization and globalization in India. The increasing flow of commercial goods and images from the West led to a "feeling of displacement" among many Hindus. Middle class Hindus felt another threat of displacement, when the left-wing Prime Minister V. P. Singh in 1990 declared that he intended to implement the recommendations of the Mandal Commission, which would reserve substantial proportions of educational seats and government jobs to the so-called "other-backward classes". Finally, it was during the 1980s that new mass media made new forms of mass mobilization possible. This became evident during the *yatras* of the 1980s and culminated in the campaign to demolish the *Babri Masjid* (Hansen 1999: 134, 140, 159, 164). In this particular political juncture, Hansen argues, the strategy of the Hindu nationalist organizations to focus on places like Ayodhya as sacred places within a new national geography "proved to be an apt reading of the conditions of possibility for ideological intervention provided by the majoritarian democracy of the 1980s" (ibid.: 157).

Hansen's emphasis on the particularities of Indian politics in the 1980s does not mean, however, that reflections over references to an integrated Hindu civilization are absent from his analysis. On the contrary, the theme of Indian civilization was brought into play as Ayodhya in the Hindu nationalist rhetoric came to symbolize the "traumatic wound" in Hindu civilization. This wound was caused by the conquest of a peaceful and advanced civilization by "primitive" Muslim invaders. Hindu nationalism succeeded in making Ram the central metaphor of the essential Hinduness of Indian culture, and what better way of healing the wound than restoring his alleged birthplace to a place of Hindu worship and at the same time tear down a structure bearing the name of the villain Babar, founder of the "alien" Mughal Empire. Through this symbolic act of healing, Hansen argues, the Hindu nationalists seeks recognition and respect as the "civilizational other" of the West (ibid.: 172–81, 243).

Despite the difference in focus, Veer and Hansen agree to explain Hindu nationalism as a recent occurrence, which cannot be properly understood as the pure inheritor to the ancient Indian civilization. The concept of an Indian civilization is no doubt important for current developments in Indian politics and society. Not because an historical continuity between the presumed ancient, golden days of Hindu civilization and its present reinvigoration can be convincingly demonstrated, but because the idea of an integrated Hindu civilization has been a potent rhetorical trope in processes of identity formation over the last two hundred years. The onset of globalization has, it seems, only amplified its resonance within Indian society.

Acknowledgments

This chapter is based on a lecture given at the Centre for Cultural Research, University of Aarhus, November 1997 as a part of a lecture series entitled "Europe and the other Civilizations". Apart from the literature referred to in the text, I am inspired by the article "Fra den indfødtes synsvinkel – og andre kultur-relativistiske paradokser" [From the natives' point of view – and other cultural relativist paradoxes] by Sören Christensen published in Danish in the Danish journal *Den jyske Historiker* vol. 66 (1994). I am grateful to Professor Prasenjit Duara for providing me with a copy of his manuscript "The Discourse of Civilization and Pan-Asianism" before it was published, and to my colleague in Aarhus, Jens Chr. Manniche, for a critical reading of the text.

Notes

1   This anomaly leads Samuel P. Huntington to speak of "torn countries" and to mention Russia, Turkey and Mexico as prime examples (Huntington 1997: 139–54).

2   Max Weber was perhaps the most influential writer who elaborated on this idea (Weber 1958), but it was also adopted by William McNeill (as illustrated above), by Jawaharlal Nehru and by Louis Dumont (as will be illustrated below).
3   This religious populism was not exclusively directed towards Hindus, but attempted to accommodate both Hindu and Muslim communal forces (Hansen 1999: 148).

References

Ajami, Fouad (1993) "The Summoning", *Foreign Affairs*, vol. 72, no. 4, pp. 2–9.

Anderson, Benedict (1983) *Imagined Communities. Reflections on the Origin and Spread of Nationalism*, 2nd rev. edn, London, Verso.

Bayly, C.A. (1985) "The Pre-history of 'Communalism?' Religious Conflict in India, 1700–1860", *Modern Asian Studies*, vol. 19, no. 2, pp. 177–203.

—— (1988) *Indian Society and the Making of the British Empire*, Cambridge, Cambridge University Press.

Bayly, Susan (1989) *Saints, Goddesses and Kings. Muslims and Christians in South Indian Society 1700–1900*, Cambridge, Cambridge University Press.

—— (1999) *Caste, Society and Politics in India from the Eighteenth Century to the Modern Age*, Cambridge, Cambridge University Press.

Brimnes, Niels (1999) *Constructing the Colonial Encounter. Right and Left Hand Castes in Early Colonial South India*, Richmond, Curzon Press.

Chandra, Satish (1997) "The Indian Perspective", in Robert W. Cox (ed.), *The New Realism. Perspectives on Multilateralism and World Order*, Basingstoke, Macmillan, pp. 124–44.

Chatterjee, Partha (1986) *Nationalist Thought and the Colonial World – a Derivative Discourse*, London, Zed Books.

Dirks, Nicholas B. (1987) *The Hollow Crown: Ethnohistory of an Indian Kingdom*, Cambridge, Cambridge University Press.

Dirks, Nicholas B. (1992) "Castes of Mind", *Representations*, vol. 37, pp. 56–78.

Dumont, Louis (1980) *Homo Hierarchicus: The Caste System and Its Implications*, rev. English edn, Chicago, Chicago University Press.

Duara, Prasenjit (1995) *Rescuing History from the Nation: Questioning Narratives of Modern China*, Chicago, University of Chicago Press.

Duara, Prasenjit (2001) "The Discourse of Civilization and Pan-Asianism", *Journal of World History*, vol. 12, no. 1, pp. 99–130.

Eisenstadt, Shmuel N. (1982) "The Axial Age: The Emergence of Transcendental Visions and the Rise of Clerics", *Archives européennes de sociologie*, vol. 23, no. 2, pp. 294–314.

—— (ed.) (1986) *The Origins and Diversity of Axial Age Civilization*, Albany, State University of New York Press.

Eisenstadt, Shmuel N. and Wolfgang Schluchter (1998) "Introduction: Paths to Early Modernities – A Comparative View", *Dædalus*, vol. 127, no. 3: "Early Modernities," pp.1–18.

Fisch, Jörg (1972) "Zivilisation, Kultur", in O. Brunner *et al.* (eds) *Geschichtliche Grundbegriffe*, vol. 7, Stuttgart, Ernst Klett Verlag.

Freitag, Sandria B. (1989) *Collective Action and Community: Public Arenas and the Emergence of Communalism in North India*, Berkeley, CA, University of California Press.

Gandhi, M.K. (1963) "Hind Swaraj", in *The Collected Works of Mahatma Gandhi*, Delhi, Government of India Publications Division, vol. X, pp. 6–68.

Hansen, Thomas Blom (1999) *The Saffron Wave: Democracy and Hindu Nationalism in Modern India*, Princeton, NJ, Princeton University Press.

Hobsbawm E.J. and Ranger, T. (1983) *The Invention of Tradition*, Cambridge, Cambridge University Press.

Huntington, Samuel P. (1993) "The Clash of Civilizations?", *Foreign Affairs*, vol. 72, no. 3, pp. 22–49.

—— (1997) *The Clash of Civilizations and the Remaking of World Order*, New York, Touchstone.

Inden, Ronald (1990) *Imagining India*, Oxford, Blackwell.

Jones, William (1807) *The Collected Works of Sir William Jones*, vols I–XIII, London, Stockdale and Walker.

Khilnani, Sunil (1998) *The Idea of India*, London, Penguin.

Kulke, Hermann and Rothermund, Dietmar (1998) *History of India*, 3rd edn, London, Routledge.

McNeill, William H. (1963) *The Rise of the West: A History of the Human Community*, Chicago, Chicago University Press.

—— (1990) "The Rise of the West after Twenty-Five Years", *Journal of World History*, vol. 1, no. 1, pp. 1–21.

Marshall, P.J. (ed.) (1970) *The British Discovery of Hinduism in the Eighteenth Century*, Cambridge, Cambridge University Press.

Mayer, Peter (1993) "Inventing Village Tradition: The Late 19th Century Origins of the North Indian 'Jajmani System'", *Modern Asian Studies*, vol. 27, no. 2, pp. 357–95.

Metcalf, Thomas (1994) *Ideologies of the Raj*, Cambridge, Cambridge University Press.

Mill, James (1826) *The History of British India*, vols I–VI, 3rd edn, London, Baldwin, Cradock and Joy.

Mukherjee, S.N. (1968) *Sir William Jones*, Cambridge, Cambridge University Press.

Nehru, Jawarharlal (1947) *The Discovery of India*, 2nd edn, London, Meridian Books.

Pandey, Gyanendra (1990) *The Construction of Communalism in Colonial North India*, Delhi, Oxford University Press.

Perlin, Frank (1985) "State Formation Reconsidered", *Modern Asian Studies*, vol. 19, no. 3, pp. 415–80.

Prakash, Gyan (1992) "Writing Post-Orientalist Histories of the Third World: Indian Historiography is Good to Think", in Nicholas B. Dirks (ed.), *Colonialism and Culture*, Ann Arbor, MI, University of Michigan Press, pp. 353–88.

Raychaudhuri, T. and Habib, I. (eds) (1982) *The Cambridge Economic History of India, c. 1200–1750*, vol. I, Cambridge, Cambridge University Press.

Richards, J.F. (1993) *The Mughal Empire*, Cambridge, Cambridge University Press.

Subrahmanyam, Sanjay (1992) "The Mughal State: Structure or Process? Reflections on Recent Western Historiography", *Indian Economic and Social History Review*, vol. 29, no. 3, pp. 291–321.

—— (1997) "Connected Histories: Notes Towards a Reconfiguration of Early Modern Eurasia", *Modern Asian Studies*, vol. 31, no. 3, pp. 735–62.

Thapar, Romilla (2000) "Imagined Religious Communities? Ancient History and the Modern Search for a Hindu Identity", in *History and Beyond*, Delhi, Oxford University Press, pp. 60–88.

Veer, Peter van der (1994) *Religious Nationalism. Hindus and Muslims in India*, Berkeley, CA, University of California Press.

Weber, Max (1958) *The Religion of India*, New York, Free Press.

Wink, A. (1986) *Land and Sovereignty in India. Agrarian Society and Politics under the Eighteenth-century Maratha Svaraya*, Cambridge, Cambridge University Press.

Wiser, W.H. (1936) *The Hindu Jajmani System*, Lucknow, Lucknow Publishing House (reprint New York 1979).

Wiser, W.H. and Wiser, C. (1932) *Behind Mud Walls*, London, G. Allen & Unwin.

Index